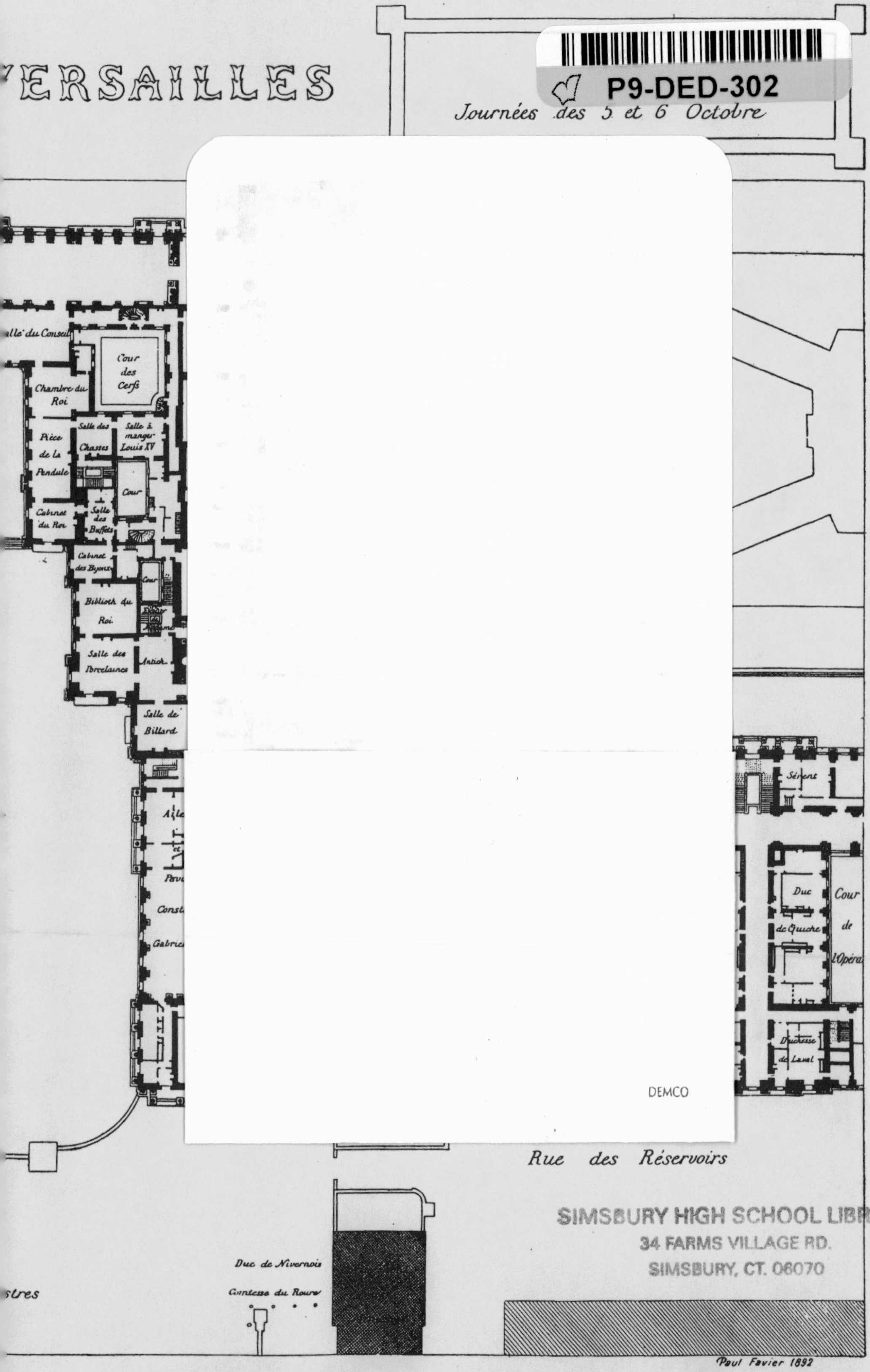

ERSAILLES

Journées des 5 et 6 Octobre

Salle du Conseil

Cour des Cerfs

Chambre du Roi

Salle des Chasses

Salle à manger Louis XV

Pièce de la Pendule

Cour

Cabinet du Roi

Salle des Buffets

Cabinet des Bijoux

Cour

Biblioth. du Roi.

Salle des Porcelaines

Antich.

Salle de Billard

Serent

Aile

Pavi

Duc de Quiche

Cour de l'Opéra

Const

Gabrie

Duchesse de Laval

Rue des Réservoirs

Duc de Nivernois

Comtesse du Roure

stres

Paul Favier 1892

MARIE ANTOINETTE

BY THE SAME AUTHOR

Madame de Pompadour (Paris, Perrin, 2000)

Philippe Egalité (Paris, Fayard, 1996)

Mémoires du Baron de Breteuil (Paris, Bourin, 1992)

Marie-Antoinette (Paris, Fayard, 1991)

Louis XVIII (Paris, Fayard, 1988)

Louis XVI (Paris, Fayard, 1985)

Histoire de la guerre d'Algérie (Paris, Editions du Seuil, 1982)

MARIE ANTOINETTE

THE LAST QUEEN OF FRANCE

EVELYNE LEVER

TRANSLATED FROM THE FRENCH
BY CATHERINE TEMERSON

FARRAR, STRAUS AND GIROUX
NEW YORK

Farrar, Straus and Giroux
19 Union Square West, New York 10003

Library of Congress Cataloging-in-Publication Data

Lever, Evelyne.
    [Marie-Antoinette. English]
    Marie Antoinette : the last queen of France / by Evelyne Lever ; translated from the
French by Catherine Temerson.
        p. cm.
    Includes bibliographical references and index.
    ISBN 0-374-19938-8 (alk. paper)
    1. Marie-Antoinette, Queen, consort of Louis XVI, King of France, 1775–1793.
    2. Queens—France—Biography.   3. France—History—Louis XVI, 1774–1793.
I. Title.

DC137.1.L4813 2000
944'.035'092—dc 21
[B]   00-028763

In memory of my grandmother,

Mathilde Annibali (1876–1973)

CONTENTS

1. Daughter of Maria Theresa 3

2. Great Expectations 11

3. A Royal Marriage 20

4. The Versailles Court 27

5. Madame la Dauphine 36

6. End of a Reign, End of an Era 46

7. A Happy Accession 54

8. "Little Twenty-Year-Old Queen" 61

9. The Coronation 69

10. The Queen's Circle 77

11. Venus and Vulcan 87

12. The Queen's Intrigues 95

13. The Brother's Visit 104

14. Motherhood 113

15. Fersen 122

16. Queen of Trianon 129

17. Birth of a Dauphin 138

18. Fersen's Return 147

19. Last Illusions 155

20. Scandal in the Air 163

21. The Diamond Necklace Affair 173

22. "Madame Deficit" 183

23. "My Fate Is to Bring Bad Luck"   191

24. "Do You Know a Woman More to Be Pitied Than Me?"   200

25. The Fall of the Bastille   208

26. The Last Summer at Versailles   216

27. The Tragedy of October 1789   223

28. The Tuileries   233

29. Escape Plans   242

30. The Varennes Drama   250

31. The Impasse   260

32. The Last Show of Strength   269

33. The Fall of the Monarchy   277

34. The Death of the King   285

35. The Conciergerie   292

36. Trial and Death of the Queen   299

    Epilogue: What Became of Them?   306

    Abbreviations   313

    Notes   315

    Bibliography   331

    Index   345

SIMPLIFIED GENEALOGY

OF THE FRENCH ROYAL FAMILY

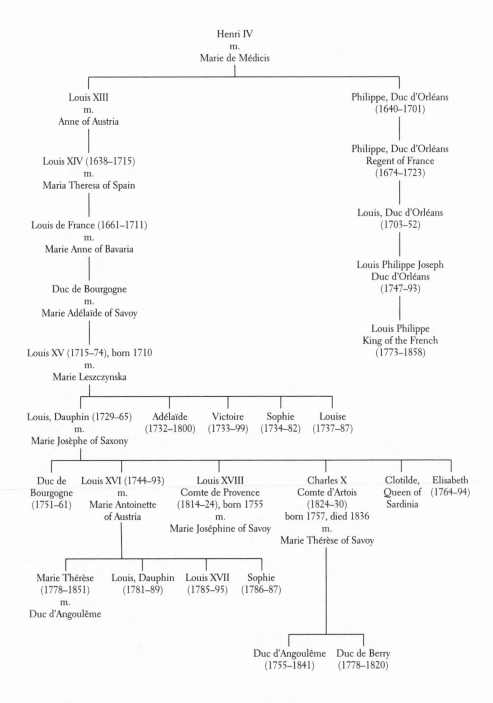

Henri IV
m.
Marie de Médicis

Louis XIII
m.
Anne of Austria

Philippe, Duc d'Orléans
(1640–1701)

Louis XIV (1638–1715)
m.
Maria Theresa of Spain

Philippe, Duc d'Orléans
Regent of France
(1674–1723)

Louis de France (1661–1711)
m.
Marie Anne of Bavaria

Louis, Duc d'Orléans
(1703–52)

Duc de Bourgogne
m.
Marie Adélaïde of Savoy

Louis Philippe Joseph
Duc d'Orléans
(1747–93)

Louis XV (1715–74), born 1710
m.
Marie Leszczynska

Louis Philippe
King of the French
(1773–1858)

Louis, Dauphin (1729–65)
m.
Marie Josèphe of Saxony

Adélaïde
(1732–1800)

Victoire
(1733–99)

Sophie
(1734–82)

Louise
(1737–87)

Duc de
Bourgogne
(1751–61)

Louis XVI (1744–93)
m.
Marie Antoinette
of Austria

Louis XVIII
Comte de Provence
(1814–24), born 1755
m.
Marie Joséphine of Savoy

Charles X
Comte d'Artois
(1824–30)
born 1757, died 1836
m.
Marie Thérèse of Savoy

Clotilde,
Queen of
Sardinia

Elisabeth
(1764–94)

Marie Thérèse
(1778–1851)
m.
Duc d'Angoulême

Louis, Dauphin
(1781–89)

Louis XVII
(1785–95)

Sophie
(1786–87)

Duc d'Angoulême
(1755–1841)

Duc de Berry
(1778–1820)

MARIE ANTOINETTE

1

DAUGHTER OF MARIA THERESA

*V*ienna, November 2, 1755. Her windows wide open, as was her habit, regardless of the rigors of the season, the Empress Maria Theresa worked without respite. She was busy annotating reports, signing decrees, dictating her orders when the first pains suddenly made her wince. The thirty-eight-year-old sovereign, ruler of an empire, was to give birth for the fifteenth time in her life. Nature had reclaimed her rights and the female head of state could do nothing but stoically await her deliverance. But since Maria Theresa hated wasting time, she took advantage of the momentary inconvenience to have a decayed tooth extracted. Once that operation was disposed of, she settled, following German custom, into the low armchair where she would give birth to her child. Word was rushed to her husband, Francis of Lorraine, that the birth was imminent. The Prince was attending the All Souls' Day mass with his son Joseph at the Augustinian church. After arranging for the young man to be escorted back to his apartment lest he hear "improper things," he ran to his wife's bedside. It was a difficult labor, but at around seven-thirty in the evening, a perfectly formed infant girl came into the world. On the following day, she was baptized Maria Antonia Josephina Johanna. Since all the archduchesses were given the first name of Maria, they were usually addressed by their second name. Maria Theresa would refer to her youngest daughter as Antonia. It was the French who would call her Marie Antoinette.

Antonia was brought to the wing in the Hofburg palace reserved for the imperial couple's children. There she joined her young brothers and sisters: Johanna, who was barely five years old, Josephina, who was four, the two-year-old Carolina, and Ferdinand, who had just celebrated his first birthday. Her older siblings lived on other floors: the frail Maria Anna, who was already seventeen, and Joseph, who was fourteen. Maria Christina and Elisabeth, born in 1742 and 1743, were nearly young ladies. Their marriages were already being thought about. As for Charles Joseph, Amalia and Leopold, they had reached the age of reason and fully enjoyed their carefree childhood. Maria Theresa was very proud of this fine progeny, her "henhouse" as she sometimes liked to call it. In a time when infant mortality took a grievous toll on all families, the imperial couple was exceptional in having lost only three children in early childhood. And the Empress would still have another son in 1756, Maximilian Francis, the future Archbishop of Cologne. Meytens, official painter of the Viennese court, showed the brood of archdukes and archduchesses between the husband and wife, who are seated on sumptuous armchairs and dressed in ceremonial regalia. The painting was retouched regularly; the artist would add the newcomers and take account of the elders' changing appearance.

Since succeeding her father, the Habsburg Emperor Charles VI, in 1740, Maria Theresa had done her best to reconcile the exercise of government with her duties as a wife and mother. In 1736, at nineteen, she had married Francis of Lorraine, a prince who had been educated at the Viennese court and was considered one of the handsomest men of his day. His full face and regular features bespoke of a well-balanced personality and an even temper which he never betrayed. Amiable, frank, devoid of ambition and authority, he had known how to attract this princess, who both loved and dominated him. Wishing him never to feel inferior to her, she behaved with him as a submissive wife. She never put up the slightest resistance to his amorous ardor, even if this meant getting pregnant regularly for nearly twenty years.

She had known from earliest childhood that she was destined for the highest function. Disregarding every tradition, her father the Emperor had decided by the Pragmatic Sanction that his daughter would succeed him (he had no son). He had managed, not without difficulty, to get this act recognized by his own states and the foreign powers. However, when he died, the people did not hail Maria Theresa's accession as they might have hailed a prince; they were deeply troubled to be governed by a woman. As for the European sovereigns, they forgot their promises. They each coveted some segment of the empire that had been given over to the young, inexperienced twenty-three-year-old, who was incapable, they felt, of ruling over the destinies of a portion of Central Europe. Populated with nationalities speaking different languages and governed by dissimilar laws, her states were indeed spread far and wide: they included what constitutes present-day Austria, Bohemia[1] (Prague), Hungary[2] (Budapest), part of northern Italy (Milan, Mantua, Florence) and present-day Belgium, which was called the Austrian Netherlands. Far from letting herself be discouraged by such unfavorable circumstances, Maria Theresa took power with the title Queen of Bohemia and Hungary. She made her husband coregent but, convinced of the legitimacy of her rights as an absolute sovereign, she accorded him only the semblance of monarchical power.

Two months after her accession to the throne, she had to face the invasion of one of her provinces and confront a European coalition. "I am but a poor queen but I have the heart of a king," she cried out.[3] With indomitable energy, a sharp sense of reality, unintimidated, unshaken and never discouraged, she succeeded in rallying her subjects to her cause. She raised armies, negotiated alliances and set her enemies at odds with one another. After eight years of war, her legitimacy was no longer challenged. The Pragmatic Sanction was universally recognized. Maria Theresa then pretended to give way to her husband. She let Francis be crowned and given the title of Emperor, but continued to govern alone with the counselors of her own choosing. She then devoted herself entirely to ensuring her empire's independence and security.

During those troubled years, Francis had hardly ever left Maria Theresa's side. Despite the vicissitudes of war, their family life had developed harmoniously. The Empress had given birth to six children, among whom were the future emperors Joseph II and Leopold II. In that time, the imperial couple had adopted the lifestyle which would be theirs until the Emperor's death. The Empress rose very early every morning: six o'clock in the winter, four in the summer. Although her high functions absorbed her, she did not neglect her family. Compelled to delegate her maternal authority to tutors and governesses who looked after the legion of archdukes and archduchesses, she left nothing to chance. She maintained a daily, punctilious correspondence with their teachers. Nothing concerning her children was to be concealed from her. Furthermore, she demanded to be summoned should any serious incident arise concerning any of them—or any incident that might be construed as such. Interested in scientific progress, she had engaged in her service one of the most reputed physicians in Europe, Dr. van Swieten. He alone, in their parents' absence, had the right to make decisions concerning the young princes. Maria Theresa ordered his subordinates to follow his prescribed treatments and diets with the utmost diligence. Like his Swiss colleague, the renowned Tronchin, van Swieten advocated a healthy, outdoor life; physical exercise, such as walking and riding, were an important part of his program. He also tried to impose on his illustrious patients a nutrition that was far from standard at the time. The imperial children were to eat soup, eggs, vegetables and fruit. They ate very little high game and stew. They usually ate their meals in private, as did the Emperor and Empress, who tended to neglect van Swieten's advice when it came to themselves. The honest doctor warned them several times that an overly rich diet might be detrimental to their physical well-being. Maria Theresa probably felt that her life was sufficiently difficult without having to sacrifice the innocent pleasures of the table. Graced with robust good health, she allowed herself a few hours of relaxation in all seasons, and rode to the outskirts of Vienna. She went either to one of her many residences or to see some of the great servants of the crown, who were very flattered by her visit.

The imperial family liked the simple joys of intimacy. A somewhat naïve gouache painted by the Archduchess Maria Christina takes us into the home on Saint Nicholas' day, 1762, when the children receive gifts. Nothing about it recalls the Meytens painting described above. In a small drawing room with light-colored walls and polished wood furniture, the kind of room that could belong to a good middle-class family, the Emperor is reading in front of a blazing fire. He is seated at a table, wearing a dressing gown, nightcap and slippers, and is being served hot chocolate (or tea) by his wife, who is standing behind him looking resplendent in a simple sky-blue wool dress. Four children are making merry by their side, two girls and two boys. Maximilian, the youngest of the archdukes, is eating sweetmeats and playing with a cavalryman mounted on a boiled cardboard steed; Ferdinand, who has found only birch rods in his shoe, is crying his eyes out, while his older sister, Maria Christina, who almost looks like a young mother, is holding out a plate of cakes to console him. Finally, behind Maria Theresa's skirts, a beaming, proud little girl is holding up a magnificent doll—it is little Antonia! She is barely seven years old.

Maria Theresa had had comfortable apartments built in the ancient Hofburg palace, which still looked a bit like a medieval fortress. But when the summer season came, the Empress preferred to move to Schönbrunn Castle with her entire family. This palace, built a few miles away from Vienna, was modeled on Versailles, which had fascinated European sovereigns for half a century. As of 1749, the Empress stayed more and more frequently in this pleasant, relatively small residence, which she enjoyed altering according to her taste—a very reliable, very feminine taste. She chose panel decorations in the rarest woods, commissioned artists to paint bright landscapes filled with flowers and birds and wanted the allegories illustrating her reign to be done with more grace than grandeur. She also liked creating many precious exhibition rooms, a Chinese room, a room of lacquerware, a porcelain room . . . The imperial family lived in brightly colored rooms decked with baroque mirrors endlessly reflecting delicately shaded pastels.

Though the Empress liked finding respite from the obligations of government in the simplicity of family life, she did not disdain splendor. In Vienna she presided over a brilliant court whose entertainments remained legendary. Antonia made her first official appearance on the occasion of the Emperor's name day, on October 5, 1759. Swathed in a low-cut court dress, she sang several couplets in French, Ferdinand beat the drum, Maximilian recited a compliment in Italian, Joseph played the cello, Charles the violin, Maria Anna and Maria Christina the piano. The following year, in spite of her very tender years, the little Archduchess attended the celebrations of Joseph's marriage to Isabella of Parma. A huge painting kept at the Kunsthistorisches Museum in Vienna portrays a concert given in honor of the young married couple. Sitting quietly in the first row on each side of their parents, the imperial children, in gala attire, are listening to the music. Several of them are still so small that their feet do not touch the floor. Watched over discreetly by her governess, Antonia, her hair powdered and well groomed, is sitting erect and gracious in her dress à paniers.

Music held an important place among the august family's entertainments. Maria Theresa's father, Charles VI, was an excellent harpsichordist and did not consider it beneath his dignity to conduct the court orchestra. Maria Theresa enjoyed singing; Francis liked her warm contralto voice. The imperial family encouraged musicians. Wagenseil was the court music master, but the works of Haydn and Gluck were preferred over his. When word came to them about a certain Mozart, a child prodigy from Salzburg, who was coming through Vienna in 1762, Maria Theresa invited him to the Hofburg. Surrounded by their progeny, Maria Theresa and Francis listened to the little Mozart and his sister for three hours. They then questioned them at length about their art. The princes showed themselves to be particularly affable. "We were received with so many marks of favor by Their Majesties that if I told you

about it in detail, my account would be taken for a fairy tale," Mozart's father
would write to one of his friends.⁴ In the artist's family, they told the story of
how the little prodigy had slipped and fallen on the well-polished drawing-
room floor, and how Antonia, the youngest of the archduchesses, who was
exactly his age, rushed to help him up and kissed him. "You are kind, I would
like to marry you," he said to her. "Out of gratitude," he replied to the
Empress when she laughed and asked why he wanted to marry her daughter.
The anecdote has been told many times, and though it cannot be authenti-
cated, it is perfectly plausible. In Vienna, it was possible to deviate from protocol and the archdukes' education did not crush their spontaneity.

Antonia led the most carefree life imaginable. The lenient Countess of
Brandeiss, who was in charge of her education, was content to merely instill in
her the religious and moral principles that every archduchess had to possess.
To please her charming pupil, she shortened the hours devoted to reading and
writing. Antonia preferred racing around madly in the park grounds or riding
by sleigh in winter with her older sister Carolina and the Princesses of Hesse
and Mecklenburg. Her mind was only on amusing herself. Her mother gave
very little thought to her education, and her father, though he was very attentive to his sons' education, was far less demanding as far as his daughters were
concerned. So long as they were virtuous and proficient in the female arts such
as music, tapestry work and watercolors, they would know enough to make
accomplished wives. What more could be asked of them? When he was in the
prime of life, the Emperor wrote a kind of spiritual testament for his children.
Inspired by the principles of the Catholic religion, which the imperial household observed devoutly, he reminded them that their illustrious birth should
not lead them to forget that they were on earth to earn their salvation. Moreover, this debonair Epicurean warned them against all worldly vanities and
implored them to be wary of flatterers and false friends.

The year 1765 marked a turning point in the life of the imperial family.
Early that year the court celebrated Archduke Joseph's second marriage, to
Josephine of Bavaria—in sadness, for the Prince still mourned his first wife,
who had died of smallpox in 1762. Then other preparations were underway
for Leopold's marriage to one of the daughters of the King of Spain, much
to the Empress's delight. At the beginning of August, the imperial couple
and their children went to Innsbruck to celebrate this union. But everything took a rapid turn for the worse. Leopold fell sick with inexplicable
malaises which made them fear for his life. Several days were spent in
anguish. On August 17, the Prince seemed fully recovered and Maria

Theresa decided to go to the theater with the entire family. Feeling unwell during the performance, the Emperor left his box without saying a word. Joseph left with him. When he arrived in his apartment, he collapsed in his son's arms. Attempts were made to revive him, but in vain. He was dead.

Utterly grief-stricken, for the first time in her life the Empress was at a loss what to do. She refused to see anyone for several hours. She thought of retiring to a convent and leaving the empire to Joseph. But she soon recovered her wits and resolved to pursue her work. Her children were too young to be entrusted to even the most devoted servants. And above all she could not leave the empire—one of her purposes in life—to Joseph, who was too inexperienced. She decided to include him in her government with the title of coregent. He thereby succeeded his father. It seemed reasonable to assume that this young man of twenty-four would not be as submissive as Francis. Assertive, innovative, educated for the exercise of supreme power, he would likely clash with his mother, whom he both revered and feared.

We don't know what feelings overcame the young Antonia at the death of her father, who treasured her as he did all his children. But her daily life certainly changed. There were fewer moments of family intimacy. She saw her mother less frequently, and suddenly she now seemed an imposing and distant elderly lady. The governing of her states claiming her attention more than ever, Maria Theresa took refuge in ostentatious mourning. Dressed entirely in black, her face hooded in a lace bonnet tied under the chin, she would not allow concerts or entertainments. For long months, a deathly silence was cast over the Hofburg and Schönbrunn. In 1766, however, the Empress wanted merry celebrations for the wedding of her daughter Maria Christina to Prince Albert of Sachsen-Teschen. It was the culmination of a true love story. But the joy was short-lived. An epidemic of smallpox soon decimated Vienna and the imperial family was not spared. Nor was it the first time the dreadful disease struck the Hofburg. It had already taken the lives of Archduke Charles Joseph, Archduchess Johanna and Joseph's first wife. Now the illness afflicted Maria Theresa, Josephina of Bavaria, Maria Christina and Albert of Sachsen-Teschen as well as Archduchess Elisabeth, all at the same time. Though his wife was in critical condition, the Emperor never left his mother's bedside. Maria Theresa recovered but her daughter-in-law died. No one lamented her passing. Maria Christina and Albert survived; Elisabeth pulled through but her beautiful face was irreparably pockmarked.

As soon as she had regained her strength the Empress had to set about preparing the marriage of her daughter Josephina to the King of Naples. This

would be the fruit of skillful diplomatic schemes which the sovereign had carried out in a masterly manner. Before celebrating the ceremony by proxy,
which was to be held in Vienna, the Empress demanded that her daughter
meditate at the grave of her recently deceased sister-in-law, in the forbidding
crypt of the Capuchin church. Overwhelmed by a dread presentiment,
Josephina saw this command as a death sentence. Upon her return to the
Hofburg, she began shivering: it was the onset of smallpox. Two weeks later,
all the churches in Vienna tolled their bells. Josephina had passed away. She
had just turned sixteen. Antonia would never forget this tragic death.

Josephina had barely joined her countless relations in the Habsburg
necropolis when the King of Spain, "without hesitating, or losing a minute,"[5]
asked Maria Theresa for another archduchess for his son, the King of Naples.
Disregarding her own emotional state, the Empress let him choose between
Amalia and Carolina. He chose Carolina, the youngest. Nothing could have
brought greater sadness to Antonia. The two sisters were bound by deep
affection. They were always whispering and laughing together, observing the
failings or ridiculous ways of some of the people around them and making
fun of them mercilessly. Maria Theresa had previously wanted to separate
the two adolescents to avoid hurting feelings provoked by their attitude. But
the two accomplices had continued their games. Carolina's departure for
Naples, in April 1768, put an end to this close bond. Finding "a husband
whose face was very ugly" and whose behavior was often peculiar, the new
Queen of Naples's conjugal life had a distressing beginning.[6] In her letters to
her governess, Countess of Lerchenfeld, she always asked for news of Antonia, whom she said she "loved extraordinarily. When I think her fate may be
like mine," she said, "I would like to write her entire volumes on the subject . . . for I must say the agony suffered is all the greater in that one must
always appear happy."[7] In writing these lines, in August 1768, Carolina was
fully aware that negotiations were progressing over Antonia's marriage to
Louis XV's grandson.

2

GREAT EXPECTATIONS

*A*fter she had become a widow, the Empress no longer gave much thought to personal happiness; her main preoccupation was the future of her states, and she saw her children as destined to serve the dynasty. Each was meant to help consolidate her achievement as best he or she could. Having included Joseph—who thereby became Emperor Joseph II—in her government, she hoped to fashion him in her own image and make him into a sovereign who would be worthy of her. She had entrusted the government of Tuscany to Leopold. As for the archduchesses, they were to enter into unions that would be profitable to the House of Habsburg or would consolidate preexisting alliances. In this respect, Maria Theresa acted no differently from the other European sovereigns. However, none of the others had made nuptial politics into a systematic policy. Through their marriages, the young princesses were sacrificed to their mother's diplomacy. The prospective husband's personality was irrelevant so long as the Empress considered him a major player on the political scene. Wanting the Habsburgs represented in Naples, she had offered one of her daughters to a sovereign who was considered feebleminded. "So long as she fulfills her duty toward God and her husband and earns her salvation, even if she is to be unhappy, I will be pleased," Maria Theresa wrote concerning her young daughter.[1] In 1769, she gave Amalia to Ferdinand, Duke of Parma, a simpleton and sensualist who was five years her junior. This hardly mattered considering that the presence of a Habsburg in Parma would strengthen the power of the illustrious House in Italy.

For over ten years Maria Theresa had been nursing a plan that was to be the crowning achievement of her nuptial politics: the union of one of the archduchesses with the heir to the French throne. In 1756, the Empress had managed a tour de force in winning the alliance of the French King, Louis XV, against the King of Prussia and the King of England. France's foreign policy was thereby given a new orientation after centuries of trying to subdue Austria. This tie, which had served her interests to the detriment of Louis XV's, meant a great deal to the Empress and she saw a marriage as a way of making it durable. On Austria's initiative, the two courts began to engage in vague negotiations on the subject in 1764. Antonia had been designated by her mother for this great destiny quite simply because her age matched that of the Dauphin, Louis Auguste, who was to succeed his grandfather, Louis XV. That Antonia become Queen of France was Maria Theresa's greatest wish.

But Louis XV had to be coaxed. The alliance with Austria was sharply criticized in France and was still extremely unpopular. During their lifetime, Louis Auguste's parents had not concealed from the sovereign their repugnance at the consummation of such a union. Louis XV seemed to hesitate. In Vienna, the Empress cajoled the French ambassador and repeatedly made him admire the gracious blond girl with the porcelain complexion in the hope that he might make a decisive pronouncement in his master's name. Mindful of the instructions he had received, the diplomat kept a cautious reserve. During a reception, one of the Austrian ministers asked him point-blank what he thought of Archduchess Antonia. "Very attractive," the ambassador answered simply. "She will make a charming wife for Monsieur le Dauphin," the Austrian went on. "She is a dainty morsel and will be in good hands, if it is to be,"[2] replied the Frenchman somewhat enigmatically. No progress was made. Maria Theresa was fuming.

In 1768, with Louis XV suddenly a widower, the Empress hatched a new plan: why not organize a double marriage? She would give her daughter Elisabeth to the monarch, who was not yet sixty, and Antonia to his grandson. The idea of this new match did not trouble the pious sovereign in the least; she would have no hesitation in marrying off one of her daughters to an aging sovereign whose libertine morals were widely talked about. However, in Versailles, Louis XV had just taken a certain Madame du Barry as mistress, a young woman who was highly accomplished in the voluptuous skills needed to excite the senses of the blasé sensualist. There was no question of another marriage for the King of France, certainly not with a princess whose face was pockmarked.

Maria Theresa then concentrated all her energies on her younger daughter's marriage, which still had to be confirmed. She decided to round off her education. More to the point, it was time to begin this education, for though the young thirteen-year-old had the gift of charm and grace and performed her courtly roles to perfection, Antonia hardly knew how to read and write in the three languages that were in use at the Viennese court—German, French and Italian. Attending first to the priority required by the prospect dearest to her heart, Maria Theresa arranged for her to take diction lessons from two French actors who were staying in the Austrian capital. This was sufficient to rouse Louis XV. Entrusting the future Dauphine to actors was bound to shock the monarch. Maria Theresa was exultant. The King of France's discontent was proof that he had not given up the great plan. It was therefore legitimate to ask him to send the ideal tutor to Vienna for the future Dauphine.

Several weeks later, the Abbé de Vermond arrived at the Hofburg. The odds seemed slim that this unimpressive-looking clergyman who was passionately fond of belles lettres could hold the attention of the petulant and lazy Archduchess, who thought only of having fun. But contrary to all expectations, the maiden and the Abbé got on extremely well. The little Princess soon charmed her teacher, who succeeded in imposing a curriculum on her that included the study of religion, the French language and French literature and history. The clever Abbé immediately understood that the only way he could hope to educate the Archduchess was by amusing her. So he invented an educational approach designed for her. He shortened her hours of study and replaced them with long conversations. He told her anecdotes that would help her commit to memory the habits of the court and the histories of the great families she would be meeting. The Abbé was surprised by the encouraging results he obtained from his student; she showed herself to be more gifted than he had originally thought. "She understands me well when I present her with clear ideas; her judgment is always good but I cannot accustom her to delve into things, though I feel she is capable of it," he noted, quite captivated by her.[3] As for Antonia, she so liked the Abbé's company that she wanted him to be present when she played. The Empress was the first to congratulate herself on this good relationship. She flattered Vermond, admitted him into the imperial family's intimate circle and lavished thoughtful attentions on him. She was already planning to use him when her daughter would be in France. Without the little Princess knowing it, at Ver-

sailles he would still be her mentor-spy in the service of Austria. When she
became Dauphine and Queen, she never suspected her confidant's duplicity.

In the meantime Antonia blossomed. She grew and developed harmoniously. Elegantly dressed, she never missed a ball, a concert, a reception or a
performance at the opera. At the Hofburg, she was seen once a week at the
Empress's card table, though she clearly preferred the games of *cavagnole*[4] and
the lotteries organized in the archdukes' apartments. But everything paled
compared to the joyful sleigh rides on the outskirts of Vienna during the winter
of 1768–69. The social whirl almost made her forget her imminent marriage
and departure for faraway, unknown France and the mythical Château de Versailles depicted to her by the Abbé in the rosiest terms. If not for the sessions
imposed by the French dentist who had come from Paris to straighten her
pretty but badly aligned teeth, her life would truly have been a fairy tale.

In April 1769, dressed in a lovely blue silk dress brightened with ribbons
of the same material and lace trimmings, the Archduchess posed for the
pastelist Ducreux, who had come expressly from Paris. The artist found it difficult to render the radiance of her transparent skin that glowed in the light.
With her oval face, her big blue eyes, her small, slightly disdainful mouth,
her powdered hair swept up in curls and held with pearls, the adolescent girl
already seems to know who she is and what is owed her. But her still childish
expression, the gentleness exuding from her little being, plead for leniency.
She posed to project an image and not as she really was. "One can find faces
with more regular beauty," wrote Vermond, "I do not think one can find
more pleasant ones."[5]

Negotiations between the two courts were being actively pursued. At last,
on June 13, 1769, the Empress received the French King's official marriage
proposal. She responded with alacrity, assuring him of her joy at giving her
daughter to his grandson, whom, she hoped, Antonia would have "the good
fortune of pleasing." In the meanwhile, the wedding date was set for May 16
of the following year. Antonia would be fourteen and a half, and the
Dauphin, who was born on August 23, 1754, would not even have celebrated
his sixteenth birthday.

But who was this Dauphin, heir to such a glorious kingdom? It seems his
young fiancée had been told very little about him. In fact, the reports Maria
Theresa received about him might have distressed his future spouse. "Nature
seems to have denied everything to Monsieur the Dauphin. In his bearing
and words, the Prince displays a very limited amount of sense, great plainness
and no sensitivity."[6] So spoke Count Mercy-Argenteau, the Empress's ambas-

sador to the court of Louis XV. This diplomat, who would play an important part in the future Queen's life, tended to denigrate the French royal family and was often very critical of the Louis XV's politics. However, if Mercy had found the Dauphin attractive, he would have made it his duty to describe him in flattering terms.

It is true that the future Louis XVI was hardly a shining light in his grandfather's court. Though tall, this young man had grown up too quickly and did not have an imposing appearance. Not yet portly, he nevertheless waddled as he walked, as though hampered by a graceless body. Louis Auguste's regular facial features and gentle, myopic blue eyes might have attracted sympathy if he had been able to look people straight in the face, but he dared not. When he spoke, his muted, nasal voice and guttural laugh were an unpleasant surprise. Sad, timid, full of feelings of inferiority, the Dauphin seemed to bear the weight of shameful torments on his frail shoulders. Unloved by his parents, who had preferred his older brother—a child endowed with all the qualities of an ideal prince but who died at ten—he believed he was unworthy of his royal destiny, as if he had usurped his rank. The untimely deaths of his father and mother from tuberculosis left him in the hands of a pretentious, narrow-minded tutor, the Duc de La Vauguyon. He completed the task of "castrating" the personality of this boy who already had a tendency to withdraw into himself from early childhood. Convinced that no one was interested in him and that he was the object of countless court jeers, Louis Auguste dared not love anyone, confided in no one and withdrew into a silence that might have seemed offensive to those around him if they hadn't considered the heir to the throne an idiot and regarded him with condescension. And yet Louis Auguste had a thorough knowledge of French history and the history of the European states; he had acquired a solid grounding in law, could translate Latin writings quite competently, spoke Italian and English and was passionately interested in geography, overseas travel and scientific discoveries. But the inhibited adolescent was distressed at the prospect of his marriage. His tutors had depicted women to him as the cause of all public and private evil. Though he did not have a detailed knowledge of his grandfather's depraved way of life, he had heard enough cryptic comments on the subject to feel a mixture of fear and disgust for anything connected with sex. To compound matters, before dying, his father and mother had had time to convey to him their aversion for the Austrian alliance. And La Vauguyon had continued to educate him along those lines.

Naturally, Antonia knew nothing of all this. Very curious by nature, the

Archduchess must have asked countless questions about this husband selected for reasons of state. The replies must surely have been heartening. Louis Auguste must have been described to her in the most conventional terms, as an excellent prince, true to the religion of his forefathers, serious and hardworking, sensitive to the misfortunes of the humble—all of which was perfectly true. To help her in her reveries, the future Dauphine was sent a colored print representing the heir to the throne plowing! Bent over a cart driven by a robust peasant, modest and pensive, the Dauphin is plowing a furrow under his tutor's approving gaze while his two younger brothers seem amused by this utterly incongruous situation.

The last months in Vienna flew by for Antonia in a daze of celebrations and the future plans with which she was lulled. On April 3, 1770, she was given two official portraits of her betrothed. Apparently delighted to become acquainted with this face which she had been forced to imagine up to then, the Archduchess asked for permission to hang up one of the paintings in her room. Before her departure for her new homeland, the Abbé de Vermond decided to organize a three-day retreat for his student. In spite of all the excitement of preparations, she succeeded in gathering her thoughts. "I would need more time to explain all my ideas to you," she sighed after her meditations.[7] But time was running out and the thought of letting this inno-cent, naïve child go to the most corrupt court in Europe suddenly worried Maria Theresa. In a seeming attempt to make up for the time she had never been able to devote to her, she had her sleep in her bedroom for the last nights she spent at the Hofburg.

On April 15, Easter Sunday, the official ceremonies began. As Louis XV's representative, the French ambassador made a public entrance into the capi-tal in order to make a second request for the Archduchess's hand. The events of the day were to be a lavish demonstration whose purpose was to assert the French monarch's power: a cortege of forty-eight coaches, each drawn by six horses and accompanied by a hundred and seventeen footmen, rolled through the streets of the capital to the imperial residence. From the balcony of an aristocratic mansion, little Antonia watched this impressive procession organized in her honor. In the evening, wearing a miniature of the Dauphin on her bosom, she took part in the gala reception given by her mother. A short while later, Maria Theresa led her guests to the performance of Marivaux's *La Mère confidente* and a ballet choreographed by Noverre. It was he, inciden-tally, who had introduced Antonia to the subtleties of French dances.

On April 17, the Archduchess renounced all rights to succeed her mother. Two days later, at six o'clock in the evening, wearing a silver brocade dress with a long train, radiant and misty-eyed, she followed her mother and brother Joseph as they entered the austere Augustinian church. She knelt next to her brother Ferdinand, who stood in for the Dauphin in this wedding by proxy held in Vienna. After the mass, the young bride, now regarded as Dauphine of France, was seated at the place of honor, on the right side of her brother the Emperor, at the sumptuous feast in her honor.

Antonia lived these last Vienna days in a feverish state. Letters were written. For the last time, the Archduchess signed with the first name "Antonia" the affectionate and deferential missive she addressed to Louis XV, under the Empress's dictation. From now on her name would be Marie Antoinette. Maria Theresa wrote to the King of France as well, requesting that he show indulgence for her daughter's youthfulness and flightiness. Some last confidences were shared. Kisses were exchanged. And on April 21, before the entire court, the Dauphine got into a coach that looked like a jewel box and set off for the kingdom of France.

The journey would be a long one. She had to cross through some of the Habsburg states and several German principalities and free cities before reaching Strasbourg, the French city where the large Austrian retinue accompanying the Dauphine would have to part with her. Forever. Only the Abbé de Vermond and the Prince of Starhemberg were allowed to continue the journey to Versailles, residence of the Kings of France. The long row of coaches drove down the roads of Germany under driving rain. The carriages were met with nothing but cheers, applause and celebrations along the way, but each stage of the journey lasted eight hours. Every evening, after an exhausting day on the road, she had to be on show, smile and respond to compliments. Tired and suffering from a very bad cold, the Dauphine sometimes fell asleep as she sat through the theatrical performances and concerts given for her—or imposed on her—wherever she went. Marie Antoinette adored entertainments, but on this occasion they exceeded her capacity for endurance.

On the evening of May 6, they stopped in Schüttern just across the river from Strasbourg. The Princess slept on German soil for the last time. The following day at eleven-thirty, the imperial coach crossed a newly constructed bridge over the Rhine. It led to the Ile des Epis, an island considered neutral territory for the *remise*—transfer—of the Dauphine to the French authorities. In the course of several weeks, a wooden pavilion had been built designed to look exactly like a small château. It included five rooms: two antechambers on the Austrian side, two on the French side, and a central drawing room between the two. It had been furnished as well as possible, by calling upon the generosity of Alsatian families, who had lent furniture, paintings and tapestries.

Before retiring to her dressing room to change clothes, Marie Antoinette said goodbye to all the people who had accompanied her up to then. She took off her traveling clothes and put on a ceremonial dress in a golden fabric. It is worth pointing out that the Princess was not required to strip naked in public and offer her virginal body to the lustful gazes of the dignitaries in her retinue, as some historians, inspired by a lewd imagination, have written. Choked with emotion, dressed according to French fashion, Marie Antoinette saw the door of the large, brightly lit drawing room open before her. Led away from the Austrian delegation which had also entered this solemn hall, the Princess was taken to a majestic armchair placed under a canopy. The French devoured her with their eyes while the welcoming speeches succeeded each other and the formalities of the *remise* proceeded. Did she look at the tapestries illustrating the tragic love of Jason and Medea, which the day before an unknown young student by the name of Goethe had found horribly shocking? It is unlikely. Marie Antoinette had very little knowledge of mythology. She was surely more responsive to a tragicomic incident: the driving rain had leaked through the cracks in the ceiling onto the ceremonial clothes and hairdos of the French ladies who had come to welcome her. Yet it was hardly the time to laugh. With the deeds signed, the compliments recited, the door to the French side opened and a crowd of noble strangers appeared before our ingenue's eyes: her future subjects. Marie Antoinette turned her head the other way. The Austrians had disappeared. Distraught, she ran toward the first lady in the row and threw herself, sobbing, into her arms. Once this emotional moment had passed, this woman, who was none other than the Comtesse de Noailles, her lady-in-waiting, introduced her to all the people who had come to welcome her and escort her to France.

The spectacle offered by the city of Strasbourg allowed the Dauphine to recover her serenity very quickly. Young girls from the best Alsatian families, wearing regional costumes, strewed rose petals in her path as her coach crossed a jubilant city. The crowd acclaimed Marie Antoinette, who politely greeted all these unknown people who had come to pay homage to her. In celebration of her arrival, the most beautiful tapestries were hung at the windows, orchestras played at the crossroads, beef was roasted on the Place de l'Hôtel de Ville and fountains of wine flowed in the streets. This was certainly enough to make anyone forget fatigue, a cold and secret feelings of distress.

3

A ROYAL MARRIAGE

verywhere jubilant crowds ran out to meet the young Princess and she began to develop a taste for these vibrant tributes. With beating heart, her hair done in French fashion, wearing a gorgeous dress with hoops, she approached the Château de Compiègne,[1] where the King, the Dauphin and the court awaited her arrival. Several equerries rode out to meet her coach. They preceded the Duc de Choiseul, who came to compliment Madame la Dauphine. Louis XV's principal minister, Choiseul had negotiated her marriage. "I will never forget, monsieur," she said, "that you made my happiness." "And that of France," Choiseul replied.

The big moment was drawing near. The King and his grandson waited for Marie Antoinette a short distance away, near the Berne bridge. The procession started moving forward again. The Princess soon saw the monarch's imposing silhouette in a clearing up ahead. By his side, a young man she could not as yet make out well; further along several women's silhouettes and, at a more respectful distance, a large group of people in court attire. The coach came to a halt and two noblemen helped the Princess step down. Her clothes were unruffled. She looked admiringly at the sovereign and, after a moment's hesitation, disdaining protocol, she ran up to him as fast as her enormous gown and small silk shoes would allow. Blushing, she bowed in a perfect curtsy before Louis XV, who gently helped her up and kissed her.

Such youth, naturalness and spontaneity conquered the King, who immediately introduced the charming Dauphine to Louis Auguste. Dreadfully intimidated, the Prince gave this young unknown girl, who in three days would be sharing his bed, a tiny kiss on the cheek. Marie Antoinette then made the acquaintance of three mature princesses, the King's daughters, Madame Adélaïde, Madame Victoire and Madame Sophie. The fourth, Madame Louise, had just retired to a convent, to expiate the sins of her father.

In the royal coach, seated between the King and the Dauphin, Marie Antoinette expressed herself easily and smiled uninhibitedly. A great lover of women, Louis XV was captivated by his new Austrian granddaughter and immediately felt a great tenderness for her. The Dauphine was not impervious to the aura of this majestic grandfather, who was still considered the handsomest man in the kingdom. Indeed, she felt much more comfortable with him than with her future husband, who seemed to be sulking and did not even look at her. "Meeting with Madame la Dauphine," was all he noted in his diary that evening.

At the Château de Compiègne, which generally served as the court's summer residence, the princess met the other members of the royal family—first and foremost, Louis Auguste's two younger brothers, the chubby Comte de Provence, who, at fifteen, already looked full of solemn self-importance, and the Comte d'Artois, his junior. At thirteen and a half, he already resembled his grandfather. With his lively, mischievous air and impish gaze, he attracted Marie Antoinette's sympathy at once. Then came the turn of the kind, corpulent Duc d'Orléans, first royal prince, and his son Louis Philippe Joseph, Duc de Chartres. This slim-waisted young man, older than the Dauphin by seven years, stood out thanks to his attractive expression and conquering air. By his side, his wife seemed self-effaced, her attention riveted on her husband, with whom she was madly in love.

The following day, the coaches drove slowly toward the capital. But the Dauphin and Dauphine were to make a solemn "entrance" there at a later date. Today, after stopping off at the Carmelite convent of Saint Denis to pay Madame Louise a visit, the imposing royal procession bypassed the city and headed for the small Château de la Muette[2] in the Bois de Boulogne. Hundreds of carriages were parked along the road, whose occupants had come to see the new Dauphine and pay tribute to their sovereign.

In the evening, only the members of the royal family were invited to supper at La Muette. However, Marie Antoinette noticed a beautiful young woman whom no one thought to introduce to her. Very embarrassed by the

Archduchess's questions, Madame de Noailles replied that she was a lady in charge of amusing the King. To which Marie Antoinette answered rashly that she would like to become her rival! Seeing her chaperon's look of dismay, she realized she had just made a faux pas: the pretty woman was none other than Madame du Barry, the King's official mistress. Moreover, the entire court would soon cry out in indignation on learning that Louis XV had invited his favorite on such an occasion. After the supper, the King and princes returned to Versailles while the Princess retired to the apartment that had been prepared for her. The most magnificent surprise awaited her. Spread out on her dressing table were the late Dauphine's priceless jewels, which she would wear on the following day, May 16, 1770, the day of her wedding.

Madame la Dauphine rose early that morning. A warm, spring sun shone down on the road between La Muette and Versailles—the Versailles so often described and imagined. Already at dawn the roads had begun to fill with people and the rivers with boats. The Princess encountered a joyful, bustling crowd all along the road, for the common people, too, were invited to the royal nuptials. All decently dressed people were to be admitted into the castle and gardens. Food would be distributed in the streets and squares, and there would be fountains of wine for all those who wished to drink to the royal family's health.

By ten o'clock, when she rode through the gates of the famous palace, it resembled a busy beehive, with carpenters, upholsterers, pyrotechnists, cabinetmakers and cooks bustling about inside and out. Was she dazed by all this coming and going? Was she surprised by the relative austerity of the marble courtyard? Did she expect greater splendor? The entrance facing the city is certainly far less grand than the facade facing the grounds. Did she compare Versailles with Schönbrunn? No one can say. On arriving at the ground-floor apartment that had been temporarily assigned to her, the Dauphine felt a bit lost but ladies-in-waiting, chambermaids and hairdressers took possession of her, leaving her no time to brood over her first impressions. Her toilette would take nearly three hours! While she was being dressed, the King had himself announced. He came to introduce the Dauphin's younger sisters to his new granddaughter—two little girls, the already portly Madame Clotilde and Madame Elisabeth, who was only six years old.

At one o'clock, Marie Antoinette, in her white brocade dress, entered the King's room, where the Dauphin was waiting for her, ill at ease in his suit of gold fabric studded with diamonds. Louis XV smiled. It had been quite a while since he had beheld such a pretty bride. Her adolescent charm and candid blue eyes could only attract the hearts of all. However, her slightly haughty carriage and natural aloofness already offered a foreshadowing of the regal woman who would become Queen of France. As for the Dauphin, he still looked as glum as on the previous days. He took the Dauphine's hand, as protocol required, and the young couple appeared before the bedazzled eyes of the courtiers who had been waiting in the Hall of Mirrors—the huge hall which was the talk of all Europe. Followed by the King, the princes, the princesses and about sixty handpicked nobles, Louis Auguste and Marie Antoinette slowly made their way to the chapel, which was filled with people. They took their position at the foot of the altar and knelt down on two red velvet cushions. Slightly set back, the King, on his prie-dieu, gazed tenderly upon these two children who were being united for better or for worse. The great organs rang out; the Archbishop of Rheims conducted the service. Louis Auguste very solemnly slipped the wedding ring on the finger of the Dauphine, who still looked as radiant as she had that morning. The ceremony ended at two o'clock. While the guests could take a rest, the new bride had to receive the oaths of the officers of the house—that is, of all the gentlemen and ladies that were part of her immediate entourage and in her service.

Soon everyone gathered in the hall for the King's game while they waited for the evening festivities. Lanterns were to illuminate the groves in the park; the triumphal arches built over the grand canal were to form a blazing vault for the canopied gondolas which would ferry the guests around; a grandiose display of fireworks was to light up the sky and bring the evening to a close. But toward the end of the afternoon, the sky suddenly darkened, a violent storm broke out and torrential rains drenched the gardens. The King had to cancel the extravaganza and postpone it for two days, weather permitting.

While the common people who had come by the thousands returned home greatly disappointed, the royal family, followed by all the courtiers, walked down to the Opera House, newly completed by the architect Gabriel. As soon as the doors opened, exclamations of admiration arose from this normally jaded group. In a perfectly proportioned oval theater, gold-embroidered blue silk drapes hung from the boxes and mirrors behind the colonnades reflected the gilded sculptures to infinity. The parquet floor of the stalls, raised to the level of the stage which extended over the orchestra pit, had been made into an immense drawing room. A table had been set at the center solely for the royal family. Indeed, that evening, the courtiers remained standing, watching the spectacle of the wedding feast. All eyes were fixed on the Dauphine and her husband, seated on either side of the

King. Marie Antoinette hardly touched the food she was offered, but Louis Auguste's hearty appetite surprised his grandfather, who advised him to exercise self-restraint. "I always sleep better after a good supper," the young man replied blandly.

When the meal was over, it was time to proceed to the ancient ceremony of the *coucher*. Custom required that the court be present when the princes of the House of France went to bed. Many legends abound on the subject. Contrary to what has often been said, the princes and princesses did not undress publicly. The King—as a mark of honor—handed the Dauphin his nightshirt, but the Dauphin went into a changing room to slip it on and came back to the bed in night attire. The Queen—or in her absence the princess of royal blood[3] closest to the bride—gave the nightgown to the young bride, who also changed in private. This was the protocol that was quite naturally adopted for Louis Auguste and Marie Antoinette. Louis XV gave the nightshirt to his grandson and the Duchesse de Chartres, daughter-in-law of the first prince of royal blood, handed the nightgown to the Dauphine.

When the couple was ready to retire, the Archbishop blessed the bed. Throughout the entire ceremonial, Marie Antoinette remained perfectly self-possessed and smiled like a good actress, while Louis Auguste, to whom the King whispered some bawdy remarks, looked increasingly gloomy and embarrassed. Finally, the couple got into the large bed, before the crowd of courtiers, and the curtains were drawn. But Louis Auguste and Marie Antoinette were not left alone yet: the curtains were drawn open so the court—and the entire world—would see that the Dauphin of France was sharing his bed with Maria Theresa's daughter. The curtains were drawn shut again. Everyone retired. The newlyweds were not to be disturbed again. "Nothing," the Dauphin wrote in his journal for the day of May 16. The fact is nothing had happened during that wedding night. The Dauphine soon confided to her dear Abbé de Vermond that the Prince had not kissed her once or so much as held her hand.

Even if tired, they were not to linger in bed the following morning. The day was devoted to introducing hundreds of people to Madame la Dauphine, who had to smile and greet them with a few amiable words. The endless procession had wearied her and in the evening she nearly fell asleep while pretending to admire the performance of Quinault and Lulli's *Perseus* at the Opera, now changed back into a theater.

Two days later the court met again at the Opera, now transformed into a ballroom. That evening the festivities reached their apotheosis. Marie Antoinette danced gracefully, unaware of the scandal that had broken out shortly before the start of the ball—a matter of precedence as so often occurred at Versailles, where each person held his rank dearer than anything else. Since the Dauphine was the daughter of a Prince of Lorraine, the French representatives of the House of Lorraine had requested the King grant them the honor to dance immediately after the princes and princesses of royal blood. This put them ahead of the dukes and duchesses! By granting their request, Louis XV literally caused a palace revolution. Offended by this special dispensation which went contrary to custom, the dukes took grave counsel among themselves and persuaded much of the court not to take part in the ball! For the first time—quite inadvertently—Marie Antoinette angered the court nobility. Soon she would be all too familiar with the tenacity of resentments. However, for the time being, the Dauphine was completely unaware of this court drama. She knew she was being admired and it gave her inexpressible joy.

While they were dancing in the Opera, a growing crowd streamed into the illuminated grounds where the fountains offered the spectacle of the *grandes eaux* as in the time of Louis XIV. In the groves there were orchestras inviting people to dance, the thousands who had come from Paris and its outskirts eager to enjoy the nocturnal extravaganza. Actors were cheered on as they performed short scenes; there were tumblers, funambulists and jugglers who executed somersaults, acrobatics and a variety of other stunts; then came the great fireworks display, which the King and royal family watched from the windows of the château. So excited was the Dauphine that she clapped her hands and wanted to go down into the gardens and mingle with the crowd. But Louis XV, who feared that the frail adolescent would exhaust herself, advised her to go to bed, for the celebrations were still to go on for several days. Later there would be a masked ball where the Dauphine came as a domino and a series of theatrical performances that would familiarize her with the French repertoire.

The celebrations continued in Paris as well. They were to conclude on May 30 with a gigantic fireworks display and illuminations. The Dauphine, who was very eager to see the capital, succeeded in obtaining the sovereign's permission to go there with Mesdames Adélaïde, Victoire and Sophie, her husband's aunts, or *Mesdames Tantes* as they had now become for her. She boarded the coach joyfully with the daughters of the King; the Dauphin preferred to stay in his apartment. On the road, the princesses saw several rockets shoot up into the sky. Marie Antoinette's impatience grew as the carriage arrived at Cours-la-Reine,[4] which ran alongside the Seine and led to the just completed Place Louis XV (the present Place de la Concorde), marking the entrance into Paris from the west. But a strange clamor arose from the city. The horse and carriage slowed its pace. The bodyguards became apprehensive on seeing some men in tattered clothes running like madmen. They were questioned: a terrible tragedy had just occurred. On the Place Louis XV, after the fireworks, a dense crowd, impatient to get to the festivities on the boulevards as quickly as possible, had been caught in a dreadful trap. In the dark, dozens of people had fallen into the gaping ditches of the rue Royale, which was still under construction. In the general panic, they had been suffocated, crushed and trampled, and coachmen had tried to force their way through, adding to the confusion and horror.

The princesses had to return to Versailles. The following day, the Dauphin and Dauphine learned that the dead numbered one hundred and thirty-three. They immediately sent assistance to the victims' families, to whom the celebration of their marriage had brought grief.

THE VERSAILLES COURT

$\mathscr{D}$ azzled by this whirlwind of festivities, Marie Antoinette had no time to think about the instructions which her mother had given to her before her departure from Vienna. However, the Empress would surely have been pleased with her daughter. Maria Theresa might merely have raised an eyebrow on learning that Madame la Dauphine had neglected her spiritual readings after her daily morning prayers. She could not disrupt the sacrosanct protocol which left no time for intimacy or meditation, even though mass was attended daily.

The Princess was still getting to know the strange and fascinating world of Versailles. Nearly a century had gone by since Louis XIV had decided to make this palace his residence as well as the seat of government and the court. Built for the Sun King's great glory, the château had become the temple of royalty where the cult of the monarch was celebrated on a daily basis. The sovereign and his family were on perpetual show from the moment they woke up. Admitted by an extremely strict order of precedence, the courtiers attended the King's *lever* (rising) and watched him dress. In the evening, the same dignitaries returned for the King's *coucher* (bedding) ceremony and competed for the honor of handing him his nightdress or holding his candlestick. During the day, the King of the realm was rarely alone. Taking inspiration from a set of rules laid down by Henri III at the end of the sixteenth century, Louis XIV imposed a rigorous etiquette on the court and on himself, and regarded it not as a simple ceremonial matter, but as an instrument of domination. He felt that the respect shown to the sovereign was proportional to the distance he put between his subjects and himself, and he used the requirements of protocol to underscore that distance and decide on the rank he wished to give each person.

Louis XV endured the daily monarchical ritual painfully and continued to perform it with conscientious weariness. In contrast to his predecessor, he led somewhat of a double life. His official life took place in the state apartments, but he arranged to live his personal life away from prying eyes in a private apartment. A hidden door in the paneling of his official Bedchamber led to a row of chambers and reception rooms furnished with meticulous taste, giving out on the château's inner courtyards. Only a few privileged friends were admitted there. His mistress's apartment, which was just as refined, was connected to his by an inner stairway. Louis XV thereby escaped the burdens of his life as a sovereign. As for the members of his family, they all lived in comfortable and elegant apartments redistributed according to marriages and bereavements.

The château did not just house the King and his family. It was crowded with ten thousand people every day. The royal residence was open to all. Anyone could enter into the inner sanctum provided they were decently dressed, though men were required to wear a sword at their hip—an accessory that could be rented at a stall near the gates. Moreover, it was surprising to see a great many small sheds in the courtyard. The King allowed the sale of souvenirs and wares supporting a fruitful commerce.

The palace was entered by a marble stairway that opened out onto an impressive row of drawing rooms and antechambers. But these huge rooms had nothing that recalled a museum. The Guardroom, for instance, where soldiers lived around the clock, looked more like a barracks than a reception room. Beds, screens, and piles of weapons made for a very unroyal-looking chaos! The King's Antechamber, called *Oeil-de-boeuf* because of its oval-shaped window, was home to a huge, bulky Swiss guard. He drank, ate and slept in this very room where all the notables of the kingdom converged. His duty consisted of opening the door to the royal apartments giving out onto the Hall of Mirrors. He had to remember nine resonant words in order to perform his task: "Gentlemen, proceed! Gentlemen, the King! Withdraw. No entry, Sir!" And Sir would dash away without uttering a word. His rich, sonorous voice put to flight counts, marquis and dukes in droves. No one intimidated this commoner from the Swiss mountains who spoke in the monarch's name.

Though bewildered by the permanent bustle of this immense household, visitors admired the painted ceilings, monumental fireplaces, resplendent sculptures. In the Hall of Mirrors, they were dazzled by the play of light which further enhanced the magnificent decor. They walked by the most important personages in the kingdom strolling about nonchalantly. With a bit of luck, they could see the King on his way to the chapel for mass and attend His Majesty's public meal, on the days of *"grand couvert."* Aside from the throng of onlookers and supplicants who were immediately recognizable, there were countless administrators and servants of all ranks who took great pride in their employment.

Three to four thousand courtiers were constantly promenading and rushing in the sovereign's footsteps. The court, which these aristocrats disparaged and claimed to find boring, remained the seat of all prestige for them. To be "presented" at court, the King's genealogist had to be able to certify, with concrete proof, that an applicant's nobility dated back to the year 1400, at least! Nor would this necessarily suffice to be admitted into the monarch's intimate circle, which usually included only the oldest families in the realm. But a person's destiny could be changed at the whim or favor of the King. Everyone secretly dreamed of being singled out by the all-powerful ruler. In the meantime, a person who was "presented" had the right to ride in the King's coaches, hunt in his company and be invited to his balls and entertainments. But these were costly privileges, requiring that a person live according to his or her rank—in other words, luxuriously. A woman could not be seen wearing the same dress or jewels on several consecutive occasions. One had to follow fashion, have a coach, entertain in style. With a great deal of luck—and connections—one might be given one of the 226 apartments in the château, or more modestly one of the 500 rooms. These were tiny attic quarters, devoid of conveniences, freezing in winter and stifling in summer, where the courtiers lived crammed with their unavoidable servants—quarters they would never have tolerated in any other circumstances. But even living in a garret at the Château de Versailles was considered a mark of the highest favor and immediately made the happy beneficiary into one of the most prominent of privileged persons. However, the wealthiest among them owned mansions in town and only stayed at the château for certain occasions; others preferred to commute between Paris and Versailles and regarded their quarters at the château as just a pied-à-terre. This was the case for the princes of royal blood and the notables of the kingdom even though they had the best lodgings.

"Life at the court is a serious, melancholic game . . . One must have a plan of action, pursue it, forestall one's rival's plan, be prepared to take chances and act on a whim; and following all these dreams and calculations, be put in check, or occasionally checkmated." Such were the words of the moralist La Bruyère a century earlier. Nothing had really changed under Louis XV. The courtier's life was ruled by a confining etiquette. He knew every detail of the ceremonial and observed it scrupulously. He would greet distractedly, ask questions looking the other way, glide lightly along the floor, speak in a loud voice. But this would not necessarily bring him royal favor, which was his sole goal, on which all his energy was concentrated. He would try by every means to be intimate with the sovereign. Everything depended on the monarch, who could raise one individual's rank and lower another's at whim. The person who reached his goal was attentive to the sovereign's smallest desires; better yet, he anticipated them. Without engaging in truly sincere conversation, he instinctively knew how to say what the monarch wanted to hear, knew how to reassure him or entertain him, boredom being a permanent threat to princely lives. Whoever had acquired this priceless honor, which was the envy of so many noblemen, became obsessed with retaining it, for royal favor was fickle.

No one could escape the requirements of protocol with all its own peculiarities; it hindered the princes even more than those who served them, for the latter were only briefly inconvenienced. Madame de Noailles tried to explain its many subtleties to the Dauphine, but Marie Antoinette was exasperated by these lessons whose usefulness she failed to see, and was quick to nickname her lady-in-waiting "Madame Etiquette." Moreover, she had trouble accepting that everything concerning the royal family constituted the main subject of interest at the court.

Idle and scheming, no public was greedier for gossip and scandal than the courtiers at Versailles. The new couple formed by the Dauphin and Dauphine was fodder for all their conversations. Would Louis Auguste soon consummate his marriage with the blond Archduchess? This was the burning question on everybody's lips. At Versailles, everything was public knowledge. The morning after the wedding night it was already known through the servants, who had been bribed to report on the condition of the bed linens, that the prince had not honored his wife. Furthermore, the young husband's coolness had escaped no one's notice. Though he shared his wife's bed, everyone knew he left her early in the morning to go hunting for hours. "Did you sleep well?" he asked her when he returned. "Yes," she answered simply. And he left, while she played with her little dog. "It breaks my heart," sighed the Abbé de Vermond, who hastened—without the Princess knowing it—to report to the Austrian ambassador, whose duty it was to inform the Empress on every last detail concerning her daughter's life.[1] Maria Theresa, who intended to control Marie Antoinette's behavior from Vienna, had given the diplomat the task of sending her detailed reports on this subject. Hence they exchanged secret letters in addition to their official correspondence.

As the Empress's loyal servant, Count Mercy-Argenteau had set up an information system in which the Abbé de Vermond was a key player. Marie Antoinette confided in the Abbé with candor and was pleased to receive Monsieur de Mercy. He alone could speak to her in the name of her mother. This tall, thin, unfailingly elegant and impassive-looking forty-three-year-old man succeeded in winning the Princess's friendship in spite of a standoffish-ness which sometimes gave him a slightly unpleasant, haughty air. In her youth and naïveté, she saw in him a kind of fatherly friend. She would never know that Vermond and Mercy were the first to betray her. Indeed, how could she suspect them, since it was through Mercy that she received the letters which the Empress refused to entrust to ordinary couriers?

"True happiness in this world is a happy marriage. Everything depends on the wife being obliging, gentle and amusing," she wrote her in her first missive.[2] Marie Antoinette probably knew this little talisman sentence by heart since it came from the all-powerful mother whom she loved and had to keep happy at all costs. And yet Maria Theresa had no illusions concerning the husband she had given to her daughter. The letter sent to her by the Prince of Starhemberg, who had stayed in Versailles for the wedding cele-brations, had dissipated her last illusions—if she ever had any—concerning the Dauphin. "The first nights went by without any interesting event. It is rather natural to attribute the cause of this coldness to embarrassment, timid-ity and a kind of imbecility that shows in the Prince's entire countenance," he declared callously.

Some people spoke of "mental frigidity,"[3] others of impotence. The King, who was not unduly worried about the young couple's future, acknowledged nonetheless that his grandson was "not very caressing."[4] But had not Louis Auguste's father taken six months to consummate his marriage? The Dauphin and Dauphine needed time to get to know each other. So, following the advice of her dear mother, Marie Antoinette tried to domesticate this timid husband who remained impervious to her charms.

It was during a stay in Marly, where Louis XV liked to retire with a small retinue, that the ice began to break between the two young people. This residence, not very far from Versailles, had twelve pavilions laid out around the small royal château, symbolizing the sun, emblem of Louis XIV, and the twelve signs of the zodiac. In Marly,[5] as in Choisy,[6] where they went immediately afterward, they lived almost without constraint. In this relative tranquillity Marie Antoinette and Louis Auguste spoke frankly with each other for the first time. Very solemnly the Dauphin declared to his wife "that he was not ignorant of what was involved in the state of marriage"[7] and that he would live in marital intimacy with her during the court's traditional long summer stay in Compiègne. "Since we must live in intimate friendship," she replied, "we must trust each other in speaking about everything."[8] She won the sympathy if not the love of this strange, brusque-mannered boy who hastened to confide to his aunts that he found his wife "very charming."[9]

However, when they arrived in Compiègne, the Dauphin had a serious case of indigestion and decided to sleep separately, deserting his wife though he had been more attentive to her than previously. Secretly relieved, perhaps, to escape embraces whose clumsiness she feared, Marie Antoinette sang Louis Auguste's praises to her mother. "As for my dear husband," she wrote her, "he has changed much and all for the better. He shows me a great friendliness."[10] Such considerations exasperated Maria Theresa. Once again, her daughter's happiness mattered little to her. She had but one goal: maintaining the Franco-Austrian alliance. The nonconsummation of their marriage jeopardized what she regarded as her masterpiece of diplomacy. That the Dauphin lacked brilliance hardly bothered her—quite the contrary. She wanted her daughter to show herself clever enough to gain influence over him. Then she could easily dictate what she expected from France. Mercy-Argenteau was full of hope in this respect: "There is no doubt that Madame l'Archiduchesse will succeed in completely subjugating Monsieur le Dauphin," he wrote to the Empress.[11] But for that to happen, the Prince would have to give up his amorous passivity! Careful not to rush matters, Maria Theresa heaped advice on her daughter, preached patience and told her to "lavish more caresses."

The young couple continued to live separately like two good-natured relatives with different, indeed opposing tastes, but brought together by an incontrovertible family will. For the time being Louis Auguste and Marie

Antoinette felt rather lonely. They each had an overwhelming need for tenderness. Louis Auguste because he had never been loved; Marie Antoinette because she felt homesick. She realized very soon that Louis XV was not "the most tender of fathers" as her mother had told her. The King loved his children and grandchildren, but being completely absorbed in his passion for Madame du Barry, he kept them at a distance. He liked the Dauphine's spontaneity and was amused by her youthfulness, though he found her "lively and a bit childlike."[12] He certainly showed more interest in her than in his other grandchildren and his demonstrations of affection were not devoid of a certain flirtatiousness, as when he took her on his knees or kissed her little hands. However, his open liaison with a young woman thirty years his junior who was said to come from the gutter deeply shocked Marie Antoinette. This dashing grandfather who had initially captivated her now left her with feelings of shame and disgust. She avoided meeting him and manifested a certain embarrassment in his presence. Accustomed to living in a society where the least deviation in morals was severely punished, the Dauphine was strict in judging the King. "It is pitiful the weakness he has for Madame du Barry, who is the stupidest and most impertinent creature,"[13] she wrote, deeply shocked, to her mother, who had carefully avoided mentioning such an indelicate subject to her.

Docilely following the advice of the Empress, who had praised the piety and virtue of the elderly demoiselles, Marie Antoinette grew closer to her aunts. Little loved, devoid of influence and avidly fond of intrigue, Louis XV's three daughters, who had always ruled over the Dauphin, had apparently given his wife a warm welcome. However, the eldest, Madame Adélaïde, who dominated her younger sisters, had been hostile to the alliance with Maria Theresa and had not hidden her resentment when the King told her of his determination to marry Louis Auguste off to the Archduchess. She had immediately nicknamed her "*l'Autrichienne*," the Austrian woman. This pretty, petulant little girl who played with her dogs and the children of chambermaids, who hid behind her fan giggling and refused to wear a corset, annoyed the Princess, who was wedded to her starchy principles and jealous of Marie Antoinette's radiant youthfulness. She was appalled at the thought that this saucy girl would one day accede to the throne. But eager to maintain her influence over her nephew, the future monarch, Madame Adélaïde behaved affectionately with Marie Antoinette. She soon gave her the key to her apartment so she could come by whenever she wished. Marie Antoinette was duped by these sham manifestations of tenderness. Very soon Mesdames' quarters became a kind of haven of intimacy for the young couple. The Dauphine carelessly revealed her most intimate secrets in front of the three sisters, who were titillated by these secrets of the alcove. "You're my husband, when will you be my man?"[14] she was bold enough to ask Louis Auguste in their presence. Having acquired their niece's trust, they proceeded to encourage her natural laziness. When the Dauphine complained of having "to hold court," they offered to take her place, giving themselves the opportunity to play a far more glamorous role. That their niece live in their shadow and the young couple remain under their tutelage—these were the three princesses' wishes.

Finally Mesdames took great pleasure in openly fostering Marie Antoinette's and Louis Auguste's animosity against Madame du Barry. They had been responsible for telling Louis Auguste of his grandfather's depravities. Though the two spouses were brought closer by their tacit condemnation of the sovereign's private life, their disapproval also greatly contributed in estranging them from him. No attitude could be more dangerous in a world where everything depended on one ruler, the absolute monarch. Provoked by Mesdames' comments, Marie Antoinette decided to snub the King's favorite; she vowed to herself that she would ignore her disdainfully and never address a word to her.

Adored by Louis XV, Madame du Barry ruled over the court and organized all its entertainments. She also supervised the renovations that were being done in the château. Thus, when the Dauphine wanted improvements made in her apartment, her requests were carefully studied by the all-powerful Comtesse. When the King of Sweden came to visit Versailles, he spent much more time with her than with the Dauphine. People waited patiently in the Comtesse's antechamber to request favors from her. The sovereign had no hesitation about receiving his ministers in her apartment. It seemed she had usurped the role of queen, which by right belonged to the young Princess.

Then political quarrels further embittered relations between the still virgin Archduchess and the royal hetaera. The two women had inadvertently become the women counselors of two rival factions: Choiseul's, advocating a monarchy tempered by what was called the "intermediate bodies,"[15] and that of the Duc d'Aiguillon, who declared he was in favor of reinforcing absolutism. The first faction supported the Austrian alliance; the second was against it. Choiseul's supporters—he had been in power since 1758—praised the Dauphine to the skies, while Choiseul's opponents paid assiduous court to the King's favorite. The people flattering Madame du Barry wanted the standing minister dismissed, while the Dauphine's admirers saw her as the future queen capable of lending support to Choiseul and his principles. The political stakes, however, were way above these two pretty heads who saw in politics mere palace intrigues.

To Marie Antoinette's great surprise, for she did not follow political developments, on December 24, 1770, Louis XV dismissed Choiseul on the pretext that he was likely to drag France into a risky war with England over the Falkland Islands. Then the King called in the representatives of the opposing clique to replace the dismissed ministerial cabinet. While Madame du Barry rejoiced, Marie Antoinette was clever enough not to show her sorrow. On the other hand, while the Dauphin and Mesdames were sorry to see the royal mistress triumph, they were openly delighted by Choiseul's departure; they hated him, for, among other things, being responsible for the famous alliance in which Marie Antoinette was the innocent pawn!

As naïve as she still was, it was beginning to dawn on the Princess that she was far from universally liked at Versailles; the treaty which her mother was upholding with all her might was not as popular as she had been led to believe. She understood that Louis Auguste had married her only because he had had no choice; he had been forced into it. Perhaps this helped explain his odd behavior which kept her in a state of inexpressible disquiet.

5

MADAME LA DAUPHINE

*U*ntil then, Louis XV pretended not to know about the open war the Dauphine was waging against his mistress. Aware of his grandson's shortcomings, he wanted Marie Antoinette to have fun. He allowed her to learn to ride, which she did against the will of her mother, who still kept an eye on her every move. She could then follow the royal hunts. On these occasions, she invited the young participants to picnics where all protocol was banished, which made Madame de Noailles— whom the Dauphine had been careful not to invite—very indignant. Marie Antoinette was becoming more independent. Louis XV allowed her to throw a ball every Monday in her apartment at which women wore white dominoes and men court attire. Madame de Noailles also organized parties in her honor. Marie Antoinette appeared for the first time escorted by her husband, who was very proud of the fact that he had taken dancing lessons in order to look good in public. However, in private the Prince was still just as inhibited. After several unfruitful attempts at consummating his marriage, he withdrew into his usual apathy.

In May 1771, the Comte de Provence's marriage failed to spur him to accomplish his conjugal duty. He invariably came up with good reasons for postponing the fateful moment. When he found his wife in tears in his bed on the night of his brother's wedding, "he promises her that she will really be his wife and if the moment has been postponed for reasons of health, she has

no cause to worry . . . He believes that a man who is too young when he con-
summates his marriage runs the risk of becoming a libertine and that children sired by fathers who are too young have weak constitutions and do not
live long."[1] At least this was what Mercy reported based on what the Princess
had confided to the Abbé de Vermond! If Marie Antoinette feared that her
new sister-in-law might become a mother before her and thereby fulfill the
dynasty's hopes, her mind was soon put at rest. The Comte de Provence
turned out to be just as ungifted in lovemaking as Louis Auguste, though he
boasted of having been "happy four times" during his wedding night. This
was a hollow boast and everyone knew it. He, too, was secretly laughed at.
And it was not the taciturn Princess of Piedmont, Marie Joséphine of Savoy,
who would ever succeed in awakening his slumbering Eros.

The Dauphine had little sympathy for the Comte and Comtesse de
Provence. She did not like her brother-in-law at all. Endowed with a physical
appearance that was even less attractive than the Dauphin's, this fat and conceited prince exuded hypocrisy. Caustic and sometimes witty, Louis Stanislas
Xavier envied his elder's position and saw him as lacking in all the qualities of
a future sovereign. He would willingly have usurped his place. Hence relations between the two brothers were often rather tense, with the younger
brother taking a malicious pleasure in asserting what he regarded as his intellectual superiority over the Dauphin. His marriage to an unassuming
princess, whom the court would always consider to be unworthy of attention,
deeply mortified him, though he was careful not to show it. Indeed, the fact
that this sister-in-law was a nonentity completely reassured the Dauphine,
who had feared finding a rival in her. She tried to make her into an ally if not
a friend. But Marie Joséphine was more cunning than people thought and
deceived everyone. She followed her husband's advice blindly, even though
he was completely scornful of her, and paid court to the King and the King's
favorite, who cajoled her.

Encouraged by Mesdames, the little war between the Princess and the
King's mistress maintained its course. Marie Antoinette never missed an
opportunity to denigrate Madame du Barry and show her the full weight of
her contempt. She adopted a haughty attitude toward the new ministers, pre-
sumed to be the favorite's protégés. This irritated the King. "Madame la
Dauphine is being given bad advice,"[2] he sighed. Her mischief was certainly
badly timed: the Princess was annoying Louis XV at a time when her mother
needed her. Indeed, the Empress needed France's benevolent neutrality, for
she was getting ready to carve up Poland with Prussia and Russia. As far as the

Austrian sovereign was concerned, that the Dauphine dared anger Louis XV under these circumstances was almost tantamount to high treason. Though Mercy lectured the young woman and Maria Theresa raged in Vienna, Madame la Dauphine remained inflexible. She did not want to request an audience with the King and refused to say a few innocuous words to Madame du Barry in order to calm matters. To lower herself by talking to this woman whom she had been defying for months seemed to her the height of humiliation. For weeks she resisted Mercy, who begged her to talk to the favorite. To get her to agree, Maria Theresa would have to personally send her a strong reprimand. Shaken by her mother's tone, the unhappy Princess tried to defend herself. "You can be assured that I need no one's guidance in anything concerning propriety,"[3] she bravely replied, and went on to describe in detail all the intrigues she was wrestling with.

However, subdued by her mother's rebuke and Mercy's objurgations—for he had let her know that her obstinacy was endangering the alliance—she admitted to the ambassador, "The Empress knows very well that I will do whatever she wants."[4] Capitulation was then inevitable. On January 1, 1772, while several ladies of the court were accompanying Madame du Barry to the Princess's, the Dauphine turned casually to the favorite. "There are a great many people at Versailles today," she said to her enemy. This was sufficient to send the favorite back to her lover in triumph. And the news spread in Versailles like a powder trail. "I have spoken to her once," said Marie Antoinette to Mercy, "but I am determined to leave things there. That woman will never again hear the sound of my voice."[5]

The short sentence the Dauphine had addressed to the favorite had created a sensation. The partisans of the royal mistress, who were called the *"barrystes,"* temporarily stopped making their usual unkind comments about the young Princess. However, in taking sides, Marie Antoinette had unknowingly attracted a great many feelings of animosity. The ministers in power loathed her, starting with the Duc d'Aiguillon, who was Minister of Foreign Affairs. The Dauphin's former tutor, the Duc de La Vauguyon, an opponent of the famous alliance, was unsparing about her as well. In refusing a position of lady-in-waiting to Madame de Broglie, because the Broglies had not supported Choiseul, the Dauphine had also alienated that powerful family. These were influential people, belonging to the oldest noble families in the realm, and staunchly supported by many loyal relatives and friends. The Dauphine had therefore set against her several coteries starting with Mesdames, who now considered themselves betrayed.

Marie Antoinette was ignorant in the art of humoring people. She did not realize that the effects of wounded pride ran deep, and she had already offended several elderly duchesses by neglecting to treat them with proper deference. On several occasions, she had been seen bursting into insolent laughter behind her fan. Elderly people bored her. She ignored them, preferring the boisterous company of young people. Nothing could have made a worse impression in a court that was used to respecting customs—from which she had decided to free herself once and for all!

However, early in that year 1772, Madame la Dauphine, unaware of the passions she provoked, was almost happy. Never had the King been more attentive to her, and she thought she had recaptured her mother's love. Ever since she had agreed to talk to Madame du Barry, Maria Theresa had changed her tone; she stopped scolding her and showed affection, a great deal of affection. Convinced that the Empress ceased loving her when she rebelled against her, Marie Antoinette had panicked. Now she breathed freely again. A sweet emotion had taken possession of her. Convinced that the relations between France and Austria depended on her goodwill, she was prepared to obey Vienna's injunctions blindly to help fulfill the wishes of a mother who demanded complete compliance from her. "It would be the misfortune of my life if a breach occurred between my two families,"[6] she exclaimed. Mercy-Argenteau triumphed. "Your Majesty can be more and more certain of guiding Madame l'Archiduchesse on all matters relating to the essentials of your position," he declared, satisfied, to the Empress. "There is no longer any doubt about how effective we can expect to be later on."

Vienna had grasped that the Princess would become a true ally so long as she was threatened with losing her mother's love. Austrian Chancellor Kaunitz was no more troubled by this emotional blackmail than Maria Theresa. They took no account of the young woman's feelings or real interests. They viewed her as a pawn for Austria in the diplomatic game of chess. Maria Theresa was extremely cold-blooded in judging her daughter. Her docility failed to satisfy her; her affection left her unmoved. Marie Antoinette was too wanting in the gifts and skill which the Empress had wanted her to possess. Like Kaunitz, she believed in "getting as much as one could from a bad debtor."[7] With this in mind, she would manipulate her daughter with lofty sentiments, and the Princess would show herself incapable of rebelling.

Maria Theresa's correspondences with Marie Antoinette and her ambassador were kept secret. Louis XV suspected, however, that attempts were being made to manipulate the Dauphine. He did not fret over this. He knew his granddaughter had no head for politics and no gift for intrigue. Though she always kept her distance from him, he liked this sincere, impulsive child whose outbursts of gaiety were often followed by bouts of sadness. Nevertheless, the young couple's strange marital situation was beginning to worry him. A good friendship existed between the two spouses even though they were rarely together. The Prince spent his entire days hunting. He would return from his endless rides staggering from exhaustion, with just enough energy for a copious meal, before going to bed and instantly falling asleep. This rigorous physical exercise probably provided an outlet for his frustrations. To his wife's astonishment, the Dauphin did not despise manual labor. He had had a forge installed above his apartment and enjoyed making keys and dismantling locks under the guidance of a professional in the craft. He could sometimes be seen helping the laborers who were working at the château, and it was not unusual for him to appear with his clothes in disarray and his fingers blackened by such menial tasks. These activities did not prevent Louis Auguste from spending hours reading history books and travel memoirs, or from studying geographical maps. He was always most unhappy when he had to be on show at court. His wife shared none of his tastes. She regarded hunting as a pleasant pastime which gave her the opportunity to be surrounded by a group of young women and men. She only enjoyed balls, fetes and excursions with a select group of people who were to her liking. She could not bear solitude or any activity that required some degree of seriousness. The Abbé de Vermond found it extremely difficult to read to her.

However, when Marie Antoinette was with Louis Auguste, she had no misgivings about discussing their intimate problems. The physicians whom they consulted advocated some treatments, to which the Prince graciously submitted. He took baths, drank some potions and even ingested iron filings! Still nothing. The possibility of a small medical operation was mentioned but in the end the surgeons claimed "that the consummation of the marriage depended on the young prince's volition; no physical obstacle would stand in the way when his mind was made up."[8]

Louis XV had never broached this sensitive subject frankly with his grandson. He had only written and asked him to explain "the lack of eagerness he showed in consummating his marriage."[9] The Dauphin had not dared answer. Unable to contain himself anymore, on October 28, 1772, the monarch summoned the couple and demanded a detailed confession from them. With less embarrassment than might have been anticipated, Louis Auguste admitted that he had made several attempts to consummate his marriage but that painful sensations had prevented him from reaching the desired conclusion. Louis XV dismissed the young couple, but summoned the Dauphin to his study two days later. He wanted personally to check whether his grandson had a malformation. The examination completely reassured him: "The tiny obstacle that remained was merely a very common occurrence among adolescents and did not require an operation."[10]

At Versailles, everyone could guess why the King had wanted to have a conversation with the Dauphin and Dauphine and they became, once again, the focus of attention for the entire court. Convinced, quite rightly, that his failings were the sole subject of conversation, the unhappy Prince continued to behave like the clumsiest of spouses. Humiliated by an impotent husband, the Princess was less and less willing to partake of embraces that were both labored and disappointing. And the thought that Madame du Barry learned all about her intimate misfortunes from the King himself magnified her feelings of distress.

Assuming "some clumsiness and some ignorance between the two youths,"[11] Louis XV asked the Dauphine's physician to instruct his grandchildren. The practitioner offered a great deal of advice, encouraged the Dauphin, watched the young couple's frolics and noted, with astonishment, that the Prince, in spite of his goodwill, was "of surprising nonchalance and laziness."[12]

For months Louis Auguste still tried to become Marie Antoinette's true husband. In each of her letters, the Princess kept her mother apprised of the tiniest details of her sexual life exactly as if they were matters of day-to-day business. "My husband is a little more forward than usual," she wrote her on May 15, 1773. Remarks of this kind succeeded one another as the weeks went by. Finally, in Compiègne, on July 22, Louis Auguste could proclaim victory. Before going off to hunt, he went to see the King in order to introduce "his wife," and he assured his grandfather that the Princess had truly become his during the night. Very moved, the King took his children by the hand and kissed them. The Princess immediately announced the big news to her dear mother, news that brought "everyone," she said, "great joy."[13]

It was high time. Several months later, Charles Philippe, Comte d'Artois, married Marie Thérèse of Savoy, Marie Joséphine's younger sister, and consummated his marriage on the very night of the wedding even though the young bride was not much more attractive than her older sister! But the Prince was already reputed to be a ladies' man and had lost his virginity long ago with charming opera girls. Marie Antoinette was very fond of this young brother-in-law who thought only of amusing himself and brightened family reunions with his gaiety and liveliness. There were now three young couples in Versailles. A great intimacy soon developed among them in spite of the Dauphin and Dauphine's suspicions concerning the Provence couple. Though she did not let herself be taken in by her pedantic brother-in-law's obsequious compliments, Marie Antoinette was cordial with him and pretended not to notice that he was consumed with jealousy. With the two Piedmontese sisters, she had adopted the tone of a protective and authoritarian older sister. Excursions, hunts, balls, theatrical performances punctuated their carefree lives. The family ambiance is rather well re-created in a letter written by Marie Joséphine on the eve of a departure for Compiègne: "I don't know why I haven't gone crazy," she wrote to her parents. . . . "I'm surrounded by caskets, papers, books on the floor; my casket was ready; now it's been knocked over. I must start all over again. I get angry, they laugh, they grab the paper from me . . . I'm in a little corner surrounded by baggage. Madame la Dauphine is knocking everything over, the Comte de Provence is singing, the Comte d'Artois is telling a story that he's already started telling ten times and he's shouting at the top of his voice and laughing loudly, and on top of everything, Monsieur le Dauphin is reading a tragedy aloud. I think he thinks we're deaf. There are also two birds singing and three dogs making a deafening racket, one is mine, two are Madame la Dauphine's . . ."[14]

Like Marie Antoinette, the Comte d'Artois had a true passion for theater. They both dreamed of getting the King's permission to go to the great theaters in the capital. In the meantime, they had to be content with the performances that were presented at the château, which were not always to their taste. Since Madame de Pompadour had started the trend, private theatricals were all the rage. Many aristocrats presented plays for their friends at their residences. Marie Antoinette and the Comte d'Artois were yearning to follow their example and decided to perform in the Dauphin's apartments. Louis Auguste and Marie Joséphine did not feel they were gifted for the stage, so they were assigned the part of the audience while the Dauphine, the Comte de Provence and the Comte and Comtesse d'Artois were to make spectacles of themselves. Since Louis XV would probably not have granted permission had his grandchildren requested it, they decided to do without it. The princely troupe began rehearsals excitedly and in great secrecy except for the complicity of two servants as stage managers. The fledgling actors performed in an entresol room, on a stage that could be hidden away in a closet. They staged all the great scenes of the French classical theater. Provence always knew his parts to perfection, Artois recited his with style, Marie Antoinette injected a lot of feeling into hers. Alas, Marie Thérèse of Savoy was dreadful! But it did not matter! The Dauphin had great fun, applauding noisily, or whistling unmercifully when he disapproved of a performance.

These innocent games failed to completely satisfy Marie Antoinette. Her empty heart and unappeased senses drove her to seek new distractions constantly. Ever since her arrival at Versailles, she had wanted to see Paris. She was fascinated by this huge capital she had just had a glimpse of on the night of the fireworks tragedy. With its population of 600,000, Paris was then the largest city in Europe, a modern metropolis steeped in history where all conceivable pleasures could be found. The royal family went there only on exceptional occasions. In response to the Dauphine's repeated entreaties, the King granted her permission to go to the opera ball during the carnival of 1773.

On February 11, 1773, wearing masks and long black dominoes like all the other participants at the ball, the Dauphin, the Dauphine and the Provences made a discreet entrance in the immense illuminated room, the site of countless intrigues and of all classes of society mingling indiscriminately. The opera ball resembled no other ball. The large crowd of dark dominoes crushed together and swaying to the rhythm of the music created an amazing impression. Conversations between the sexes—all the women being masked and very few of the men—were carried out in hushed voices, with each man trying to guess the identity of the woman under the disguise. This was an ambiance that surpassed anything the Dauphine had imagined. She delighted in not being recognized and was amused by everything, but her whims exhausted her husband and the Provences, who took far less pleasure in this unusual entertainment. Afraid of antagonizing the King, the Dauphine turned down the Duc de Chartres's invitation to continue the evening in his residence, at the Palais-Royal. It was seven in the morning when the young people returned to Versailles; they went to mass and then to bed.

From now on, Marie Antoinette's most ardent wish was to return to the capital. Louis XV gave her complete freedom to do so after the traditional "entrance" into Paris, which the heir to the throne and his wife were required to make with great pomp and circumstance. Indeed, it was customary for the Princes to be introduced to the people according to a rigid code of solemn

celebrations which were meant to exalt royal grandeur amid popular jubilation. The Dauphin and Dauphine willingly accepted to submit to this ritual
on the date set by the King, June 8, 1773.

On that day, at around eleven-thirty in the morning, the trumpets
sounded and the cannon at the Invalides thundered as Louis Auguste and
Marie Antoinette, wearing formal ceremonial attire, arrived at the gates of
the capital. They were welcomed by the Duc de Brissac, Governor of Paris,
as well as the Lieutenant of the Police, the Prévôt of Merchants and a delegation of market women carrying flowers and fruits. The young couple and
their retinue settled inside the six coaches of the city of Paris to the cheers of
the public. The fishwives were particularly enthusiastic, and, having always
been outspoken with the sovereigns, shouted: "Monsieur le Dauphin, make
us a child!" Some had no hesitation about extending their ample forearms
toward to Prince: "We wish you one like that Monseigneur," they yelled,
"and that's not too much for such a pretty woman. When you have one like
that, you should certainly carouse." These ribald comments provoked mirth
in the Dauphin and Dauphine and allowed them to fully appreciate the feelings of "their good people," as they called them.

The festivities proceeded with a solemn mass celebrated at Notre-Dame.
From there, the cortege went to the new church of Sainte Geneviève (today
the Panthéon), where they gathered before the relics of the patron saint of
Paris. On the way, the carriage stopped in front of the famous Collège Louis-
le-Grand, where the princes received compliments from the university,
phrased in the requisite learned language. Lost in the crowd of older stu-
dents, a pale young man with a tormented look stared greedily at the heir to
the throne: his name was Maximilien de Robespierre! Louis Auguste and
Marie Antoinette could never have guessed that they would meet him many
years later in the most tragic circumstances in their lives. For the time being
all was for the best in this best of all possible worlds. Or so they thought.

To the cheers of the Parisians, the Dauphin and Dauphine then made
their way to the Palace of the Tuileries,[15] which served as an occasional
dwelling place for the French kings. After a sumptuous dinner, Louis
Auguste and his wife appeared on the balcony to greet the huge crowds that
had assembled under the palace windows in anticipation of this special
moment. The cheers intensified when Marie Antoinette responded with her
engaging smile. The Dauphin greeted his future subjects, less self-
consciously than usual, though clearly cutting a pale figure next to his wife.
Though she had a certain aversion for the crowd, Marie Antoinette agreed to

go down to the terrace of the Tuileries gardens with the Prince. "There you have two hundred thousand people who love you," the Duc de Brissac whispered in her ear. Then the Parisians rushed forward madly, broke through the police barriers and crowded around the heroes of the day, who were soon engulfed by the human tide. Crushed by their adorers and unable to move for nearly three-quarters of an hour, the Dauphin and Dauphine instructed the law-enforcement forces not to retaliate against any excessively enthusiastic onlookers.

The couple, exhausted and delighted, returned to Versailles in the evening. Guilefully, Marie Antoinette said to the King: "Sire, Your Majesty must be greatly loved by the Parisians, for they feted us well." The Princess was not so innocent as to still believe in Louis XV's popularity. She fully realized that the Parisians had feted their future sovereigns because their accession was seen as offering the promise of a new golden age.

Intoxicated by her success, she wrote her mother: "Last Tuesday I had a day which I will never forget as long as I live; we made our entrance into Paris. As for honors, we received every conceivable one; but although this was very well, it was not what touched me the most, but rather the tenderness and eagerness of the poor people, who, in spite of the taxes which oppress them, were carried away with joy on seeing us . . . I cannot tell you, my dear mother, what transports of joy and affection we were shown at that moment. How lucky we are, in our position, to win the friendship of an entire people so cheaply. Yet there is nothing so precious; I felt it deeply and will never forget it."[16]

6

END OF A REIGN,

END OF AN ERA

"Every day I am aware of how much my dear mother did to place me,"[1] the Dauphine wrote the Empress. For the first time since being at Versailles, Marie Antoinette was enjoying life to the full. Though she was completely ignorant of love, the Parisians' welcome had healed her secret wounds. She had fallen in love with the people for honoring her like a long-awaited sovereign. She forgot the Dauphin's coldness, Mesdames' pettinesses, Provence's hypocrisy, her absurd rivalry with du Barry, the courtiers' suspicious whispers, the sulking elderly duchesses and Versailles's unbearable etiquette. In Paris, she was sought after; she was not accused of having a taste for intrigue; she was not called *l'Autrichienne*. Indeed, people had forgotten that she was the pawn in an unpopular alliance. Peace had been restored for ten years and since there was no threat of war she seemed rather like the symbol of reconciliation between the two powers. In short, she was loved; she was loved for her grace, her charm, her natural nobility—in a word, for herself.

Louis Auguste and Marie Antoinette soon returned to the capital. They were seen at the Opera, at the Comédie-Française and at the Théâtre des Italiens. As soon as they appeared in their box they were given lengthy ovations. Their simplicity and good humor immediately erased the distance imposed by protocol. Moved, blushing with pleasure, the Dauphine always responded to the cheers with gracious bows and gave the public the signal to applaud the performance. Though the Prince had not yet acquired much poise, he did not seem quite as embarrassed as before. He looked at his wife with tenderness and was attentive to her in many small ways that pleased her. He did not take umbrage at her success, for it clearly reflected well on him and on the monarchy as a whole.

Evenings in Paris with the Dauphin did not completely satisfy the Dauphine. She wanted to move about the large metropolis as she pleased. The King, without any coaxing, granted her permission to go there informally, in the company of her sisters-in-law or Mesdames, who were once again currying her favor. Marie Antoinette took full advantage of this unhoped-for freedom. In relatively simple attire, she stopped to look at the Bibliothèque Royale (the present Bibliothèque Nationale) and the Savonnerie tapestry workshop; she also roamed about the painting salon where the best artists were exhibited. But none of these visits amused her so much as her errands in stores or her strolls around the stalls of the Saint Ovid's fair held on the Place Louis XV. She discovered an unknown world which gave her the illusion of starting a new life. She would return to Versailles exhilarated by her discoveries and by the love of the Paris population, for she was always greeted with the same ardor as soon as she was recognized. In Paris, Marie Antoinette became a desired woman and thereby found fulfillment in her own way. It was her best revenge.

Confident of her charm, Marie Antoinette was finally asserting herself as the real queen of Versailles. The King congratulated himself on this apparent happiness. The *barrystes* kept cautiously silent. Many courtiers, first and foremost the most powerful among them, now treated the Dauphine with all the interest usually shown a future sovereign. As for the favorite, she had to content herself with the favors of her lover. The King was aging. "He could soon be absent," said Mercy.[2] Louis XV would soon be sixty-four, which was considered old at a time when the average life expectancy was hardly more than forty-five. The monarch, who was known to be obsessed with the idea of death in spite of being in good health, was closely watched. He had recently been shaken by the sudden death of three people in his entourage. He had been seen in his apartment on his knees, praying. When Madame du Barry was informed of this by pious souls concerned with the sovereign's salvation, she said she would leave the court should the King have the intention of devoting his remaining days to preparing his salvation. Some people started hoping for the favorite's prompt dismissal.

A subtle observer of cabals, Mercy looked after the Dauphine. In his own way. As the Princess's sole intellectual guide, he continued to train her to defend the interests of the august House of Habsburg. Without clearly explaining to her the great political issues of the day, he instilled anti-French prejudices in her and generally gave her a rather negative view of the King and his government. Moreover, he intimated that she would be called upon to play an important role in the near future. Convinced of Louis Auguste's complete incompetence, he liked to think that Marie Antoinette would actually be the one to wield power after Louis XV's death. "There is no doubt that Madame l'Archiduchesse will one day govern the kingdom," he wrote the Empress.[3] So he carefully groomed her for her future responsibilities. However, the Dauphine was not as docile a student as her mentor claimed. She was afraid of compromising herself and feared making the wrong move. "They torment me and worry me, but in the end I'll understand politics," she said, weeping.[4] These were reactions that astounded the diplomat. "She won't let herself take into account that she may one day have power and authority," he sighed.[5]

Mercy pursued his plans inexorably. For the time being, Marie Antoinette was to charm the elderly sovereign, who was consumed with boredom and the fear of death. And Mercy believed—with some conceit—that under his skillful guidance the Dauphine would succeed in subjugating Louis XV. In this, he underestimated her craving for pleasure and how unattracted she was to power. She had no intention of spending time trying to entertain a libidinous grandfather whom she respected only out of obligation. She preferred her marvelous outings in Paris, the court entertainments and even her innocent amusements with her brothers- and sisters-in-law.

The 1774 carnival was a case in point, offering the young princes new distractions. That year, they went to the famous opera balls as often as they wished. The Dauphine, who delighted in starting up conversations with strangers, now went to these parties to see people rather than to dance. On January 30, 1774, the three couples, wearing masks and dark dominoes, made their usual discreet entrance into the large room. Taking particular pleasure in being incognito that evening, Marie Antoinette struck up a conversation with a very handsome man who responded without the slightest embarrassment. Quite obviously, the stranger was seeking his fortune. It was odd to see them conversing at length without knowing each other. Though he had been to several balls at the court, not for a second did he suspect she might be the Dauphine. But the enchanted moment was soon disrupted. A circle formed around them. The Princess had been recognized; she took refuge in a box, leaving the attractive nobleman dazed by the flattering encounter he had just had.

Count Axel Fersen, heir to one of the most powerful Swedish families, was eighteen—exactly the same age as Marie Antoinette. He was finishing his European "Grand Tour," an educational requirement for all young aristocrats. He had left his native country in the company of his tutor and traveled around Germany, Switzerland and Italy prior to arriving in France, where he was thoroughly enjoying the delights of his Paris stay. The Swedish ambassador, who was chaperoning him, sang his praises. Since January 1, Axel Fersen had not missed a single ball at the court, and Marie Antoinette had certainly noticed this exceptionally handsome foreigner who did not possess either the arrogance or the conceit of young French courtiers. "Of all the Swedes who have been here in my day, he is the one who has been best received in high society. He was extremely well received by the royal family," the ambassador remarked in a letter to Gustavus III.[6]

Fersen returned to Versailles regularly, but he does not mention any conversation with the Princess in his journal. She had not lost sight of him, but her attention was then focused on Chevalier Gluck, her former harpsichord teacher. He wished to give performances in Paris of an opera he had recently composed, *Iphigénie in Aulide*, directly inspired by Racine's tragedy. Having first made his fame in Austria, Gluck's music had been performed in Milan, Venice, Prague, Leipzig, Hamburg, Munich and London. He still had to conquer Paris. Encouraged by Empress Maria Theresa and Emperor Joseph II, he had composed his *Iphigénie* with a French libretto and sent it to the directors of the Paris Opera. These gentlemen showed no enthusiasm at all for the work, for it broke with the tradition of Italian opera, which favored music over the text. Gluck, on the contrary, wanted the music to serve the poetry. The administrators' polite refusal could only be overruled by very high patronage. After some difficulty, Gluck managed to approach the Dauphine. She received him courteously and made it her duty to help him triumph. There were two reasons for this: first of all, her mother had urged her to help him; second, if she failed to champion him, Madame du Barry, whom the maestro had also appealed to, would probably do so in her place. Her honor was truly at stake.

As soon as she gave her support to the composer, all opposition from the Opera vanished miraculously and rehearsals began under the baton of this demanding, meticulous composer-conductor. Accustomed to working with docile musicians whose primary concern was performing well, Gluck refused to put up with the whims of the French singers, who all benefited from high patronage and rebelled against the demands of a maestro who did not treat them with the usual deference. However, in spite of tantrums and angry quarrels, the work progressed. Marie Antoinette encouraged Gluck; she listened to him tell of his unpleasant dealings with the musicians, and calmed his wrath. She had promised him she would attend the "premiere," which showed signs of being the event of the season.

On the eve of the great day, news came that the tenor had lost his voice. For the Opera management, postponing the performance was unthinkable; the ailing singer would have to be replaced by his understudy. Chevalier Gluck flew into a violent rage. He had not rehearsed the tenor for weeks merely to have another tenor sing in his place! The Dauphine's intervention was his only recourse: she set another date for the first performance and the Opera management complied.

On April 19, as the curtain rose on *Iphigénie*, the atmosphere was very tense. Accompanied by all the youthful members of the royal family, the Dauphine gave the public the signal to applaud. As soon as a recitative began, she clapped her hands with such enthusiasm that the chronicler Bachaumont wrote that she looked like a member of a cabal! The performance was a great success. All the music lovers, first and foremost Jean Jacques Rousseau and Julie de Lespinasse, sang the praises of the Dauphine for having successfully introduced an original work that furthered a new conception of opera.

Marie Antoinette reveled proudly in her triumph, with no fear for the future. But on the afternoon of April 27, to her astonishment, she was told that the King was ill. Two days earlier, Louis XV had decided to spend several days with Madame du Barry in her small Trianon residence. Though he had shivered with fever during the night, the sovereign had not wanted to cancel the next day's hunt, so he had followed it in his carriage—something he never did. Feeling increasingly unwell, he had consulted a physician and a surgeon. "It is at Versailles, Sire, that one must be sick," said the latter. The King complied. Throwing a coat over his dressing gown, he cried to the coachman: "To Versailles, full speed ahead!" The princes and princesses immediately rushed to his bedside. He sent them away, saying he wished to be alone—in other words, with Madame du Barry. Aside from the physicians, no one was alarmed.

On April 28, the fever had not abated and the illustrious patient complained of bad migraines. Six physicians, five surgeons and three apothecaries were at his bedside. Helpless and unable to make a diagnosis, they took turns taking his pulse and examining his tongue. Out of desperation they decided to bleed him. Not just once, but twice, which suggested that the disease was much more serious than originally thought.

Versailles was in a state of turmoil. In the afternoon, anxiety gave way to anguish. At around ten o'clock in the evening, just as the Dauphin and Dauphine were about to leave the patient's room, a torch was brought close to the King's face. The physicians looked at each other. The red spots covering his forehead, cheeks and hands left no room for doubt: it was smallpox. No one had thought of making this diagnosis, for the sovereign himself was convinced he had contracted the disease in childhood. The Dauphin was immediately led out of the room and told the awful news. Since none of Louis XV's grandsons had been inoculated, they ran the risk of infection. Louis Auguste and his brothers were told to retire to their apartments. Inoculated in Vienna after the epidemic that had decimated a part of the imperial family, Marie Antoinette bravely offered to stay by the King. She was advised—by Mercy first—to rejoin her husband. Mesdames, though they had never had the disease, decided to look after their father regardless of what might happen to them. As for Madame du Barry, faithful in her duties, she stayed by her lover's bedside at night and, at his request, caressed his feverish forehead.

Should the monarch be told the truth? Some feared that the news would crush him. Others felt that he ought to be told the nature of his illness so that he could make peace with God. No one thought of consulting the Dauphin and the Dauphine. Everything was decided among Mesdames, the Duc d'Aiguillon and the Duc de Richelieu. They opted for silence. They let the King believe that he was suffering from a virulent case of miliary fever.[7] However, when he saw the pustules appear on his hands and arms, he expressed surprise: "If I had not had smallpox," he said, "I would be convinced I have it now."[8]

From the comfortable camp bed that had been set up at the foot of his ceremonial bed, Louis XV continued to receive those princes of royal blood and courtiers who had been immunized against smallpox. No one dared speak freely. Everyone held their feelings in check and intrigues were rampant. The *barrystes* knew they were doomed if the King died. Convinced that Marie Antoinette would dominate her young husband, they feared she would dismiss the ministers in power and appoint Choiseul and his friends in their place. They also worried about the small acts of revenge she would take against those who had openly supported the King's favorite. On the other hand, the *choiseulistes* hoped for a fatal outcome.

Marie Antoinette and the Dauphin kept their distance from all this agitation. Deeply distressed by the King's illness and its possible consequences,
the three young couples had cloistered themselves in the Dauphin's apartment. Only in the evening did they emerge, each one returning to his own
quarters. They saw no one except the Duc de Chartres, who, since he had
been inoculated, went back and forth between the King's room and the
Dauphin's, conveying the latest news. On the alert, Mercy and Vermond
mounted guard. Nothing escaped their vigilance. Only the people recommended by them had access to the Dauphine, who set the pace for the royal
family. Mercy continued to prepare the Princess for her role of Queen as he
conceived it. "She must start to secure the authority that Monsieur le
Dauphin will wield only in precarious fashion," he said to the Empress
before urging her to write to Marie Antoinette so that "she would agree to listen to him concerning the great objectives relating to the union and the system of the two courts."⁹ He could not have stated matters more clearly. The
ambassador obviously had the intention of governing France—at least in foreign affairs—through the future Queen.

The King's disease followed its course and no one dared tell him the
truth. Not even the Archbishop of Paris, who came to celebrate mass in his
room. Only the Abbé Maudoux, the parish priest of Saint Louis de Versailles
and Marie Antoinette's confessor, had wanted to brave the orders and go in to
see Louis XV. He was upbraided by the Duc de Fronsac, who took him by
the shoulders and sent him back to his church. Unperturbed, the priest
answered: "When the lord of the castle is sick, his priest has the right to see
him." The Abbé complained to the Dauphin and refused to leave the palace,
convinced that he would eventually be summoned.

On May 3, the King finally understood what everyone had gone to so
much trouble to hide from him. The physicians stopped misleading him. At
around midnight, he summoned Madame du Barry. "If I had known what I
now know," he said to her, "you would not have been admitted. I must devote
myself to God and my people. Therefore you must depart." The favorite wept
and left her lover. The very next day, the Duc d'Aiguillon took her to her
château, Rueil, not far from Versailles. If Louis XV were to recover, she could
be quickly recalled. However, to everyone's surprise, Louis XV, whose condition was worsening, still did not ask for the holy sacraments. The Abbé Man-
doux still waited. Finally, on May 7, at around two-thirty in the morning, the
King summoned the priest, who stayed with him alone for about twenty minutes. After hearing his confession, he asked Madame Adélaïde to wake his

grandchildren for the viaticum ceremony[10] which he had given instructions to prepare.

By six o'clock, the château troops were called up. The bodyguards and the Cent-Suisses[11] were lined up in rows all along the courtyard, from the chapel to the entrance to the King's apartment. As the drums sounded, the canopy of the Holy Sacrament was carried out. The Dauphin, his brothers, the princes and princesses of royal blood walked behind the canopy. Distraught, his eyes swollen from tears and fatigue, Louis Auguste walked unsteadily through the palace galleries. Though pale and distressed, Marie Antoinette kept all her dignity. The Dauphin knelt at the foot of the marble staircase while his wife and the princesses took seats in the Council Room. The disease the monarch was dying of would keep his grandchildren away from him to the end.

With a rustle of silk and lace the Grand Almoner and his retinue walked up to the bed where the King—once the handsomest man in the kingdom— now lay, his face swollen and covered with scabs. Versailles fell silent. Time stopped. Before giving the monarch communion, the Grand Almoner had a long conversation with him. "Would Your Majesty like me to state publicly what you said to me?" The dying man breathed yes and the prelate said that the King asked his people forgiveness for his scandalous private life. The ceremony ended. Louis Auguste and Marie Antoinette walked slowly back to their apartments under the worried and critical gazes of the courtiers. They knew that the reign of Louis XVI would begin in a matter of hours. The future sovereign decided that he would leave for Choisy with his family and the entire court as soon as his grandfather had breathed his last. The carriages were ready; the pages and equerries waited for a candle burning near one of the windows to be extinguished: this would be the sign that Louis XV had died. The elderly King wrestled against the disease. His body resisted annihilation. But on May 9, his condition suddenly worsened. His face turned to bronze, like the mask of a Moor with a gaping mouth, a terrifying sight for the people who still went near him. A pestilential stench wafted from his room and infected the palace air. This mortal agony became an endless nightmare for all.

7

A HAPPY ACCESSION

*M*ay 10 was a radiant spring day; the cabarets and open-air dance halls were overflowing with people; there was not a soul in the churches to pray for the King. Louis XV died amidst total indifference. During these endless death throes, Marie Antoinette and Louis Auguste remained secluded in their quarters with their brothers, sisters and sisters-in-law; from moment to moment, they expected the fateful news which would put an end to the exhausting tension.

Suddenly, at half past three, the Dauphin and Dauphine heard an indistinct noise that grew louder and louder, more intense, and changed into a thundering rumble. The doors to the Prince's apartment were flung open onto a crowd of courtiers who had come to congratulate Louis XVI on his accession to the throne. Faltering, dabbing her eyes with a handkerchief, Marie Antoinette was at her husband's arm, looking beautiful in her grief and youth. The new sovereigns immediately kissed Mesdames Clotilde and Elisabeth. "We will not part," the King said to them. "I will be all things to you."

After the first moment of emotion had passed, Louis XVI and Marie Antoinette, followed by the Comte and Comtesse de Provence and the Comte and Comtesse d'Artois, walked through the palace halls between the two rows of courtiers, who bowed as they went by. As in a dream, the Princess heard the request for "the Queen's horses" without realizing that this title, which sounded so strange to her ears, seemed to arouse dismay in most of the members of the royal family.[1] Clearing its way through a silent, sympathetic crowd, the royal couple's carriage took the road to Choisy. The gilded coach glittered in the sun as they drove slowly by, amidst a people who paid homage to them as the new royal couple in whom they placed their hopes.

Suddenly bereft of the elderly King's tutelage—for in spite of his tumultuous personal life, he had been like a father and had exercised a debonair, yet real authority over them—the young princes suddenly felt like orphans. This was particularly true of Louis XVI, since he was called upon to take on the highest government function without being prepared for the task. However, halfway to Choisy the oppressive tension they had felt since the beginning of the King's illness was suddenly dispelled when the Comtesse d'Artois amusingly mispronounced a word. All six broke into nervous laughter, which was both incongruous and liberating. In spite of the solemn mourning that was to be imposed on the court, their arrival in Choisy was greeted like a return to life.

Meanwhile, Louis XV's mortal remains were left in the care of a few servants who performed the last rites at their own risk and promptly placed the corpse in a double lead coffin filled with alcohol. Because of the danger of contagion, they had decided to do without the usual ceremonial. Two days later, after nightfall, the catafalque would leave the deserted palace and briskly make its way to the royal sepulcher at Saint Denis. In Choisy, it was already far from anyone's thoughts.

After a sixty-year reign marred by many disappointments, the reign of youth was now beginning! Louis XVI was called Louis le Désiré (Louis the Desired One) and the French expressed joy at finally having a Queen worthy of that title. Louis XV's devout wife, who had died in 1766, had left no impression on her subjects, nor had Maria Theresa of Spain, Louis XIV's wife. Modest and lacking in charm, crushed by their all-powerful husbands, these women had lived at the court like virtual recluses. Louis XIV and Louis XV honored their beds solely to ensure descendants and imposed official mistresses on them whom they were obliged to treat with respect. Lavished with gifts and privileges, the kings' favorites ruled as the true Versailles sovereigns, though the clergy thundered from their pulpits rebuking these scandalous, adulterous relationships. They were accused of leading the kings into sin, surreptitiously giving them the worst possible advice on governing the kingdom, getting their protégés appointed to the highest positions and squandering public funds for their own pleasure. The people's hatred had been focused on them for over a century.

While the French naïvely expected their sovereign to ensure their happiness—in other words, bring peace, a reduction in taxes, a more comfortable standard of living, a more equitable judicial system and, at least for the more enlightened among them, some kind of participation in public life—they could not have articulated exactly what they expected from the King's wife. No power was assigned to the Queen. The fundamental laws of the kingdom, which stood in lieu of a constitution and were invoked by jurists, granted her no authority whatsoever, unless the King died prematurely and left an heir who was a minor. The King's widow could then be called upon to act as regent until her son reached his majority. This had occurred twice in the seventeenth century: Marie de Médicis had ruled during Louis XIII's childhood and Anne of Austria during Louis XIV's. These extremely troubled periods had left a very unflattering view of female government in the French collective memory. Defamatory lampoons and crude caricatures had tarnished the images of these two queen regents who had tackled the ungrateful tasks of government.

Indeed, the role assigned to the monarch's wife was rather frustrating. She had to be a shining incarnation of virtue, gifted with all the feminine attributes, and be content with providing her husband with a large, healthy progeny. As the sovereign's first subject, she was required to be completely submissive to him, refrain from showing concern for the interests of her native country, maintain a perpetual reserve and never express any opinion. If she was young and beautiful, like Marie Antoinette, she enhanced the monarchy's prestige and was willingly granted a representative role. It was thought that Marie Antoinette could play that part. With her charm and natural modesty she could prevent any other woman from exercising control over the King. She could thus ensure the triumph of good morals at Versailles, something unprecedented except in the time of the austere Madame de Maintenon, the aging Sun King's secret wife. However, this uncrowned queen had been rigid and devout and had contributed to making court life oppressive. As the power behind Louis XIV's throne, she had been hated as much as his former mistresses and was often blamed for France's misfortunes.

In the collective unconscious, the Queen was supposed to incarnate the people's happiness in prosperous times and take on the traits of a compassionate sister of charity when misfortune struck the kingdom. This was asking for the impossible. Besides, though Henri IV was still held up as the model of the benevolent king, no queen remained dear to the French heart. There was not a single prior queen with whom Marie Antoinette could try to identify, even if she had wanted to. While the office existed, the role still had to be created; Marie Antoinette was too young and inexperienced to realize this. In any case, the young Queen saw only one female sovereign worthy of admiration—her mother.

Exhilarated by the euphoria sweeping France, the Queen was far from suspecting that she had very little margin for error and that her popularity was very fragile. Having no lust for power, she naïvely imagined that her new status gave her complete freedom to lead the life she pleased, satisfy her whims and be adulated and loved. "I cannot help but admire the disposition of Providence which chose me, the youngest of your daughters, for the finest kingdom in Europe. I am more than ever aware of how much I owe to the love of my august mother, who took such care and effort to get me such a good settlement," she wrote the Empress, four days after Louis XV's death.[2] She was far from suspecting Maria Theresa's despondency. "My daughter's fate . . . can only be either completely great or very unhappy . . . I count her halcyon days as over," she confided to her ambassador.[3]

While Marie Antoinette was enjoying the delights of her new power, her husband was plunged in deep perplexity. He had absolutely no factual knowledge of the kingdom. His grandfather had never given thought to his succession. Haughtily ignoring his grandson, he had never discussed the governing of France with him or invited him to sit in on the Council. The young Prince had talked to the ministers only on rare occasions, at a time when he was considered an insignificant entity. And now, to make matters worse, he could not see them for several days. They had spent too much time with Louis XV and might have contracted the disease. The new sovereign hesitated to pick an adviser in the Duc d'Aiguillon's entourage, for he had been too close to Madame du Barry. Moreover, he knew that if he asked Marie Antoinette, she would suggest summoning Choiseul. But he could never under any circumstances forgive this man for having fought openly with his father. Since he distrusted his brothers, particularly the Comte de Provence, he went to his aunts as a last resort.

After much pleading, Mesdames had obtained from Marie Antoinette permission to stay at Choisy, instead of Trianon, even though they were exposing the royal family and its entourage to the danger of contagion. In spite of her obligatory semi-seclusion, Madame Adélaïde had not stayed inactive. She very soon informed her nephew that she had a list of trustworthy persons, formerly drawn up by the late Dauphin, Louis XVI's father. Immunized against smallpox, very proud of being given a mission, Marie Antoinette transmitted the aunts' messages to her husband. Discussions were carried out in the utmost secrecy, and after careful consideration, the King decided to summon the Comte de Maurepas, Louis XV's minister who had been dismissed from the court in 1740 for his nasty ditty against Madame de Pompadour, the official mistress at the time.

This elderly man's return to the court, after living in gilded exile in his Château de Pontchartrain about fifty kilometers from Versailles, had something dreamlike about it. Admirably informed on the affairs of state, experienced in the mysteries of power, he had a long conversation with Louis XVI and promised to be "his man," in other words, his adviser, or, as some would soon say, his mentor. In fact, though he did not hold the title, he acted as Louis XVI's Prime Minister until his death in 1781.

The presence of this amiable, discreet, aged aristocrat by her husband's side did not inconvenience the Queen. On the contrary, she was very pleased that he could help Louis XVI bear his crown, a burden which seemed to weigh heavily on him. Mercy's worried comments did nothing to change her mind. The Austrian ambassador, whose intentions had been plain to the entire court and who had been the cause of many complaints during Louis XV's last days, had decided he would be wise to spend several days in Paris. But, alarmed by Maurepas's arrival at Choisy, he rushed to the Princess's side to caution her against Prime Ministers whose "profession," he said, "had always been to destroy the influence of Queens."[4] To his amazement, these admonitions did not trouble the young woman at all. Piqued at not being understood as he had hoped, Mercy left again but nevertheless implored her to "never sleep separately from the King."[5]

Vienna was making its intentions clear. Chancellor Kaunitz had just sent Mercy a long memorandum regarding the Queen's conduct. He hoped that she could influence her husband's decisions without his realizing it and quickly gain complete control over the rest of the royal family. She was to stay out of petty court intrigues which could destroy her influence and use all her authority to get appointed to high office, particularly to ministerial positions, men who would become her future protégés. Kaunitz had no hesitation about naming the ministers who would favor the interests of the Viennese court. Choiseul, for example, whom Marie Antoinette was prepared to ardently support, was not Austria's ideal candidate. Maria Theresa and Kaunitz feared he would give France a preponderant place. On the other hand, the Duc d'Aiguillon, whom the Queen hated and Kaunitz viewed with contempt, he still regarded as the best minister. "For lack of knowledge and mental courage, he will dare nothing great or bold in the political field," the Chancellor asserted cynically.[6]

Maria Theresa wanted to be apprised of Louis XVI's every decision. "It is important for me to be informed on time and with accuracy of what is going on in France in these decisive moments and by the same token transmit what suits my interests," she wrote Mercy.[7] "The Queen should never for a minute lose sight of all the possible ways of ensuring her complete and exclusive control over her husband's mind," she had already commanded. To her daughter, whom she inveigled with affectionate messages, she declared without hesitation: "Mercy is as much your minister as mine."[8] The Empress hoped that Marie Antoinette would be docile in obeying her and would bend her husband to her will, a husband whom everyone took pains to depict to her as a spineless idiot.

For the moment, the young Queen was too busy with the delightful fringe benefits of power to want to enjoy power itself. She vaguely sensed that her influence would grow but, for the time being, she had no real desire for this to happen. With all her heart, naïve as she still was, she dearly wanted to please her mother, like a loving, grateful, fearful child. But she did not want to be prevailed upon to meddle in affairs of state. Besides, she would not always have a clear understanding of her mother's requests via Mercy and would often interpret Vienna's injunctions ineptly. As for Louis XVI, who pretended to be unaware of this secret correspondence involving the Empress, the Queen and Mercy-Argenteau, he abstained from confiding in his wife about political matters. Maria Theresa would soon realize this. "Some of his behavioral traits make me also doubt that he will be very compliant and easy to control," she would soon note, not without resentment.[9]

In spite of Mercy's saber rattling, which bored her, Marie Antoinette savored her newly acquired happiness. The King had just given her the Petit Trianon, the perfectly proportioned pleasure house; it had been built by the architect Gabriel for Madame de Pompadour, but she had not lived to see it completed and Louis XV had inaugurated it with Madame du Barry. Louis XVI handed his wife the key to her new kingdom, a true work of art finely chiseled and studded with precious stones. In this pavilion, situated a quarter of a league away from the château, Marie Antoinette could indulge her fantasies far from society, ignore etiquette and live with no constraints. She immediately came up with thousands of plans for redesigning the area around her new residence. In the meanwhile, in order to properly celebrate this happy event, she invited the King, and her brothers- and sisters-in-law, to supper.

Marie Antoinette had other reasons to be satisfied. Following her entreaties, the King had just sent Madame du Barry to the Abbaye de Pont-aux-Dames. She was now working on obtaining the exile of the favorite's most faithful ally, the Duc d'Aiguillon. On June 3, indifferent to Mercy's sad expression, the Queen was exultant: the Duc had handed in his resignation. Thereafter, she was far less interested in his successor in foreign affairs, Comte de Vergennes, than in her dear Choiseul, whose return to court she had just obtained. To please his wife, Louis XVI lifted the order of exile against the former minister. He immediately left his castle, Chanteloup.[10] Still dashing, he presented himself at the court. While Marie Antoinette greeted him eagerly, the King showed more than the usual reserve. "Monsieur de Choiseul, you have put on weight," he said to him. "You have lost a lot of hair; you are going bald." The former minister instantly understood that he had no hope of being reappointed. The very next day, he set off for Touraine again, which did not cause the Queen the slightest grief. Did she not have her whole life before her?

At La Muette, where the court went in great haste after Mesdames came down with smallpox, the honeymoon between the new sovereigns and the people continued. The Queen and her sisters-in-law strolled unescorted in the Bois de Boulogne, which, exceptionally, was open to the public. One day, during a brief ride between two meetings with his ministers, the King saw the princesses sitting on the grass eating strawberries and cream. He dismounted from his horse, took the Queen by the waist and kissed her on both cheeks like a good bourgeois. Applause broke out. Never had the monarchy offered such a spectacle! And when Louis XVI and Marie Antoinette joined the procession of Corpus Christi on the hill of Chaillot, the crowd went wild. Paris sang the praises of this virtuous Prince who refrained from exacting the "right of the happy accession"[11] and his ever so gracious Queen who refused to levy the "right of the belt."[12] All the poets scribbled exuberant verse on the new era of prosperity dawning on the kingdom. The young royal couple's fame spread beyond the frontiers. Even the pessimist Maria Theresa joined the chorus of praise: "Everyone is ecstatic, everyone is mad about you; there are expectations of great happiness; you bring new life to a nation which was in desperate straits and sustained only by its attachment to its princes."[13]

8

"LITTLE TWENTY-YEAR-OLD

QUEEN"

*S*oon some discordant notes were heard amidst this chorus of praise. At court, the Dauphine's old enemies had not laid down their arms. Madame du Barry's exile would not have upset them had it not been followed by the Duc d'Aiguillon's resignation. The Queen's fierce crusade against this minister, the scathing contempt she openly showed him and her overt joy when his dismissal was officially announced, revived old hatreds. The former *barryste* clan, which included many families from the most ancient nobility, were prepared to use any expedient to fight the young woman.

In the first weeks of her reign, quite unwittingly, Marie Antoinette alienated the formidable Rohan family as well as all its relations, friends and connections—in other words, everyone with close or remote ties to the family. The conflict had originated in a diplomatic matter that did not concern her. Cardinal Louis Edouard de Rohan-Guémémé, who had been hostile to the Franco-Austrian alliance, had been appointed French ambassador to Vienna at the recommendation of the Duc d'Aiguillon. This attractive, lax and libertine prelate had antagonized the Empress, who saw him not only as a political opponent but also as a kind of devil who might debauch the chaste ladies of Vienna. Though Maria Theresa hated him, her son Joseph was not averse to his company—which led the elderly Empress to moan over the French diplomat's "naughty pranks" and to try many times to get him recalled. Privately Rohan did not deny himself the pleasure of mocking the virtuous sovereign. When Poland was being divided, in 1772, in a letter addressed to du Barry's friends, he had poked fun at the hypocritical tears she had shed over the unfortunate country's fate though she had no qualms about invading it. His letter had been read at the favorite's, in Louis XV's presence, and the Empress had been sneered at. This had made Marie Antoinette indignant. She also knew that the ambassador made venomous remarks about her conjugal difficulties and was unsparing toward her. He claimed that her coquetry would prove detrimental to the future of the monarchy. At Louis XVI's accession, it was easy for the young Queen to obtain the Cardinal's recall and he was replaced by the Baron de Breteuil. But when Rohan returned to the court, Marie Antoinette haughtily refused to speak to him. She could not forgive his comments against her mother and herself.

Her insolent youthfulness, Mercy's constant presence by her side, her flaunted contempt for etiquette already provoked doubt about her future conduct. Convinced that since she was Queen, her whim should prevail over any other consideration, Marie Antoinette refused to see the dangers that surrounded her. She immediately adopted the attitude of a spoiled child without realizing that her enemies were on the lookout and would certainly exploit any errors she would make. At La Muette, the ceremony of the "mourning bows" reinforced her detractors' prejudices. On that occasion the new Queen received all the ladies of the court. In their long black dresses and odd black coifs with long fringes, for once these ladies could not vie with one another in elegance. Though the younger ones laughed at their ridiculous attire, at least they managed to make the best of it. But the older women looked like they had come out of a ghost story in which pathos contended with comedy. Some of the venerable dowagers looked truly grotesque. During the procession, the Queen kept a dignified bearing until the young Marquise de Clermont-Tonnerre, who was standing in back of her, decided the spectacle was exhausting and that she would be more comfortable sitting on the floor, hidden behind the row of dresses formed by the Queen and other ladies. Though this was a solemn occasion, Madame de Clermont-Tonnerre made many facetious remarks. Marie Antoinette, who had no trouble hearing all these comments, had to put her fan to her face several times to conceal an irresistible urge to laugh. The contingent of elderly ladies never forgot this affront. The very next day, rumors spread that the Queen flouted all the rules of propriety. Soon a song went around, evidently originating at the court, with the following refrain:

"*Little twenty-year-old Queen / Since you treat people with no shame / You'll go back from where you came.*" Marie Antoinette paid no attention to it.

Several days later, the King and his two brothers decided to get inoculated against smallpox. At the time, this procedure, which was not always successful and sometimes ended with tragic consequences, was considered extremely dangerous. In the royal family no one had submitted to it, except on the Prince d'Orléans's side. That Louis XVI and his two brothers (who were then, respectively, first and second in line to the throne) should be inoculated simultaneously seemed utterly mad to the older members of the court. Marie Antoinette, who had encouraged her husband in his decision, was sharply blamed for her recklessness. The triple inoculation, however, turned out for the best. When the three brothers were declared out of danger, Voltaire made a point of complimenting the enlightened princes in his way: "History will not omit that in being inoculated in the bloom of their youth, the King, the Comte de Provence and the Comte d'Artois taught the French people that it is necessary to brave danger in order to avoid death. The nation was moved and educated." The public had indeed followed the course of the King's illness attentively, for his popularity was at its height. The Queen's was already beginning to decline. This became apparent during the stay in Marly, where the sovereign and the court had gone for the inoculation.

After the monarch's convalescence, distractions not allowed during the period of mourning were resumed. The Queen went riding or took drives in a barouche with her sisters-in-law, the Princesse de Lamballe, the Comte d'Artois and the Duc de Chartres. Several young noblemen followed them. Concerts were given in the evening. Marie Antoinette, who had never seen the sunrise, suggested to her husband that they climb the hills of Marly at three in the morning and watch nature's wondrous spectacle. Louis XVI needed no coaxing to grant permission, but refused to join the party. He liked to go to bed early. The Queen watched the dawn break in the company of the Princesse de Lamballe and Madame de Noailles and delighted in it. "How beautiful! How beautiful!" she exclaimed repeatedly.[1] Several days later, a virulent lampoon entitled *Le Lever de l'aurore* (The Rising of Dawn) denigrated her morals. This nocturnal excursion, so consistent with the court's taste for a return to nature, was depicted as an orgy during which Marie Antoinette had disappeared in the groves in gallant company. "The Queen is the target of vicious attacks, there is no end to the horrors being

spread and the most contradictory things are accepted by some people,"
asserted an impartial witness, the Abbé Beaudau, as early as July 13.[2] According to this chronicler, the King found some anonymous writings under his
table napkin including a fierce epigram saying "Henri[3] was not resurrected
but the woman of Samaria was."

In the summer the court left for Compiègne, as it always did, where Mesdames, who had recovered by then, joined their nephews. The Queen was the
center of all entertainments. The Duc de Croÿ, who had not seen her since
Louis XV's death, found her "taller and plumper" and noted that she exercised unmistakable authority over the rest of the royal family.[4] Marie
Antoinette continued to amuse herself almost childishly with the Provences
and the Artois, granting them liberties ordinarily given in families, but suddenly, remembering she was the Queen, "she indulged in remarks on the
superiority of her rank and slightly mortifying comparisons for the other
princes and princesses."[5] They felt—particularly the two Piedmontese sisters—that they were merely her playthings and nothing more. Though the
Comtesse de Provence and Comtesse d'Artois affected to treat her with polite
deference, they actually joined forces with Mesdames (relegated to a semi-
retirement by Marie Antoinette) and openly denigrated her. The Comtesse de
Provence and the Comtesse d'Artois withdrew to their aunts' quarters, where
they took pleasure in commenting on all the details of the Queen's private life
and distorting them. "Whatever was put forward by one of the princesses was
confirmed by another, then a third made the anecdotes incontrovertible."[6]

During the stay in Compiègne, Louis XVI seemed very much in love
with his wife. On several occasions, husband and wife dined together in the
utmost intimacy. However, when they were together in the conjugal bed, the
King still showed the same lethargy. The Spanish ambassador, who paid spies
to inform him on every last detail of the couple's "matrimonial state," assured
his sovereign that Louis XVI suffered from phimosis and that a dauphin
might still be long in coming. At the time neither the Comtesse de Provence
nor the Comtesse d'Artois showed any signs of being pregnant. If the elder
branch were to die out, the King of Spain would be in a position to assert his
(albeit questionable) rights to the French crown, which was why his ambassador was so determined to penetrate the secrets of the conjugal bedroom.
Probably thanks to his concerned efforts, a lampoon had just been printed in
London and Amsterdam that was injurious to the Queen and whose publication the King wanted to prevent at all cost. Marie Antoinette was designated
as an Austrian agent and denounced as the kind of woman capable of engag-

ing in the most criminal intrigues in order to give the kingdom an heir, since her husband was notoriously impotent. Austrian, perfidious and libertine — this was already the way the Queen was portrayed, just two months after Louis XVI's accession to the throne. Wounded by this attack, the young woman had demanded clarifications, which one tried to provide. Mercy took advantage of the opportunity to exhort her to greater caution in her behavior. Nevertheless, she knew it was impossible to prevent people from chattering about her relationship with Louis XVI. This caused her unspeakable suffering, which she tried to forget by escaping into a life of unbridled pleasure.

The King and Maurepas were most heartened that the Queen still seemed to take no interest in politics. By the end of August, Louis XVI had dismissed his grandfather's ministers and formed a new cabinet without any interference on her part. The new ministers — including two reformers, Turgot and Malesherbes — succeeded men with ruined reputations. Their appointment seemed to portend an era of prosperity and justice. On hearing the news, the people, according to one chronicler, "were exuberantly joyful," while Marie Antoinette was busy driving cabriolets at lightning speed with the Comte d'Artois. Neither showed any concern for the future of the kingdom. Besides, the Queen could soon be satisfied with Turgot, the new Finance Minister. He doubled her annual allowance without her requesting anything.

After the stay in Compiègne, the court went to spend the autumn, as was customary, in the Château de Fontainebleau, about sixty kilometers southeast of Paris. Marie Antoinette liked this residence with its heterogeneous architecture. When she went there for the first time, she had been particularly interested in its history. Perhaps because Fontainebleau, like Schönbrunn, meant "beautiful fountain." As Dauphine, before learning how to ride horseback, she had lured Madame de Noailles and her ladies-in-waiting into endless donkey rides around the grounds and forest, from which she returned delighted and her attendants exhausted. Those seemed like very distant times.

In Fontainebleau, Marie Antoinette continued to disregard court protocol. She easily succeeded in getting her husband to abolish the custom of dining in public every day and being served by her ladies-in-waiting kneeling by her side. She now further refused to be followed by two of her ladies as she moved about the palace. A valet and two footmen were appointed to the task. Finally, after repeated pleading, Louis XVI permitted the Queen and the princesses of royal blood to take their meals with men who were not of the royal family. With the King choosing the male guests and the Queen the female ones, the young sovereigns initiated this new type of gathering, in the absence of Mesdames, who would certainly have been gravely shocked by such a disruption in customs. Louis XVI and Marie Antoinette were delighted by their first reception and decided to make it a twice-weekly event. Mesdames, the vestal virgins of court tradition, were confronted with a fait accompli. Once again they fumed against their niece, whose palace revolutions were endangering the kingdom's stability! But why should the gracious sovereign care about the grumbling of these embittered, vindictive old maids?

The Queen was clearly happy as she returned to Versailles. The mourning period was coming to an end. She knew Louis XVI would give her complete freedom in planning court entertainments and she rejoiced ahead of time. She was determined to rouse this palace lulled by two exceedingly long reigns and impose her own style on the court. She dreamed of *fêtes galantes* in the style of Fragonard paintings, and wanted to live sheltered from prying eyes, in refined surroundings molded to her tastes, in a social set chosen according to her personal affinities. Her mind was also on her Trianon estate, which she wanted to remodel. Keeping the garden as Louis XV had conceived it was unthinkable, even if it filled all Europe with admiration. She was completely indifferent to the exotic plants, pineapples, coffee trees, aloes, geraniums, fig trees from the Barbary Coast, jasmine, dwarf peach trees, orange, apricot and cherry trees, and to the heated glass greenhouses where early-season fruits and a great many rare plants were grown. Yielding to fashion, Marie Antoinette dreamed of an Anglo-Chinese garden copied from nature. The Duc de Chartres had created one on his property in Monceau[7] and the Comte de Caraman, on the rue Saint-Dominique in Paris. The Queen had spent long hours in those gardens and had finally asked Richard Mique, Gabriel's successor, to submit plans to her. She waited impatiently for them.

The court returned to Versailles in prematurely cold, bitter weather. Wrapped up in her furs and wearing an extravagant hat, Marie Antoinette went on long sleigh rides with the Comte d'Artois and the Duc de Chartres. As soon as she had arrived, she had summoned Papillon de La Ferté, the Intendant des Menus-Plaisirs (Steward of Small Amusements), as the position was fetchingly called. This nobleman had the task of organizing all the court festivities, the sovereigns' trips when they left Versailles, weddings, mourning ceremonies and all prestigious events. He was then immersed in the books by the grand masters of ceremonies in preparation for Louis XVI's coronation, which was to take place in the spring. He had to review all the files relating to the coronations of previous monarchs and submit a plan to the King on how the formalities should unfold; he also had to oversee the preparation and decoration of the cathedral, draw up the guest list, make sure the coaches were in good repair, see to the sovereign's attire and that of all the official personalities, both secular and ecclesiastical. In sum, the Duc de La Ferté was overloaded with work!

The preparations for the coronation certainly interested the Queen, but first she was determined to bring off her winter season. Here, as in all other areas, she wished to innovate. Besides the suppers she gave twice a week with the King, the performances at the Opera, the Comédie-Française and the Théâtre des Italiens—which they were to see in Paris (as a measure of economy!)—the Queen wanted to hold two balls a week at Versailles. The Monday-night balls were to be costumed. The evening of February 9 was inaugurated by a quadrille of dancers disguised as Lapps. The King made his entrance to the ball at around nine o'clock, strolled among the guests and retired much earlier than his wife, who tarried for a protracted period among a large circle of courtiers. It had been ages since Versailles had seen such crowds. The preparation of costumed balls was incredibly time-consuming. Monsieur de La Ferté had never had to deal with such a whirlwind before. His staff was under enormous pressure. With the utmost urgency, they had to make complicated, extremely costly Indian and Tyrolean costumes, or clothes from the time of Henri IV. They had to put up with the Queen's whims, while bills rapidly piled up in her offices. Mercy tried to curb these follies. Maria Theresa and Joseph scolded her from Vienna. Marie Antoinette took no notice of them.

The Austrian Empress, who grew increasingly anxious with each passing day, wanted opinions other than Mercy's concerning her daughter. Since her youngest son, Archduke Maximilian, had to make his Grand Tour, she asked his chaperon, Count Rosenberg, to send her a detailed report on the Queen's conduct. Maximilian, who was noted neither for his appearance nor for his intellect, arrived at La Muette on February 7, 1775. Marie Antoinette was thrilled to see her younger brother and welcomed him warmly. To brighten his stay, she increased the number of entertainments. At the balls, they could be seen laughing gleefully with the Comte d'Artois, who had become the Queen's pleasure companion. A protocol incident marred this brilliant carnival. Maximilian was traveling incognito under the name of Comte de Burgau. His sister had introduced him to the King and his brothers without any formality. Mercy had presented him to the ministers, but had neglected to introduce him to the Duc d'Orléans, first prince of royal blood, his son the Duc de Chartres, or the Condés and Contis. They considered themselves offended.

In the hope of rectifying this blunder, Louis XVI put the matter into the Queen's hands. But she sided quite strongly against the princes. Feeling that they owed her brother the first visit, she said things that were "pleasant neither for princes nor for the nation," wrote the wise Abbé de Véri.[8] The Duc d'Orléans and his son took umbrage and abstained from going to the court, making ostentatious appearances in the capital instead. They were applauded.

By claiming a status for her brother independent of the etiquette in force at Versailles, the Queen had wanted to emphasize the preeminence of Habsburg blood over that of the Bourbons. Though the nation did not take sides in the ceremonial issue involved, it detected, for the first time, a contemptuous attitude on the part of the Princess for things French. This attitude was all the more offensive in that the Queen was beginning to neglect the King and take definite pleasure in the company of attractive noblemen. Unmindful of her own reputation, Marie Antoinette had no compunctions in judging the reputations of others quite harshly—that is to say, the reputations of people who did not belong to what was already called her coterie. She thus excluded several people from her balls, either because they lacked discretion or because their birth did not meet her lofty standards. There were complaints and whispers at the court, and the city started paying heed to the myriad stories being told about her. Yet she continued to lose herself in amusements. She was still acclaimed when she appeared at the theater. At the Opera, when Gluck's *Iphigénie* was performed, applause broke out when the chorus started singing the lovely tune:

> *Let us praise, celebrate our Queen.*
> *Hymen chains her under his laws*
> *And will make all happy.*

In the parterre, the audience had joined in and cries of "Long Live the Queen" had rung out from all sides. Marie Antoinette bowed to the public with tears in her eyes, and when she left the theater, a huge crowd accompanied her coach amidst ovations. Taking bows before her subjects like a charming queen in a play, Marie Antoinette moved in a world which she tended to reduce to the most wondrous of theatrical stages.

9

THE CORONATION

*T*he queen in a play—Marie Antoinette had become just that even down to her way of dressing. Being recognized as the prettiest woman in the kingdom seemed to her a most enviable title. As Dauphine, she had followed court fashion and worn the gowns suggested by her lady-in-waiting, "Mistress of the Robes." She had indulged in no follies in dress. But at Louis XVI's accession, the Duchesse de Chartres introduced her to Rose Bertin, the dressmaker—or "modiste," as she was called—who was venerated by all the fashionable ladies. This commoner, who had been catapulted by an uncommon talent to the rank of supreme master of the frivolous, came to see her and unpacked a dizzying array of gorgeous outfits and hats. The Queen was filled with breathless admiration.

Mademoiselle Bertin, who had a shop in Paris called the Grand Mogol, dressed lavishly kept actresses, several prominent bourgeoises and the prettiest ladies at the court. As with the other modistes of her day, the dresses and hats she designed were made in her own workshops. She also sold "ready-made pieces" in her shop—large bonnets, hats trimmed with flowers or feathers, mantelets, pelisses, collars, ties, silk handkerchiefs, gauze fichus, muffs, fans, belts, gloves, shoes, embroidered slippers and thousands of other knickknacks. It was impossible to come out of the Grand Mogol empty-handed.

In the spring of 1774, Mademoiselle Bertin launched the fashion of "poufs," which became all the rage. Set on top of a towering mound of hair, like gauze scaffolding, these poufs were strewn with the most extraordinary objects: flowers, fruits, vegetables, birds and ornaments of all kinds; some even supported miniature theater stages or boats. Marie Antoinette had proudly sported the unbelievable "inoculation pouf." It consisted of a rising sun, an olive tree with olives and a snake wrapped around the tree threatened by a blossoming club. This outrageous artistic composition was meant to represent the symbols of a new era: science triumphing over evil and bringing the golden age. Hairdressers and modistes competed in extravagance in inventing these thematic, illustrative coiffures, so indicative of the aesthetics of the period. The female head of hair had itself become an art object, incorporating the most unexpected objects. Some women were seen wearing English-style gardens, ruins and myriad other follies. This was really pushing to the absurd the metaphor of female hair, so dear to poets.

That summer Marie Antoinette became the Grand Mogol's biggest customer. She got into the habit of receiving the dressmaker twice a week. At each meeting, Mademoiselle Bertin showed her ever more tempting original creations. And she had no equal in her ability to convince the Queen to buy, and buy again. In company, Bertin spoke arrogantly of "her work with Her Majesty," and she was soon disparaged as a ruinously expensive "minister of fashion" whose pretensions were equal only to the eccentricities of her outfits. In the first year of the reign, while Turgot preached thrift, the Queen incurred serious debts, partly due to these purchases. However, this was not the cause of the state's budgetary deficit.

The Queen was thrilled by the new style dictated to her by Mademoiselle Bertin. She looked like a dream princess and might have been mistaken for an actress except that she always retained the distant grace that would be hers to the end. "You know that I have always believed that fashions should be followed in moderation and not unduly," wrote her mother. "A young and pretty queen, full of charm, does not need all these follies; on the contrary, simplicity of attire is more suitable to the rank of queen."[1] And the Empress expressed her surprise that her daughter could wear a hairstyle adorned with feathers and ribbons rising thirty-six inches above her forehead! Marie Antoinette answered blithely that the height of the feathers had just been lowered and that since "everyone wore them, it would seem strange for her not to wear any."[2]

The Queen was sinking a fortune into Trianon. Richard Mique was finishing the project of the famed English garden. Up to then, Marie Antoinette, by an odd whim, had restricted herself to redesigning according to reigning fashion the immediate area around the small château. She had a strange Chinese-inspired game of rings constructed—a kind of carousel with peacocks and multicolored dragons instead of wooden horses; these were mounted by the select group of ladies and gentlemen of the court who were admitted into the Queen's entourage.

That the Queen was preoccupied by all these trifles suited the King and his ministers. Intent as they were on applying Turgot's new economic and commercial legislation, the last thing they wanted was for her to meddle in the affairs of the kingdom—particularly then, since it was a perilous moment. Misunderstood and sharply criticized, the Finance Minister's program was responsible for some serious disturbances. A fervent supporter of liberalism, Turgot had decided to institute free trade in grain. By abolishing internal customs duties and allowing foreign grain imports, the minister's aim was to bring down the price of bread, which was then the staple food of most of the French. However, in April 1775, speculators who had an interest in stockpiling wheat forced the price of bread up artificially since the harvest had been bad the preceding year. Riots broke out in markets nearly everywhere in France and bakeries were looted. The "flour wars" raged, causing the Queen no particular distress. Nevertheless, the disturbances served as a pretext for the Choiseul clan to launch an offensive in favor of their great man. His most zealous partisans submitted a memorandum to the Queen directly attacking Turgot's management and stating that Choiseul was the only man capable of restoring France's economy. Marie Antoinette submitted the memorandum to the King and tried to plead this highly compromised cause before her husband. His response was cold, and without mincing words, he told her that the former minister had better expect nothing from him.

There was more talk at court about the coronation than about the "flour wars," which were regarded as a banal "Jacquerie." Ever since he had succeeded his grandfather, Louis XVI was preparing for this ceremony which celebrated the monarchy's union with the Church and the nation. By receiving the grace of the sacred unction, the young sovereign was to become the lieutenant of God on earth. In France, where absolute monarchy by divine right had been instituted centuries earlier, this rite granted the sovereign a supernal quality in exercising his civil authority. This sanctification of power was being seriously challenged at the time. While some enlightened minds tolerated this antiquated tradition in the hope that it helped the sovereign understand his duties to the nation, others saw it as the expression of puerile magic used to keep the population subordinate. Still others wanted the ceremony to be given the character of a national election, sealed by a pact between the King and the people, for which God would be the sole guarantor. But for this irresolute, sincerely religious Prince who was strongly attached to tradition, the deep meaning of the coronation could not be called into question. He would be a true King of France only after the holy unction. He was convinced that the divine grace conferred upon him on that occasion would help him bear the heavy burden of the monarchy.

While her husband pondered the meaning of the coronation and the commitments it implied for a Christian monarch, Marie Antoinette saw this grand ceremony as the opportunity to be acclaimed and admired, though she was given no official role. Since queens did not participate in government, they were not even required to attend their husband's coronation. Not since the sixteenth century had a female sovereign been present at this solemn ceremony. In fact, the three previous kings—Louis XIII, Louis XIV and Louis XV—had ascended to the throne so young that they had been crowned before being married. Monsieur de La Ferté had to refer to the ceremonial at Henri II's coronation in 1547 for the protocol that had been adopted for Queen Catherine de Médicis!

Mercy, more than anyone, worried about the role that would be assigned to Marie Antoinette. He felt the circumstances should definitely be taken advantage of to increase the young woman's prestige in the eyes of the nation. Having commissioned a clergyman to write a treatise on the coronation of queens, he gave one copy to Marie Antoinette and another to the King. The Queen could not be bothered with this boring booklet despite all the energy Vermond expended explaining the advantages she might derive from being crowned along with Louis XVI. The Abbé found her "completely indifferent in this regard."[3] Actually, Marie Antoinette had no particular desire to take part in this ceremony which really concerned only her husband. It was therefore decided that she would attend as a simple spectator, as had Catherine de Médicis. But she was well aware that she would be a focus of attention at this fete, which seemed to her the most splendid show staged by the monarchy.

Traditionally, the kings' coronations were held in Rheims Cathedral, in Champagne, but for the sake of economy, Turgot wanted the celebration to take place in Paris. Festivities of unparalleled magnificence would thereby have been offered to the Parisians. By attracting scores of foreigners to the capital, the coronation would have stimulated commercial activity and made the people feel closer to their King. Louis XVI, however, chose to have the ceremony take place in Rheims. In spite of their disappointment, in the first days of May crowds of Parisians rushed to admire the exhibit of royal ornaments prepared for the coronation. And many of them began thinking about how they could get to Rheims to join in the festivities, even from afar.

On June 5, Louis XVI and Marie Antoinette left Versailles for Compiègne, followed by the entire court. The bells of all the churches rang out along the way, as the sumptuous procession made its way through rows of marveling onlookers. Dazed eyes looked on as a procession of splendors, exemplifying an unknown and inaccessible world, paraded by—the source of dreams for some, of grim amazement for others.

The King, the Queen and their large entourage stopped in Compiègne for two days of rest prior to the exhausting solemn ceremonies in Rheims. On June 8, Louis XVI left early in the morning for the small town of Fismes, near the coronation city. Marie Antoinette did not accompany him. She left Compiègne at around eight in the evening with her brothers-in-law and the Comtesse de Provence.[4] A magical journey was in store for her. A surreal vision, lit by torches and moonlight, her bosom glittering with precious stones, like an idol adorned for worship, she appeared to an entire people who waited to acclaim her, heedless of the night falling on the countryside.

The next day, early in the morning, in the Rheims archdiocese, people streamed into the Queen's small apartment opposite the King's quarters. Since Louis XVI had not yet arrived, Marie Antoinette was alone in accepting the tributes of the province of Champagne's courtiers and representatives. Perfectly at ease in this sea of elegant people, she greeted some, complimented others, omitted no one and unfailingly found the right thing to say to each. She reigned magnificently over this small world of adulators, among women dressed in the latest style who—much to the amazement of the provincials—had coiffures topped with feathers so tall that "they all seemed to have grown a foot and a half."[5]

At around one in the afternoon, the Queen took her seat on the balcony of a residence near the cathedral so she could watch the King's arrival. The streets were decked with garlands, leafy arches, symbolic statues. The crowd shuffled impatiently until a sudden clamor from the outskirts heralded the royal retinue's slow advance amidst increasingly loud ovations. As he passed in front of the Queen in his coach, the King greeted her. The cheers intensified. Welcomed by the highest ecclesiastical authorities in the kingdom, Louis XVI made his way into the cathedral for the celebration of the *Te Deum*, which the Queen did not attend. She waited for her husband in the

archiepiscopal palace, where they were to receive all the provincial delegations one after the other. With a radiant smile, Marie Antoinette listened to
the speeches praising her virtues and those of the young monarch.

On the following day, Saturday, June 10, there were solemn, pre–coronation day Vespers, but no other ceremonies. The next day, starting at four in
the morning, the first guests began to file into the cathedral, which had been
transformed into a kind of baroque opera house. Between the pillars of the
nave, hidden by Corinthian columns, were rows of boxes surmounted by cof-
fered ceilings. All the features belonging to what the century of the Enlightenment called "the awful Gothic" had been covered up. There were statues
of angels in Greek dress supporting heavy torchères and of children holding
up flame burners. The entire polychromatic decor, highlighted by purple
satin and velvet draperies with brocade fleur-de-lis and gold fringes and trimmings, conferred unbelievable luxury on this grandiose ceremony. Behind
the Queen's grandstand, the Menus-Plaisirs had installed a real apartment
with all the conveniences, including—a supreme luxury in those days—
"English-style facilities." Indeed it was to be quite a long ceremony.

At five-thirty, the Queen, beautifully dressed, and accompanied by the
ladies of her household, took her seat in the grandstand. All eyes were upon
her until the sovereign entered. The great organ soon sounded and Louis XVI
appeared silhouetted against the light of the cathedral entrance. Wearing a
long silver robe, the King seemed transfigured by grace. With a bishop on
either side of him, he walked toward the altar with manly assurance while the
hundred-man orchestra accompanied the thundering chords of the organ.
Marie Antoinette's eyes were riveted on her husband, usually so clumsy, who
seemed inhabited by a strength she had never seen in him before. Then the
ancestral ritual began, during which the sovereign was successively anointed,
crowned and enthroned. At the most solemn moment, when he received the
sacred unctions, tears of emotion streamed down the Queen's cheeks. The
King raised his head and looked at her. "An unmistakable air of contentment
was then reflected in the monarch's appearance," Mercy-Argenteau would
note.[6] Unable to contain her agitation any longer, Marie Antoinette retired to
her apartment to weep freely. When she returned to her seat, applause broke
out, an unprecedented event in this sacred building. Emotion spread to all
present. Even the envoy from Tripoli broke down in noisy sobs. The ceremony ended in great joy. Outside, volleys of artillery shots, musketry salvos,
the chimes of bells from all the churches and convents and the clamorous
merriment of the city announced to France that Louis XVI had been

crowned. Radiant, the King returned to the Archbishop's palace at eleven. Etiquette still required a dinner, which the Queen could attend only from a small balcony located in an angle of the room. Fortunately, no other ceremony was scheduled for the afternoon. The King and Queen were able to rest. But in the evening, at around seven, having taken off his heavy coronation clothes, the King took his wife's arm and led her to a gallery overlooking the church square and then down into the square to mingle with the crowd. The young couple were given an ovation for over an hour.

The stay in Rheims had not yet come to an end. The Queen admired Count Eszterhazy's marching regiment and the charge led by her brothers-in-law at the head of their squadrons. Once again she was applauded in a final ceremony in the cathedral. During each of her public appearances, she could savor the love shown her by her subjects. She returned to Versailles convinced that the country's heart beat in unison with her own. Not without condescension toward the people, whom she saw as a faceless, voiceless mass of men and women on occasion thoughtless enough to rebel, she hastened to write to her mother. "The coronation was perfect in every way," she wrote to her. "It seems that everyone was very pleased with the King; all his subjects must have been pleased; great or humble, they all showed him the utmost interest; the church ceremonies were interrupted at the moment of the coronation by the most touching cheers. I couldn't contain my emotion; tears rolled down my face in spite of myself and people took kindly to it. I did my best during the entire trip to respond to the people's enthusiasm, and though there was much heat and many crowds, I do not regret my fatigue, which, by the way, did not upset my health. It is at once amazing and most fortunate to be so well received two months after the rebellion and in spite of the high price of bread, which, unfortunately, continues. It is a remarkable trait in the French character that it lets itself be carried away by evil suggestions and then returns to the good right away. It is certain that having seen people treat us so well in spite of their misfortune, we are even more obligated to work for their happiness. The King seemed to be imbued with this truth; as for me, I know that I will never forget the day of the coronation (even if I live to be a hundred)."[7]

Marie Antoinette's emotion was surely not insincere, but the Queen was not telling the Empress the whole truth. She carefully omitted telling her about her long meeting with Choiseul. In the hope of still seeing the former minister return to power and encouraged by her small coterie, she had very much wanted to meet him. Knowing that her husband could refuse her nothing at a time of such perfect happiness, she had asked him for permission to give Choiseul this audience. Louis XVI, who saw no harm in it, granted his wife's wish quite naturally. "You will never guess the skill I used so as not to appear to be asking for permission," she wrote to Count Rosenberg. "I told the King that I wanted to see Monsieur de Choiseul and that I was only wondering on which day. I managed it so well that the *poor man* fixed the most convenient hour for me to see him. I think I took full advantage of my female prerogatives at that time."[8]

What a difference in tone between the two letters! We have every reason to believe that the Queen was more sincere in talking to Count Rosenberg than to her mother. This was not a thoughtless slip on her part. For the first time, Marie Antoinette was expressing her true feelings toward her husband, this *poor man* who had been imposed on her for reasons of state.

10

THE QUEEN'S CIRCLE

*T*hat her own daughter, the Queen of France, should call her husband "the *poor man*" was unthinkable for Maria Theresa. The elderly Empress was deeply shocked. "What style! What a way of thinking! This only confirms my fears; she is heading straight for her ruin," she confided to Mercy.[1] Indeed, Rosenberg had thought the young girl's behavior too dangerous to keep the letter secret and it had made the rounds of the imperial family. The Emperor was assigned the unpleasant task of reprimanding his sister. "Could anything more unreasonable, more improper be written than what you wrote to Count Rosenberg?" he fulminated. "If a letter of this kind ever got lost, if you ever let words or comments of this kind slip in front of your intimate confidantes, as I am nearly certain you do, I can see the misfortune it will bring you, and I admit that, being attached to you, I am greatly distressed by it. It is your enemies and those who most want to see the destruction of all the influence you could have who drive you to such steps."[2] After having seriously rebuked Marie Antoinette, Joseph called upon her to get closer to the King in order to win his esteem and trust. "Read, keep busy, improve your mind, give yourself talents and ready yourself to have inner resources when you reach a more advanced age and in case that vast public approval which fulfills all your present desires and pleasures were to leave you, as is bound to happen."[3]

The letters from Vienna deeply affected the Queen. While she listened to her mother's reprimands like an obedient child, saying, "When she speaks, I can only bow my head,"[4] she was angry at her brother. She accused him of wanting to control her and found the hard tone he had adopted with her intolerable. Seeing her discontent, Mercy-Argenteau calmed her down and got her to listen to reason, but he also tried to point out the dangers of what he called her *"entours"* (entourage), so lacking in good advisers. Indeed, in a little under a year, the Queen had surrounded herself with a circle of friends who literally formed a little coterie isolating her from the rest of the court.

During Louis XV's reign, she had been able to become intimate friends only with Marie Thérèse de Savoie-Carignan, Princesse de Lamballe, a young widow whose husband, well known for his profligacy, had died of syphilis. Madame de Lamballe's idle life was divided among the many castles of her father-in-law, the Duc de Penthièvre, and the courts at Versailles and at the Palais-Royal, where she enjoyed the company of the Duchesse de Chartres, her late husband's sister. Marie Antoinette had felt an immediate strong attraction for this discreet, pleasant woman, who was so sensitive she fainted at the slightest thing. The Dauphine had needed a companion her own age and the docile Princesse de Lamballe had filled this role perfectly. But her unimaginative loyalty had started to weary the Queen. She was bored with Madame de Lamballe, who lacked wit and whose private life was as unexciting as her own. Ever since she saw herself as free to live as she pleased, Marie Antoinette sought not just a tearful confidante but a social set that could entertain her. However, touched by the Princesse's affection and eager to prove she could wield influence, she was very insistent in asking the King to restore the position of Superintendent of the Queen's Household for her friend. This was an honorary function that offered lavish benefits to the holder and which Louis XV's wife had chosen to abolish. Using all his diplomatic skills, Turgot—with the support, in fact, of Mercy-Argenteau—tried to argue against the Queen's expensive plan. To no avail. Louis XVI finally gave in to his wife and she felt triumphant. "Picture my happiness," she wrote to Rosenberg. "I will make my intimate friend happy and I will benefit even more than she."[5]

However, Madame de Lamballe's star was fading. She retained only the outward prerogatives of intimacy. The Queen preferred the company of the Princesse de Guéméné and Madame Dillon. Madame de Guéméné, who had inherited from the Princesse de Marsan the position of Governess of the Children of France, had very few obligations in this capacity since Madame Elisabeth, the King's youngest sister, was already eleven years old. Madame de Marsan's private life had been above reproach. This was not the case with the new governess, who maintained an official liaison with the Duc de Coigny—without causing her husband, the Prince de Guéméné, the least displeasure, for he was passionately in love with the charming Madame Dillon. Furthermore, these two ladies were the best of friends and saw each other every day. Madame de Guéméné organized extraordinarily refined evenings in her small château of Montreuil, very near Versailles, and in her apartment in the Tuileries in Paris. The best actors and musicians in Paris performed in her little theater, and it was a delight to stroll in her English-style garden; one path led to a hill from which there was a magnificent view of the capital.

This tall, haughty woman was a striking eccentric. Attracted to illuminism, she claimed to be in communication with the next world through her dogs and they never left her side. Her salon was a center of intrigue, a meeting place for supporters of Choiseul (*choiseulistes*), and she was the mastermind behind the group. No sooner had Louis XVI's coronation taken place than Marie Antoinette seemed to them an ideal prey. They wanted to sway the mind of this young Queen, who was idle and inexperienced and had always shown concern for Choiseul. Madame de Guéméné had no trouble attracting her; Marie Antoinette made it a habit to spend her evenings at the house of the governess, who—to everyone's surprise—treated the sovereign as an equal. The Queen took no offense at this and showed as much interest in this odd princess as in the gentle and fragile Madame Dillon.

Madame de Guéméné's social circle included several attractive gentlemen. Among them was the Chevalier de Luxembourg. Unconventional, full of wit, fascinated by magic, he stimulated the Queen's curiosity. But his weird projects—he wanted to put the Comte d'Artois on the elective Polish throne—made her keep her distance rather quickly. The young Queen was said to have had a weakness for the Duc de Coigny, who was old enough to be her father. But what she liked most about him was that he represented the accomplished gallantry of noblemen from the old court and was polished in the art of paying compliments. The Baron de Besenval, colonel of the Swiss Guards, immediately impressed her. This protégé of Choiseul, who was over fifty, was a brilliant conversationalist, known for his juicy anecdotes, biting repartee and mocking gaiety. A man of considerable writing talent, the author of two successful novels, he left memoirs that provide interesting observations on the courts of Louis XV and Louis XVI. An acute observer of this small society's mores, he depicted himself as a courtier who loved intrigue. Rather domineering behind a playful appearance, he knew how to attract the confidences of the Queen, whose frustrations he was expert at guessing. "By talking to her in a language suitable to a twenty-year-old woman, I was merely concerned with giving her the standing most suitable to her glory and assuring her happiness," he claimed.[6] It was he and his friends who gave Marie Antoinette the idea of having an audience with Choiseul in Rheims. We can assume that the Queen made imprudent remarks to this over-the-hill Don Juan whose life centered on schemes and cabals.

As yet, no man had deeply aroused the Queen. Though they were often seen together, the Comte d'Artois was not the kind of person who could move her heart and sensuality. Glowing with health and impulsiveness, incapable of reflection, his mind exclusively on amusement, he was nonetheless thought to be her favorite companion. At Versailles, the Prince always came up with ideas for fetes. He accompanied the Queen in her rides and strolls; at balls, he played the role of chaperon and official escort. Mercy deplored that he "was concerned only with frivolity" and accused him, quite rightly, of dissoluteness: Artois neglected his wife and spent a great deal of time with opera girls. The Austrian ambassador worried about his being constantly seen with the Queen. Besides, malicious gossip was beginning to spread concerning their intimacy, which was really only a fraternal, complicitous frivolity. However, in his exceedingly detailed correspondence with the Empress, the diplomat carefully avoided mentioning the Queen's relationship with the Duc de Lauzun.

At thirty, this nobleman was the very embodiment of male seductiveness. A very highborn aristocrat and former darling of the Marquise de Pompadour, he had won greater fame in the bedroom than in the diplomatic career he had chosen. His reputation for romantic love affairs had crossed the border and given him an unparalleled aura of prestige in women's eyes. He returned from Russia in March 1775 and was in a hurry to go back to St. Petersburg with a treaty of alliance between Louis XVI and the Empress Catherine the Great. His impatience stemmed in large part from his desire to be reunited with Princess Czartoryska, with whom he was passionately in love. As he waited for an answer from the Minister of Foreign Affairs, he resumed his usual life as a French aristocrat. He had barely arrived in Paris when his old friend the Duc de Chartres invited him to take part in a horse race on the Sablons plain. It was attended by the King and Queen. According to Lauzun, Marie Antoinette was "as beautiful as the day and the day was lovely." The Queen noticed this new, pleasing face. Since Lauzun's horse won the race, she went up to congratulate the happy owner, whom she had first met in 1770. In the evening, she saw the hero of the day again at Madame de Guéméné's, for he was one of her regular visitors. The Queen longed to be acquainted with this charmer whose amorous exploits had often been recounted to her by Madame de Guéméné and Madame Dillon.

Could Marie Antoinette resist the charm of this man to whom so many women had already succumbed? Drawn to the court by her, he became her attentive escort. He went hunting and rode in the forest with her. Of course, the Queen was always followed by an equerry and several ladies of her household, but she would often spur her mount and ride ahead with a charming rider. This is what she did with Lauzun. In a matter of weeks he was thought of as her favorite. He did not want to invite slander and was extremely reserved with her. He was also diligently attentive to Louis XVI, whose hunting parties he never missed. But in the evening he would see Marie Antoinette again at Madame de Guéméné's, where the King hardly ever came. When he had to leave Versailles and return to his regiment in the provinces because of the "flour war" unrest, the Queen offered to have him called back near Paris. He refused, alleging the transfer would be damaging to his legion. "You're a fool," she said to him, laughing. She repeated her offer. To no avail. They went hunting together in the Bois de Boulogne. "She never stopped talking to me," he said, "and then my favor drew so much attention that it was probably fortunate for me that I left that very night."[7] He left for his garrison and did not attend the coronation in Rheims. During his exile in the provinces, his beautiful Polish princess sent him a farewell letter, and he consoled himself in the arms of a German baroness, but his heart was free.

At the end of the summer, when he had finished his military duties, he joined the Queen in Fontainebleau. As soon as he arrived at court, Marie Antoinette demonstrated the same interest in him as she had in the spring and they resumed their private conversations. The Queen, who could no longer do without his presence, showed irritation with anyone who interrupted their discussions. She asked Madame de Lamballe to invite Lauzun, saying to her, "I'm asking you to love like a brother the man I like most, and to whom I owe the most: may your trust in him be boundless, as is mine."[8] In order to permanently bind this nobleman to her, for she found him irresistibly attractive, she wanted to offer him an important position at the court. Though the Queen's wishes were commands, Lauzun preferred to decline this flattering offer. When she asked him why he was turning it down, he answered: "The reason, madame, is that I want to be able to retire as soon as I stop being well treated there, when Your Majesty no longer shows me the same kindnesses."[9] Marie Antoinette objected, Lauzun pledged fidelity to her, but that is where they left things. The truth of the matter is, he was too fond of his freedom to stay at the court in the service of an inaccessible woman who was all too visibly attracted to him. He found her charming, no doubt desirable, but he did not love her. A libertine as fickle as he could not contemplate an affair with a Queen, whose virtue had to remain above suspicion. He would be exposing himself to the greatest dangers.

Yet Madame de Guéméné and her friends urged him to take advantage of his situation. If the Queen had yielded to Lauzun, she would have been at their mercy. They could have manipulated her at will and obtained their hearts' desires. But Lauzun did not want to be a part of this game, which he felt was unworthy of a nobleman. He had tried to make use of the Queen only once, when he had realized that Vergennes was not giving attention to his plan for a Franco-Russian treaty. He had asked Marie Antoinette to intercede with Louis XVI. But she had shown so much "dismay" at the suggestion that he had retreated immediately. However, tongues were wagging.

One day, the insinuations of both the Princesse de Guéméné and the Princesse de Bouillon were such that Lauzun decided to discuss matters personally with the Queen. She received him in her private apartment. He told her that the kindnesses she honored him with invited malicious gossip and begged her to allow him to take temporary leave of her in order to silence the slander. "Do not abandon me, I beg you. What will become of me if you abandon me?" she whispered, on the verge of tears. Lauzun threw himself at her feet, she held out her hand and he "kissed it ardently several times." "She was in my arms when I rose. I clasped her in my arms, close to my heart, greatly moved. She blushed but I saw no anger in her eyes," Lauzun said. The Queen gently broke away from his embrace. "You are my Queen, the Queen of France!" he stammered. "Her gaze seemed to request another title. I was tempted to grasp the happiness which seemed to be offered to me," added Lauzun.[10]

Marie Antoinette continued to show Lauzun the same favor, though his plan was to return to Russia and offer his services to Catherine the Great. Once again, Marie Antoinette offered him a position at court, as her First Equerry, since the Comte de Tessé was about to resign. But again Lauzun refused to enter in the service of the Queen, holding that such an honor would invite even more malicious gossip. The Queen wept. She then tried to entice him with the prospect of another position, tutor to the Dauphin, were she so fortunate as to one day have a son. Lauzun answered that he did not possess the talents required for educating a great king. In desperation, she requested Madame de Guéméné to ask him to give her the beautiful heron plume which he wore on his helmet on the day he had come to take leave of her. Lauzun answered that he would never dare give the plume directly to the Queen, but would be happy for her to receive it from the hands of Madame de Guéméné. The next day, Marie Antoinette wore the plume publicly at dinner. "Never have I been so well adorned," she said to Lauzun. "I feel like I own invaluable treasures!"[11]

Word spread. People chattered so much that Lauzun felt it would be prudent to withdraw from the court. He left for Chanteloup, where he was warmly received by the Choiseuls. The Duchesse de Gramont, the former minister's sister, who was extremely well informed on everything that went on at Versailles, was convinced that Lauzun's favor would vouchsafe her brother's return to power. "The Queen's fondness for you is obvious and the outcome is inevitable," she said to him. "At the opportune moment, you will have Monsieur de Choiseul called back to the ministry."[12] Exasperated by Madame de Gramont's persistent assaults, for he knew her to be consumed with ambition, Lauzun returned to the court, where he continued to enjoy a favor that aroused growing jealousy.

With every passing day, Marie Antoinette gave herself over to the whirlwind of pleasures that had become her life. In spite of a flu epidemic, the winter season looked extraordinarily promising. As during the previous year, the Queen presided over the organizing of balls and fetes with Papillon de La Ferté, who was more and more overwhelmed by her avalanche of impatient and sometimes contradictory orders. Youth reigned at Versailles. The Queen's gibes, her tastes, which were judged extravagant, and her contempt for etiquette drove away the courtiers of Louis XV's time. The giddy girl had dared to say that she could not understand anyone presenting themselves at court after thirty and referred to middle-aged women as "centuries" or "straitlaced." Hence Madame de Noailles had retired, as had the Princesse de Marsan and the Duchesse de Cossé, her Mistress of the Robes. Many others had followed their example. The Queen was not distressed in the least by these departures, for she was happy to see only attractive faces around her.

The Queen's perpetual restlessness, her whims and infatuations, her fits of trumped-up authority concealed a state of great confusion. She was inclined to *spleen*, which was just then beginning to be fashionable. And she was homesick: she wished she could see Vienna, her mother, her brothers, her sisters again. She had to hold back tears on hearing that the Comte and Comtesse de Provence were accompanying Madame Clotilde to Chambéry for her marriage to the Prince of Piedmont. This meant that Marie Joséphine would be reunited with her family for two weeks. She envied her brother Ferdinand, who had spent several days in Vienna with his wife. Austria was still very much the Queen of France's homeland; it seemed she had left all her childhood dreams in her native land and—in spite of her formidable mother's scoldings—an ever so sweet sense of security. Vienna appeared to her as a protected haven, the preeminent sanctuary.

Disappointed by a husband who could not satisfy her and by a family lacking in charm, she was in desperate need of a person whom she could truly love and who could reciprocate her feelings in a relationship that would not cause a scandal. Since love was prohibited, she sought refuge in friendship. She wished to be loved for herself and not for what she represented. She needed another Princesse de Lamballe more suited to her new life. Though she still had affection for her, the Princess, she felt, was like a childhood friend with whom one no longer has tastes in common. Marie Antoinette, who attributed the utmost importance to life's private pleasures, had never known true moments of abandon with Madame de Dillon or Madame de Guéméné. Though she liked their company, these women were too fashionable, too worldly, too jaded and too scheming to be her confidantes. Though she was dazzled by Madame de Guéméné's social set, she had an ill-defined sense that she could become the plaything of many a cabal. Her flirtation with Lauzun had been proof of this.

She was convinced that she had finally found a friend after her own heart in the person of the unnerving Comtesse Jules de Polignac. With her angelic face that could have inspired Raphael, her large, candid blue eyes, her innocent smile and melodious voice, this twenty-six-year-old woman fascinated the Queen by her nonchalant grace. Madame de Polignac was not admired for an uncommon intelligence or witticisms, but her remarks were always to the point. Even-tempered and playful, she had a pleasant way of contributing to conversations without ever being self-serving or eclipsing others. Sensitive, indolent, extremely forthright, she was always perfectly natural. Her modest fortune prevented her from coming often to the court, and she spent most of her time at her estate in Claye[13] in the company of an extremely obliging husband, who accepted her liaison with the Comte de

Vaudreuil. For the Queen, who could only experience certain emotions vicariously, this woman's experience with love endowed her with an unquestionable superiority.

Marie Antoinette became very taken with her in the summer of 1775. Besenval encouraged this attraction, which he was the first to notice. On friendly terms himself with the Polignacs, he immediately saw all the advantages he could derive from such a relationship, though he claimed the opposite in his memoirs. If Madame de Polignac became Marie Antoinette's intimate friend, he hoped to exert control over the Queen and influence her actions using the charming Countess as his intermediary. Marie Antoinette refused to listen to Mercy's repeated warnings. In Lauzun's absence, the only person whom she was happy to be with was Madame de Polignac and they had more and more intimate conversations together, to the great chagrin of the Princesse de Lamballe, who suffered to see herself so neglected. In fact, the Queen met her new friend more often at Madame de Guéméné's salon than at the Superintendent's. She shared her time between these two circles, both of which feigned to be utterly devoted to her, though they were actually just greedy for favors of an ever more exorbitant nature. Happy to dispense such gratifications, the Queen began interceding with the ministers to please those who adulated her.

At the end of her stay in Fontainebleau, Madame de Polignac alleged that because of her limited financial situation she had to leave the court and return to her estate. She came to take leave of the Queen. "We do not love each other so much yet that we will be unhappy when we are separated," she said to her. "I feel it coming. Soon I will be unable to leave you: let us prevent this from happening. Allow me to leave Fontainebleau. I am not made for the court." Madame de Polignac's carriage stood ready to depart. Distraught, "the Queen wept, kissed her, grasped her hands, entreated her, urged her and threw her arms around her neck." In seeing the scene from a door left ajar, the Comte d'Artois burst out laughing and walked away saying: "Don't stand on ceremony!"

This story, reported by the Prince de Ligne,[14] was immediately known to the entire court. It inspired particularly spiteful comments because Madame de Polignac gave in to the Queen's entreaties. Several days later, she and her husband moved into an apartment at the Château de Versailles. Marie Antoinette was already thinking about all the privileges she would shower on her friend, whom she treated as a favorite. The passionate friendship she displayed for her gave rise to more nasty gossip. "We are in the midst of an epidemic of satirical songs," she wrote to her mother on December 15. "These are being written about everyone at court, men and women, and the French in their levity have even included the King. As for me, I have not been spared."[15] The *Nouvelles de la cour* attributed to the Queen a taste for both female and male lovers!

11

VENUS AND VULCAN

*M*y tastes are not the same as those of the King, who cares only for hunting and mechanical work. You must agree that I don't really fit in near a forge; I could not play Vulcan and the role of Venus might put him off much more than my tastes of which he does not disapprove."[1] This was how Marie Antoinette spoke to Count Rosenberg; the tone was entirely different from the one she used with her mother. After the euphoric period following Louis XVI's accession, relations between the two spouses had noticeably slackened. They saw each other more and more infrequently, the King being taken up with matters of state and the Queen with her amusements, in which he did not share.

Marie Antoinette rose late every morning in the bedchamber that had formerly belonged to Marie Leszczynska and which Louis XV had modernized for the Dauphine shortly after her arrival in Versailles. She disliked the huge formal room, where every small detail reminded her of her eminent position—the ceilings were adorned with high reliefs representing the arms of France and the eagles of Austria; the sumptuous bed, covered with brocade, was set on a platform behind a golden balustrade and under a canopy decorated with sculptured cupids and garlands of lilies. The tapestries decorating the back of the room and the mirrors framed with festoons of gilded bronze flowers also contributed to the room's stateliness. On moving in, the Queen's only contribution had been to replace the portraits that were there with portraits of her Empress mother and Emperor brother.

Marie Antoinette would lounge in bed, drink her coffee or chocolate and nibble on a slice of Viennese bread and butter; then she would get up. On the days she took a bath, she would slip into a long flannel dress buttoned up to her neck and dip into a bathtub that had been dragged into the middle of the room. When she had finished her ablutions, two bath assistants helped her come out of the water; she requested that a sheet be held in front of her during that time so she would not be visible to her ladies. Then the dressing ceremony began. "It was a masterpiece of etiquette," Madame Campan tells us. "Everything was regulated. The Lady-in-Waiting and the Superintendent of the Household—both took part if they were there together—helped by the First Woman of the Bedchamber and two ordinary Ladies, performed the main function; but there were distinctions among them. The Superintendent of the Household helped her with her petticoat and presented her dress. The Lady-in-Waiting poured the water when she washed her hands and helped her with her chemise. When a princess of the royal family was present at the dressing ceremony, the Lady-in-Waiting surrendered her function to her, but she did not surrender it directly to princesses of royal blood; in their presence the Lady-in-Waiting handed the chemise to the First Woman of the Bedchamber."[2]

This elaborate protocol regulating her every gesture was a torment to the Queen and poisoned her daily life. Had she agreed to follow it without protest, she would have had no right to retain Mademoiselle Bertin. She would have been obliged to order her dresses from the dressmakers who held the court appointments entitling them to dress the sovereign. The same thing was true of her choice of her hairdresser. She preferred to have her hair dressed by the renowned Léonard, who came to Versailles every morning but continued to practice his art with the most elegant women in Paris. This guaranteed that the Queen was always in step with the very latest fashion. And Léonard had to collaborate with Mademoiselle Bertin in balancing the most unlikely structures on his august mistress's lofty head.

Once she was dressed and coiffed, the Queen opened a door near the head of her bed and vanished into her inner rooms, a suite which she planned to remodel into a private, warm, comfortable apartment where none would enter unless invited. In these rooms, decorated by the late Queen, she would hold her late-morning meetings with her "minister of fashion," receive the painters who wanted to paint her portrait, grant audiences to musicians and see a select group of friends. Time went by fast. She was not to be late for mass. The Queen crossed the Peace Room leading to the Hall of Mirrors, followed by all the ladies of her household who had waited for her in her bedchamber. Together they looked like a moving forest of feathers. Marie Antoinette greeted some and smiled faintly at others, as she made her way to the chapel, where the royal family was already seated, except for Louis XVI, who always arrived last, as etiquette required.

It was nearly one o'clock. This was the Queen's first meeting of the day with her husband, unless he had paid her a discreet earlier visit, which during that period was rather unusual. The sovereign had worked all morning. He had awakened in the bedchamber of the inner apartments, formerly occupied by Louis XV. After a copious breakfast, he had sat at his desk at the window, with papers scattered about him and several books lying on the floor. In the distance, outside the window, he could see the crowd hurrying into the palace courtyard. He was in seclusion, far from the infernal Versailles ceremonial, which he detested as well. He examined his dossiers for the Council. If the day's agenda was not too full, he allowed himself a few distractions: he devoured travel narratives, studied geography maps, drew up his personal accounts and prepared the afternoon hunting party. Hunting was his outstanding passion. Only serious events or exceptionally poor weather conditions could prevent him from indulging in this pastime—a preeminently royal pastime, to which his ancestors before him had also been ardently devoted. Hunting cannot be improvised. The King saw to its preparations personally. In the silence of his study, he anticipated the strong and pleasurable emotion that would grip him as he chased deer, sometimes for hours at a time. He read the reports he had requested on the royal forests so he could gain knowledge of the animals' hiding places; he drew up the best tactics of pursuit and attack, preparing hunting plans as if they were battle strategies. He was tireless on the terrain, chasing his prey in headlong pursuit until it surrendered, exhausted.

During those quiet mornings, Louis XVI spent a few minutes admiring the mechanisms of his timepieces and the many devices in his physics cabinet. And this solitary man often liked to take refuge in a retreat where a very restricted number of people were allowed, the forge installed above his library. Here in this den he enjoyed playing Vulcan, making the occasional key or a padlock. The walls of the room were covered with marvelous locks, peerless examples that the King would never be capable of matching. Through lack of time, his know-how remained limited, though he benefited from the advice of Gamain, "Locksmith to the King's Chambers," and of Ambroise Poux-Landry, a former soldier in the French guards who had raised the locksmith's art to a high degree of perfection.

The King's contemporaries, starting with the Queen, were surprised to see the King indulge in such a plebeian occupation. However, there have been few attempts to explain this particular inclination. Why locksmithing rather than cabinetmaking or cooking? Psychiatrists contend that the compulsive need for manual labor in nonprofessionals is evidence of an obsessional neurosis. The hypothesis can quite plausibly be applied to Louis XVI, who had many other compulsions, such as minute record keeping. He kept count of the number of nights spent away from Versailles, his monthly and yearly walks and rides, and his hunting catches, listing everything from swallows to deer, as well as any dog or squirrel killed by accident.

However, other interpretations can be suggested that might shed light on the King's behavior. Two French psychoanalysts, Nicolas Abraham and Maria Torok, have used the term "cryptophoria" to describe the psychology of a person who carries within himself (in his crypt) the ghost of a dead relative, usually a sibling. This ghost, buried deep inside, feeds on the life of the person he inhabits, completely inhibiting him so long as the "host" does not succeed in expelling the ghost. It will be recalled that the King had an older brother, the Duc de Bourgogne, a radiant, handsome and precociously intelligent child, who died of tuberculosis when he was barely six. His parents, in their despair, unconsciously never forgave the future Louis XVI—who was next in line to the throne after the Duc de Bourgogne—for living and taking the place of the deceased child. It is impossible to say how the young Prince really felt about this tragedy, but he probably saw himself as usurping a place that belonged to his older brother, who possessed all the royal virtues. He felt the full weight of his unworthiness and the burden of his uncomeliness that those around him took a perverse pleasure in making him aware of. One could well ask, in the case of Louis XVI, whether the working on locks and keys did not represent a desperate quest, at once unconscious and symbolic, of a person seeking a liberating "open sesame."

But let us return to the forge, which the King soon had to leave for the State Bedchamber, where the immutable ceremony of the official *lever* (rising) took place in the presence of the princes of royal blood, the high dignitaries of the crown and all those who were admitted to attend the royal toilette, consisting really of the finishing touches of the actual toilette. Once he was dressed, and his hair coiffed and powdered, the sovereign crossed the balustrade separating his bed from the rest of the room and recited a brief prayer; then the mirrored door to the Hall of Mirrors swung open: the King appeared.

Louis XVI had an imposing stature accentuated by a slight portliness. Even after the dancing lessons he had taken to please the Queen, he still waddled as he walked, and his appearance always looked neglected in spite of all the care lavished on him. People who saw him for the first time were astonished when they saw his hands, blackened by the forge. Yet it was hard not to be struck by the noble, melancholic, distant expression in his gentle, slightly shortsighted blue eyes and his unsettled gaze that seemed lost in an endless dream.

What a remarkable contrast between the two spouses! Everything, or nearly everything, set them apart. Tall, shapely, with a full bosom and a lovely, radiant complexion, the Queen was gracious in her movements. Despite her disdainful mouth and slightly protruding blue eyes, Marie Antoinette, though not conventionally beautiful, was what would commonly be called a pretty woman. To be found attractive was the Queen's greatest wish, though according to her page, the Comte de Tilly, she had "something worth more on the throne than perfect beauty, the appearance of a Queen of France, even when she most sought to look like just a pretty woman."[3] Yet the witty, skeptical Tilly, who left memoirs that were admired by Stendhal, was not among those who swooned over her, as did Horace Walpole, who did not hesitate to write: "It was impossible to see anything but the Queen! Hebes and Floras, Helens and Graces, are streetwalkers compared with her. She is a statue of beauty, when standing or sitting; grace itself when she moves!"[4] Tilly, whose lucidity is beyond question, had to admit: "If I am not mistaken, just as one offers a chair to other women, one would almost always have wanted to draw up her throne."

Louis XVI was intimidated by his wife's majestic grace, just as the petulant charm of the little Archduchess who had bowed graciously at the feet of Louis XV in the clearing of the Compiègne forest had made him feel awkward when he was a boy of fifteen. "The King fears her rather than loves her, for he is never more visibly gay, or more at ease, than in the hunting parties where she is absent. This impression of fear, no matter how absurd, often has a greater effect than that of affection," asserted the Abbé de Véri, confidant of Maurepas and friend of Vermond.[5] The presence of this coquettish, self-confident woman made him lose his nerve. Though brought up by the most austere sovereign in Europe, Marie Antoinette had a whimsical, impulsive nature and none of the self-restraint of previous queens. Her predecessors, whose modest charms could not measure up to their husbands' power, lived and breathed solely in the shadow of the revered monarch. Not so the young Queen who wanted to live like a heroine in a novel of the period. She retained from her readings a certain idea of happiness—a kingdom limited to the gardens of Trianon, the estate given her by the King, friends chosen after her own heart, a prince charming who would always astonish her and rescue her from her own self under the delighted gazes of this ideal and loving little court.

The prince charming was the very thing that Marie Antoinette cruelly lacked. In spite of all her efforts since arriving at Versailles, her heart was never stirred by her husband though she acknowledged his uprightness, sincerity and seriousness. His self-consciousness and indecision exasperated her. She was condescending toward him, and betraying her thoughts, as we know, called him a *poor man*. She barely regarded him as a sovereign. True, there were reasons for her attitude. For years her Empress mother and Mercy-Argenteau, without really disclosing their full intentions, had been urging her to gain ascendancy over her husband, while simultaneously preaching utter submissiveness to him. With very different intentions, Choiseul, during his infamous audience, had had the audacity to advise her to use "gentleness to win the King and fear to subjugate him."[6] As for Besenval and his associates, they let her believe that she was to play a major role in the state. All these instructions contributed in convincing the young Queen of her superiority over her husband—this man whom she could not admire and whose clumsiness in love was a continued source of humiliation. Louis XVI's inability to behave like a true husband and enable her to bear Bourbon heirs kept her perpetually, it seemed, in the situation of a spoiled child.

Up until the spring of 1775, Louis XVI had shared his wife's bed regularly. But their embraces had never been crowned with success. Several times it had been suggested to Louis XVI that a small operation could eliminate the pain that hampered the King in his sexual relations with the Queen and prevented him from procreating. Unfortunately, the King hesitated over having the operation. When he learned of the Comtesse d'Artois's pregnancy, however, he decided to consult his physician again. The physician, noting "great changes for the better," no longer thought the operation necessary. He believed that "the only obstacles were a lack of self-confidence, fear and childish timidity, aggravated by a cold, late-blooming temperament which gave definite signs of gradually maturing and left no doubt that a real physical potency was developing." But for Marie Antoinette the conjugal bed had become the site of a trial that she decided to avoid as often as possible. She used the pretext of a bad cold to ask her husband not to join her in her room. This was at the time of the "flour wars," when the Queen was beginning to show an interest in Lauzun. The separation between the two spouses extended beyond Marie Antoinette's recovery; she showed no eagerness to resume conjugal life. Mercy tried to get her to listen to reason by repeatedly telling her that her casualness might cool the King's affection and undermine his trust in her. She paid him no heed. In the hope of bringing about an intimacy that he believed was threatened, the ambassador suggested building an underground corridor between the King's apartment and the Queen's. They both applauded this suggestion. For since the two apartments did not communicate, whenever Louis XVI wanted to join his wife after the official *coucher* ceremony, he had to cross the Second Antechamber in his bathrobe and be seen by dawdling courtiers. The secret passageway would enable the couple to meet whenever they wanted without anyone knowing about it.

By the time they returned from Rheims, the two bedrooms were linked by a fabric-lined corridor. But Louis XVI rarely availed himself of it. Marie Antoinette kept later and later hours and the King disliked being awakened in the middle of the night. Consequently, they more or less continued to live separately. Marie Antoinette had nevertheless felt intense disappointment when the Comtesse d'Artois gave birth to a son, on August 6, 1775. The child, who was given the title of Duc d'Angoulême, was now third in line to the French throne.[7] If the Queen did not become pregnant soon, the Comte d'Artois's progeny could very well ascend the throne in the decades to come, for it was extremely unlikely that the Comtesse de Provence would have children. "I need not tell my dear Mother how much I suffered in seeing an heir who was not mine,"[8] sighed Marie Antoinette, who had to endure the aggressive cries of the market ladies who pursued her all the way to her apartment demanding a dauphin!

The possibility of an operation for the King was again raised, but no one seemed to be in a rush. Not even the persons most directly concerned. Though Marie Antoinette maintained to her mother that "any nonchalance was not due to her," her "wedded state" hardly evolved. Louis XVI's indecision and fear grew as the Queen became more distant from him. Maria Theresa and Mercy could scold all they wanted, telling her repeatedly that childless queens have always been in a precarious position at the French court, but Marie Antoinette turned a deaf ear and continued to lose herself in a whirlwind of entertainments. She so dreaded finding herself in the arms of her husband again that she even began wishing he would take a mistress to acquire the experience he lacked. Thus the elderly Duc de Richelieu, Louis XV's former romantic confidant, who could have offered the King some valuable advice, thought he had found a solution—he wanted to introduce the King to Mademoiselle Contat, an actress whose performances he enjoyed. The plan was not worth pursuing. The young monarch had no interest in a dalliance. He had eyes only for his wife, this wife whom he could not satisfy. In his inability to express his love, he showered her with generous gifts. Time and again she exerted a very feminine form of despotism over her husband, harassing him in order to gratify her whims and those of her friends. As for her intimate relations with him, she was now determined to "leave matters to Providence and wait submissively for some happy outcome."[9]

12

THE QUEEN'S INTRIGUES

A frenzied need for pleasure had taken hold of the Queen. She was seen in all the fashionable places. She never missed a ball or an evening at the Opera or the theater. Often she would leave Versailles when the King retired to bed, rush to Paris and stay there until dawn. She would return to the château to hear mass and then sleep until noon. One night, the wheel of her carriage broke and she had to continue her trip in a hackney. She boasted of this escapade the next day, with peals of laughter: "Imagine me in a hackney!" Of course, the story made the rounds of the court and the city. Rumor had it that Marie Antoinette was actually on her way to an amorous appointment with the Duc de Coigny, who seemed in greater favor at the time than Lauzun. In court, she surrounded herself openly with young people; the Duc de Croÿ, who observed her, noted sadly that she easily sniggered in the face of courtiers as she listened to that old roué Besenval, who knew how to entertain her better than anyone.

Besenval, the Swiss baron, had succeeded in his objectives: he could manipulate the Queen and the Comtesse de Polignac, her inseparable friend, just as he pleased. The Queen liked the social set gathered at Madame de Polignac's; the supremely discreet Comte de Polignac allowed his wife's official lover, the Comte de Vaudreuil, to act as the host in his wife's salon. A witty man, fond of literature and the arts, Vaudreuil took pleasure in playing the part of Maecenas and knew how to talk to women.

Madame de Polignac could not resist him. Immensely greedy, Vaudreuil often took advantage of his mistress's situation. Marie Antoinette kept up a front but did not like him. Some people claimed she was jealous of him. She certainly preferred the Duc de Coigny, who now neglected Madame de Guéméné and paid discreet court to her. The Comte d'Adhémar—personable enough to charm but not brilliant enough to frighten anyone—was a pleasant conversationalist. The Comte de Guines, who had just been called back from his embassy in London, was one of the Comtesse's most devoted guests. She also liked to invite foreigners like the Prince de Ligne, a witty Belgian aristocrat who was secretly in love with the Queen, whose "white soul" he would defend to the last, and the Count Eszterhazy, whom Marie Antoinette would trust even in the darkest moments of her life. Madame de Polignac attracted all her relatives to Versailles of course; first and foremost her aunt, the Comtesse d'Andlau, who had a scandalous reputation; and her sisters-in-law—the scheming, free and flirtatious live wire, the Comtesse Diane de Polignac, and the evanescent Comtesse de Polastron, who conquered the Comte d'Artois's heart.

The Queen's increasingly exclusive friendship with the Comtesse aroused many jealous feelings. Mercy was the first to take offense at this favor, which he regarded as undeserved and as possibly having detrimental consequences for the Queen. In his eyes, Madame de Polignac was a young lady whose presence at the court was unwarranted and whose reputation was tainted by rather dubious conduct. He saw her as having "a very slender intellect," capable only of urging the Queen further along the path of dissipation. Completely trusting, Marie Antoinette opened her heart to her friend and confided her most intimate thoughts to her "with unreserved candor." When Madame de Polignac left the court for Paris or her country estate, the Queen wrote to her and Mercy feared that the content of her letters might be divulged. "Such letters do not remain secret . . . I have exhaustive proof of the countless abuses they result in, but it is useless to think of stopping the Queen in this matter," he said to the Empress.[1] The ambassador had grasped the situation; the standing enjoyed by Madame de Polignac conferred on her a small amount of power which her entourage began to exploit shamelessly. She was already being courted with the aim of getting her to obtain favors and advantages. As for the Comtesse's family, they sought positions for themselves.

Vermond, who was in the habit of speaking frankly to the Queen, tried to warn her against this dangerous infatuation. "You have become very lenient concerning the morals and reputations of your male and female friends," he said to her. "I could prove to you that at your age such leniency, especially toward women, makes a bad impression; but let me just say that I can overlook your disregard of a woman's morals or reputation, your making her your social companion and friend merely because she is charming, though this may not be the morality of a priest; but that shocking behavior of every variety, bad morals, tainted and lost reputations are requirements for admission into your social circle—this is something that causes you infinite harm. For some time, you have not even had the prudence to maintain ties with some women who have the reputation for being sensible and having good conduct."[2] Marie Antoinette listened to this sermon very obligingly, admitted almost laughingly that the Abbé was not wrong and returned just as flippantly to her usual occupations.

Her friends did not just confine themselves to amusing her. They wanted her to play a central role in their intrigues to bring Choiseul back to power. The pleasant circle cared not a scrap about their great man's governmental program (indeed, did he have one?); the only thing they cared about were the benefits they stood to gain. By compromising Marie Antoinette in their cabals, they gravely contributed to tarnishing her image in the eyes of the public and they also exhibited a lack of political acumen. The Queen's influence over her husband remained limited, and though the King could often be accused of weakness, his hatred for the former minister was such that it was pointless to hope for his return to power. Moreover, Choiseul had understood this perfectly well. He had had two opportunities to gauge the depth of the King's contempt for him: first, when the Queen had intervened to lift his order of exile, and second, at the coronation. However, his partisans refused to admit defeat. During the "flour wars," it will be recalled, they had tried to circumvent the sovereign by using the Queen and she had thereby angered Louis XVI. But it was thanks to their advice that the Queen had succeeded in getting the Duc d'Aiguillon exiled. Since then, all their intrigues inevitably revolved around soliciting her intervention with the King to obtain appointments, pensions and other advantages. And Marie Antoinette often committed herself thoughtlessly, simply to oblige a small social set whose greediness she had underestimated.

At that time, the Polignac coterie openly showed great contempt for Turgot, who was considered the principal power in the cabinet. During the uprisings the previous spring, he had taken needed measures to maintain order while Maurepas had been both weak and indecisive. The King listened to his Finance Minister, who was leading him on the path of innovative and bold reforms. But Turgot did not just draw up economic and fiscal projects; he also wished to implement measures that did not directly fall within his own ministry: he wanted to grant civil status to Protestants and secularize education and public assistance. All these proposals threatened a number of privileges; indeed the minister did not conceal that he wanted to impose drastic cost-cutting policies that would first target the court. The Queen's friends were therefore in an agitated state. Marie Antoinette had to serve their purposes.

Besenval had been making violent attacks against Turgot for several months, claiming, ironically, that he was "consumed with the rage of public welfare." He did not hesitate to tell the Queen that this minister, with "his vain character," was showing "real incompetence." It was easy for the old roué to make her dislike this "man with a system, this arrogant philosopher, mediocre and weak," who had been opposed to her projects on several occasions—he had not wanted to release the funds required for the redesign of her Trianon garden, and he had dared to turn down pensions for some of her protégés. Marie Antoinette did not easily forgive what she saw as "crimes of lese majesty." It was not a difficult task for the Baron to persuade her that Turgot had to be dismissed and replaced by a successor who would be fully devoted to her. For Marie Antoinette, who was really more interested in people than in politics, Turgot's dismissal became a kind of game. She put all her pride into winning.

By the beginning of 1776, Turgot was completing work on four bills that, in the long run, would have drastically changed the structure of the monarchy. Directed against privileges, the new legislation would eventually have established equal rights for all Frenchmen. Turgot was meeting with strong opposition from his colleagues within the cabinet. Maurepas, the King's "mentor," was silently jealous of this still youthful man who seemed to be leading the monarch toward reforms that were contrary to his principles. Indeed, Louis XVI believed that he should pass the kingdom down to his successors exactly as he had received it. Though he accepted, on principle, limited reforms, he was reluctant to adopt structural reforms. And these were the very ones involved in Turgot's projects. Overcoming his fears, the monarch nevertheless imposed his Finance Minister's edicts.

There were cries of indignation at court. No one had harsh enough words for "le Turgot," who was threatening, it was said, the established order. The Queen was the first to inveigh against the minister. The King's brothers and all her friends joined her in a chorus against him. Frightened by his own boldness and the tempest he had caused, Louis XVI very soon gave signs of discouragement. Whenever, by chance, he said anything about current affairs in the Queen's presence, he had to put up with the worst criticisms of this minister and his measures. Goaded on by her friends, Marie Antoinette declared a merciless war against the Finance Minister, whose edicts she had not even read. She merely repeated all the salon comments she had heard about them here and there. One day, as he galloped by her side under pouring rain in the Bois de Boulogne, the Prince de Ligne heard her complain bitterly of Turgot. "Madame," he said to her, "let us return and hunt him instead of deer, for the weather is dreadful." And the Queen burst out laughing.

There were other influences hostile to the Finance Minister that exerted pressure on the King. Maurepas, who lived in Madame du Barry's former apartment and could therefore communicate with Louis XVI without anyone knowing, denigrated his colleague systematically. The other ministers did nothing to conceal their disapproval. Certainly, there was no shortage of lucid observers prepared to defend the reforms, but they carried little weight compared to the cohort of privileged people who were all up in arms against Turgot. The populace, though, directly affected by the edicts, remained unorganized, too preoccupied by daily difficulties and the high cost of bread. Soon Louis XVI lacked the strength to support Turgot. After much procrastination, he decided to dismiss him.

An explosion of joy broke out in the ranks of the *choiseulistes* when they heard of this dismissal, on May 10, 1776. The Queen exulted, her friends congratulated themselves. A second news item seemed to confirm the little coterie's triumph: the Count de Guines was made a duke. This diplomat had been accused of serious mistakes during his ambassadorship in England and the King had heard damaging criticism of him from Vergennes, his Minister of Foreign Affairs, as well as from Turgot. But the Queen had secretly pleaded the cause of this staunch *choiseuliste* to her husband. Seeing him as a victim of the Finance Minister, whom she blamed for all evils, she had improperly linked the two unrelated affairs—the minister's dismissal and the diplomat's resounding rehabilitation. "The Queen's plan was to demand that the King dismiss Monsieur Turgot and even send him to the Bastille on the same day that the Comte de Guines was declared a duke, and it took the strongest and most insistent appeals to appease the Queen's anger, which has no other basis than the steps Turgot had to take to recall the Comte de Guines," Mercy wrote to the Empress. "No doubt Your Majesty will be surprised to learn that this Comte de Guines, for whom the Queen has no personal affection and cannot have any, should nevertheless be the cause of such great movements."[3] Through cajoling and threats, Marie Antoinette had succeeded in getting the King to send Guines a sort of certificate of good conduct along with his nomination to the title of duke. She had even made him rewrite the letter twice, because she thought the two first versions were not warm enough.

Though Marie Antoinette was indeed responsible for Guines's undeserved elevation, her role in the Finance Minister's dismissal had been negligible. For months she had acted as the spokeswoman for the privileged and harassed her husband with diatribes against his minister. But it was Maurepas who, through insinuation and persuasion, had obtained the Finance Minister's disgrace. He had succeeded in convincing the young monarch that Turgot was endangering the fundamental laws of the monarchy, to which the King was viscerally attached. However, public opinion assumed that the Queen had much greater influence than she actually had and attributed this grievous decision to her.

To her friends' great disappointment, the Queen did not meddle in the appointment of the new Finance Minister. Had she wanted to, her husband would have silenced her. Strikingly incompetent, Turgot's immediate successor did not long remain in power. Marie Antoinette worried very little about this, but she sank into a profound state of melancholy. She was bored, and found Versailles sad and deserted. And Mercy told her that her incessant trips away from the château and perpetual mockery put off a great many courtiers. Thus it was that for the first time since her arrival in France, she was overcome with an attack of religious fervor. She could be seen spending more time in the Versailles churches. She grew closer to the King, accompanied him on his hunts, dined alone with him several times and probably shared his bedroom on a few occasions.

That summer Louis XVI did without the traditional stay in Compiègne, which was deemed too costly. The court moved to Marly, where the Queen spent her days peacefully, surrounded by her dear friends. They constantly did their utmost to cleverly denigrate the handsome Lauzun, whom she still seemed interested in despite the unremitting attentions of the Duc de Coigny, who was visibly hurt by this obvious preference. Lauzun's love affairs were once again the talk of the town. He had been having a tempestuous liaison for several months with the beautiful Lady Barrymore, whose favors he shared with the Comte d'Artois. Yet, being an assiduous courtier, he remained a loyal servant to the Queen while she feigned to be ignorant of his love affairs, whose notoriety could only make her suffer. Having heard that Madame de Lamballe was afflicted with a very bad case of measles in the spa town of Plombières, he immediately suggested to the Queen that he go see her friend so he could bring back accurate news of her. Indeed, Marie Antoinette feared that she was not being told the truth about the seriousness of her friend's illness.

Lauzun's departure allowed the little social set to scheme freely. Madame de Polignac requested the position of First Equerry to the Queen for her husband, the position that had formerly been offered to Lauzun. Since she still felt obligated to Lauzun, Marie Antoinette asked him if she could make the position available to the Comte de Polignac. Though his pride was slightly wounded, Lauzun replied that he was happy to please his sovereign. The Polignacs triumphed, but when Lauzun returned from his trip, the Queen welcomed him more graciously than ever and spoke to him in a low voice for a long time, thereby shocking the good company. "You have not kept your word; you promised not to speak to him at length and to treat him like every one else," Coigny complained to the Queen.[4] Lauzun overheard him, so when she came up to him again he said: "Beware, you will get scolded again." With a slight embarrassment, she laughingly had to acknowledge that he was right.[5]

During the stay in Fontainebleau, to the great disappointment of the Polignacs, Lauzun's favor never diminished. To distract the court, the Duc de Chartres organized a horse race. A lover of England in his day, he had been converted to this new fad by Lauzun himself. Chartres, Artois, Lauzun and a number of French noblemen had taken to racing their magnificent Thoroughbreds in Spa and Ipswich before they could do so in France. The Queen had soon shared their passion for races and betting. Mercy was horrified to see her climb into a sorry-looking wooden structure which was both a grandstand and a registration office and move about among noisy young people who were not sufficiently respectful of her royal majesty.

On November 13, 1776, the Comte d'Artois's horse was to run against the Duc de Chartres's. A solicitor recorded fabulous wagers. Marie Antoinette bet against the Duc de Chartres and Lauzun against the Comte d'Artois. Chartres's jockey won. After the race the Queen went up to Lauzun. "Oh! Monster! You were sure of winning!" she said to him.[6] She was heard. This way of speaking, which led people to assume they shared a certain intimacy, was all that was needed to alarm the Polignac circle and, according to Lauzun, they swore to bring about her downfall.

The Queen did not just gamble at the races. During her stay in Fontainebleau she indulged in a new passion for card games. Like the queens who had preceded her, Marie Antoinette "presided over her card game," going in for lotto and *cavagnole*, which exposed players only to small losses. Lansquenet and faro, which were forbidden even among princes of royal blood who lived in high style, seemed to her infinitely more exciting. After much coaxing she overcame her husband's objection and succeeded in getting "gambling bankers" to come from Paris. Delighted to please his wife, the King claimed it would not matter as long as they played for only one evening. The bankers arrived on October 30 and held the bank until five in the morning at the Princesse de Lamballe's. The next day, Marie Antoinette played from evening to three in the morning. It was All Saints' Day, a solemn holiday. This made an unfortunate impression on the public. "The Queen got out of it by joking. She told the King that he had allowed a gambling session without specifying its length, and that therefore they had the right to make it last thirty-six hours," Mercy recounted. "The King burst out laughing and answered gaily: 'Go on, you are all a worthless bunch!' "[7] The Queen had lost a lot of money but she had had a wonderful time. Attentive to his wife's every wish, overcoming his aversion for games of chance, Louis XVI soon offered to bring back the bankers. On November 11, they played faro again. Marie Antoinette spent another evening and night gambling. These games attracted a great many brazen young people who were oblivious to protocol and thought nothing of addressing her as they would a commoner. Flushed with excitement, she answered them laughingly, paying no heed to the people of high rank who stood in a respectful circle waiting for her to speak to them. For Marie Antoinette, the results announced by the bankers and the remarks of the young people were far more important. The custom of playing for high stakes started that year in Fontainebleau. It became very costly to pay court to the Queen, for one had to be able to pay gambling expenses.

The stay in Fontainebleau had never before been as dazzling. Fetes, balls, all sorts of entertainments succeeded one another at a mad pace. The Queen's melancholy seemed to have completely vanished. She had regained her insatiable appetite for pleasure, which her friends cleverly encouraged. They were extremely free in conversation with her; they cursed some individuals and schemed against others. All this elegantly spun chatter inevitably agitated and influenced the imprudent princess. According to Besenval, who knew her well, her coquettishness and lack of natural gaiety prevented her from presenting the image of herself that was expected, given her physical appearance and genuine natural qualities. "Her overfamiliarity," he added, "detracted from her standing. It led to everyone being displeased with her on occasion and saying derogatory things about her, to their own astonishment."[8]

13

THE BROTHER'S VISIT

E nthralled by her little social circle, Marie Antoinette listened to neither Vermond nor Mercy. Her letters to her mother were increasingly brief—and perfunctory. She even forgot to wish her a happy birthday for the year 1776! The Abbé considered leaving Versailles, and Mercy had the utmost difficulty in reporting on the young Queen's conduct to his august employer. He was reduced to praising the Queen's exceptional social skills, her ability to think up lovely compliments when she received new ambassadors or distinguished guests. But what more could he say in her favor? The unhappy diplomat carefully concealed from Maria Theresa the offensive gossip about her daughter that had spread to the courts of Berlin as well as Turin. It was rumored that the Duc de Coigny had access to her apartment at night and that one of her chambermaids had preferred to resign rather than be a party to such disgraceful behavior. Though he carefully avoided those particular subjects, Mercy nevertheless did have to report to the Empress that there were complaints about the Queen's excessive expenditures. During the last year she had doubled the number of horses in her stable to three hundred. She had spent enormous sums in remodeling the Trianon gardens and on her constant fetes and suppers. She demanded that her husband and the ministers pay exorbitant pensions to her friends and friends of her friends. Hence Madame de Lamballe's brother, the Comtesse d'Andlau—Madame de Polignac's aunt—the Marquis de Polignac, Cardinal de Polignac, the Chevalier de Luxembourg and many others became the lucky beneficiaries of the royal manna though they had done nothing to deserve it. Without giving up her fashion excesses, Marie Antoinette developed a passion for jewelry. After having bought magnificent diamond girandoles which she tried to pay for, as best she could, on an installment plan, she purchased two bracelets that cost as much as a Paris mansion!

The Queen was beginning to be blamed for all the things the royal mistresses had been blamed for in the past. And Louis XVI, unable to oppose his wife's whims, behaved with her like the most attentive courtier. He even offered to pay the debts she could not meet from his own privy purse. Maria Theresa was indignant that her daughter, the Queen of France, was behaving like a favorite. Lucid and utterly unsentimental, she made no mystery of her feelings about her: "I have always found her frivolous," she said to Mercy, "unreflective, with no interest in serious occupations, prone to attaching herself to people who cleverly comply with her inclinations and dissipations."[1] She begged Vermond, however, not to abandon the Queen. Flattered and touched by the Empress's request, the clergyman submitted to her will and tried, in turn, to defend the young woman. "Her youth and her fondness for touching lightly on things without ever delving into anything—therein lies the cause of her faults. She will get over it," he prophesied.[2]

However, with the Queen, the elderly Empress maintained the tone of a grumbling but very affectionate mother. "Do not lose through frivolities the credit you have won for yourself," is all she said to her, almost tenderly.[3] "So my bracelets have reached Vienna,"[4] the charming featherbrain cried out, slightly stung, on reading this letter. Far from suspecting Mercy, Marie Antoinette was convinced that Maria Theresa was informed of her every movement by the Belgian newspapers, which she considered incredibly malevolent in their treatment of her. In her replies to her mother, she defended herself feebly, always claiming that the reports about her were exaggerated.

Increasingly worried about her daughter's fate—to which was linked the fate of the famous alliance—Maria Theresa urged her son Joseph to go to France. She wanted him to make his sister see reason and tighten the ties between Austria and France. Serious talk about this trip began in the fall of 1776. Marie Antoinette felt torn between the joy of finally seeing a member of her family again and the fear that the meeting might turn into a disaster for her. She knew her brother's character. Authoritarian, austere, serious to the point of pedantry, the Emperor had great simplicity in his manners but was quick to take on a curt tone at the slightest hint of an argument. Twice widowed, he looked down on women and took pleasure in exercising a kind of moralizing authority over his sisters, which exasperated them. Marie Antoinette had not forgotten the scathing letters he had written to her.

As soon as she understood that Joseph's trip was more than a vague project, she forestalled matters by assuring her mother that her "greatest happiness would be that, having seen things as they were, he would disabuse my dear mother of the prejudices people are trying to give her against me."[5] Yet Marie Antoinette was well aware that her brother would inevitably criticize her. The question was how far he would go. She opened her heart to Mercy. And he relayed her fears to Vienna.

At the Hofburg, many secret meetings took place between Maria Theresa, Joseph and Chancellor Kaunitz. The latter's prime concern was maintaining the alliance. He was indifferent to the Queen's private behavior so long as it would not harm Austrian diplomacy. He warned the Emperor against brotherly reprimands that might have regrettable repercussions on the relations between the two states. It would be better to secure Marie Antoinette's good graces by a conciliatory attitude. "Either my daughter will win over the Emperor by her kindnesses and charms or he will be impatient," the Empress moaned. However, the die was cast. Joseph was to go to France the following spring.

Marie Antoinette, her heart beating with excitement, rose early on that April 18, 1777. She was expecting her brother, who insisted on maintaining a very strict incognito. As he wished to be known as Count von Falkenstein, he would not be given any of the honors due to his rank. At nine-thirty in the morning, his carriage entered the gates of the palace. The Abbé de Vermond, who went to meet the illustrious visitor, took him to a hidden stairway that led directly into the Queen's inner rooms, avoiding the crowded antechambers. Brother and sister fell into each other's arms and remained locked in a silent embrace for a long time. How many memories streamed into the Queen's mind! Seven years had gone by since she had seen her family. The visit of the oafish Maximilian, at the beginning of the reign, had not really brought her the affection of her family and the atmosphere of Vienna. Though usually perfectly self-possessed, the Emperor was as overwhelmed as she by this emotional reunion. He found the Queen of France a very pretty woman. In jest he said to her that if she had not been his sister, he would gladly have married her.

Marie Antoinette led him into another inner room and opened her heart to him for nearly two hours; skipping from one thing to another, she poured out all the small details and facts of her existence, her joys and disillusionments. He listened to her, captivated by the charm of her lively conversation, and his sullenness vanished. The censor had turned into a compassionate brother. Soon the Queen led the Emperor to the King. The sovereigns, who did not know each other, embraced good-heartedly. Overcoming his timidity, Louis XVI appeared confident and cordial, and Joseph, amiable. The Queen then took her brother to the princes and princesses. He was to see the ministers later.

For once the immutable Versailles protocol was disrupted. With the courtiers in attendance, the French sovereigns lunched with the Emperor at a table set at the foot of the Queen's bed. This was a unique instance in the annals of the French court—the Queen having a meal with a man who was not a member of the royal family. Perched on two tall folding stools propped against the bed, Louis XVI and Marie Antoinette sat facing their guest, who was seated just as uncomfortably. The Queen, usually very concerned about her appearance, had been so excited by her brother's visit that she had not taken the time to finish her toilette. She wore a simple mourning dress (the King of Portugal had just died), and her hair was minimally coiffed. On the other hand, the King had made an effort to look elegant. He cut a fine figure in his purple suit, and his hair, for once, was meticulously powdered. As for the Emperor, who was dressed in black wool, he looked like a respectful and stiff foreigner. The elderly Duc de Croÿ, comparing his master with Joseph II, noted, not without satisfaction, that "the King's style was very good, very noble and simple, and at least as good as the other one's."[6]

The Emperor wanted to see everything, get to know everything, understand everything, both in Versailles and in Paris, like an inquisitor who would later pass judgment without mincing words. Hence, he would reproach his brother-in-law for never having been to the Invalides[7] and the Ecole Militaire. He would express surprise that he had never traveled around his kingdom. He had the French financial systems explained to him and he circumspectly observed the habits and morals of citizens from all the social classes. He visited the administrative offices of the Ponts-et-Chaussées (the highways department), the Louvre storerooms, the Imprimerie Royale (royal printing press), the Manufacture des Gobelins,[8] the Savonnerie[9] and the establishment created by the Abbé de l'Epée for the education of deaf-mutes. He also conversed with the ministers and honored most of the Paris salons with his presence. All in all, in a few weeks he would do more to acquaint himself with the French capital than Louis XVI would do in the course of several decades.

The Emperor saw everything, took note of everything, criticized everything. These interesting and self-interested visits did not prevent him from spending several hours a day with his sister. The Queen confided in him immediately. She dared tell her brother all the things she had hidden from her mother. Joseph listened and was careful not to voice the slightest opinion, thereby encouraging the young woman to increasingly intimate confessions. Then suddenly, on May 9, Joseph moved onto the attack. Now that Marie Antoinette had told him what he considered essential, he started to bully her. Indeed, he wondered "if more could not be obtained through force than through gentleness." In the evening, in the presence of the Comtesse de Polignac and the Duc de Coigny, he ordered her to fetch her husband. The Emperor found it inexcusable that his sister should spend her evenings without showing any concern for her husband. Perhaps he had been told that sometimes a member of her little circle would take pleasure in maliciously setting the clock forward so the sovereign would return to his apartment as soon as possible. That evening, at least, the Queen was as gentle as a lamb and she ran to fetch her husband. On the following day, the Emperor launched into a caustic critique of the Queen's entourage. Madame de Polignac, in his opinion, was an insignificant young woman of easy virtue; Madame de Lamballe, a pedigreed fool; Madame de Guéméné, a schemer whose salon was a real "dive." The Emperor was put off by the entire frivolous circle of gossips and did not hide from his sister his distaste for her friends. Deeply wounded by his abrupt judgments, she stood her ground; she openly continued to go to Madame de Guéméné's, where high-stakes gambling was held, and treated Madame de Polignac just as affectionately as before. However, despite his altercations, Marie Antoinette did not tire of listening to her brother, who wished to recall her to her duties as a wife and queen.

After spending three weeks in Versailles, Joseph could assess the seriousness of the conflicts that kept Louis XVI and Marie Antoinette apart. He was now ready to broach the thorniest problem with his brother-in-law—his relations with the Queen. And oddly enough, the King, who was usually so secretive, abandoned all prudishness with this foreigner, this man whom all Europe feared and admired. He finally confessed the shameful facts. Mercy's and Joseph's letters clearly reveal the tone and nature of the King's disclosures. "The Emperor has succeeded in removing from the King's mind the extraordinary idea that he was endangering his health by fulfilling his conjugal duties," Mercy reported to the Empress. But it was in a letter to his brother Leopold that Joseph divulged the sad secret of the royal bed; with the cold eye of a professional, he exposed the French sovereign's "nuptial predicament" in very specific detail:

"In his conjugal bed, he has normal erections; he introduces his member, stays there without moving for about two minutes, then withdraws without ejaculating, and still erect, bids good night. This is incomprehensible because he sometimes has nocturnal emissions, but while inside and in the process, never; and he is content, and says quite frankly that he was doing it purely from a sense of duty and that he did not like it. Oh, if I could only have been present once, I would have taken care of him; he should be whipped so that he would discharge sperm like a donkey. My sister, moreover, has very little temperament and together they are two complete fumblers."[10]

Things could not be clearer. This letter, written in the Emperor's rough French, allows us to gauge the full extent of the royal couple's problem. We find it easier to understand Marie Antoinette's demoniac drive to spend her nights far from such a husband. His fruitless endeavors would today warrant professional psychotherapy. Under the circumstances, the Emperor was the one to play therapist with the King of France. He spoke to him at length, as a brother and friend. Though he thought that "laziness, clumsiness and apathy were the only impediments" to their achieving normal sexual relations, he was clever enough to let Louis XVI believe that a small surgical operation would solve all his problems. He thereby relieved the King of any inhibiting feeling of guilt.

Joseph was severe in his judgment of this strange brother-in-law. "He is absolute sovereign only to pass from one form of slavery to another," he said to Leopold. "He is badly brought up; his appearance works against him, but he is honest; he is weak to those who know how to intimidate him and consequently he is ruled with a rod of iron. The man is weak but not a fool. He has ideas, judgment, but is apathetic in body and mind. In sum, the *fiat lux* [let there be light] has yet to come; it is still undeveloped."[11] It would be hard to be more contemptuous.

With regard to his sister, the Emperor did not err on the side of leniency. Despite all the unfortunate rumors about her, he could see that her "virtue had remained intact."[12] He nevertheless criticized her insatiable appetite for futile and dangerous pleasures, though it was understandable given what they had divulged to him. He blamed her "for fulfilling neither her duties as a wife nor her duties as a Queen in satisfactory fashion . . . She is empty-headed and driven to run all day from dissipation to dissipation. She thinks only of having fun. She feels nothing for the King. She is a likable and honest woman, a bit young, unreflective, but deep down honest and virtuous."[13]

At the end of his Versailles stay, Joseph gave his sister a long Instruction[14] recapitulating her duties as wife and queen. Presented in the form of a self-examination, this document is even more revealing of the Queen's character, sentiments and behavior than Mercy's letters and the memoirs of the time. Addressing himself directly to Marie Antoinette, the Emperor requested that she search her heart and lucidly consider her situation. The questions he asks make it easy to infer her answers. "Look into yourself," he says to her. "Do you put all your efforts into pleasing him? Do you study his desires and his character and try to conform to them? Do you try to make him enjoy your company—beyond all other objects or amusements—and the pleasures you can grant him, where, without you, he would find only a void? Do you make yourself essential to him? Have you persuaded him that no one loves him more sincerely than you, or takes his glory and happiness more to heart? Does he see your affection focused exclusively on him?" We know the answer to that last question. Joseph was very forceful in warning his sister against the casualness she showed toward Louis XVI. "Only in relation to him are you allowed to have desires, he alone can impose his will—both on your person and on the affairs of his country. With one word, he can determine your fate. Do not forget that," he said to her, speaking both as a man and as a sovereign. It was clear to the Emperor that the Queen had to yield to the will of the King, even if he were the least enlightened ruler of his day. The King's personality is superseded by his office, an office Joseph, an absolute monarch himself, naturally held in the highest regard.

Without any false prudery, the Emperor broached the subject of the couple's intimate relations. Insensitive to the traumas of a wife who has been sexually frustrated, not to say humiliated, he reminded her of her duties as a woman in the strictest sense of the term, as though he considered her solely responsible for her husband's difficulty. "Are you not cold or absentminded when he caresses or talks to you? Do you not seem bored, or even repelled? If so, how could you expect a cold man who has never experienced carnal pleasures to get close to you, be aroused, love you and successfully complete his great act, or at least taste the possible pleasures of his position with you? This point requires all your attention, and whatever you do to reach this great goal will be your strongest link to happiness in life. Never get discouraged and always give him the hope that he will still be able to have children; don't ever let him give up or despair of it. You must avoid this idea and any separation of beds with all your powers, which consist only of your charms and your friendship."

We wish we knew what advice Joseph gave to his brother-in-law. However, we can assume that Marie Antoinette's problems were not taken into consideration. The King, the man, was supposed to impose himself on the woman; she was born to satisfy her master's desires and give him beautiful progeny! Thus, all would be for the best in this best of all possible worlds.

In his long epistle, Joseph broached the subject of the Queen's friendships and her most glaring follies; he cautioned her against a superficial, egotistical social circle with exceedingly loose morals. He asked her if she had seriously weighed the "dreadful fecklessness of her passion for gambling." Finally, he pointedly referred to her mad nights at the Opera, "of all the pleasures, surely the least appropriate. Be so good as to think for a moment of the inconveniences you met with there and the adventures you yourself told me about," he said to her. "What is it you want? To be unknown and play the role of a person different from yourself? Why the need for adventures and naughtiness? Why mingle with a crowd of libertines, girls, strangers, listening to their conversation and replying in kind? What *indecency*! The King left alone for a whole night at Versailles and you mixing with all the Paris riffraff!"

He implored her to educate herself and stop reading the licentious books which seemed to give her such intense pleasure: "Forget the rubbish you've filled your imagination with from this reading," he scolded. Joseph did not conceal his fears for the future. And he urged her to "tear off the blindfold that prevented her from seeing her duty and true happiness."[15]

Deeply distressed by this long epistle, Marie Antoinette tried to justify herself. However, she soon acknowledged that her brother was right and promised to mend her ways. His tutelary presence had brought her back to the path of duty. She wept bitterly when the Emperor left her. "His departure gave me a cruel jolt," she wrote to her mother. "I suffered as much as possible and I can only console myself with the thought that he shared my sorrow. I would be very unfair if I said that my pain and the emptiness I feel left me nothing but regrets. Nothing can pay for the happiness I experienced and the signs of friendship he gave me. I was quite sure that he only wanted my happiness and all his advice proves it."[16]

Very sensibly, the Queen put Joseph's advice into practice. She held court in exemplary fashion, avoided showing any favoritism and thought of singling out all those who deserved it. She grew closer to the King, who demonstrated unusual tenderness toward her. They secluded themselves for two hours each day in their apartments. Once again, the court whispered. Everyone watched for the slightest clue. On the morning of August 18, Louis XVI came to his wife at ten o'clock as she was emerging from her bath and finally succeeded at what Joseph called "the great act." On the thirtieth, Marie Antoinette wrote to her mother: "I am now enjoying the most essential happiness of my entire life. It has already been more than eight days since my marriage was perfectly consummated; the event has been repeated and again yesterday more completely than the first time . . . I do not think I am pregnant yet, but at least I have the hope of being so any day."[17]

A week later, the Queen gave a fete in honor of the King to inaugurate the Trianon gardens. The grounds were converted into a huge fair with stores kept by the ladies of the court selling precious objects. Dressed up as a café keeper, Marie Antoinette offered beverages while music was played by the musicians of the French Guard. It was an ephemeral late-summer frolic. The King and Queen had the satisfaction of having accomplished their duty. But nothing more!

14

MOTHERHOOD

The bright interval was short. Louis XVI and Marie Antoinette were never to become a pair of lovers. But they were under the obligation to procreate and the conjugal duty was a real trial for them. The King "does not like sleeping with anyone," the Queen asserted.[1] Tiring very soon of her husband's exploits, she once again seized any excuse to shun the conjugal bed. She had resumed her mad life of pleasure and stayed up until all hours. Strangely accommodating, Louis XVI seemed to applaud her dissolute activities. Some people even insinuated he was the first to provoke them. When by chance she went to bed early, Marie Antoinette refused to give herself to him. Proof of this came during a trip to Fontainebleau. Louis XVI met with the closed door of her apartment and went quietly back to his own bedroom in front of a crowd of surprised and embarrassed courtiers. It was surely not the first time he encountered this kind of setback, but at Versailles the secret passage kept such disappointments away from the public eye.

Marie Antoinette made no secret of her revulsion at satisfying the desires of a husband who was still extremely clumsy. She sometimes still wished he would take a temporary mistress. To Mercy's great displeasure, she told her closest friends about this wish. The dangers for her if the King were swept into dalliances scarcely troubled her. She would accept anything to avoid the onslaughts of such an inept lover who, furthermore, was not very appetizing.

However, no other woman appealed to the King but his wife. He had sworn to himself that he would attain his objective and live up to his duty as sovereign by making her a mother. Besides, he was now convinced he had "done what was required and hoped that the following year would not go by without his having given a nephew or niece" to the Emperor. "We owe this happiness to you," he said to him, "for since your trip, it has become steadily better and better until it has reached a perfect conclusion."[2] Several weeks later, around mid-April 1778, Marie Antoinette became pregnant.

When the first hints of pregnancy became apparent, the Queen stayed confined in her apartment. She allowed herself only a few short walks on the grounds of the château and carefully avoided riding in carriages. During the day, she divided her time between music and conversation, chattering tirelessly with Madame de Polignac, in whose company she still delighted. She went to bed early and led a carefully regulated life. She was immensely relieved that the King interrupted all carnal intercourse with her, and as soon as the hope of a happy event was confirmed, she gave free rein to her joy. "I think this is all only a dream, but the dream continues," she confided to her mother.[3] This long-desired pregnancy consolidated her position as a sovereign and gave her considerable importance, for she now carried the hopes of the dynasty. Maria Theresa was right in her assumption: she saw her daughter as "more solidly established for the future." However, on this occasion, there were ulterior motives behind the compliments and demonstrations of affection the elderly Empress lavished on her. Maria Theresa and Joseph needed Marie Antoinette.

The matter engaging them was complex. Wishing to expand his states, Joseph II had decided to take possession of Lower Bavaria, an independent German principality where the sovereign's recent death left no direct heir. In the name of accords that had been signed while that prince was still alive, the Emperor invaded his territory in January 1778. Since his initiative endangered the European balance of power, it met with hostility from Frederick II, King of Prussia. He threatened Joseph II with an armed conflict if he refused to withdraw his troops from Bavaria. For the Emperor and Empress this was the opportunity to test their alliance with France. But neither Louis XVI nor his Minister of Foreign Affairs, Comte de Vergennes, had any intention of supporting what they called a "policy of armed robbery." They informed their ally not to count on France. Furious at seeing himself rebuffed by a brother-in-law for whom he had contempt, Joseph appealed to Marie

Antoinette to intercede. As he saw it, the alliance was an instrument for the advancement of imperial ambitions which the Queen had to serve.

Marie Antoinette hesitated as to what attitude to adopt. Fearing that her brother "would cause trouble" (as she put it to Madame de Polignac), she could not bring herself to act in spite of Mercy's urgings. What worked was the Empress using the old refrain of motherly love. "A change in our alliance would kill me,"[4] she wrote her, with more pathos than ever before. The Queen blanched on reading this letter. Deeply distressed by her mother's fears, she listened to Mercy's explanations very docilely. With incredible bad faith, the ambassador succeeded in persuading the unsuspecting young woman of the legitimacy of Austria's ambitions, for she was still viscerally attached to her family and utterly ignorant of the European stakes involved.

Marie Antoinette was astonished to find that her husband was adamant. This man, usually so weak with her, was unexpectedly unyielding in resisting her will. "Your relatives' ambition will upset everything. I am very sorry for you,"[5] he said to her simply, as a way of denouncing Joseph II's politics. The Queen no longer knew which way to turn. The views expressed by her husband and his ministers were the exact opposite of those of the Empress and her ambassador. Harassed by her mother and Mercy, she pressed her family's case repeatedly with Maurepas and Vergennes. She raised her voice each time in the hope of making herself heard, but the answers she received were respectful if evasive. Mercy urged her to spend every night with her husband. In March, she followed his advice and we know the result.

Maria Theresa and Joseph saw the Queen's pregnancy as an unhoped-for opportunity. The Princess would finally be able "to put to good use the influence she had over the King." However, the Habsburgs' hopes were quickly dashed. Though Louis XVI had finally succeeded in being a true husband with his wife, he had no intention of behaving as Austria's accommodating ally out of sheer love for her. He refused once again to give in to her demands. Marie Antoinette was very distressed. Her brother had no hesitation in trying to make her feel guilty for her "inaction," while her mother showed her more tenderness than ever before. "I am so worried about my mother," she sighed.[6] "It is the ministers' dreadful weakness and the King's extreme lack of self-confidence that are the cause of the problem," she claimed.[7] Her letters to the Empress reflected the ambassador's lessons admirably. Skillfully manipulated by this mentor who was under the Habsburgs' orders, the Queen of France sided with Austria. The warmth with which she spoke of the alliance, her long conversations with Mercy, her acrimonious comments about the King of Prussia, her appeals to Vergennes and Maurepas, her ties with the *choiseulistes*, who still railed against the ministry—all this contributed in discrediting her with the court and the public. People erroneously attributed to her a power and influence that she was very far from possessing. Already, in February, at the Opera, a large number of spectators managed to silence the ones who applauded her. The ambassador from Sardinia informed his sovereign of the Queen's budding unpopularity, accused now of "not liking the French." She was nicknamed *"l'Autrichienne"* by a growing number of people.

Yet Marie Antoinette really only wished to think about the child she was carrying. She scrutinized herself, saw her waist fill out and was surprised, in the beginning of June, at having added "four and a half inches." She marveled at not feeling the slightest discomfort. Her daily life remained just as quiet, and she seemed not to suffer in the least. Like all women in her situation, she talked about the first months in the lives of infants and inquired about the best ways of bringing them up—something not a single queen of France had ever done. Previous queens had been content to produce heirs to the throne, and had never shown much concern about the care they would receive. Helped by an impressive number of subgovernesses and servants, the Governess of the Children of France took complete charge of the royal progeny—boys to the age of six, when they would be entrusted to a tutor chosen by the King, and girls to the age of fifteen or sixteen. The queens paid very little attention to their children before they reached the age of reason; they saw them only when their obligations permitted. Marie Antoinette had other intentions. She vowed to herself to take the greatest care of her child. "The way they are brought up today," she said to her mother, "they are far less uncomfortable; they are not swaddled anymore, they are always in a wicker crib or held in the arms, and as soon as they can be outdoors, they are accustomed to it gradually and end up being outdoors all the time. I think this is the healthiest and best way to raise them. Mine will be housed downstairs, with a little railing separating him from the rest of the terrace, which may teach him faster to walk on parquet floors."[8] The Queen then wondered if she herself would breast-feed her firstborn rather than give the baby to a wet nurse, as was the custom.

These gentle preoccupations delighted the King. Louis XVI was in high spirits. He had lost that air of fearful submission he had so often shown in his wife's presence. On the other hand, Mercy was impatient. He thought it his

duty to rouse the Queen from her bourgeois daydreams, and lamented seeing her fall into what he called inaction. Perpetually goaded by the ambassador, who wanted her to believe that she would lose all her influence if she
stopped intervening with the King and the ministers, Marie Antoinette
resolved to speak out once again against Frederick II. This time, war between
Prussia and Austria seemed imminent. Furious, the Emperor openly called
Maurepas and Vergennes "imbeciles" for refusing to take Austria's side.[9]

When Frederick II invaded the Austrian states, on July 7, Marie
Antoinette burst into tears. She "wished she could mingle her tears with those
of her mother."[10] She was misled by her entourage into thinking that her husband's tenderness should make him submit to her personal will not just in private matters but also in state affairs. She had no excuse other than her
ignorance of the realities of international politics, which she always reduced
to family intrigues. How could she possibly question the deliberately simplify-
ing explanations of a Mercy, the man whom her mother had designated as a
most devoted adviser? For years so much effort had gone into persuading her
of her superiority over her husband and demeaning Louis XVI's ministers that
she really believed she had the right to impose her family's views—which she
saw as the only correct views. She had feelings of tenderness, admiration and
submission for her mother, her brother and even Austria, that, try as she
might, she just did not have for her husband or the kingdom of France.

As she waited for news from the Empress, the Queen wanted to give up
all her amusements for as long as the situation in Austria looked critical.
Indeed, the King of Prussia had succeeded in rallying a good number of
allies to Germany and his army was twice as powerful as the Emperor's.
Mercy had to insist that she continue her usual way of life. A letter from her
mother, dated August 6, deepened her anguish. Maria Theresa begged her
daughter to "support Mercy to save your House and your brothers."[11] Every
missive from Vienna to Marie Antoinette overflowed with the same worried
tenderness and brought pressing calls for help.

Shamelessly mixing family contingencies with interests of state, the
Empress dramatized the situation, stressing the dangers and sufferings her
sons were exposed to by war, and begging her daughter to intercede again
with the King. But did not France's interest and glory, which the Empress so
liked to invoke with her daughter, require maintaining the European balance of power, even at the risk of displeasing an ally with whom France had
never had a particularly happy collaboration? Stepping in to help Austria
defend her unbridled ambitions would have been a very grave error on the

part of Louis XVI. And it is surprising that this perceptive mother, this pessimistic and lucid sovereign who gave her daughter judicious advice concerning her position as queen, could have led her to commit such errors.

In the end, it was the Russian Empress Catherine II's threat to enter the war on the side of Prussia that convinced the Austrian sovereigns to negotiate a peace that was not entirely unfavorable to them. Indeed, Austria acquired part of the territories it had laid claim to. Marie Antoinette was relieved. The torments she had been put through in the last few months had brought her closer to her Austrian family and made her feel a rancor edged with contempt for her husband's ministers. "I was born to owe everything to my dear *maman*. I owe her again the tranquillity reborn in my soul, thanks to her kindness, gentleness and I dare say patience with regard to this country," she unabashedly wrote her mother when the peace was concluded.[12]

The Bavarian episode did her a grave disservice. Before then she had generally been thought of as a charming scatterbrain; now public opinion suddenly shifted and she was seen as an Austrian archduchess rather than a queen of France. She had been criticized for her frivolity and her expenses. Now, there was the suspicion of treason.

Many slanderous rumors circulated concerning the legitimacy of the child she was expecting. Evil gossips claimed that the Duc de Coigny was the real father. But Louis XVI and Marie Antoinette were completely indifferent to these offensive tales. The King unexpectedly proved as much during a cabinet meeting. A dispatch from Sweden had just been read tending to substantiate the rumor that King Gustavus III, a notorious homosexual, had pushed his favorite equerry into his wife's bed in order to ensure a royal descendant. Somewhat embarrassed, the ministers could not refrain from looking at the King. They could see, from the relaxed way he reacted to the anecdote, that it had no bearing on his own situation.

The King of France a cuckold? Certainly not. The endless correspondence exchanged between Versailles and Vienna and the foreign ambassadors' secret reports prove the exact opposite. Moreover, the Comte de Provence and the Comte d'Artois would have been all too thrilled to let such a scandal erupt. It is not impossible that the hypocritical Comte de Provence, heir apparent to the throne at the time, paid a few lampoonists a handsome sum to spread the calumny.

Grave as it was, the Bavarian episode had not altered the affectionate relationship that now existed between the spouses. The King was pleased not to have yielded to his wife, a tendency for which he was too often reproached.

He had stood up to her without making any hurtful comments and this was something for which she was grateful. The monarch's newly acquired self-confidence, since the beginning of this so intensely desired pregnancy, struck all those who knew him. He showed Marie Antoinette great tenderness and tried to entertain her in every possible way, allowing a great many fetes to be organized for her pleasure.

The Queen was in excellent health. Since July 31, she often felt her child moving, "which caused her great joy," each movement "adding to her happiness."[13] Oddly enough, she did not seem to fear the dreadful trial of childbirth, so often fatal even to young women enjoying the best of care. No doubt her mother's example was reassuring to her. Marie Antoinette had chosen Vermond, the Abbé's brother, as her obstetrician. His talents were recognized, though he was considered greedy and vain, and had no qualms about forsaking a bourgeois lady for a duchess. He had been caring for the Queen since the beginning of her pregnancy.

The time of the delivery was approaching. For the queens of France, childbirth included a barbaric ceremonial and was a hideous ordeal. Helped by an accoucheur, physicians and midwives, they gave birth to their children in public, for it was of paramount importance that there be not the slightest shadow of a doubt concerning the legitimacy of their child: the newborn had to be seen still attached to his mother by the umbilical cord. In spite of her loathing for etiquette, Marie Antoinette did not protest against this custom even though it was more constraining than any other.

During the second week of December, more than two hundred titled people, who usually lived in Paris, came to stay at Versailles for the Queen's confinement. The city and the château were swarming with visitors. On December 18, Marie Antoinette went to bed at around eleven o'clock; around twelve-thirty, she started to feel the first pains. At about one-thirty, she gave orders to notify the King. Madame de Lamballe, Superintendent of her Household, immediately informed the royal family, the princes and princesses who were at Versailles, and sent letters to those who were in Paris or in their nearby castles. She was still in her large bed when Louis XVI came to her bedside. She got up and walked around her bedroom until eight o'clock. Her pains having started again at that point, she lay down on the little labor bed that had been especially erected near the fireplace. News of the delivery had spread throughout Versailles. The Queen's Antechamber, the King's Council Room and the Hall of Mirrors were overflowing with people. At around eleven, when the double doors of the bedroom were opened, a horde of curious spectators rushed in all the way to the foot of the bed. Two little chimney sweeps climbed up on the furniture to get a better view of the spectacle. Stoical, Marie Antoinette made an effort not to cry out. "The Queen is in labor," Vermond soon announced.

For a brief moment, since the child did not scream, it was thought to be stillborn. But soon cries were heard. And when applause broke out—a habit the Queen had established almost everywhere—it was thought that the child was a boy. Alas, the child was merely a girl, who was carried off into another room to be washed. While the King accompanied the newborn, the Queen lost consciousness. She lay inert, her mouth twisted, and the natural contractions following childbirth stopped. She had to be bled very urgently. Vermond yelled for hot water to be brought to him, but since it was impossible to get a basin through such a dense crowd, a surgeon made a dry incision. Marie Antoinette regained consciousness and the labor continued normally. She wept a long time when she was told the child's sex.

Louis XVI, who had attended mass after his daughter's birth, learned only later of the threat to his wife's life. As soon as he saw her, he showed her great tenderness and the immense joy he felt in having a child. The little princess was brought in to her mother, who was pleased to see her. "A son would have belonged more particularly to the state. You will be mine; you will receive all my care; you will share my happiness and soothe my sorrows," were the words the Queen is said to have pronounced, if Madame Campan is to be believed.[14] Such solemn language does not resemble the language of Marie Antoinette as we know it, but it is possible Madame Campan transposed into slightly pompous speech the spontaneous words which the young mother uttered with greater simplicity. The Queen seemed happy. The child was named Marie Thérèse and given the title "Madame Royale" or "Madame, daughter of the King," so that she would not be confused with the Comtesse de Provence, who by custom was also called Madame, just as the Comte de Provence was called "Monsieur, brother of the King."

Exhausted by her difficult childbirth, Marie Antoinette rested for several days. At the time it was considered dangerous for new mothers to get up before three weeks. Aside from her physicians and her personal servants, only Madame de Lamballe and Madame de Polignac were allowed into the Queen's bedroom, and they took turns at her bedside. The King, overjoyed, spent long hours by his wife's side and showered her with every possible consideration. He felt no shame in taking a seat near the little Marie Thérèse, to whom "he showed the most touching tenderness," assured Mercy.[15] As required by tradition, the child was placed in the hands of the capricious Princesse de Guéméné, who had the position of Governess of the Children of France. Of a common accord, the King and Queen wanted their daughter to have a simpler education than the one usually received by the princesses of France. They had reduced the number of servants assigned to the child and did not want her subjected to antiquated protocol. Hence, they refused to let her be harangued by representatives from the different parts of the body politic, or for the ambassadors and court dignitaries to be presented to her. Marie Antoinette took no account of her mother's objections. Indeed, the Empress believed it was never too soon to accustom princes to life in the public eye.

The end of the year went by very quietly at Versailles. On January 3, 1779, the Queen, sitting on a sofa with her legs stretched out, received all the ladies of the court as they filed by to congratulate her. After this ceremony, Marie Antoinette hosted a performance of a comedy for them, the King having fitted out a theater in the gaming salon.

One month later, on February 8, Louis XVI and Marie Antoinette made a solemn trip to the cathedral of Notre-Dame in Paris and attended the *Te Deum* mass celebrated in honor of the sovereigns on the occasion of Madame Royale's birth. However, in spite of the munificence of the festivities organized in the capital, in spite of money by the fistful distributed generously among the crowd and fountains of wine flowing at the intersections, the Queen was not warmly received. The crowds were driven much more by curiosity than by feelings of affection. Absorbed in their joy, the young sovereigns did not seem to realize that public opinion was beginning to turn against them.

15

FERSEN

*T*he Queen was happy. Maternity was not the sole reason for this happiness. Since the previous summer, Marie Antoinette was in love. In August, a tall Swedish gentleman, with regular features, who looked exactly like the hero of a novel, asked to be introduced to her. This was a common occurrence at Versailles. But the Queen instantly recognized Count Axel Fersen, with whom she had had a flirtatious conversation during an Opera ball a few weeks before Louis XV's death. "Ah! He is an old acquaintance!"[1] she cried out. And while Fersen bowed respectfully before her, the equerry who was holding her hand felt her tremble against her will.

Just twenty-three and disappointed by his idle life at the court of Gustavus III, Fersen had decided to place his sword in the service of a European monarch who would employ him. His father in his day had served Louis XV. His family having maintained very good relations with France, he had decided to try his luck with Louis XVI. At the time, Swedes were very much in fashion and always well treated by the Queen. Though flattered by the Queen's greeting, Fersen rarely went to pay court to her. She complained about this to the Swedish ambassador, Count Creutz, and the young man soon visited Versailles assiduously. Having heard of the extraordinary uniform Gustavus III had imposed on his officers, Marie Antoinette asked Fersen to come see her wearing his uniform. He created a sensation with his open white tunic and blue doublet, tight-fitting chamois trousers, Hungarian-style booties and black shako topped with a blue-and-yellow aigrette. Nothing could have been more flattering to his self-esteem than to appear dressed this way before the Queen of France. Very fond of women, he found the young Queen, with her advancing pregnancy, charming. "She is the most delightful princess I know," he said to his father.[2] Thus did Fersen soon become the most popular man. "All Versailles is talking only about a Count Fersen, who came to court wearing the Swedish national dress, which the Queen, I was told, examined with great care,"[3] wrote a Swedish traveler who did not know Fersen but happened to be in France at the same time.

Just as the young man arrived at Versailles, Lauzun was leaving to con-quer Senegal, which was then a British possession. His favor had worn off, Marie Antoinette having finally surrendered to the Polignacs' treacherous attacks against him. The Queen's heart was free. This foreigner's irruption into her life, a life made monotonous by an excess of frivolity, would turn everything topsy-turvy. As soon as she had completely recovered, she made Fersen come to Versailles as often as possible and admitted him into her inner circle. In the evening, she invited him to her small suppers in her pri-vate apartment. Very reserved, he always showed a perfect simplicity and replied to her questions without the slightest affectation. She wanted to know everything about him and showed such interest in him that before long she was regularly asking after his father, Senator Fersen. By the beginning of 1779, he was thought of as the Queen's favorite, though she did not treat him the same way as a Lauzun or a Coigny. Contrary to these seductive courtiers, experienced in intrigues of every kind, eager to please and to impress their entourage with amusing witticisms, Fersen possessed the art of being himself. He had an innate presence and had no need to play a role or even speak. Women were captivated by his virile beauty and the mysterious quality he radiated. They could not resist him, yet thus far none had captured his heart. Like most aristocrats of his rank and age, he thought of marrying. But he had to find a good match—in other words, a young woman of his rank and, in addition, very wealthy. Feelings were not a factor in this projected union and marriage would not have prevented him from having mistresses.

Unable to master her agitation in the young Swede's presence, the Queen was encouraged by her coterie and especially by Madame de Poli-gnac and Besenval to give in to this gentle attraction. According to the Comte de Saint-Priest, Louis XVI's future minister, Fersen "captured the Queen's heart . . . No doubt Vaudreuil and Besenval worked out that an isolated foreigner, who did not have a very enterprising character, suited them far better than a Frenchman surrounded with relatives who would win all the favors for these relatives and possibly end up as the head of a clique that would eclipse them all."[4]

Since the birth of her daughter, the Queen had shown no desire to resume conjugal life. Her delivery having left a very painful memory, she told her husband that she had no intention of becoming pregnant again for several months. Fortunately Louis XVI was not at all demanding. Indeed, he seemed not to notice Marie Antoinette's fondness for the handsome Swede. That the King had no predisposition for gallantry fully reassured the young woman. Let Maria Theresa grumble. The Empress ironically asked if it would be necessary to wait another eight years for the birth of a Dauphin. Nor did she pay any attention to the sermons of Mercy and Vermond, who wanted to drive her into the King's bed.

Fersen did not let the exceptional favor he enjoyed go to his head. He very much wanted to pursue his military ambitions. It seemed like an opportune moment. Louis XVI had just entered the War of American Independence and many young French noblemen dreamed of going to fight in America by the side of the insurgents who were rebelling against England. Fersen was ready to join them. On February 6, 1778, the King of France had recognized the United States of America and concluded a military alliance as well as commercial accords with the young republic. On the following March 13, France and England broke off diplomatic relations. As the English ambassador returned to London, Louis XVI received Benjamin Franklin, Silas Deane and Arthur Lee at Versailles.

The reception of the Americans in the Hall of Mirrors had caused a true revolution at Versailles. "Substituting Franklin, rebel and leader of the rebellion, for the English ambassador on the very day of his departure, recognizing the rebels who were not yet completely free, being the first to recognize them, what an example!" The Duc de Croÿ could not "get over his astonishment." Yet this descendent from a long line of tradition-bound aristocrats greeted Franklin with the words: "Only the person who discovered electricity could electrify two worlds."[5] The philosopher, with his shiny bald head ringed with thinning long hair and his rustic suit, felt perfectly at ease under the gilded paneling of Louis XVI's palace, surrounded by courtiers wearing richly embroidered clothes trimmed with gems. Versailles was more astonished by him than he by Versailles. Louis XVI had greeted the Americans with warm words of welcome in front of a breathless, surprised and ultimately delighted court. The "Roman" virtue of the old sage, citizen of the new world, and the austere virtue of the young King, heir to one of Europe's most venerable monarchies, formed a most touching and unusual sight for this jaded, gossip-prone crowd.

Hostilities between France and England began the following June 17. In early 1779, Fersen wanted to join the French expeditionary corps which was to leave for America. Thanks to the King of Sweden's intervention, he was appointed aide-de-camp of Comte de Vaux, who was to be commander-in-chief. Before embarking, Fersen came to bid the Queen farewell. Upset by this departure, for which she seemed unprepared, Marie Antoinette could not hide her emotion. With a trembling voice, she began singing an aria from *Dido*, accompanying herself on the harpsichord: "*Ah, what a happy thought led me to admit you to my court.*" Each word was clearly addressed to Fersen and she did not take her eyes off him for a second. Perfectly aware of the folly she was publicly committing, he listened to her with downcast eyes. "Anyone watching them at that moment could have no more doubts regarding the nature of their feelings," Sir Richard Barrington wrote in his memoirs.

The Queen's disquiet had escaped no one. "I must tell Your Majesty that the young Count Fersen was so well received by the Queen that several people were offended by it," wrote the Swedish ambassador to Gustavus III. "I admit that I cannot refrain from thinking that she had a fondness for him: I saw signs of this that were too clear to leave any doubt. The young Count Fersen's behavior on this occasion was admirable in its modesty and restraint and especially in his decision to go to America. By leaving, he removed all dangers, but of course wisdom and resolve beyond his years were required to overcome this seduction. The Queen could not take her eyes off him these last few days; as she watched him they filled with tears. I beg Your Majesty to keep this a secret for her sake and Senator Fersen's."[6] When they heard of the Count's departure, all the favorites were delighted. The Duchess of Fitz-James said to him: "What! Monsieur, you are deserting your conquest?" "If I had made one, I would not desert her," he replied. "I am going away free, and unfortunately without leaving behind any regrets."

The day after Fersen's departure, the Queen fell ill. She had the measles. Her chest was heavy, her throat on fire, her skin red, and she surrendered to the disease. But with the fever abating after several days, she felt an imperious need for amusement. Since Madame de Polignac was ill with the same disease, she could not give herself over to their sweet confidential conversations.

So she decided that four nurses would take turns at her bedside from eleven in the morning until eleven at night. To the court's indignation and surprise, she appointed the Ducs de Coigny and de Guines, Count Eszterhazy and the inevitable Baron de Besenval. Under the pretext of being contagious, she kept her door closed for the King. The genial quartet thus recounted to her all the latest stories from the town and the court. These gentlemen denigrated some people and showered praise on others. Together, they laughed merrily, and time passed more quickly in their company than in any other. Reluctantly, Marie Antoinette did have to accept visits from the Comtesse de Provence and several courtiers who bored her to death. While hinting at their own petty desires, her four gallant knights dared insinuate that the King had failed in his duties by not disobeying her prohibitions about not coming to see her. She was weak-minded enough to believe them and began nurturing resentments toward her husband.

Once again Marie Antoinette deeply shocked the court. People wondered maliciously which ladies the King would choose to nurse him if he were to become sick. Mercy and Vermond had to make the rash girl see reason. They urged her to write to her husband and she did so without further delay. She wrote to him that "she had suffered much, but that what annoyed her the most was to be deprived of the pleasure of seeing him for a few more days."[7] Did Louis XVI believe in these fond feelings? No one can say. However, several days later, at Mercy's instigation, she came out on a balcony to speak to her husband, who placed himself underneath the balcony in order to talk to her. This tender duet (was it all that tender?) never occurred again.

When she recovered from her illness, the Queen decided to convalesce at Trianon, and she settled there on April 12 along with her inevitable nurses. She led a relatively quiet life: "small, simple fetes in a charming place, in a beautiful season, excursions in a barouche or on the water, no intrigues, no high-stakes gambling; only the grand splendor reigning there could make us suspect we were at court,"[8] Eszterhazy recalls in his memoirs. During that period, the King did not ask after her. There were plots to find him a mistress. Thanks to Mercy and Vermond's entreaties, the carefree young woman finally agreed to return to Versailles and resume her life with Louis XVI, which had been interrupted for a year. After coaxing him, she extracted amorous confessions from him, which she confided triumphantly to the ambassador. "He told her that he loved her with all his heart and that he could swear to her that he had never had sensations or feelings for any other woman besides her."[9]

The Queen resumed her conjugal duty. "I am too aware of the necessity of having children to neglect anything on that score," she told her mother. "If I was wrong in the past, it was due to childishness and irresponsibility, but now I am much more levelheaded." However, the royal couple's good intentions were not crowned with success. The physicians were worried by this sterility and prescribed a treatment of iron filings for the Queen. When this appeared fruitless, they considered the possibility of a thermal cure. The Queen, in those days, spent a great deal of time taking care of her daughter, whose progress she followed attentively. "The poor child is starting to walk quite well in her dress à paniers. She started saying 'papa' a few days ago; her teeth are not out yet, but you can feel all of them. I am very pleased that she has started naming her father, this is one more tie that binds him to her."[10] Marie Antoinette wrote these lines when Madame Royale was just eight months old.

The Queen had developed a sudden interest in the American war— though Franklin's visit the year before with the representatives of the young republic of the United States had left her completely indifferent. But ever since Fersen had joined the French officers and enlisted in the expeditionary corps that was to land in England, she was eager for any news. She dreamed of a peace that would bring the handsome Swede back to Versailles. And, as it happened, Maria Theresa offered to mediate between France and England. Never had Marie Antoinette supported her mother's proposals with greater enthusiasm. She spoke with emotion of that peace which would bring her "the greatest happiness. My heart wants it more than anything in the world,"[11] she said to the Empress. With unexpected solicitude, she referred to the fate of those who were going to fight. "They are on the English Channel! And I cannot think without shuddering that at any moment their entire fate will be decided. I also fear the approach of September, when the sea is no longer passable; in sum I am laying down all my worries on my dear mother's bosom. God grant that they be for naught! But her kindness encourages me to speak my thoughts."[12] Maria Theresa must have thought that her daughter had suddenly developed a new interest in international relations. She undoubtedly congratulated herself for it. Naturally Mercy had carefully refrained from telling her about the Queen's fondness for Count Fersen.

The King and his Minister of Foreign Affairs truly had the intention of doing battle with England by coming to the aid of the United States. They turned down Maria Theresa's mediation, but gave up the idea of landing on the British Isles. The Queen's relief was compounded by the fact that she had learned with alarm that a dysentery epidemic was decimating the troops. Disappointed at not seeing battle, Fersen returned to the court. The Queen welcomed him effusively. And they were seen together throughout the winter in Versailles and Paris. She often took him to the Opera balls and sat in a loge talking with him at length. She even saw to it that he was invited to the suppers in the inner rooms of the King's private apartment. To silence the nasty gossips, she pretended to favor another Swede, Count von Stedingk. Naturally, Fersen attended all of Madame de Lamballe's and Madame de Polignac's parties. The Queen never organized a single fete without him and he proved to be particularly gifted—at the game of blindman's buff.

A serious romance developed between Marie Antoinette and Fersen during that winter of 1779–80. However, the young man was too aware of the risks of such a liaison to truly commit himself. Intoxicated with freedom, he very much wanted to face the baptism of battle and be acquainted with military life. The steps he took with Maurepas and Vergennes finally bore fruit, and thus he departed for the second time. The Queen concealed her distress as best she could. She found a roundabout way of expressing her anguish to her mother: "It is certain that we cannot risk this big convoy without being certain of the sea," she said to her. "It would be dreadful to endure further misfortune from that; I admit that I cannot think about it in cold blood."[13] Marie Antoinette probably hoped that the war would be brief and that her hero would return very soon. No one knows what they said to each other in parting. Though their letters have been destroyed, we know they wrote to each other and that the Queen saw to the promotion of the man she loved.

16

QUEEN OF TRIANON

*T*he Queen, who was not yet twenty-five, was at the peak of her beauty. Madame Vigée-Lebrun, who became her appointed painter, immortalized her, as she was then, in a famous portrait known as *Marie Antoinette Holding a Rose*. In a rural setting that suggests the foliage of Trianon, a young woman wearing a blue silk dress with panniers and trimmed with lace is holding, in her long hands, a rose in full bloom — symbol of the ephemeral. She is offering this flower just as she seems to be offering her voluptuous bosom, whose delicate contours can be seen through a light chiffon flounce. A long, supple neck adorned with two rows of pearls gives her elegant silhouette majestic grace. Her fleshy mouth, in her long, oval face, is mischievous, but her blue gaze, which could express benevolence or aversion with remarkable intensity, betrays a touch of melancholy. The Queen loved this image of herself. Madame Vigée-Lebrun had represented her as a desirable woman without making any allusion to royal grandeur. Though the painter had certainly flattered the model, contemporaries were unanimous in finding the portrait her perfect likeness.

The sovereign's beauty, often extolled, was primarily due to her lovely fair complexion, her height and her imposing look, which her admirers called dignity and her detractors, haughtiness or disdain. Her every gesture exuded a gentle femininity. "She had two ways of walking — one firm, slightly hurried and always noble, the other more indolent and swaying, almost caressing, though it did not inspire any lapse in respect. No one ever curtsied with as much grace, greeting ten people and bending just once, giving each his due with her head and gaze," asserted the Comte de Tilly, one of her pages.[1]

Marie Antoinette continued to lead her life as she saw fit, devoting a minimal amount of time to her state obligations. Claiming that a queen had the right to a private life, Marie Antoinette intended to behave as freely as her privileged subjects, whose society delighted her. Etiquette, for her, was the symbol of a barbarian age; she could not accept that she was not her own person, but belonged entirely to the kingdom of France; that she ranked above common mortals in a society that was hierarchical in the extreme, her every gesture having the impact of a public act.

The enemy of all constraint, she constantly asserted her independence. Not only had she succeeded in paring down the ceremonial but also in creating a realm, within Versailles itself, where she saw herself as the sole mistress. Though it was extremely difficult to hide from indiscreet gazes in the château, she had almost succeeded. Since the state rooms were the ones that really counted in this palace, conceived as the temple of the monarchy, the Queen kept her official apartment, but went about rejuvenating it while respecting its timeless structure. In order to imagine her room as she envisioned it—and as it is now restored—we need only look at the painting of the miniaturist Gautier-Dagoty which shows Marie Antoinette posing for the painter in her morning negligee, plucking the strings of a harp, sitting between her dress merchant and several close friends who have been summoned to give their opinion. For this state room, which she did not like, the Queen first chose a blue-and-white brocade of flowers and butterflies, designed by the Lyon silk manufacturer Pernon. Disappointed by this first renovation, she ordered the decoration, which is called "*meuble*," transported to her room in Fontainebleau and replaced by a white *gros de Tours*[2] brocaded and embroidered with flower bouquets, ribbons and peacock feathers, made by Desfarges, an equally well reputed silk manufacturer. In order to tone down the formality of the Antechamber of the Great Dining Hall, where she held her balls and concerts, she removed the tapestries devoted to the glory of Louis XIV and put up new ones of more pleasing subjects, like the *Gallery of Saint-Cloud* after Mignard. In 1786, she very much wanted to renovate the famous Peace Room, a continuation of the Hall of Mirrors, which served as her gaming room and on occasion as a theater thanks to some movable adjustments. Wanting "by all possible means to confer cleanliness and gaiety" on this sumptuous room, she asked the Buildings Administration to suggest some modernization projects. It took the Comte d'An-giviller's[3] utmost resolve and all his powers of persuasion to convince the Queen to keep Le Brun's ceilings, Le Moyne's large oval, the Louis XIV fire-place and the marble with bronze ornaments. The Queen had to limit her-self to replacing the furniture and the hangings.

Louis XVI and Marie Antoinette seriously considered rebuilding Ver-sailles at the time. Starting in 1780, at the King's request, several architects drew up grandiose plans[4] which would have drastically changed the architec-ture of the castle and made the Queen's apartments as spacious as those of the King. Because of financial considerations, these projects were never imple-mented. The royal couple had to limit themselves to upkeep and redecora-tion work.

Marie Antoinette could more freely indulge her desire for change in her private apartment. She began by overhauling Queen Maria Leszczynska's inner rooms circling a sad, sunless courtyard. To create an impression of brightness, she used light wood paneling and mirror effects, particularly in her boudoir, called the "Cabinet de la Méridienne" or Sofa Room, a small drawing room with diagonal cutoff corners and a sofa placed in the center of a mirrored recess. The mirrors are framed with sprays of roses whose bronze foliage is echoed in the paneling, along with the Habsburg eagle and sym-bols of love. The "Méridienne" gives on to the Library, collected by Mon-sieur Campan, Secretary of the Queen's Cabinet. It could be said that Marie Antoinette showed more interest in the container than the thing contained; the room is paneled with glass cabinets displaying an impressive alignment of Morocco-bound books with her coat of arms: these include a great many novels, light poems and all the newest literary publications that had been presented to the young sovereign. The Library leads into the main room of this private apartment, "the Queen's large Inner Room," with its white-and-gold paneling and its arched mirrored recess draped with silk. A harpsichord and a harp stand amidst the armchairs and the many tables overloaded with knickknacks. It was in this drawing room—where no one was admitted with-out special permission—that Marie Antoinette held her private audiences, received the King and her dearest friends, sang in her unsteady voice as she accompanied herself on her favorite instruments, posed for Madame Vigée-Lebrun or simply rested. This suite, which was far smaller than the King's private apartment, also included a few more tiny drawing rooms, furnished with refinement, and some inner rooms on the mezzanine floor. Marie Antoinette always felt cramped in these quarters. This is why, after Madame

Sophie's death in 1782, she would take possession of her ground-floor apartment, which looked out on the marble courtyard, and connect the two apartments with an inner stairway. From then on, the Queen would prefer sleeping in the green-damask-covered bed of her spacious and soberly decorated new bedroom. After this expansion, it was common to refer to "the Queen's new apartment" at Versailles.

In Fontainebleau, which she liked more than the other royal residences, Marie Antoinette redecorated her apartment entirely. Her boudoir is considered a masterpiece of the Louis XVI period, with its piers decorated with Pompeian arabesques on a golden green background and framed with tawny gold, and its four doors with cutoff corners crowned with stucco clusters. Among other innovations, she redecorated a second boudoir called "the Turkish boudoir," which was coveted by all the actresses. "It was furnished in the Oriental style and lit by lamps placed in the wardrobe separated by a large mirror lined with taffeta in a different chosen color," wrote Félix d'Hézecques, one of the King's pages.[5] In 1785, as an economical measure, the court gave up its yearly autumn sojourn in Fontainebleau and Marie Antoinette never saw the completion of the redecorating work that was underway there. She would have time only to draw up plans for the Château de Saint-Cloud, which the King bought for her from the Duc d'Orléans in 1784.

Marie Antoinette never overlooked a single detail in decoration or furnishing. But she had no particular attraction to painting; she considered it a purely decorative art. At the beginning of her reign, she let several mediocre artists paint her portrait. The only merit she saw in portraits was resemblance. Madame Campan reports that when she went to the painting exhibitions at the Louvre, she would look at the small genre paintings very quickly and leave without even glancing at the large compositions. Madame Vigée-Lebrun's talent attracted her because it agreed with her own sensibility. She spurned the cold representations of Roman antiquity which inspired artists such as Vien, Suvée and David, and which contributed to making the 1785 Salon truly revolutionary. She paid some attention to Greuze, Lépicié and Aubry, but preferred Hubert Robert. Though the Queen ordered a large number of painted panels for the royal castles from excellent artists, she did not enrich the Crown's collections with important acquisitions. On the other hand, she showed a definite predilection for new furniture designs. She liked pure, geometric lines, whose rigor was softened by bronze decorations shaped to look like draping. She sometimes had her chest of drawers adorned with brightly colored Sèvres porcelain plaques. Loyal to her suppliers, she ordered most of her furniture from Riesener, the most famous cabinetmaker in Paris, trained by Oeben. He made an impressive number of chests for her, as well as secretaries, corner cupboards and tables in various shapes, often working in collaboration with the bronzesmith Gouthière. Among his pieces are the marvelous mechanical table delivered in December 1778 for the private apartment of the château, and now in the Metropolitan Museum in New York, and the unusually voluminous drop-front secretary designed for Trianon, but which can be admired today at the Wallace Collection in London. Several pieces of furniture with intricate mechanisms were also ordered from Mercklein, such as the bed with an adjustable back, at Madame Royale's birth. The Queen also occasionally bought some rare pieces from collectors or private individuals. From the sales after the Duc d'Aumont's death, she acquired sumptuously finished metal tables supporting green jasper plaques. She ordered her armchairs from Georges Jacob, whose sober workmanship she liked. But she sometimes asked him to give up his usual style and embark on rural fantasy, as can be seen in what is left of the furniture of the "latticework bedchamber," designed for Trianon. This set of chairs with polychromatic carvings of lily of the valley, jasmine, pinecones and other rustic motifs, covered with tapestry embroidered with wool flowers, suited the Queen's pastoral fantasies. The decorations designed for her always included nature at its sunniest. Since she wished she could live in the midst of flowers, she wanted them woven or embroidered on her hangings, her curtains and her bedspreads. She also had flowers made in porcelain, gauze and enamel and placed them in her inner rooms, which she liked to fill—indeed overfill—with knickknacks. She collected lacquerware, Chinese porcelain, shells mounted in gilt bronze settings, crystals, jasper, sard, petrified wood. Grancher and Daguerre were her main purveyors. From Robin, she ordered clocks with chimes to commemorate the bright hours of her life as a sovereign. Careful about the finishing touches in her intimate decor, she liked brocade curtains and hangings to be trimmed with braids, fringes, tassels, and canopies to be adorned with bouquets of plumes. Blue, green and lilac would always be her favorite colors.

But above all, it was at the Petit Trianon that Marie Antoinette really succeeded in creating the intimate decor she liked. Trianon remains the symbol of her taste and the favored scene of her legend. What interested her most— more than Gabriel's architectural masterpiece—was the garden. At the beginning of her reign, she had no thought of living in the pavilion as Louis

XV had done. She simply wanted to take walks in an environment that fit her conception of landscape. She felt there was nothing grimmer than the monotonous layout of paths and flower beds in Le Nôtre's gardens. Marie Antoinette dreamed of replacing Louis XV's famous botanical garden with a living nature that would not be imprisoned in greenhouses. By 1778, her wishes were fulfilled. Her English garden was almost completed. Nothing was missing—it had tortuous paths, ornamental ponds, waterfalls, statues. The Temple of Love, built on an island overgrown with rosebushes, connected to the grounds by two rustic bridges, and the Belvedere, an octagonal pavilion on a hill, guarded by four marble sphinx couples, completed her dream landscape. The only thing still to be built was a grotto in a rock shaded with pine trees, thujas and larches. This den, intended for tender private meetings, was entered by way of a low opening next to a small waterfall. Couples settling on the deep bed of moss would never be startled by intruders: through a hollow made in the rock, it was possible to see without being seen, and to take flight through a narrow stairway leading to the other side of the garden.

Marie Antoinette really felt at home only at Trianon, where the King came as a simple visitor. At Trianon, the Queen made all the household arrangements. In her little estate, where she forgot all about royal grandeur, she set the rules and decided everything. To the great outcry of the courtiers, rules were posted inside the gardens. They were "by order of the Queen," instead of "by order of the King." While the castle and grounds of Versailles were, as we know, open to the public, no one was allowed to enter the estate of Trianon without a special invitation from the Queen. Speculation arose as to the depraved acts that might be taking place in such a well-guarded place. And tongues wagged when it was learned that the Queen had put in "moving glass panels," which allowed her to shutter her windows by an ingenious system of mirrors rising from the floors! What encouraged the gossip was that ever since her famous case of measles, Marie Antoinette had got into the habit of staying at Trianon frequently over the summer months. The King never slept there, even though a bedchamber had been prepared for him. He was content to dine there every night with his wife. Only Madame Elisabeth and her dear Polignac stayed overnight there with her.

At Trianon, Marie Antoinette wanted to behave like a simple chatelaine. "Here I am myself," she liked to repeat. During that summer of 1780, she stopped wearing complicated court outfits, plumes and pompons, and launched the style of white lawn dresses drawn in at the waist with a large silk ribbon. She now wore her hair loose under a simple wide-brimmed straw hat. When she entered the drawing room, no one was to rise. Conversations continued, ladies did not interrupt their embroidery, tapestry work or music making. The Queen would take a seat among her guests, wherever she wished, would join conversations or take up some needlework. No one was to feel any constraint. "If you want to come at noon, I will give you lunch. I will be all alone; I therefore kindly request that you not come in formal attire, but in country dress," she wrote to the Princess von Hesse-Darmstadt, a childhood friend visiting France. However, her close friends happily made it their duty to keep her entertained. In the daytime, they took walks, and if the weather was good they lunched outdoors. They played all the parlor games and had a particular fondness for blindman's buff. In the evening, if they were not gambling for high stakes as at Versailles, they played music.

The Queen received artists both at Versailles and at Trianon, where she often held concerts. She continued to protect Gluck, whose reputation she had helped establish, but this did not prevent her from welcoming Piccini, his great rival, whose work she found very appealing. The first time he came to see her, she wanted to honor him by asking him to accompany her on the harpsichord. Thoughtlessly, she chose an aria from Gluck's *Alcestis*. Though vexed, the musician had to comply. The next day, Marie Antoinette laughed and blushed as she recalled the incident. She also extended her protection to Grétry, Salieri and Sacchini, but seems to have ignored Mozart, who had given her a few enchanted hours in her Viennese childhood.

The Dauphine, it will be remembered, had very much enjoyed playacting with her brothers- and sisters-in-law, behind the King's back. Ten years later, the *"théâtre de société"* was still all the rage: the Duchesse de Bourbon gave performances for her friends; Madame de Montesson, the Duc d'Orléans's morganatic wife, played the great classical roles marvelously well; and theater was performed at the houses of many other ladies of the court. Up until then, only the great official troupes had performed at Versailles. Since the use of Gabriel's Opera, which had been inaugurated for their marriage, proved to be too costly, the King and Queen had an auditorium built inside the château's Orangerie. Marie Antoinette soon had her husband agree to the building of a small theater in the Trianon gardens. It was inaugurated on June 1, 1780. With its gold ornamentation, effective trompe l'oeil, walls hung with blue moiré, *gros-bleu de Tours* silk curtain and ceiling painting of

Apollo sailing through the clouds with his entourage of Muses, Graces and Cupids, this tiny theater, designed by the architect Mique, was like a modest, intimate replica of the Versailles Opera.

Marie Antoinette could not resist the temptation of performing on a stage which had been built especially for her. She recruited her brothers-in-law and closest friends and formed her own company, soon called the *"troupe des seigneurs."* In June, after combing through the entire repertoire, they decided that on August 1 they would stage *Le Roi et le fermier* and *La Gageure imprévue* by Sedaine.

The first of these plays is a comedy with ariettas about a king who gets lost while hunting and is taken in by a farmer who satirizes the court for him. Comte d'Adhémar played the king and Marie Antoinette a shepherdess who is in love with the farmer Vaudreuil but has to put up with the assiduous attentions of a young libertine lord. In *La Gageure imprévue* she portrayed Gotte, the soubrette accomplice of an idle marquise who has admitted a charming gentleman into her room and hidden him in a cupboard when her husband returns unexpectedly. "We complain, we domestic servants," were her first words to the public, before starting to embroider sleeves for her suitor, the valet Lafleur, played by the Comte d'Artois. The Comtesse Diane de Polignac had the part of the fickle wife and young Princess Elisabeth played the minor parts. The little amateur troupe rehearsed for entire days under the supervision of professional actors and singers. Campan was the prompter, to the great displeasure of the Duc de Fronsac, who felt that he was entitled to this position, as Gentleman of the King's Bedchamber in charge of the court's Menus-Plaisirs, or entertainments. "You cannot be First Gentleman when we are actors," the Queen is said to have replied; "besides, you know my wishes concerning Trianon; I do not hold court there: I live like a private individual and Monsieur Campan will always be in charge of my instructions relating to the fetes that I want to hold there."

The *troupe des seigneurs* did not give itself a moment's respite. On August 10, it performed Sedaine's *On ne s'avise jamais de tout* and Berthe's *Les Fausses Infidélités*; on September 6, Favart's *L'Anglais à Bordeaux* and Poinsinet's *Le Sorcier*; on September 19, Sedaine's *Rose et Colas*; on October 12, Jean Jacques Rousseau's *Le Devin du village* and a repeat of *Le Roi et le fermier*. The Queen and her friends worked nonstop. All their time was spent learning and rehearsing the plays in an atmosphere of heightened excitement. The magic of the stage allowed Marie Antoinette to escape from her role as Queen that at times seemed to weigh so heavily on her. And it was not by chance that she took the parts of the bourgeois ingenues or soubrettes, like Lise in *On ne s'avise jamais de tout*, who has the contents of a dustbin poured on her head, or Agathe in *Le Sorcier*, who is seen ironing a heap of laundry and trying to avoid the gallant solicitations of an enterprising villager.

The King attended all the performances and enjoyed them enormously. Contrary to what Mercy misleadingly told the Empress, the Queen did not just invite the King and the royal family to these performances. She had tickets distributed to all the people whom she wanted to honor, and thereby wounded many feelings. She preferred to favor her friends' protégés rather than some courtier with a prominent name who had the unfortunate luck of not being liked by her. She did not realize that she was alienating a nobility that was jealous of its prerogatives—prerogatives that may seem surprising in the context of our present-day societies, but which were then considered tokens of extraordinary honors.

Most of the courtiers began to feel offended by such lack of deference. Some deserted the court. In trying to live like a princess without a kingdom, she avoided being seen by the people admitted into the inner sanctum of the Château de Versailles. Her absence or bored presence contributed to feeding the rumors that were already spreading regarding her mad life of dissipation and lust. People whispered that it was in order to better satisfy her desires and give herself over to shameful pleasures that she hid from the public gaze! And so were dark legends spun about a Queen who only dreamed of the sweet joys of intimacy.

17

BIRTH OF A DAUPHIN

*T*he summer came to an end as gaily as it had started. The Queen extended her stay in Trianon to the beginning of September in the company of Madame de Polignac, who was at the height of her favor. Marie Antoinette, unable to do without her presence, gave her most of her time, thereby fostering the court gossip.

Had she not imposed a trip to La Muette the previous May only because the charming Countess had given birth to a son in the village of Passy? The situation was particularly improper in that the Comte de Polignac, absent for many long months, was clearly not the child's father. But this hardly mattered to the Queen since her favorite seemed supremely happy. Marie Antoinette went to see her every day. She even managed to bring Louis XVI to her bedside. Since the King never visited his subjects, this favor created a sensation. Madame de Polignac had obtained much greater rewards from her august friend—an enormous dowry for her thirteen-year-old daughter, who was to marry the Duc de Guiche; the repaying of her husband's debts; the Abbé de Polignac's appointment to a bishopric; an honorary position for her sister-in-law; considerable compensation for Vaudreuil, whose interests in the West Indies were adversely affected by the American war. For the Polignacs and their protégés, the royal manna seemed inexhaustible. Coming at a time when there was beginning to be serious talk of reducing expenses, these generous, undeserved gifts were shocking. And to crown matters, in

October 1780 the favorite's husband was given the title of duke, which entitled his wife to the privilege of a *tabouret* (a folding stool) at court. This high distinction, allowing duchesses to sit in the presence of the sovereigns, was among the most sought-after honors. "There are few examples of a favor which became so useful to a family in so short a time," Mercy lamented.

In Vienna, the Empress was distressed that her daughter had become the plaything of a swarm of intriguers. She tried to warn her gently, without adopting her former authoritarian tone. Marie Antoinette, on the other hand, minimized the influence of her small social set and reassured her mother, promising her she would return to court life with all the constraints it entailed. "I am most pleased you intend to resume being on show for state functions at Versailles," replied Maria Theresa. "I am aware of how tedious and empty they are; but, believe me, when there aren't any, the resulting inconveniences are far more consequential than the small drawbacks of being on show."[1]

For months, the elderly sovereign, who sensed she was declining, had been insistently pressing her daughter for a Dauphin. Tired of strife, the Queen finally admitted to her dear mother that she had not shared Louis XVI's bed in a long time. "It is a very common practice here between husband and wife and I did not think I should torment the King on this point, for it would go against his way of being and his personal taste. I would be all the more in error to insist on it in that we live together very maritally," she added to justify herself.[2] Greatly disappointed, the Empress had answered that she regretted that the royal couple had adopted such habits and she praised the advantages of the "German style" conjugal bed for the intimacy it encouraged between spouses.

The young woman did not realize that the Empress was at death's door. Maria Theresa complained of rheumatism and the physicians had diagnosed what they called "a hardening of the lungs." Joseph refused to believe in the seriousness of his mother's ailment, which, though she suffered physically, did not prevent her from working. Surrounded by several of her children, Maria Theresa died piously on November 29, 1780. A few days later, Louis XVI learned of the death of his mother-in-law, whom he had never met and who meant so much to his wife. He did not have the courage to announce the sad news to her. Perhaps he felt he was not close enough, not intimate enough with her, to tell her something that would deal such a blow to her heart. He assigned the task to the Abbé de Vermond. As the man of the Church who was closest to Marie Antoinette, was he not meant to fulfill this kind duty? However, the King was by his wife's side a quarter of an hour after the Abbé had spoken to her. Though clumsy in appearance, Louis XVI was capable of thoughtfulness and tact. Marie Antoinette was aware of this and especially grateful to him on this occasion. Shattered by the death of her mother, she had an attack of convulsions and remained prostrated for several hours. As soon as she recovered her senses, she wrote to Joseph: "Overwhelmed by the most dreadful grief, I am writing to you in tears. Oh, my brother! Oh, my friend, you are all that is left to me in a country which is and always will be dear to me! Be careful, look after yourself; you owe it to all . . . Farewell, I can no longer see what I write. Remember that we are your friends, your allies. Love me. I kiss you."[3]

For several days she was disconsolate. Pathetic in her grief—such a rare occurrence in princes—Marie Antoinette was touched by her husband's thoughtfulness. She showed him more affection than usual. No doubt she had a feeling of guilt toward this man who was so lenient with her. As though wanting to grant her mother's wish beyond death, Marie Antoinette drew closer to her husband and by February there was talk of another pregnancy: the Queen expected a happy event in October 1781. Her health was excellent and she would have fully surrendered to the joy of prospective motherhood except that her Emperor brother, seconded by Mercy-Argenteau, forced her to intervene in political matters which she disliked being involved in.

Now sole master of his empire, Joseph II wanted to inaugurate his reign with an outstanding, brilliant action. He dreamed of appearing as the arbiter of Europe. He thought the American War of Independence, which pitted France and Spain against England, could give him the opportunity. He wanted to preside over a European congress where he would be the mediator among the belligerents. Actually, the Emperor was reviving a plan which had already been suggested by Maria Theresa at the beginning of the conflict and which Marie Antoinette had supported enthusiastically. So once again, he solicited his sister's good offices. As she was praying for a rapid resolution to the conflict so she could be reunited with her dear Fersen, she was eager to support her brother.

At Versailles, the only person to respond favorably to the Emperor's suggestions was Necker, who was then Director of Finance. He felt it was dangerous to continue the war because of the costs involved. But Louis XVI and his Minister of Foreign Affairs did not share his fears. They rejected a peace without winners or losers, and were determined to prevail over England. In fact, they had just accepted the plan for a new naval campaign suggested by the Minister of the Navy. He promised to settle American independence by a test of strength. His plan consisted in striking a decisive blow against the British where the greater part of their troops were concentrated, which required a combined land and sea operation.

Louis XVI and Vergennes were evasive in their reply to the Emperor. When they were alone, the King dodged his wife's insistent requests affectionately. Unwilling to admit defeat, Joseph decided to make another European trip, a trip that would naturally bring him to Versailles. Though awkward for the King and his ministers, this visit was a source of great joy to the Queen.

Joseph's stay was shorter than his previous one. He arrived in Versailles on July 29 and left on August 5. The King saw little of his brother-in-law, leaving him in the care of his wife. Dressed in the simple white dresses that she liked to wear in summer, Marie Antoinette spent entire afternoons strolling arm in arm with the Emperor. Joseph was frank in speaking with her and did not refrain from harshly criticizing her friends. She let him talk, and feebly attempted to defend her little social set whose company she so enjoyed. Her brother's reprimands were much more moderate than in 1777. He thought the Queen seemed more sensible. He was pleased to see that she hoped to give France a Dauphin. Besides, the Emperor needed her help in his diplomatic aspirations. She promised to assist him.

For Marie Antoinette, those days went by too quickly. On the eve of her brother's departure, she gave him a tasteful fete at Trianon. The evening began in her little theater, with a performance of Gluck's *Alcestis* by musicians from the Opera. Afterward, the Queen personally welcomed her two hundred and sixty-three guests for a walk through the illuminated gardens. A sumptuous dinner followed. And once again, she wounded many feelings by excluding part of the court from the reception. Let those who were disgruntled go to the devil! The evening was in honor of her brother. And she found this kind of evening infinitely more pleasant than an official reception. When Joseph left, she cloistered herself in her apartment so she could weep without constraint. Several days later, she was displeased to learn that the King had officially rejected the Emperor's mediation. Her husband's reassuring remarks concerning the future of the French-Austrian alliance helped her recover her serenity.

The last months of her pregnancy went by quietly. She showed no fear at the prospect of this birth, in spite of the unpleasant memory of her first delivery. The King, in fact, did not want to subject her to the same painful trial that she underwent with the delivery of Madame Royale. So he completely modified the protocol. Only members of the royal family, a few ladies of the Queen's Household and the Lord Chancellor were to be present in the Bedchamber. The rest of the public would wait in the adjoining drawing rooms and halls.

On the morning of October 22, the Princesse de Lamballe, Superintendent of the Queen's Household, gave orders to inform the princes and princesses that labor had started. After an hour and fifteen minutes, she gave birth to the much hoped-for Dauphin. But when the Lord Chancellor bent over the child to see its sex, the room was so still that everyone thought it was another girl. Exhausted, the Queen remained silent. The King sobbed with joy. The newborn was taken away to be washed and dressed and the Queen learned the happy news only when an emotional Louis XVI said to her: "Monsieur le Dauphin begs permission to enter."

In the neighboring drawing rooms excitement was at a high pitch. A disheveled woman had been seen emerging from the Queen's Bedchamber. Holding a finger up to her mouth, she had said, "A Dauphin, but you must not say anything yet." Then she immediately vanished. People instantly began rejoicing and embracing each other; the King had an heir! The news spread like wildfire. When the sovereign appeared with Madame de Guéméné holding the sumptuously dressed infant in her arms, the crowd went wild. People wanted to touch the child and they followed him to the chapel where the Cardinal de Rohan, Grand Almoner, baptized him Louis Joseph Xavier.

The little Duc d'Angoulême, the Comte d'Artois's eldest son, expressed astonishment: "My God, Papa, how small my cousin is!" "You will certainly find him big enough someday, my son," replied the Prince, who saw the crown slipping away from his own children. Nor did the Comte de Provence, until then heir apparent to the throne, partake of the general rejoicing. The King wept profusely during the ceremony and everyone present was moved by his tenderheartedness. As for the Queen, she rested. Her son, who weighed 13 *livres* and measured 22 inches, was put in the arms of a buxom peasant woman chosen for her superior qualities as a wet nurse—a job for which she seemed predestined by her name: Madame Poitrine (Mrs. Breast). Though she had to wear a wet-nurse outfit worthy of Versailles, she still had a country look, which in a court so in love with nature, conferred ineffable charm on her function.

The birth of the Dauphin was soon known in Paris. There was a general explosion of joy. People stopped in the streets and embraced. The festivities began. For three days, the capital was illuminated at the King's expense and fountains of wine flowed at the crossroads. At Notre-Dame, a *Te Deum* was celebrated in the presence of the King, who was greeted with cheers as he crossed Paris.

According to custom, the representatives from the different trades and crafts in the city came to Versailles to pay homage to the newborn Dauphin and congratulate the happy parents. They formed a long procession in the marble courtyard of the château. The Queen, alas, could not attend. The guilds all competed in ingenuity in celebrating the birth of the heir to the throne. Butchers and pastry cooks had composed extraordinary confections of meat and cake; chimney sweeps carried a beautiful chimney from which a young boy emerged and delivered an appropriate compliment to the sovereign; chair bearers carried a sedan in which was seated a wet nurse suckling a baby; knowing the King's passion for their craft, the locksmiths had designed a lock with a secret: when successfully opened, a dauphin emerged.

The market women, dressed in black silk, were received by the Queen, who was still bedridden. The writer La Harpe had written a speech for them which one of them recited fluently, with only a few furtive glances at her fan, where the text was inscribed. Afterward, the fishwives recited some couplets they themselves had composed. Their sauciness cheered the King and Queen, who requested several encores before treating all the women to a copious meal. The Queen was enjoying herself; she was happy. She had accomplished her most sacred duty by giving the kingdom an heir.

Marie Antoinette's happiness was short-lived. It was impossible to hide from her for very long a growing number of scurrilous lampoons casting doubt on the legitimacy of the Dauphin and for the most part naming the Duc de Coigny as the child's real father. Had they been commissioned by England, the princes or some vindictive aristocrats? The investigation ordered by Louis XVI led to nothing. However, the Queen's reputation, already considerably tainted by the gossip provoked by her free and easy manner, was damaged even further.

Mercy, for his part, had several good reasons for not leaving the young Queen in peace. Maurepas was on his deathbed. Always concerned with defending Austrian interests, the ambassador had his heart set on the nomination of a minister favorable to the alliance who would also owe his promotion to the Queen. Her enforced period of rest gave the diplomat ample time to indoctrinate her. He presented Maurepas's death as a good opportunity and suggested she press for the nomination of the Archbishop of Toulouse, Loménie de Brienne, a philosopher prelate and a friend of the Abbé de Vermond. Marie Antoinette hesitated and replied that there was no rush. Meanwhile, Joseph II informed his sister that it would be preferable for the King to govern alone. The Queen, who had had conflicts with Maurepas on several occasions, concurred, for it suited her well. She encouraged her husband on the path which he had actually chosen himself. Louis XVI felt he could rule without a Prime Minister.

When Mercy understood that Marie Antoinette agreed with her brother and that Maurepas would have no successor, he saw all that Austria stood to gain from such a godsend. He therefore lectured the Queen even more than usual; she was to be attentive and clever enough to impose her own choices on the King without giving him the impression that she wanted to govern. And Mercy began to dream of seeing the Habsburgs rule over France thanks to an intermediary named Marie Antoinette. He would soon be sorely disillusioned.

Indeed, Louis XVI and Vergennes had every reason to be pleased. After several months of indecisive maneuvers, the French and Americans had just won a clear-cut victory which would allow a profitable peace to be negotiated without having to resort to Austria's mediation! The British had just surrendered at Yorktown. There, in southeastern Virginia, at the mouth of Chesapeake Bay, the British general, Cornwallis, had been taken by surprise by the French and American troops. The allies had taken 7,500 prisoners! Lauzun was immediately dispatched to France to announce this important news to Louis XVI. News of the French military success, several days after the Dauphin's birth, was greated with enormous enthusiasm. There was a great demand for the Abbé Raynal's book, *La Révolution de l'Amérique*, published a few weeks earlier, which vindicated the revolutionaries. Franklin saluted Louis XVI in French for bringing about the happiness of so many people, and wished him the greatest prosperity. Philadelphia held a grand celebration for its liberators, foremost among them the Marquis de Lafayette. Disregarding the royal prohibition, this young aristocrat had joined the revolutionaries prior to France's official involvement in the American war. Appointed a major general in the United States Army by Congress, he had gained Washington's confidence, had distinguished himself in the battle of Monmouth and had greatly contributed to the illustrious Yorktown victory. Convinced that this success would bring the war to an end, he had just declared: "The play is over, the fifth act is just ended." In France, Lafayette was now universally regarded as a hero. Paris was preparing great festivities in celebration of the King, the Queen, the Dauphin and the Yorktown victory.

Under a pale winter sun, in dry, cold weather, on January 21, 1782, the Queen made her solemn entrance into the capital, with Madame Elisabeth, Madame Adélaïde and three other princesses by her side. As she made her way across the jubilant capital—where large quantities of money had been distributed—the Queen was radiant; she was cheered all along the way to Notre-Dame, where her churching ceremony was held. Like the humblest Frenchwoman, Marie Antoinette knelt on the flagstones of the cathedral and thanked the Lord for the birth of the Dauphin she had so ardently desired. The ceremony resumed. It was very grand. Now she was no longer a simple penitent at Notre-Dame, but clearly the Queen of France, to whom the Church and the faithful had to pay the honors due to the crown. When the ceremony was over, Marie Antoinette went to pray at the Church of Sainte Geneviève before going to the reception put on by the municipal magistrates of Paris at the Hôtel de Ville. For the occasion, a kind of wooden palace had been built which could accommodate hundreds of guests. No expense had been spared, particularly not on the decoration.

The royal family took their seats at the table with seventy-eight carefully chosen guests. Several other tables were reserved for the royal retinue and the city grandees. In the afternoon, Louis XVI and Marie Antoinette received their guests in the drawing rooms adjoining the dining room, then took their seats at gaming tables around which the public was soon allowed to mill. Thanks to the security services, under great pressure for several days, no unfortunate incidents occurred. Outside, orchestras played at the crossroads, free victuals were distributed and wine flowed in abundance. Gigantic fireworks brought the evening to a close.

A short while later, the royal coach took the rue Saint-Honoré and headed toward the Château de La Muette, where the King and Queen were to spend the night. But Marie Antoinette wanted to stop in front of the Hôtel de Noailles, where Lafayette was staying since his return from America. When the hero went up to the door of the sovereigns' coach, the crowd broke out in a long ovation.

On the following day, Louis XVI and Marie Antoinette returned to Paris[4] for the ball given in their honor. Before going to the Hôtel de Ville, they had a cheerful dinner at the Temple, a property the Comte d'Artois had inherited from the Prince de Conti. This palace, built in the seventeenth century and renovated in the eighteenth, was where the King's younger brother customarily held his pleasure parties; it had a view of a sinister medieval dungeon. Little could the King and Queen suspect that in eleven years that dungeon would be the setting for tragic moments in their lives.

Another ball in Versailles, held by the bodyguards, concluded those days of rejoicing. Marie Antoinette had fond memories of that period. Convinced that she had reconquered the love of the Parisians, she failed to see that the Yorktown victory and the unexpected arrival of Lafayette had cast the churching festivities in an unforeseen, different light. The population had greeted the soldier from America with fervor. He had been crowned with flowers at the Opera and been the true hero of the hour. His popularity had eclipsed that of the Queen.

18

FERSEN'S RETURN

arie Antoinette waited impatiently for the end of the war. However, Louis XVI and Vergennes wanted to negotiate with the British from a position of strength, and thus they decided to continue while they had the advantage. The French fleet fought the British ships relentlessly along the coasts of India; Admiral de Grasse was preparing to support the Spanish in their planned attack on Jamaica. In Europe, the French also intended to join the allies in laying siege to Gibraltar.

The continuation of the conflict rekindled Joseph II's hopes of fulfilling his dream of mediating. He harassed the Queen with his ill-timed requests. Convinced that the Emperor's intentions were well founded, Marie Antoinette implored her husband to listen to the Austrian proposals. Disappointed by his evasive answers, she summoned Vergennes and upbraided him angrily for not understanding France's best interests. However, French policy soon bore fruit. The British cabinet sent an emissary to Versailles in great secrecy proposing to enter into peace negotiations.

Overjoyed, Louis XVI immediately announced the important news to his wife, but she did not respond as he expected. She lost her temper and told him that the peace settlement was far too complex to arrange without the Emperor's arbitration. She even had the clumsiness—or naïveté—to assert that Joseph II wanted to play the arbiter not for his personal glory but in order to put an end to the dreadful bloodshed and give France proof of his undying friendship. For several months she continued to be her brother's advocate with the King, who listened to her without saying a word, and with the minister, whom she scolded shamelessly. In her opinion Vergennes was incapable of successfully carrying out the peace negotiations; she was convinced that he was only acting out of self-interest, with the aim of being appointed Prime Minister.

The Queen—who did not understand the magnitude of her brother's ambitions—was soon given another opportunity to support the Emperor's policies. He requested that she give a lavish reception for the heir to the Russian throne, the future Tsar Paul I, Catherine II's son. The Grand Duke was traveling around Europe incognito with his wife, the Grand Duchess Maria Feodorovna.[1] In spite of appearances, this was not a pleasure trip, but a disguised diplomatic mission. The Tsarevitch had been sent to Versailles by his mother to solicit France's benevolent neutrality in the partition of the Ottoman Empire she and Joseph were happily planning. Joseph had sent Marie Antoinette very specific instructions: she was to neglect no detail in making the Russians' stay in France pleasant. The steps taken by St. Petersburg, with Vienna's support, put the French ministry in a quandary, for they had no intention of backing Austria and Russia's policy of armed burglary. Louis XVI left the organizing of the festivities to his wife, for, like it or not, they were under an obligation to honor the Tsarevitch and his wife, who were traveling under the name of Comte and Comtesse du Nord.

The Nords arrived at Versailles on May 18, 1782. The Grand Duke had come to the château the day before without identifying himself. Lost in the crowd of courtiers, he observed the habits of the court, which was the talk of all Europe. When he returned to the Russian embassy, he described Versailles in such dazzling terms to his wife that the Grand Duchess was completely overawed. In the hope of regaining her self-confidence, shaken by the portrait her husband had drawn of the Queen, she quickly summoned Mademoiselle Bertin and ordered clothes to match those of the most elegant women in Paris.

In the coach, as the couple were on the way to Versailles, the Grand Duchess anxiously asked the Tsarevitch if she was as beautiful as Marie Antoinette. Meanwhile, Marie Antoinette was suffering from an acute case of stage fright. As the princely carriage passed through the palace gates, she drank a large glass of water and confessed to her lady-in-waiting that "the role of Queen was more difficult to fill in the presence of other sovereigns or princes who were themselves future rulers than with courtiers."[2] However, irreproachably self-possessed and gracious, she welcomed the Nords as a true sovereign. A concert was held in the Peace Room for her guests in the presence of the entire court. This was followed by a marvelous supper. The imperial couple left Versailles at three in the morning. They made several other visits. Marie Antoinette invited them to Trianon.

Charmed by the Queen's graciousness, the Tsarevitch mistakenly thought a certain intimacy had been established between her and him. He took the liberty of imparting some rather embarrassing things about his mother, the Tsarina, and asked her some indiscreet questions about her relations with Madame du Barry. Marie Antoinette could not have been more shocked. From that day on, she had an unspoken aversion for her visitors and was eager to see them leave. But she still had to give several performances and fetes in their honor, each more magnificent than the next. The imperial visit came to a close with a formal ball in the Hall of Mirrors. The Queen danced with the Tsarevitch and the King with Maria Feodorovna. "One of the most beautiful sights I have ever seen is the royal family's entrance at the ball, when the entire court is assembled," wrote the Baroness d'Oberkirch,[3] a childhood friend of the Grand Duchess, who felt she was living in an enchanted world. When these troublesome visitors left, Marie Antoinette was much relieved and went to rest in her dear Trianon with Madame de Polignac. Mercy was all praise for the Queen's conduct. The King and Vergennes congratulated themselves for having promised nothing of substance to the Russians.

There were fewer people than usual at Versailles. The Comte d'Artois, Vaudreuil and several other gentlemen were taking part in the siege of Gibraltar; many others had left for their landed châteaux. The Queen had moved her children as well as Madame de Guéméné and her retinue to the Grand Trianon, where she spent a few hours every day. That summer, she gave up acting and held only several small concerts. Nothing troubled the tranquillity of those fine summer days, except for the Prince de Guéméné's astounding insolvency, which compelled his wife to give up her position as Governess of the Children of France. Unmoved by this scandal, the Queen asked Madame de Polignac to succeed the Princess. The favorite accepted the nomination unenthusiastically, as it deprived her of a relative independence. Marie Antoinette thereafter lodged her children and her friend in two apartments communicating with her own.

In the meantime, peace negotiations were proceeding at a snail's pace. Many officers had come back from America, but Fersen delayed his return. By extending his time of service in the French army, he hoped to improve his chances of being given a regiment upon his return. Besides, he was also on an economic and commercial information-gathering mission for the King of Sweden. Indeed, Gustavus III hoped to acquire a Swedish colony from the young republic.

As the aide-de-camp of Rochambeau, the general in command of the expeditionary force in America, Fersen had accompanied him on all his trips, and attended the meetings with Washington and the American military commanders. He was fluent in English and often served as interpreter. His valor, particularly in the Yorktown siege, had earned him the prestigious decoration of the Order of Cincinnatus. After Yorktown, he had traveled around the American states and stayed in Virginia for an extended period. Upon seeing the huge tobacco and corn fields tilled by black slaves under the iron rule of punch-drinking "white gentlemen," he had a foreboding of the coming difficulties between the North and the South. Everywhere well received, Fersen saw Americans as frank, loyal, cheerful and likable, but being an inflexible European aristocrat, he was shocked by their sense of equality. In spite of the war, the young man had succeeded in having a good time on occasion. First, he had struck up a friendship with an engaging French aristocrat who was none other than Lauzun. We have no idea whether they exchanged intimate secrets, but we know that they got along splendidly. They probably shared their female conquests. Fersen, like many French officers, wrote enthusiastic descriptions of American women, whom he found beautiful, well proportioned and more carefully groomed than European women. They were in the habit of using soap when they washed, a relatively rare practice on the other side of the Atlantic.

On December 24 1782, after a pleasant stay in Boston, Fersen embarked for Central America. The aim was to attack the British in the Lesser Antilles, north of present-day Venezuela. After a dreadful crossing, he stepped on shore in Puerto Cabello. To use his own expression, it was "hell." "We are dying of boredom; we are drying up; we are becoming old and yellow with heat,"[4] he groaned, ailing with fever and a serious case of conjunctivitis. A French frigate put an end to these trials; he was told that the war had ended and the peace would soon be signed. After stopping in Cap-Français (present-day Cap-Haitien), he sailed for France at the end of April 1783.

During his four years in America, Fersen kept his father regularly informed of his future plans. Not long before his return to Europe, he told him he had good reason to expect a regiment in France, and that he thought he could count on the support of the Queen, who "had always been very kind and interested in him."[5] (Indeed, since 1782, Marie Antoinette had been exerting herself on his behalf with the aim of getting him a regiment.) In the hope of calming his father's fears, he assured him that the position of colonel-proprietor of a French regiment, though very "pleasant," "would not require his presence."[6] He also informed him of his marital plans. "I am at the age when marriage, regardless of my small vocation for this sacrament, becomes a necessary thing," he said to him.[7] It was time for him to find a wealthy heiress whose physical appearance was not too displeasing. He lacked ardor in searching for an ideal spouse. He thought of taking up again with Miss Leyell, an Englishwoman who had turned him down several years earlier. Foreseeing a second rejection, he considered Germaine Necker, the only daughter of the Swiss banker Necker, Louis XVI's former Minister of Finance. But then he learned that his friend the Baron de Staël was a serious suitor and he had no desire to poach on his territory.

Fersen landed in France on June 17, 1783. On the twenty-third, he went to stay in Paris with his friend de Staël, who had just been appointed Swedish ambassador to France. Suddenly, over the next few days, his life, it seems, took a new turn. The three letters he wrote on the twenty-seventh, to Gustavus III, his father and his sister Sophie, attest to the fact. He solicited the sovereign's intercession in obtaining the French regiment of the Royal Suédois and asked him "to consent to an arrangement on which his existence, his future and his entire happiness depended."[8] He asked his father for the 100,000 livres needed to acquire the regiment, to be taken from his future inheritance. "If you do not have the money readily available, dear Father, I shall go about finding it here and you must not be troubled," he hastened to add.[9] He nevertheless assured Senator Fersen that his reply "would determine whether his life would be happy or unhappy." And then he appealed to his sister Sophie to subdue the opposition he felt in his father, and repeated to her that "his entire happiness" depended on this decision.

Fersen rarely manifested such effusiveness. Was the hope of owning a regiment the sole grounds for such ardor? He had a brilliant career awaiting him in Sweden, his native country, where the King considered him a friend and held him in special esteem. But he well knew that Sweden, that cold distant land, would always be a secondary power. Though he constantly assured his father and his sovereign of his loyalty, Fersen felt not the slightest nostalgia for his family or country. Thanks to the Queen's protection, he could see a marvelous career stretch before him in France. However, if ambition and hopes of a pleasant life were powerful motives for him to stay in the French kingdom, there were "a thousand other reasons he dared not put down on paper."[10] This was as much as he could safely admit to his favorite sister.

Several days later, Axel Fersen received the answers he was waiting for. Upon Gustavus III's entreaties, his father had conceded and consented—unwillingly—to let him become the owner of the Royal Suédois. And since good fortune never strikes just once, he learned that Miss Leyell had married and that Necker had accepted the Baron de Staël as his son-in-law. "I am so happy that I can hardly believe it. I have more than one reason for that which I will tell you when we see each other," he said to his sister on July 31.[11] "In spite of all the pleasure of seeing you again," he went on, "I cannot leave Paris without regret. You will think it quite natural when you learn the cause of this regret. I will tell you, for I do not want to keep anything secret from you . . . I am very glad that Miss Leyell is married. She won't be mentioned to me again and I hope no one else will be found. *I have made up my mind. I do not want to contract conjugal ties; they are contrary to nature . . . I cannot belong to the only person to whom I want to belong, the one who really loves me, and so I do not want to belong to anyone.*"[12]

This mysterious person who "really loved" him was Marie Antoinette. Fersen had not expected that after a separation of over three years the Queen of France's love would assert itself with such force. For this aristocrat who deeply revered the monarchy, the passion of a Queen resembled no other. He tended to see her as a sovereign who had deigned to glance at him and not as a lovelorn, pathetic woman who was incapable of hiding her feelings any longer. Marie Antoinette had every power over Fersen; he was enthralled by the woman-sovereign and ready to love the woman who wore the sovereign's crown.

This sort of situation would seem unbelievable if Marie Antoinette and her friend had not remained in epistolary contact during the American war. However, aside from the official letters Fersen mentions to his father, no trace remains of personal letters from the Queen. Nor can Fersen's journal be of help. After the flight to Varennes in 1791, he deliberately destroyed the part covering the period 1776 to 1791, which would seem to confirm that it often concerned Marie Antoinette. All we have left is his correspondence notebook, in which he listed the names of his correspondents and the dates of his letters, sometimes providing brief summaries of the letters. It was in studying this document shortly after the First World War that the Finnish archivist Alma Söderhjelm discovered that one of the Swedish count's mysterious correspondents, with the banal first name of Joséphine, was actually the Queen of France. Fersen numbered only important letters—and those to Joséphine are all numbered. They form a series whose first dates always coincide with Fersen's departures (either from Paris or from Versailles) and whose last dates coincide with his return. They deal with personal matters as well as politics and military life. There is no doubt about the identity of this Joséphine, for in several instances in what remains of his journal Fersen is clearly using this name to refer to Marie Antoinette. The suddenness of the young Swede's decisions immediately after returning to France and his mysterious confidences to Sophie can thereby be better explained.

July was an extremely happy month for him. No doubt it was an equally happy one for the Queen. On July 15,1798, he would note in his journal: "I remember this day, when I arrived from Dang;[13] I stayed at Madame de Matignon's[14] and I went to Her[15] for the first time." Certainly the event must have been very important for him. Though Marie Antoinette feigned, publicly, to treat Fersen with a degree of indifference, her obvious fondness for him could not remain secret for long. Vexed that the handsome Swede did not court them, the ladies claimed that he had aged and lost his looks. However, though Fersen had lost the grace of early youth, had become thinner, and his features more chiseled, he had lost none of his charm. His natural reserve, his slightly melancholic air, the stories of his exploits, contributed to giving him a distinguished "aura."

Marie Antoinette was finally fulfilling her dream of having a private life. The man she loved came to see her almost every day and she strove to organize, for him and for herself, a kind of ideal existence. Luckily, the King seemed to see nothing, and know nothing.

During that period, the Queen freed herself even more from the burdens of etiquette. She wore only her white dresses now. Moreover, she had the idea of having herself painted in one of these dresses by Madame Lebrun. The portrait caused a scandal when it was exhibited at the Salon. There was indignation that the Queen of France dressed like a chambermaid. Some people claimed that she was conspiring with her brother to bring ruin on the Lyon silk merchants and wealth to the Brussels[16] linen manufacturers. Out of prudence, the portrait was taken down.

Fortunately for her, the Queen paid no heed to this incident, though it might have made her aware of the extent of her unpopularity. No doubt she attributed the attack to that famous French flightiness of which her mother and brother had so often complained. At the end of September, she was far more worried about the fact that Fersen was leaving on a trip to Sweden for several months.

19

LAST ILLUSIONS

*T*he Queen's happiness was once again intruded upon by the Emperor, who would not stop tormenting her, and still saw her as a pawn in the famous alliance. Marie Antoinette had received pressing letters from her brother asking her to intervene in support of an operation advantageous, he said, to both France and Austria. He and the Tsarina were planning to dismember the Ottoman Empire and Joseph needed France's obliging neutrality. In exchange for this neutrality, he offered to bequeath Egypt to Louis XVI. This offer might have tempted the King. However, he turned down the transaction and sent his brother-in-law a stern letter denouncing "the monstrous system of compensations" which caused perpetual conflicts in Europe. Angered and resentful, but convinced that France—the traditional protector of the Ottoman Empire—could turn against him with Prussia's support, Joseph was forced to back down from his plans of conquest.

Once again, Marie Antoinette sided with Austria in this affair and refused to listen to the King's arguments or those of Vergennes, on whom she inflicted more of her outbursts. It never for a moment occurred to her that her husband and his minister were acting in concert. The King gave her vague explanations and exploited his pseudo-weakness with her to avoid her fits of anger. Vergennes, on the other hand, while he kept up the respectful attitude due to her, did not shrink from responding frankly to her arguments and defending what he rightly considered to be in the kingdom's best interests. Since she failed to win them over, the Queen wrote to her brother that Louis XVI "was inadequately informed in public affairs and seemed not to fully grasp their nuances." She hoped, however, that Joseph "would forget the dishonesty of style that had been used here."

On the surface, this diplomatic conflict had not altered the Queen's good relationship with her husband. Louis XVI treated her with great kindness, continued to indulge her every whim and seemed unaware of her tender feelings for the Swedish nobleman. Malicious gossips claimed that she behaved with consummate duplicity so that he would not notice anything. When the Austrian alliance seemed to her in danger, she drew closer to him and became pregnant. But on November 1, 1783, she had a miscarriage. Several days later, she told the King that she planned not to share his intimacy for several months, despite her desire to have a second son.

Louis XVI and Marie Antoinette were beginning to be extremely worried about the Dauphin. The child was not growing and was visibly wasting away. In May 1784, he fell ill with a violent fever, stopped urinating, and his little body swelled disproportionately. It looked hopeless. Powerless, the physicians declared, not without boastfulness, that this accident had to be viewed "as one of the most powerful ways of fortifying the young Prince's constitution."[1] This optimism calmed the Queen, who believed in her son's recovery. Indeed, miraculously, the child did recover. Several weeks later, in sailor dress, too young or fragile to take part in his older sister's games, he took a few steps in the paths of Trianon with the Baroness de Mackau, his Second Governess. He was very affectionate with his mother and already spoke fluently. He was corrected when he said *I want*. "The King says *we want*," said Madame de Mackau. "Yes," he replied, "the King and I, we both want; you see I am right. My papa would not say *we* for himself alone."[2]

While the little Prince always showed a perfect good humor, such was not the case with his sister. Madame Royale, who often played in her mother's private apartment, was unbearably haughty. In the hope of sweetening her character, the Queen had given her a companion of lowly birth, with whom she was being raised. Clothed in identical dresses, the two little girls received the same education, played the same games, and Marie Thérèse was told to be very considerate of the little Ernestine.[3] The Queen had just had a flower bed prepared for her daughter and Ernestine, where they could plant whatever they wanted. They were provided with shovels, rakes, watering cans and other small garden implements. She also arranged to give them a herd of goats and sheep, placed under the care of a specially assigned shepherd.

Madame Royale did not like the Queen. This became all too obvious in a way that greatly upset Marie Antoinette. One day, she was playing next to her mother while Marie Antoinette was telling the Abbé Vermond that she had taken a serious fall from a horse. Immediately, the Abbé turned to the child and asked if she realized that she had almost lost her mother. "I wouldn't care." "Madame does not understand what cracking one's head means. The Queen would have died," the Abbé explained. "I wouldn't care," she repeated. "Then Madame does not realize what death means?" "Yes, Monsieur l'Abbé, I realize what it means. One does not see people anymore once they are dead. I would not see the Queen anymore and I would be very glad because I could do as I pleased."

When she heard her daughter make these statements with such conviction, the Queen ordered that she be taken away from her apartment and placed in penitence. Then she ran, sobbing, to Madame de Polignac's. The Duchess, horrified, blamed the child's attitude on the influence of Madame d'Aumale, one of her Second Governesses. Very upset by what she was told, Madame d'Aumale reproached the Princess for what she had said in the Queen's presence and added that she was all the more guilty in that she undoubtedly loved her mother. "No, I don't love her," said the child, "because she bothers me and pays no attention to me. For example, when she brings me to visit my aunts, she walks straight ahead of me and doesn't even look to see whether I'm following her. Whereas Papa takes me by the hand and looks after me." The authenticity of this anecdote cannot be questioned; it is drawn from the journal of the Marquis de Bombelles, who was admirably well informed on the royal children's daily life by his mother-in-law, the Baroness de Mackau.[4] It reveals the reality of the royal children's intimate life, too often distorted by hagiographic legend.

In spite of all this, in this spring of 1784, Marie Antoinette wanted to believe in happiness. While waiting for Fersen's return, she oversaw the building of her hamlet at Trianon. To complete her illusion of being a lady of the manor, or a queen without a kingdom, she wanted to create a new setting, as close as possible to reality and yet as remote as could be from her real preoccupations—the setting of a French village. The Prince de Condé had been the first to build a hamlet at Chantilly; its seven buildings—along the banks of a river at the far end of his English garden—were replicas of a stable, a dairy, a mill, a barn, a tavern and two peasant houses. Indeed, a miller had been installed to mill grain, a cowhand to take care of the cows, but the peasant houses and the rustic-looking, quasi-dilapidated barn concealed magnificent drawing rooms. It was a world of make-believe.

Marie Antoinette wanted Mique to take his inspiration from the Chantilly hamlet in building one for her at the far end of the Trianon gardens. In 1783, digging began on an artificial pond down the road from the Trianon pavilion, and by spring construction started on the houses of the village bordering the pond. Soon a looming tower could be seen, called the Marlborough Tower—an indication of the ambient anglomania—followed by two dairies, a barn which was really a ballroom, a game of bowls, a dovecote, a henhouse, a mill, a steward's house and a linen room. At the far end of the landscaped pond were two pavilions connected by a long terraced gallery and two pretty coiled exterior stairways. Conceived as Norman cottages with visible half-timbering, cracks were painted on these modest-looking constructions to create the illusion of authenticity. The hamlet would not be fully completed until 1787. This new whim seemed in questionable taste to some of the court wits. "Perhaps by spending a little more, Her Majesty would have been able to erase the look of misery worn by our real hamlets within a radius of thirty leagues and improve the dwellings that are the homes of so many decent citizens, instead of representing them in their hideous decay,"[5] wrote the Marquis de Bombelles at the time.

The area around this miniature village looked like real countryside with plowed fields. A billy goat, some nanny goats, sheep and a herd of Swiss cows were brought in; then three roosters, sixty-eight hens, eight pigeons and some rabbits were purchased. A farming couple, the Valys, lodged at the farm and managed the homestead, with the help of a gardener, a cattleman, a cowherd, a valet, assistant gardeners, a mole catcher, a ratter, a ferreter, a reaper and a girl servant. Half a league away from Versailles's luxurious splendor, Marie Antoinette supervised the work in the fields; she did not pretend to be a farmer as legend has it. She was content to stroll down the lanes of her little estate and watch the farm girl milk the cows and churn the butter. When Valy asked her for a new billy goat since the one they had was incapable of fathering offspring, she gave her consent, but added quite seriously that "the new one should not be nasty and should be all white." And here she thought she was finding out about the realities of peasant life! The swing placed in front of her house, at the edge of the pond, is the perfect symbol of this artificial enthusiasm for an unknown world which she pictured with such extreme sophistication.

The building of a hamlet in the middle of a landscape restored by gardeners and architects to mirror nature—this was indeed an idealized setting where refined luxury could blend with innocent purity, thanks to the magic connected with the soil, exalted by the loftiness of the Garden of Eden. Worldly joy and pastoral simplicity meet in this hamlet, a château and paradise where the real order of society is artfully reconciled with nature's ideal order. This stage-set village of light opera well expressed the dream of purity which consumed the happiness of the worldly-minded. Being reunited with nature through this transposition gave suggestive power to those individuals who were not particularly gifted for imagining things beyond the limits of the real. Finally, in the case of the Queen, could it not be that the conception of an innocent paradise coincided with her sudden, passionate love, and spontaneously led to the desire for a haven?

Marie Antoinette was eager for Fersen to see the first buildings of her hamlet. Axel had not been able to go to Sweden. He had stopped in Germany, where he had met Gustavus III, who was leaving for a protracted tour of Italy. The temperamental sovereign, who could not do without the company of young, handsome men, immediately asked him to give up his trip to Sweden and come with him. Fersen complied with no feelings of joy. Though he acknowledged that Gustavus had the qualities of a true statesman, and he appreciated his culture, refinement and artistic sense, he dreaded the idea of being regarded as his favorite, and could not understand his consuming, fevered love of pleasure. Gustavus wanted to see and understand everything, and never wanted to miss a single performance, reception or ball. The King, who needed very little sleep, usually exhausted his retinue, demanding absolute devotion and lively spirits equal to his own. An iron constitution was needed to keep up with him. Fersen often complained of the daily pace he imposed on his immediate entourage.

During this journey, which took him all the way to Naples, Axel wrote twenty-seven letters to the mysterious Joséphine. She pressed him to come back to Versailles before Gustavus. For the King of Sweden had the intention of ending his trip with a stay in France, a country he adored for its culture and art of living. It being impossible to leave his sovereign, Fersen noted in his correspondence notebook: "To Joséphine, May 18 and 21: no. 27, through Fontaine, that I cannot come before the King." Yet he had countless things to tell her; he had met her brother Joseph, her sister Maria Amalia, Duchess of Parma, and her sister Maria Carolina, Queen of Naples. Of course, he did not mention his amorous adventures; they were mere dalliances, but they surely afforded him some delightful moments. In Florence, he had made the conquest of a certain Emily, the sister-in-law of Lord Cooper, an Englishman who had given marvelous fetes in honor of the King of Sweden. In Naples, he had consoled Elizabeth Foster, a "very unhappy" young woman in the entourage of the pretender, Charles Edward Stuart. But his laconic correspondence notebook informs us that he had told Emily "not to think about it anymore" and "related everything" to Elizabeth.

On June 7, 1784, Louis XVI was hunting in Rambouillet when an alarmed messenger came to tell him that Gustavus III had just arrived at Versailles with no advance notice. The King rode back to the palace at a gallop. Not a single manservant was present to help him and, as ill luck would have it, the keys to the wardrobe had disappeared. Some courtiers helped him dress as best he could. Marie Antoinette, who was not at Versailles either, joined her husband in great haste. Attired with irreproachable elegance, she immediately noticed that the King was wearing two different shoes. In other circumstances, she would have been irritated by this oversight, but she was in such gay spirits that she laughed and merely asked her husband if he was dressed for a costume ball.

For six weeks, the French sovereigns provided their guests with the most tasteful and interesting entertainments. The Queen glowed with happiness and the King seemed less sullen than usual. Operas, ballets, comedies, balls, dinners and suppers followed one another at a heady rhythm. As a grand finale, there was a big fete in Trianon conceived by Marie Antoinette as a hymn to love and dedicated to Fersen. After a performance of Marmotel's *Dormeur éveillé*, with music by Piccini, the Queen invited her guests to a supper in garden pavilions in Trianon. "Respectable people" were allowed to walk around the illuminated English garden, but they had to be dressed in white. It was a "real elysian sight," according to Gustavus III. Marie Antoinette did not sit down at the table, but performed the honors at her own reception like any simple hostess, and spoke to all the Swedes, entertaining them with great attention. On July 19, Gustavus III and his suite of attendants left for Stockholm. He was satisfied: he had strengthened the ties between the two countries and obtained a comfortable income for Fersen, allowing him to live up to his rank at the court of France.

Once again, international affairs cast a shadow on the Queen's joy. Having abandoned his designs on the Balkans, Joseph II now turned to the Netherlands. He wanted the Dutch to reopen the mouth of the Scheldt River in order to permit the full expansion of the port of Antwerp as an outlet for the Austrian Netherlands. This was a violation of an article of the Treaty of Westphalia, concluded in 1648, which France abided by. The Emperor's plans infringed on the commercial interests of both Holland and France. Exasperated by the reckless ambitions of this brother-in-law, who persistently endangered the European balance of power, Louis XVI had no intention of supporting his policies. Moreover, public opinion sided with the commercial and industrious republic of Holland, and immediately flared up angrily against Joseph.

In spite of the serious diplomatic setbacks that Louis XVI had inflicted on him, the Emperor exerted new pressures on Marie Antoinette. Upon receiving truly threatening letters appealing to her sisterly sentiments, the Queen fought for her brother's cause, harped on it with her husband and upbraided the unfortunate Vergennes. One evening, Louis XVI himself had to put an end to her stormy altercation with Vergennes. Though she wept on her husband's breast and yelled at Vergennes, Marie Antoinette obtained nothing. She had no choice but to admit defeat to her brother. "I am not blind about my credit," she said to him. "I know that, particularly in politics, I have very little influence on the King's thinking. Would it be prudent of me to make scenes with his minister on subjects he can be almost certain the King would not support me on? Without any ostentation or lies, I let the public believe that I have more influence than I really do because if I did not make them think so, I would have even less. These admissions, dear brother, are far from flattering to my self-esteem, but I don't want to hide anything from you, so that you can see for yourself, as much as possible, the dreadful distance fate has put between us."[6] She could not have stated things more clearly.

Though he sensed that Louis XVI would not support him, Joseph II made a bid for power by sending an Austrian ship up the Scheldt River. After the customary warnings, the Dutch opened fire on the ship and the Emperor threatened to send an army of 80,000 men to redress what he saw as a grave insult. While all of Europe sided with Holland, while Frederick II rallied most of the German princes and while the French court grumbled against the Emperor, Marie Antoinette renewed her offensive against her husband and his minister. In vain. With bad grace, Joseph had no choice but to accept Louis XVI's arbitration. Negotiations were undertaken between Austria and Holland at Versailles. The Emperor agreed to renounce his designs on the

Scheldt, but demanded ten million florins in damages and interest. Astute businessmen, the Dutch brought the sum down to eight million. Louis XVI generously offered to pay the Emperor the other two million, out of a love for peace, he said. This unnecessary reconciling gesture was attributed to the Queen's influence.

Marie Antoinette did not see that by opposing the Emperor's expansionist policy, Louis XVI, a moderate and peacemaking sovereign, had successfully regained for France the esteem it had lost during the reign of Louis XV. Wounded in her pride, convinced of her superiority over the King, spurred on by Mercy, she focused on how to get Vergennes dismissed, as she begged her brother to excuse the "irresponsibility" of the French ministry. She thanked the Emperor for not having broken off the alliance. If he had, "it would have been the end of her happiness and tranquillity," she said to him. Very few people at court had supported Joseph II. Marie Antoinette's unconditional loyalty to the Habsburg cause seemed shocking; after all, she was the mother of the Dauphin. Within the royal family, the Comte d'Artois, without any hesitation, had suggested a rapprochement with Prussia, Austria's sworn enemy. As for the Polignacs, they had not refrained from severely criticizing the Emperor's interventions, which conspicuously cooled Marie Antoinette's friendship with the Duchess. The Queen could endure no criticism of her Austrian family, not even by her dearest friend.

20

SCANDAL IN THE AIR

*S*hortly after Gustavus III's departure, just as the frictions with Holland were beginning to assume dismaying proportions, the Queen noticed that she was pregnant. This new pregnancy seemed to distress her far more than her previous ones. For a long time, she stayed in an odd state of despondency that no one could dispel and several times she asked to make her confession. This extreme devoutness, so foreign to her habits, surprised everyone. The birth of a second son, given the title of Duc de Normandie, on March 27 1785, relieved Louis XVI, who now regarded his posterity as assured. He seemed extremely joyful as he attended the *Te Deum* sung in the chapel of the château. However, several courtiers wondered whether the paternity of this child should really be traced back to the King of France. It was impossible not to note that the birth occurred exactly nine months after Fersen's visit. People also recalled that Marie Antoinette had become pregnant just after Fersen's previous visit. When the Queen went to Paris for the traditional churching ceremony, she was met with icy silence. Upon her return to Versailles, she fell into the King's arms in tears: "What have I done to them?" she sobbed.[1]

Until recently, historians wondered anxiously whether Marie Antoinette and Fersen had been lovers and whether the royal couple's second son was actually Fersen's son. Though we can state with certainty that the Queen and the Swedish count loved each other, it is impossible to give a definite answer to these two questions. Some clues point to a platonic relationship, while others hint at more intimate ties.

If tragedy had not shattered Marie Antoinette's life, we would have had a completely different image of her. An image unclouded by the pious legend fashioned by the royalists who, starting in 1793, wanted her to be seen as a heroine who had been irreproachable in her private life. To suspect a woman who was now known as the "martyr queen" of amorous weakness was, quite simply, to commit a crime against the monarchy itself. Many memories which seemed indecent to mention were forgotten or camouflaged. Because of this, numerous doubts remained. As a result, the nature of this liaison has tormented several generations of the Queen's devoted admirers, all hopelessly infatuated with a woman made larger than life by her death at the scaffold and transformed into an untouchable myth.

Let us try to shed light on this controversial subject. As previously mentioned, when Louis XVI and Marie Antoinette lived at Versailles, many off-color anecdotes were spread about the Queen. They amounted to court gossip often based on partial truths, but greatly distorted. The Queen's unabashed contempt for proprieties, her fickleness and frivolity gave apparent substance to these rumors attacking her virtue. Cruelly picked up by lampoonists in the pay of England and Prussia, and by vindictive courtiers, these calumnies were prevalent from the very beginning of the reign. The tone of these lampoons grew to an unbelievable crescendo with the beginning of the Revolution. Marie Antoinette, who had initially scorned this literature of the gutter, ended up being very upset by it. Several lovers were attributed to her in these filthy writings, among them, of course, Fersen. These defamatory lampoons are interesting in that they afford insight into certain aspects of the collective imagination, but needless to say, they cannot be used as reliable documents when it comes to answering the questions asked by the Queen's contemporaries and the majority of her biographers.

There are few trustworthy sources. Let us start by considering the papers left by the two protagonists themselves, which we will have ample opportunity to cite. As we have said, a large segment of Fersen's journal was destroyed as well as the letters the Queen wrote to him before the Revolution. However, the journal covering the period June 1791 to 1809 has survived. There are several references to the feelings shared by the Queen and the Swedish gentleman. We will return to these below. On the other hand, Marie Antoinette's letters to Fersen during the revolutionary period and the duplicates of his answers were preserved by the Fersen family. In 1877, one of Axel's grandnephews, Baron Klinckowström, published this correspondence as well as part of the journal.[2] This publication caused much ink to flow. Very little was said about the political revelations it contained, but there was endless speculation concerning the significance of the sentences that had been crossed out and replaced by dotted lines at the beginning and end of the letters. Seeing the storm he had raised, Klinckowström refused to make his archives available and announced that he had burned them out of respect for the memory of the deceased. Because of this, the most contradictory hypotheses on the nature of Marie Antoinette and Fersen's relationship continued to fill pages of print. People were convinced that the letters would have revealed all the secrets of this tragic love story. Then, in 1982, some distant heirs of Fersen found these documents, which, contrary to stories passed down to us since Klinckowström, had never been destroyed. They sold them in London, where they were acquired by the French National Archives.[3] Few historians have held them in their hands. Upon examination, I was able to note that Klinckowström's transcriptions were generally accurate. Unfortunately, the passages of interest were so effectively crossed out that they are illegible. An ultraviolet lamp is of no use in deciphering them, nor are any of the other procedures used by the curators at the Archives de France. There can be no doubt, given where they are placed and their context, that these were crossed-out love messages. Indeed, one letter has been found that escaped the "blue pencil." The words used by Marie Antoinette could not have been clearer in expressing her feelings for Fersen: "I can tell you that I love you," she said to him.[4]

The Queen of France's love for a Swedish aristocrat, even if this love was platonic — that was the "crime" which Fersen's grandnephews tried ineptly to hide (and following in their path all the French royalists), in order to glorify her image and make her a martyr. If today we could succeed in deciphering these famous deletions, we would discover nothing more than the expression of a painful, unhappy passion, but surely no proof of physical intimacy. The letter that was preserved intact provides a key to the destroyed passages. "I can tell you that I love you and indeed that is all I have time for," wrote the Queens.[5] Though the eighteenth century was the preeminent century of libertinage, it was also a time of heightened sensibility. Marie Antoinette and Fersen are not like the heroes in novels by Crébillon, Laclos or Mirabeau. It would be a historical misinterpretation to think that

there could be any hint of eroticism in the correspondence between a sentimental young queen and an aristocrat who revered sovereigns as though
they were gods.

Let us now turn to the views of contemporaneous witnesses. At Versailles,
as soon as Fersen returned, reliable, honest courtiers wondered about the
Queen and Fersen's relationship. This can be seen in the Marquis de
Bombelles's journal, the first volume of which was not published until 1978.
He echoed the rumors according to which Fersen was the Queen's lover.
This was gossip our diarist seemed to give little credence to. The correspondences of the period, first and foremost those of the ambassadors, contain
only vague allusions to this liaison. It might be objected that these diplomats
were compelled to be cautious for fear of the "black cabinet," which thought
nothing of violating the secrecy of the mail. Conversely, it must be noted that
Mercy-Argenteau's silence concerning Fersen is suspicious. Here was a man
who was completely devoted to the Emperor and who kept him apprised of
all the intrigues at Versailles, yet he never alluded to this foreign aristocrat
who, from 1783 on, was clearly an extremely important person in the
Queen's life.

The memoirs and reminiscences of the Versailles habitués form a source
of information that should not be overlooked, but that must be viewed cautiously for the reasons stated above. Yet some of these manuscripts were published only in the twentieth century and are less evasive on the subject that
concerns us. Such is the case, for example, of the Comte de Tilly's memoirs
and particularly those of the Comte de Saint-Priest, which we will often have
occasion to refer to below. As far as this former minister of Louis XVI was
concerned, the Queen "had got the King to accept her liaison with Count
Fersen."[6] The British and Swedish memoirists entertained no doubts about
Fersen being Marie Antoinette's lover, but it is possible to object that they are
not always reliable, for they often based themselves on secondhand
accounts. Other clues exist, particularly physical clues relating to the
Queen's apartment, allowing us to suppose that the ties between the Queen
and her faithful admirer were more than just platonic. We will discuss these
presently.

Fersen had returned to France several days before the churching ceremony and had attended it. He spent most of his time at court. He was seen
at the Queen's card table, at her balls, at small dinners. He sent cryptic letters to his sister Sophie during this period, and spoke to her, in veiled terms,
of his liaison with Marie Antoinette. "I am at Versailles since yesterday, do

Marie Antoinette's mother, Empress Maria Theresa, Queen of Bohemia and Hungary, in her coronation robes. She took the throne at age twenty-three and ruled for more than forty years (School of M. van der Meytens)

The Austrian imperial family on the occasion of the Feast of St. Nicholas, painted by the Archduchess Maria Christina, one of Marie Antoinette's sisters

Marie Antoinette,
Archduchess of Austria
(Jean-Baptiste Charpentier, after
Joseph Ducreux)

Louis XV at age
sixty-three
(François-Hubert Drouais)

Madame Du Barry, Louis XV's official mistress, whom Marie Antoinette called "the stupidest and most impertinent creature imaginable" (Jean-Baptiste-André Gautier-Dagoty)

The wedding of Marie Antoinette and Louis Auguste in the chapel at Versailles, May 16, 1770. The future queen was fourteen years old; her husband was fifteen (Claude-Louis Desrais)

The great illumination of the park at Versailles and the Grand Canal, May 19, 1770. The festivities in celebration of the royal marriage included music and dancing and a spectacular fireworks display (Jean-Michel Moreau)

An official portrait that Marie Antoinette commissioned in 1775, shortly after she was crowned Queen of France
(Jean-Baptiste-André Gautier-Dagoty)

Louis XVI, painted in 1778 when he was twenty-four
(Joseph-Siffred Duplessis)

Marie Antoinette at twenty-eight
(Louis-Auguste Brun)

Germaine Necker, Baronne de
Staël-Holstein, called Madame de Staël,
daughter of France's popular finance
minister and a key witness to the
tumultuous events of the Revolution
(Marie-Eléonore Godefroid)

The Queen and her children (Elisabeth Vigée-Lebrun)

The Comte de Mirabeau responding to the Marquis de Dreux-Brézé before the National Assembly on June 23, 1789, just days before the storming of the Bastille (Alexandre-Evariste Fragonard)

The execution of Louis XVI, January 21, 1793 (Engraving, French school, eighteenth century)

Marie Antoinette being led to her execution, October 16, 1793 (William Hamilton)

not mention that I am writing to you from here, for I date my other letters from Paris," he wrote her.[7]

Overjoyed by their reunion, the Queen had forgotten the icy welcome of the Paris population. As soon as summer arrived, she secluded herself in Trianon. The houses in the hamlet were nearly finished, and she could pretend she was living in the country, far from Versailles. However, since the previous autumn, Trianon was not Marie Antoinette's only estate. Louis XVI had paid an exorbitant sum to buy her the Château de Saint-Cloud, which belonged to the Duc d'Orléans.[8] Its proximity to Paris, the beautiful design of Mansart's facades and the famous gardens sloping down to the Seine had captivated Marie Antoinette, who came up with a very good rationale for acquiring this residence: she had no intention of living at Versailles, which was going to be a chaotic building site while major renovation work was being undertaken. Though the Château de Saint-Cloud could not accommodate the entire court, it was large enough to house the royal family and a number of courtiers. Moreover, there, everyday life would be stripped of the pomp which she found so trying. Even though this expense was a folly, Louis XVI yielded to his wife's desire. He acquired the Saint-Cloud estate for her and in her name. This ill-considered purchase, made just when the Queen was overzealously supporting her brother's cause, contributed to her unpopularity, which was increasing daily.

Impervious to the criticisms that came her way, she immediately set about adapting her new residence to her needs. She began by requiring that all the domestic help wear her personal livery, and she posted rules under the heading *by order of the Queen*. This was seen as undermining the monarchy's usual practices. "My name is not out of place in gardens that belong to me; I can give orders without infringing on the rights of the state," was her reply to those who dared mention the discontent her measures provoked.[9] However, a magistrate in the Paris Parliament made a bold public statement, saying that "it was impolitic and immoral for palaces to belong to the Queen of France." This did not deter the Queen from deciding that the court would settle at Saint-Cloud in September, when Fersen had to return to his regiment in Landrecies, a dismal town located at the northeastern frontier of the kingdom, near the small city of Valenciennes.

Marie Antoinette was once again absorbed by her passion for the theater. Like most of her friends, she had nothing but praise for the talent of Beaumarchais, the seditious author of fashionable comedies. A secret agent of Louis XV, and subsequently of Louis XVI, this protean and inventive genius had played a very active role in the American War of Independence. After having convinced Vergennes and the King to take part in the conflict on the side of the revolutionaries, he supplied the Americans with arms using secret state funds. But these were activities the Queen cared little about. The only things that interested her were his imagination as a playwright and his gift for plot and staging. His latest play, *The Marriage of Figaro*, had caused a scandal the previous year. In this biting satire of the nobility and its privileges, where sentimental intrigues are hatched in the hidden alcoves and groves of a castle, the valet Figaro dares to say to his master: "Because you are a great lord, you think you are a great genius! Nobility, fortune, rank, positions, it all makes a man so proud! What have you done to deserve so many advantages? You took the trouble to be born, nothing more." Whereupon Beaumarchais attacked the social system which existed in France at the time—the magistrates, the justice system, the government.

The aristocrats who had read the play, starting with the Polignacs, saw it as nothing more than an exciting entertainment and an amusing engine of war against what they called royal "despotism." They urged the Queen to prevail upon the King to give permission for the play to be performed. "The Bastille would have to be razed!" grumbled Louis XVI and he forbade its staging.[10] This ban seemed like an infringement of liberty and people complained of tyranny and oppression. Beaumarchais promised to cut the controversial passage and the Polignacs pressed their case again with Marie Antoinette. They tried to convince her that, revised and corrected by the author, the play no longer presented any danger. The Queen trusted her friends, and did not take the trouble to reread the new text, in which the author had actually made very few changes. For the sake of peace and quiet, Louis XVI finally gave permission for the play to be produced.

The opening night of *The Marriage of Figaro* at the Comédie-Française, on April 27, 1784, was a triumph. Lords joined petits bourgeois in applauding the tirades condemning the entire existing social system. However, a lively polemic ensued—not regarding the play's political meaning, but concerning the morals and customs it depicted. Some virtuous censors attacked the immorality of the subject matter. The Archbishop of Paris forbade his congregation from going to see a work of such depravity. Beaumarchais responded to the attacks with some sharp rhetorical metaphors, which his enemies exploited. Faced with scandal, Louis XVI ordered the performances suspended, and Beaumarchais arrested. The playwright spent five days in the Saint-Lazare prison. The Queen was cross with Madame de Polignac for having been so insistent about her influencing the King.

In spite of these unfortunate contretemps, Marie Antoinette's admiration for Beaumarchais remained unshaken. She decided to perform *The Barber of Seville* in her small theater with the *troupe des seigneurs*. She even invited the playwright to come and applaud her in the part of Rosine. This comedy, which had entered the repertoire of the Comédie-Française in 1775, was not politically subversive. The Queen's part in the *troupe des seigneurs* was that of a young Spanish noblewoman who eludes the supervision of a lascivious elderly tutor to wed a dashing suitor who is madly in love with her.

In July 1785, while she thought wistfully that she would soon be celebrating her thirtieth birthday, Marie Antoinette was diligently rehearsing her role as an ingenue. On the twelfth, her jeweler, Böhmer, asked to be admitted. Marie Antoinette, who had ordered a diamond epaulette for the little Duc d'Angoulême, received this tempter who routinely showed her magnificent jewelry. But that day her mind was elsewhere, absorbed in other matters. She was merely a bit surprised to hear the jeweler whisper a turgid compliment to her about the marvelous diamonds in her possession. Certainly, Böhmer had reason to be content. The Queen had bought sumptuous jewels from him, sometimes behind the King's back. She had always tried to pay for them out of her own funds, but when she could not, Louis XVI honored her debts. Before taking leave, Böhmer left her a note, which she opened later on. She told Madame Campan that since she could make no sense of the jeweler's strange disquisition congratulating her on the purchase of an exceptional diamond necklace, she had burned it.

Several hours later, Madame Campan was astonished to find Böhmer at her house in an extremely distraught state. He explained to her that he would be ruined if the Queen did not pay for her jewel as promised. Madame Campan was flabbergasted. As far as she knew, the Queen had not bought any piece of jewelry. At which point Böhmer recounted a story that could have put doubts in the mind of even the best-informed Woman of the Bedchamber who knew every last Versailles intrigue.

About ten years earlier, the jeweler had sunk all his fortune into assembling a heavy diamond necklace made of unusually big, white, bright gems. He had first offered it to Louis XV, in the hope that he would want to give it as a gift to Madame du Barry, but the King had died. Böhmer then presented this exceptional jewel at all the courts of Europe. The legitimately high price he was asking for it—1,800,000 livres—had discouraged buyers. Shortly after the Dauphin's birth, Böhmer and his associate Bassenge offered the jewel to Louis XVI, who thought of giving it as a present to the Queen. Marie

Antoinette resisted the temptation. "France is in greater need of a warship," she is said to have remarked. And Louis XVI had returned the cumbersome item, which was known throughout Europe, back to its owners.

Madame Campan knew this story, but she was unaware of the strange sequel. Böhmer told her that the Cardinal de Rohan had bought the famous necklace on behalf of the Queen, from whom he had received notes signed in her hand. The jeweler, who had delivered the necklace to the Cardinal de Rohan in February, wanted a guarantee that the Queen would pay the first installment, which came to 400,000 livres, on August 1, as agreed. Madame Campan could make no sense of this story. Why would the Queen, after turning down the necklace from the King, arrange to buy it through the Cardinal de Rohan, a prelate she had not spoken to once since his return from Vienna? Had Madame Campan not known Böhmer, she would have thought him mad. Suspecting that he had been grossly tricked, and that this was a serious matter, she advised him to go and tell all he knew immediately to the Baron de Breteuil, Minister of the King's Household.[11]

Preoccupied by her performance as Rosine in *The Barber of Seville*, the Queen had almost forgotten Böhmer's visit. Her Woman of the Bedchamber was nevertheless obliged to tell her about the interview she had just had with him. Marie Antoinette's first reaction was to complain of the trouble caused her by all those who imitated her signature for fraudulent purposes. Then this strange business involving a prince from the House of Rohan seemed so outrageous to her that she decided she could not leave it in the hands of subordinates. She convened Vermond and Breteuil, who decided to summon the two jewelers in her presence. Böhmer and Bassenge repeated the story they had told Madame Campan. Marie Antoinette was speechless with indignation. Vermond suggested informing the King of the Grand Almoner's deed, calling it a crime of lese majesty. But Breteuil preferred to play for time. He thought the guilty party would give himself away when the first payment was due, which was very soon. In the meantime, he would try to unravel this mysterious plot. Marie Antoinette concurred with this minister who was utterly devoted to her and, like her, detested Rohan. It will be recalled that when Choiseul fell out of favor, Rohan had been appointed ambassador to Vienna, a position that Breteuil had coveted. Breteuil had had his revenge after Louis XVI's accession: Rohan had been recalled from Vienna to humor the Empress, and Breteuil had been sent in his place. But Rohan had managed things so that his successor at the embassy in Vienna was denied all the sources of information from which he had personally benefited. In short, the two men hated each other. As for the Queen, she had never forgiven the Cardinal for his comments about her mother at the time of the partition of Poland. Nor had she forgotten his venomous insinuations about her fickleness and coquetry when she was Dauphine. Not so very long ago, she had entreated the King not to give him the position of Grand Almoner. But though he had no esteem at all for this libertine prelate, Louis XVI could not grant her wishes. The Rohan clan was very powerful at court; the position was his nearly by right and the King had pledged his word long ago to the Princesse de Marsan, who had been his Governess.

Breteuil began his investigation by questioning Böhmer and Bassenge, who gave him a detailed account of the episodes in the sale. While they were desperately looking for a buyer for their necklace, they were introduced, at the end of 1784, to a very attractive young woman who claimed to be admitted into the Queen's intimate circle. Asserting she was a descendant of a bastard child of King Henri II, she went under the name of Comtesse de La Motte-Valois. She had charm, worldly wisdom and rather unusual powers of persuasion. In the course of an evening, she had hinted to the jewelers that she could convince the Queen to buy the necklace. On January 21, 1785, she told them triumphantly that she had succeeded. However, according to Madame de La Motte, Marie Antoinette keenly wanted the necklace, but would not buy it in person. She would send a nobleman to negotiate in her name. On January 24, the Cardinal de Rohan asked to be announced at the jewelers', saw the necklace, discussed its price and obtained it for 1,600,000 livres. On the twenty-ninth, the Cardinal informed them of the conditions of the sale: the sum was to be paid over two years, in installments of 400,000 livres every six months, starting August 1, 1785. The jewelers accepted the offer and brought the necklace to the Hôtel de Rohan on February 1. The Cardinal showed them a contract signed "Marie Antoinette de France." The Cardinal seemed not to have noticed this fanciful signature, unmistakable evidence of forgery, since queens always signed with their Christian names only. Rohan told his interlocutors that he was supposed to be in charge of the transaction. And to give them greater proof of trust, he took out of his secretary a small letter folded in half and read them these words: "I am not in the habit of transacting with my jeweler in this fashion. Therefore keep this paper at your house and work everything out as you think best."[12] Böhmer and Bassenge departed content: they had been freed of the unsalable item; the Cardinal had promised to request the sums owed to them at the dates set; and lastly, they were promised interest on the credit they had granted.

In the days that followed, they were surprised to see that the Queen did not wear the necklace. The Cardinal reassured them; the Queen had to bide her time before informing the King; she was waiting for the first payment to be settled at least. But around July 10, the situation suddenly took a turn for the worse. The Cardinal summoned them and announced that the Queen asked for a discount and could not honor the date of August 1. On the other hand, she promised to pay them 700,000 livres several days later. Since they had been forced to borrow money while waiting to be paid, the jewelers had no choice but to accept these conditions. Extremely worried, Böhmer decided to approach the Queen directly, which explains his giving her the note which she had found incomprehensible.

Breteuil asked the jewelers to quietly pursue their business while he had the Cardinal and his entourage secretly watched. The minister knew that this prince of the Church was deep in debt and associated with dubious, even dangerous, company. Did not the famous charlatan who went under the name of Comte de Cagliostro practically live at his house? Breteuil was convinced the Cardinal had thought up the necklace transaction in order to free himself of his creditors, and he persuaded the Queen of this. Marie Antoinette and the minister thought that in taking advantage of the Queen's name to set up a stupendous swindle, their enemy had sworn to bring about her downfall. Appearances seemed to support their view.

On July 31, Rohan summoned Böhmer and Bassenge, this time to tell them that the Queen could only pay the 700,000 livres in October. As compensation for the delay she was imposing on them, he gave them 30,000 livres on her behalf.

Another dramatic turn of events occurred several hours later. Saint-James, one of the richest bankers in the capital, was received, at his request, by the Abbé Vermond. He informed him that the Cardinal wanted to borrow 700,000 livres in the Queen's name. Saint-James was prepared to lend the sum, but wanted specific orders from the Queen before committing himself. On discovering a Machiavellian plan to cause her reputation irreparable damage, Marie Antoinette panicked. After having delayed too long in telling him about it, she now wanted to inform the King of this affair as soon as possible. After extended secret meetings with Breteuil and Vermond, it was decided that the minister would speak to Louis XVI on August 14, the eve of the Assumption, the Queen's name day.

21

THE DIAMOND

NECKLACE AFFAIR

*I*n spite of the oppressive summer heat, a large, splendid crowd packed the Hall of Mirrors at around noon, on August 15, 1785. The courtiers all vied in elegance to attend the celebration of the solemn mass in honor of the Queen. Cardinal de Rohan, magnificent-looking in surplice and cassock, strutted about as he waited for the sovereigns. To his great surprise, he was presently informed that the King expected him in the Council Room. Majestically, the Grand Almoner made his way to the royal apartment, his silk robe rustling as he walked. To his great astonishment, he found himself facing a kind of tribunal; Louis XVI, Marie Antoinette, Breteuil, Vergennes and the Lord Chancellor Miromesnil sat before him, expectantly.

Stunned by what he had just learned, Louis XVI had consulted his Minister of Foreign Affairs and his Lord Chancellor. These men disagreed with Breteuil. The latter was in favor of a public gesture against the Cardinal, who had insulted the Queen and committed a crime of lese majesty by negotiating offensively in her name. He suggested meting out an exemplary punishment. His two colleagues were more cautious, and recommended questioning Rohan before coming to any decision. The King followed their advice.

As soon as he found himself in front of the sovereigns and the three ministers, the Cardinal knew that he had not been summoned by Louis XVI to discuss the protocol of the holy mass.

"Did you buy diamonds from Böhmer?" the King asked him.

"Yes, Sire."

"What did you do with them?"

"I thought they had been given to the Queen."

"Who was it that commissioned you?"

"A lady called the Comtesse de La Motte-Valois, who showed me a letter from the Queen."[1]

Unable to contain her anger, Marie Antoinette interrupted him. Why would she ever have put him in charge of negotiating with her jeweler?

"I, who have not spoken to you since your return from Vienna; I, who have treated you with the utmost coldness and aloofness on all occasions; I, who never granted you the audiences you so stubbornly requested."

"Your Majesty gave me authorization," said the Cardinal, "with a hand-written signed document."

"Where is this document?"

"Sire, I have it in Paris in my portfolio."

"This document is a forgery," the Queen cried out.[2]

At which point the Cardinal gave her a look so lacking in respect that she blushed. As soon as Rohan left the room, Marie Antoinette burst into tears. She later admitted to Madame Campan that a frightening thought had crossed her mind in a flash. What if this whole plot had been carried out with the sole purpose of dishonoring her in the eyes of the King? The Cardinal could maintain she had received the necklace . . .

Won over by his wife's tears and Breteuil's entreaties, Louis XVI agreed to have Rohan arrested. The Lord Chancellor stepped out of the Council Room and called out in a loud voice: "Arrest Monsieur le Cardinal." Stupefaction in the Hall of Mirrors. The hour of mass had long since passed. An astonishing piece of news was expected, but certainly not the arrest of a prince of the Church, dressed in his priestly vestments, inside the Château de Versailles. This was an unprecedented scandal breaking in plain daylight. It could well tarnish the King and especially the Queen; the monarchy itself might come out shaken. Neither Marie Antoinette, Louis XVI nor Breteuil seemed to realize this.

Before being taken into custody, Rohan bent down as though he were readjusting his garter buckle, scribbled a few words for his personal secretary, the Abbé Georgel, and surreptitiously slipped the note into the hands of the valet who was with him. He asked Georgel to burn the compromising papers forthwith. Though brought to his Paris mansion under escort, the Cardinal was left alone for about an hour, which gave him the opportunity to continue burning documents. By the time Breteuil and the Police Lieutenant entered his house, the only papers they could place under seal were those Rohan had deemed useful to preserve. The following day, the Cardinal was taken to the Bastille prison. Several days later, so was the Comtesse de La Motte, who had been arrested in her house in Bar-sur-Aube in Champagne. Her husband had had time to escape.

The official investigation began. The King asked Vergennes and the Maréchal de Castries,[3] Minister of the Navy, to assemble the documents and proceed with a preliminary cross-examination of the Cardinal. Rohan was straightforward in telling his side of the story. This first confession was more or less similar to his later depositions. His unchanging version of the facts was this: In 1781, the Marquise de Boulainvilliers had recommended a young woman to him whom she had rescued from poverty, and who said she was a descendant of a bastard son of Henri II. After the death of her protectress, the young woman appealed to the Cardinal's generosity. Indeed, in spite of her marriage to a self-styled Comte de La Motte, she remained in financial difficulty. In 1784, having moved to Paris, she saw Rohan frequently, and led him to believe that she was on very friendly terms with the Queen. Knowing that the Cardinal was mortified at being held in disgrace by the Queen, she offered to intervene on his behalf. Rohan thanked her profusely when she told him that Marie Antoinette had agreed to grant him a secret interview in the gardens of Versailles, on a July night, around midnight.[4]

"At the designated hour," said the Cardinal, "I saw a woman appear, wearing a black headdress and holding a fan, with which she lifted her lowered headdress. By the light of the stars, I thought I recognized the Queen; I told her I was happy to find in her kindness the proof that she had reconsidered her prejudices against me; she said a few words in reply to me; and just as I was going to explain my conduct, she was told that Madame[5] and the Comte d'Artois were approaching. She left me abruptly and I did not see her again."[6]

Convinced, after this secret assignation, that he had entered into the Queen's good graces, the Cardinal willingly gave Madame de La Motte 50,000 livres when she claimed to be soliciting help for the needy on behalf of the Queen. In November, she requested another 100,000 livres for the same purpose. Rohan gave Madame de La Motte whatever she asked for. In January 1785, she told him that the Queen wanted him to enter into negotiations with Böhmer and Bassenge for the purchase of the famous necklace. She added that he was the only person Marie Antoinette trusted to successfully carry out such transactions. So he went to see the jewelers and gave the written sale conditions to La Motte, who brought them back, signed "Marie Antoinette de France." When Böhmer and Bassenge delivered the necklace to him, he showed them the signed contract, which he kept in his possession. On February 1, he brought the necklace to Madame de La Motte. A man dressed in black soon took the necklace to deliver it to the Queen. Several days later, Rohan was visited by the banker Saint-James, who wanted confirmation that Marie Antoinette had really bought the necklace, for the two jewelers were in need of a loan. The Cardinal was pleased to show the contract to Saint-James. From then on he heard nothing more, until that day in June when Madame de La Motte told him that the Queen found the necklace too expensive and requested new terms of payment.

After he had made this deposition, which completed the testimony of the two jewelers, the Maréchal de Castries asked the Cardinal if he had papers to substantiate his statements. Greatly embarrassed, Rohan replied that he had burned everything except the contract. Though the prelate did not admit it, Vergennes and Castries understood that he had destroyed what he believed were letters from the Queen. Indeed, how could he have shown such naïveté unless he believed he was in epistolary contact with the Queen?

Madame de La Motte was questioned. All her depositions contradicted those of the Cardinal. She had never spoken to the Queen, and Rohan had never given her the necklace. He had simply assigned her the task of selling some diamonds to some Jews. Castries and Vergennes were perplexed. Though the evidence weighed heavily against Rohan, they could not believe him guilty of such a giant swindle. On the other hand, Madame de La Motte certainly looked like the perfect adventuress; she was self-confident and seemed capable of the most outrageous lies. But at that point there was no proof against her. The contract was written in the Cardinal's name and he was convinced he had had a secret meeting with the Queen in the middle of the night. The two ministers sensed that any serious inquiry would lead to the discovery of shameful secrets.

The Queen had not interrupted the rehearsals of The Barber of Seville, but her mind was on the "Cardinal affair." On August 25, Louis XVI summoned Breteuil, Miromesnil, Castries and Vergennes to take stock of the situation. Pale and tense, Marie Antoinette was present at the meeting. She spoke: "I am being charged," she said. "The public will think I received a necklace and did not pay for it. I want to know the truth about a circumstance where they dared to use my name."[7] And she asked that the Cardinal be put on trial.

Fearing, quite rightly, the consequences of a public trial, Castries and Vergennes tried with all due respect to dissuade her. They suggested that the King, whence all justice in the kingdom emanated, settle the matter personally with the Cardinal. Breteuil and Miromesnil were of the opposite opinion. The Queen settled the matter. She asked that the Cardinal choose the jurisdiction he preferred. "May the affair proceed quickly, for I am compromised," she added, exasperated.[8]

Without further hesitation, Louis XVI ordered that this decision be sent to the Cardinal. The latter replied that he wished to be tried by the parliament of Paris. Nothing could have been more dangerous for the royal government, because this court, which was both a law court and a registration chamber for the royal edicts, had systematically opposed all of Louis XVI's decisions since 1774. Given the passions involved, the King's authority was in great danger of being weakened by this inquiry.

"It is a strange fiction, in the eyes of the entire country, that I would want to give the Cardinal a secret errand," the Queen wrote her brother, after having given him a brief account of this odd story. She complimented the "good sense and firmness" with which Louis XVI had acted in these circumstances. "In any case, I want this entire horror and all its details to be cleared up to everyone's satisfaction," she asserted, underestimating the dangers to which she was exposing herself.[9]

Relieved at the thought that her honor would be saved by the Cardinal's imminent sentencing, Marie Antoinette managed to play the part of Rosine with a grace and verisimilitude that many an actress would have envied. At least this was the opinion of the Baron Grimm. On the day after this theatrical success, the court went to live at Saint-Cloud. The Queen was delighted with this new estate. She took barouche drives with the Comte d'Artois. As in the beginning of her reign, she was often seen in the Bois de Boulogne. In the evening, the proximity of the capital permitted many escapades. Wiser than at Trianon, Marie Antoinette allowed the common people to come into the gardens. Eager to see this château which they did not know and amused by the sight of the royal family strolling around the grounds, the Parisians came to the slopes of Saint-Cloud in droves on Sundays. Outdoor cafés and dance halls opened along the Seine, attracting a mob that included unsavory individuals intensely disliked by the King. On some days, the crowds were such that Marie Antoinette thought she had regained her former popularity. She would then take the Dauphin in her arms and, radiant, show him to all the people around her, who applauded as in the theater. She had no inkling that this crowd had come for entertainment, and approached her only out of curiosity. These individuals who came to see the "Austrian woman's" fountains were vaguely curious to see if they would have a chance to penetrate the secrets of one who was so vilified.

Tongues wagged. The malicious chatter was echoed in the newspapers. People were enthralled by this strange drama, which had as its protagonists a queen of France and a prince of the Church. However, though everyone delighted in describing the libertine prelate's debauchery, Marie Antoinette was far from spared. Many people believed that she had accepted the gift of the necklace in exchange for her favors. It was even insinuated that she had used Rohan to transmit state secrets to her brother and send on boxes of gold! The most insane rumors were heard. Of all the gossip, the Queen only retained the stories concerning Rohan's private life. For her, it was a small step from debauchery to dishonesty, taken all too quickly and easily by this great nobleman, who was in addition a man of the Church. "The Cardinal used my name like a vile counterfeiter," she told her brother. "It is possible that, needing money, he thought he could pay the jewelers at the date he had fixed without anything being discovered . . . As for me, I am delighted not to hear anything more about this horror, which cannot come up for trial before December."[10] The Emperor, however, was perplexed. He was aware of Rohan's frivolousness, but could not believe he was guilty of such an enormous swindle. Yet he saw the risks involved for his sister in an affair of this kind.

Marie Antoinette tried to forget her problems. On October 10, she arrived in Fontainebleau, on a magnificent yacht which had sailed down the Seine to the thunderous sound of the cannons of the Invalides. It had been her whim to have this pleasure boat built for her; English in style, it included a drawing room with mahogany paneling, boudoirs decorated with marble and even a kitchen. This extravagance had cost a paltry 100,000 livres. Smiling and apparently relaxed, the Queen glided past her subjects like an inaccessible goddess.

In spite of the balls, concerts, plays, hunting expeditions and entertainments she had planned, Fontainebleau was no fun. She was bad at concealing her restlessness, and failed to amuse herself. One could sense that this woman, usually so gracious and self-confident, was afflicted with a weariness close to disgust. Though she did not admit it, the affair of the necklace was her foremost preoccupation. She kept herself informed daily about the judicial inquiry, which was not proceeding at all as she had hoped.

The magistrates' task was not an easy one. Breteuil had given his orders: the Cardinal was to be exposed as a swindler and forger and responsible for the whole machination; Madame de La Motte was not his accomplice. However, these gentlemen of the parliament were increasingly skeptical. By matching depositions and arresting—not without difficulty—witnesses essential to an understanding of the story, they were gradually unraveling the incredible imbroglio.

Madame de La Motte, the Cardinal de Rohan's mistress, who lived off the liberal gifts of her powerful protector, had seen in him a man gullible enough to become the instrument of a swindle which she herself instigated completely on her own. To convince him that she was on excellent terms with the Queen and that Her Highness was willing to forget the strife that had estranged her from the Cardinal, she resorted to a subterfuge. In the gardens of the Palais-Royal, on a beautiful summer evening, Monsieur de La Motte met a pretty prostitute who looked like the Queen and who went under the name Mademoiselle d'Oliva. He immediately introduced her to his wife, who promised the woman a tidy sum of money to play a part that was easy to play, at night, near the grove known as *"le bosquet de Vénus,"* in the gardens of Versailles. Mademoiselle d'Oliva needed no coaxing to accept. When the big day arrived, Madame de La Motte personally dressed the young woman and gave her strict instructions. And thus it was that Rohan thought he was paying homage to the Queen when he was actually genuflecting before a trollop. Fearing that her trick would be discovered, Madame de La Motte found a way of quickly bringing the interview to a close.

After that, it was important to avoid arousing the Cardinal's suspicions, for he might have been surprised that Marie Antoinette continued to be just as cold to him as before the nocturnal encounter. The scheming "countess" had anticipated everything. She led Rohan to believe that the Queen wanted to have a secret correspondence with him. So periodically she handed him alleged letters from the Queen, letters that were actually written under her dictation by her sweetheart, a certain Réteaux de Villette. This man confessed to having written about a hundred that were, he said, "intimate and tender." These were the letters which Rohan destroyed when he was arrested. As for the Cardinal's letters, Madame de La Motte had kept them in a trunk at Bar-sur-Aube. Comte Beugnot, who would later become Louis XVIII's minister, but was then only a young lawyer in love with Madame de La Motte, helped her burn them. He was to recall that their tone was equivocal, to say the least!

Madame de La Motte, who had until then extorted large sums of money from Rohan, now wanted more. The opportunity arose when she met the two jewelers. She next cooked up a scheme in which Rohan would be the victim. She told him of the Queen's desire to purchase the necklace and had her forger-lover write up the contract signed "Marie Antoinette de France." The prelate let himself be taken advantage of. The necklace which Rohan brought Madame de La Motte for the Queen was handed to a stooge, none other than Réteaux de Villette. With the help of her husband and Réteaux, La Motte took this exceptional piece of jewelry apart in crude fashion. And Monsieur de La Motte began to sell off the diamonds—dirt cheap. This was the scenario the magistrates had more or less pieced together.

The Cardinal, who adhered to his version of the facts, could not prove anything. His relatives and friends had fully understood that someone desired his downfall and wanted to pin the responsibility for all the crimes on him. They therefore conducted their own investigation parallel to the official one. It was they who led to the discovery of Madame de La Motte's accomplices. When they were finally arrested, they provided the needed proofs. Mademoiselle d'Oliva and Réteaux de Villette, among others, admitted their crimes and incriminated Madame de La Motte.

As the investigation proceeded, Marie Antoinette's mood darkened. Public opinion held that Rohan was the Queen's victim and persisted in believing her guilty. People seized on the defense lawyers' published speeches, reveling in this legal literature spiced with novelistic details. And the lampoonists were in their element, exploiting the grove scene shamelessly. Never before had the Queen been so dragged in the mud. She felt shattered by the avalanche of calumnies. The Cardinal's trial became her trial, a trial in which she could not defend herself by intervening before the magistrates through Mercy and Breteuil. Instead of assisting her, this attitude helped hurt her reputation. By insisting that the Cardinal be convicted of fraud, forgery and offense to the royal majesty, she was hindering the course of justice. Though some magistrates were completely devoted to the traditional monarchy and the person of Louis XVI, most of them fiercely criticized what they called "royal despotism" and refused to let a legal decision be dictated to them, particularly by the Queen. Upon rereading the instructions which had been transmitted to them by Mercy and Breteuil, the public prosecutor felt very embarrassed. "We have all reconsidered the proposed plan," he wrote the president on May 21, 1786. "It cannot be reconciled with what we have before our eyes" (in other words, with the depositions and the confessions of the witnesses and the accused).

For the magistrates, Madame de La Motte was the principal guilty party in the swindle; it was therefore appropriate to punish her and her accomplices. As for the Cardinal, his crime was one of lese majesty; he had been so foolhardy as to believe that the Queen could give him a rendezvous in the Versailles garden and ask him to negotiate a jewel in her name.

On May 30, in the middle of a tense, emotional crowd, with the entire Rohan clan attending the hearing in mourning attire, the attorney general summed up the case against the defendants. He dwelled on the Cardinal's case, gravely stressing the "insult" committed against the person of the Queen and, by extension, of the King. He denounced the Cardinal's "temerity," which he saw as "a crime requiring the most authentic and solemn reparations." The assistant public prosecutor, who spoke after him, adopted an entirely different tone, clearly insinuating that his colleague had literally sold out to the court. The testimony of the accused and the witnesses added nothing new to the case. Rohan made an excellent impression on his judges, appearing even though he was sick and declaring that he "had been completely blinded by his great desire to regain the Queen's good graces." As for Madame de La Motte, who stubbornly denied all accusations against her, she was thought to be what she was, a dangerous adventuress.

The sentencing session on the following day, May 31, started at six in the morning. An enormous crowd congregated in front of the Palace of Justice and the neighboring streets. Bets were taken. People waited for the verdict until ten o'clock at night! Few were moved by the fate of Madame de La Motte and her accomplices. Found guilty, Henri II's alleged descendant was sentenced to be publicly flogged, branded with hot irons with a "V" for *voleuse* (thief) and imprisoned for life. Her husband, who had fled to England, was sentenced to the galleys in absentia. With the exception of Réteaux, who was to be banished from the realm, their associates were "expelled from the court," which brought no real reaction on the part of the public. But when news came of the Cardinal's acquittal, the crowd broke out in jubilation. There were cries of *"Vive le cardinal!"* and several thousand sympathizers accompanied him to the Bastille, where he still had to spend one night.

For the Queen, this was truly a painful blow. She expected an ignominious punishment to be meted out against Rohan, and it was inconceivable to her that the magistrates should fail to follow the ministry's orders. That they should dare reach a verdict other than the one she had dictated seemed to her a second crime of lese majesty. She burst into tears when she heard the sentence. In an attempt to soothe her in her despair, Mercy persuaded her that it was solely through the underhanded maneuvers of Rohan's relatives that the Queen of France's honor could have been held up to ridicule.

Indignant at the verdict, Louis XVI demanded Rohan's resignation as Grand Almoner and exiled him to his abbey of La Chaise-Dieu in Auvergne. This measure gave offense to the Cardinal's partisans, both noble and bourgeois. Since the parliament had cleared the Cardinal, the punishment inflicted by the sovereign led people to cry out against tyranny. The King thereby managed to completely alienate a parliament that had already opposed him on several occasions since his accession. Criticism of royal absolutism grew stronger and the parliament gauged its power in relation to that of the King.

This incredible scandal permanently tarnished the Queen's image. She was blamed for interfering, though there was no formal proof that she had. There was speculation that she had engineered the entire thing in order to bring ruin on a man she loathed. She had been at the center of a trial during which the magistrates had tried to avoid compromising her by hardly ever mentioning her. But many questions were raised concerning her real role in the affair. The accumulation of years of irresponsibility and frivolousness told against her. The liberties she had taken pleaded in favor of the Cardinal. Had she not bought jewels behind the King's back? And was the meeting in the grove so unusual for a Queen who used to stroll around the grounds of the château incognito late at night? If the Cardinal, who was well acquainted with the court, let a schemer so thoroughly take advantage of him, it was surely because he knew the Queen was capable of depraved acts. Some people went so far as to wonder whether Rohan had not intentionally played the fool in order to save the Queen's honor.

Because of this unfortunate affair, Marie Antoinette would be seen as a perfidious and debauched woman who squandered the coffers of the kingdom for her personal pleasure, and who took advantage of the King's weakness, betraying him as a husband to satisfy her lustful instincts and as a sovereign to serve the interests of the Austrian Emperor.

22

"MADAME DEFICIT"

This ordeal had brought Marie Antoinette closer to her husband and, to her great disappointment, at the beginning of the winter she found she was pregnant. It took several weeks for her to acknowledge her new condition, which she was very unwilling to accept. Fearing her sudden changes of mood, the physicians dared not confirm their diagnosis. By February 15, she had to face up to the facts, and she made her discontent known to her brother, who lectured her once again on her wifely duties. But the reprimand left her unmoved. She was content with three children and the future of the dynasty seemed assured with two sons, even though the Dauphin's health was a growing cause for concern. The child was still frail and shivered with fever every night.

Even with Fersen present, the winter and spring were gloomy at Versailles, with everyone elegantly bored. Irritated by her unwanted pregnancy, anguished by the trial which made her a prey to the most despicable lampoonists, the Queen found she could not organize the court pleasures as was her wont. She no longer danced, but spent her evenings playing billiards and backgammon with the Comte d'Artois and his little set. She scrapped her wardrobe. She would have no more eccentricities! No more of the Polish-, Circassian- or Turkish-style dresses that she had adored up until then. No more extravagant hats. Mademoiselle Bertin had to design more classical, sensible clothes, as can be seen in Madame Vigée-Lebrun's large painting of the Queen with her children. Wearing a lush red velvet dress trimmed with dark fur and a hat of the same fabric with white plumes, Marie Antoinette is holding the little Duc de Normandie on her lap; Madame Royale is tenderly leaning on her arm while the Dauphin, in a lace-trimmed red velvet costume, is uncovering the crib, a symbol of the expected birth. The Queen looks happy; she still projects the image of a fulfilled mother in spite of the problems beginning to beset her.

When Marie Antoinette learned of the disastrous verdict in the necklace affair, Fersen had left to rejoin his regiment. As for Louis XVI, from June 20 to 29, he was away from Versailles on a propaganda trip in Normandy. He returned ecstatic, the extremely warm welcome given him by his provincial subjects leading him to believe that the monarchy had many happy days ahead. When he returned to the château, the Queen and the children were waiting for him on the balcony overlooking the marble courtyard. As soon as the little princes saw their father, all three cried out "Papa!" with touching joy. Several days later, on July 9, Marie Antoinette gave birth to a very big baby girl named Sophie Hélène Béatrice. She was to live only nine months.

The Queen recovered from her confinement rather quickly and regained a certain joie de vivre, in spite of the visit of her sister Maria Christina and her husband, Prince Albert of Sachsen-Teschen. This older sister, who governed the Austrian Netherlands in the name of the Emperor, did not receive a very warm welcome from her. Being unaware of Mercy's constant indiscretions about her, Marie Antoinette was firmly convinced that it was Maria Christina, well informed by the Brussels newspapers, who had spitefully kept the Empress apprised of her former follies. Though she did not know why, Maria Christina understood full well that the Queen of France was annoyed by her presence, and she did not insist on sharing her intimacy.

The summer was darkened by the beginnings of a financial crisis that was of serious concern to Louis XVI. Calonne had been Minister of Finance for three years. A skillful administrator, he had benefited from the trust of the big bankers. With Du Pont de Nemours as one of his foremost advisers, he wanted to develop and modernize the French economy. Shortly after the peace treaty with England, he had negotiated a free trade agreement between the two powers. He often stated that a policy of austerity was not profitable and that some expenses could actually be productive. Thus he started urban improvements in Bordeaux, Marseille and Lyon. He was having a military port built in Cherbourg, which Louis XVI had just visited. But Calonne had made expenditure into a doctrine. He had paid off the debts of the King's brother, negotiated the purchase of Saint-Cloud for the Queen and the Château de Rambouillet for the King. A member of the Polignac coterie, he had dipped into the Treasury extensively and granted scores of unwarranted pensions. He had borrowed large sums to support his policies. The loans financing the American war had put a strain on the budget. The state expenses were constantly on the rise and difficult to curtail. Interest on the debt alone represented 50 percent of the budget. As for court expenditures, though they represented a mere 6 percent, plus 2 percent for the pensions, they were particularly showy and unpopular. The shocking thing was the disproportion between the exorbitant pensions granted to the princes and favorites and the bulk of truly modest pensions given to the real servants of the state—for instance, elderly officers.

In 1786, to his great surprise, Calonne found he could no longer raise any loans. Realizing that the crisis could only be solved by overhauling the taxation system, he presented the King with a "Specific Plan for the Improvement of Finances," which amounted to making taxes equal and proportionate for all. This measure, which seems perfectly unobjectionable to us, was considered revolutionary at the time, for in the long term it threatened to upset the class society of prerevolutionary France, where each person's status was determined by birth. People who were born into the nobility had many privileges, among them being exempt from the *taille*, a tax arbitrarily assessed according to external signs of wealth. This extremely unpopular payment applied to all French citizens. It seemed obvious that equality in taxes would, in time, bring about civil equality. Louis XVI, who was quite open to short-term reforms, was wary of taking a decision whose consequences would call into question the social system to which he was still attached. However, Calonne finally convinced him that it was necessary. Foreseeing that the parliament, composed of privileged men, would refuse to support the measure, the King and the minister decided to convene, in an advisory capacity, an assembly of notables; in other words, leading personalities who were carefully chosen to approve this fundamental reform.

An unspoken anxiety plagued the King. More than ever, he needed the help of a faithful adviser. But Vergennes, who had been his mentor since Maurepas's death, was very ill. When he died on February 13, 1787, the King wept. "I have lost the only friend I could rely on, the only minister who never betrayed me," he said sadly. His death became the occasion for vicious rumors. The Queen was said to have had her husband's collaborator poisoned out of revenge—for hadn't she, a number of times, been opposed to his Austrian policy? And hadn't Vergennes timidly supported the Cardinal de Rohan? This despicable accusation was just one among many that were being spread in scurrilous lampoons throughout the kingdom.

Mercy was on the alert. His hope was that the Queen would get Saint-Priest—as the minister most congenial to Austrian interests—appointed to succeed Vergennes. But to the ambassador's great disappointment, and that of his superiors, the Queen refrained from interfering. She supported her husband, whose distress she could plainly see, and she cared more about the domestic situation than the fate of the alliance. She even said to Mercy that "it was not right for the Viennese court to appoint ministers to the court of Versailles."[1] The ambassador was furious.

Calonne's recommended convocation of notables started under the most unfavorable auspices. Though made up of handpicked men of privilege, the assembly immediately opposed the Finance Minister's reforms because these were detrimental to the majority of them. But the notables made it seem like they were attacking the minister's management rather than the proposed reforms. Louis XVI no longer knew where to turn. "He would have rescued me from this," he sighed, discouraged, recalling Vergennes. On April 4, 1787, with work suspended for a week, Loménie de Brienne, Archbishop of Toulouse and leader of the opposition to Calonne, brought the Queen a memorandum, which he begged her to deliver to the King. He requested Calonne's dismissal and, in a sense, solicited the position for himself.

Quite unwillingly, because of the circumstances, Marie Antoinette began to intervene in domestic politics by recommending Loménie de Brienne's candidacy to her husband. Though Louis XVI was hostile to this clergyman with dissolute morals, the Queen had long been favorably predisposed to him. Vermond had always praised this prelate who had been protecting him for over fifteen years. Furthermore, Joseph II, who had had occasion to exchange ideas with him, held him in high esteem. Given the King's despondent state, Marie Antoinette had no difficulty persuading him to dismiss Calonne and to replace him with the Archbishop of Toulouse. The notables applauded the change. This brightened the royal household. Alas, not for long.

Aware of the King's aversion to him, Loménie de Brienne skillfully cultivated the Queen's favor. He wanted her to play an active part in the government in order to strengthen his personal position. Appreciative of the prelate's respectful attitude, she stood steadfastly behind his reforms, and began by significantly reducing the expenses of the royal household. She thus let in the winds of change, regardless of her little social set's recriminations, for they were incensed by measures which infringed on their privileges. Calonne's friends, furious at their darling's dismissal, already resented the Queen for the appointment of Loménie de Brienne. When they realized they were to be the victims of direct measures taken by the King and the Queen, they did nothing to conceal their anger.

The first outburst occurred when Louis XVI asked the Duc de Coigny to give up his position as First Equerry. Though the request was made with great consideration, the Duke dared to lose his temper with the King. The court was shocked, but it sided with Coigny rather than with the monarch. When the Queen bitterly complained of Coigny's behavior to Besenval, he had the effrontery to reply, "Madame, he loses too much to be content with compliments. It is dreadful to live in a country where one is not sure of possessing one day what one owned the day before! That used to happen only in Turkey."[2] The Duc de Polignac had to be begged in all kindness to resign from his position as Director General of the Post-Horses. Marie Antoinette had had to entreat him in Loménie de Brienne's presence. Vaudreuil lost his position of Grand Falconer. One after the other, the favorites had to give up some of their emoluments. The Queen kept to this new policy, though it estranged her from her customary friends without reviving her popularity. She saw Madame de Polignac much less often, and now preferred to spend her evenings at the home of her Mistress of the Robes, the Comtesse d'Ossun. A relative of the late Choiseul (he had died in 1785), she often received the Queen for dinner with four or five companionable guests. She organized concerts with fashionable musicians and threw occasional small balls where Marie Antoinette still agreed to dance a quadrille.

The summer of 1787 looked bleak. On June 14, Marie Antoinette, to her great sorrow, lost her younger daughter. The Dauphin's health was worsening. Great optimism was required to believe that this unfortunate child would live. Marie Antoinette complained to the Emperor with sadness: "Though he was always weak and delicate, I did not expect the attack now afflicting him," she wrote. "His height is affected by one hip being higher than the other and by the vertebrae in his back that are slightly displaced and jut out. For some time now, he has had a fever every day and is very thin and weakened."[3] The Marquis de Bombelles was moved to pity on seeing this hunchbacked child: "I could have cried," he said, "if I had dared, over the pitiful state I found him in, bent like an old man, opening his dying eyes, his complexion pallid. He fears society, he is ashamed of showing himself."[4] The physicians, who dared not tell the unfortunate parents the truth, claimed that the Dauphin was suffering from the effects of an exceptionally difficult teething! They consulted the anatomist Petit. He persuaded them that he could straighten the young patient's body by making him wear an iron corset. He only succeeded in further torturing the child. Madame Royale, who was growing normally, was losing her childhood charm. She seemed downcast and her haughty personality gave her dignified little being a dry appearance. Only the handsome Duc de Normandie brought cheer to the Queen. "He has in strength and health everything that his brother is lacking. He is a real peasant's child, big, fresh-faced and fat," she wrote to the Emperor.[5] The physicians, alas, were less optimistic. They were worried by the young prince's frequent, violent convulsions.

Marie Antoinette's only true solace was Fersen's company. Having returned to France in April 1787, Axel divided his time between Versailles and his regiment. The bond between him and the Queen grew stronger. According to the Comte de Saint-Priest, she "had found a way of getting the King to accept her liaison with Count Fersen. She repeated to her husband all the comments she heard and which the public made about this affair and offered to stop seeing him, but the King demurred. No doubt she insinuated to him that amidst the torrent of malice against her, this foreigner was the only person who could be relied on . . . Meanwhile, Fersen went riding in the park near Trianon three or four times a week; the Queen did the same, and these meetings caused a public scandal in spite of Fersen's modesty and restraint in never revealing anything on the outside."[6]

It seems, in fact, that quarters had been installed for him above Marie Antoinette's apartment. Fersen's correspondence notebook shows that he wrote to "Joséphine" on March 3, 1787: "Plan of living upstairs; she should reply at the regiment; I will be there May 15." On April 20, he notes again: "What she must find for me to live upstairs." On October 8: "She should have a recess made for the stove; I will leave on the 18th to be in Paris on the 19th and with her in the evening; she should send me a letter at home at three or four o'clock to tell me what I must do."[7] At first glance it seems very surprising that a Swedish colonel in the service of France should be discussing stoves with the Queen! It is even more surprising to read the following note addressed to the Director General of Buildings, on October 10: "The Queen has sent for the Swedish stove maker who made the stoves in

Madame's apartment, and Her Majesty ordered him to make one for one of her inner rooms, with heating pipes to warm a small neighboring room."[8] A number of technical details follow concerning the assembling of the hearth. No doubt the Queen wanted to have a pleasantly heated room to keep the man she loved near her.

Such liberties could not fail to amaze people. Though it was known that the Queen had arranged to have a mechanism installed which allowed her to jam all the doors to her room simply by pulling a cord from her bed, the exact layout of her private apartment was not known. Besenval, one of her close friends, makes this clear. He recounts how Madame Campan led him through an incredible maze of corridors and stairways to a small apartment, separate from her inner rooms, which he had not known about. On that day, Marie Antoinette had given the old roué a secret appointment to determine the conditions of a duel between the Comte d'Artois and the Duc de Bourbon. "I was surprised," said Besenval, "not by the fact that the Queen had wanted so many accommodations, but by the fact that she had been so bold as to secure them."[9] While strolling around a deserted Versailles after 1789, the page Félix d'Hézecques was amazed to discover "a host of little apartments connected to the Queen's apartment" whose existence he had never suspected. "Most of them were dark," he said, "giving out on small courtyards. They were furnished simply, nearly all with mirrors and wood paneling."[10] The Queen protected her private life better than anyone imagined.

Marie Antoinette was becoming more and more unpopular. In the midst of the financial crisis, she was blamed for all the kingdom's woes. Her expenditures were denounced as the bottomless well that had absorbed the public resources. The necklace affair was again talked about when Madame de La Motte escaped. With the help of mysterious accomplices, this adventuress had found asylum in England, where Calonne had taken her under his protection. (The disgraced minister had chosen exile over an uncertain position in France.) It was rumored that the Queen had facilitated the schemer's departure in the hope that Monsieur de La Motte would stop publishing compromising letters. Moreover, Madame de Polignac and Vaudreuil had suddenly left for London and people said it was in order to negotiate the restitution of those papers with the La Motte couple. Though no details are known about their trip, we do know that when she returned from London, Madame de Polignac found her apartment newly repainted and refurnished courtesy of the Queen. Subsequently, Madame de Lamballe, followed by the

Abbé de Vermond, went to the British capital as well. These mysterious comings and goings on the part of the Queen's good friends gave rise to countless suspicions and further calumny.

Pamphlets and caricatures flourished. The Queen was a favorite target. She was maligned in countless prints. One of them showed the royal family seated at a table with the caption "The King drinks, the Queen eats and the people cry out." At the theater, the verses in Greek tragedy censoring cruel princesses were applauded wildly. Marie Antoinette was compared to all the wicked queens of history. At the Salon of paintings, since Madame Vigée-Lebrun had failed to meet the deadline in finishing the painting of the Queen and her three children, an empty frame was exhibited for several days. In place of the painting, a wit had written: "Here is the deficit!" "Madame Deficit," this was the Queen's new nickname. First the epigram, then the insult.

23

"MY FATE IS TO

BRING BAD LUCK"

*T*he Queen sensed that a new era was dawning. When she went to Paris, she was met with glacial silence. One evening, she found a sign posted on her loge at the Théâtre des Italiens with the terrifying words: "Tremble, tyrants, your reign is ending!" She was hissed in the theater at Versailles. "The Queen is quite universally detested," Fersen admitted. "Every evil is attributed to her and she is given no credit for anything good . . . The King is weak and suspicious; the only person he trusts is the Queen, and they say she does everything."[1] Louis XVI was in a state of deep depression from which no one seemed able to rescue him. His silence distressed his ministers. He brightened only during his endless hunting expeditions; afterward, he ate huge meals and rose from the table looking haggard, just about able to collapse in bed and fall asleep. Many people claimed that he drank, but well-informed habitués such as Mercy and Fersen denied it categorically. Never had the monarch been so oppressed by the burden of power. He seemed eager to relinquish it to anyone capable of taking it. Therefore, Loménie de Brienne needed the Queen; he had already persuaded her to sit on the interministerial committees where most decisions were made.

Marie Antoinette, as we know, never had a lust for power, in spite of Mercy's constant proddings dating back to the early days of the reign. However, since she had strength of character of the kind her husband lacked, and because the Austrian ambassador was the adviser she listened to most dutifully, she was suspected, very early on, of wanting to personally influence the affairs of the kingdom. Though they had virtually no impact, her interventions in support of Austria, inspired by her family and upheld by Mercy, had harmed her irreparably. Her scenes with Vergennes had left their mark. She was thought of as an agent for foreign interests, and had earned the grim nickname of *l'Autrichienne*, which had increasingly unpleasant connotations. Though her influence on the domestic front had been confined to a few more or less successful appointments dictated by mood, people were convinced that the Queen imposed her will on the King and that she had colluded with her favorites in bringing about France's ruin.

Loménie de Brienne's desire to have Marie Antoinette play an active role aggravated matters and further discredited her. "The Queen is governing!" became the public outcry, an outcry in which hatred was mixed with contempt. However, this woman who was completely unprepared for the realities of power suddenly felt compelled to take up the challenge. Lacking any political knowledge, or any knowledge about conditions in the kingdom, Marie Antoinette reacted by instinct. Viscerally afraid of any change in the established order, she could not contemplate any significant reforms. She rejected with horror anything that might diminish the power of the royalty, which she viewed as immutable and by nature absolute. This was her political credo. She would try to preserve the status quo at all costs. Madame de Staël, the daughter of the Finance Minister Necker, later wrote: "Since she always remained convinced that any restriction placed on the crown's authority was a misfortune, she inevitably fell under the influence of people who thought as she did."[2] Known not to be particularly lenient, foreign observers looked upon this takeover of the government by the wife of Louis XVI with alarm. "The Queen is more hated but more powerful than ever. She has left her frivolous social circle and is busy with public affairs, and since she has no head for methodical thinking she will go from whim to whim," said the new ambassador from Prussia, Herr Alvensleben, to Frederick William II.

However, the Queen did nothing more than listen to Loménie de Brienne, whose task was becoming more difficult with every passing day. Though he had criticized the management of his predecessor, Calonne, the prelate had made more or less the same proposals himself. But to his astonishment, he had met with immediate opposition on the part of the notables. It was obvious they wanted to restrict the power of the royalty. Finally, one day the Marquis de Lafayette declared that the Estates General[3] should be convened, implying this would be a "truly national assembly." Declaring themselves incompetent in tax matters, the notables implicitly invited the King to hold this grand consultation. Failing to impose his will on his former colleagues, Brienne advised the monarch to dismiss them, while promising them that he would draw inspiration from their deliberations in framing his future policy. Appointed Prime Minister, Brienne worked unremittingly to set up a vast plan of reforms in the hope of solving the financial crisis which was becoming increasingly serious.

Since the meeting of notables, public opinion ran wild. Everyone prided himself on being an "opponent." No one dared to defend the cabinet. Nor was the King himself spared. The lampoonists showed him in a pathetic light. Public affairs were debated in the recently formed clubs, and the concepts of liberty and equality exalted. Some people advocated an English-style monarchy, others the subordination of Louis XVI to the parliament. Subsidized by the banker Kornmann, several journalists employed their wit and satirical eloquence in writing incendiary pamphlets against the ministers and the court. Women threw themselves with passion into the stormy arena of political discussions. The Maréchale de Beauvau, the Princesses de Bouillon, d'Hénin and de Poix, all clamored for the return of Necker to power. The Princesse de Broglie, the Duchesse d'Aiguillon, the Marquises de Coigny and de Gontaut and the Comtesses d'Escars, de Lameth and de La Châtre, who proclaimed their "devotion to the popular cause, expressed the wish for public regeneration." The Duchesse d'Enville entertained Jefferson, Lafayette, the Duc de La Rochefoucauld-Liancourt and Condorcet in her home, where there was no end of praise for the American constitution, which had been translated into French by the very same Duc de La Rochefoucauld-Liancourt. In the Masonic lodges frequented by the liberal aristocracy and bourgeoisie, a financial reorganization was recommended, along with the suppression of all of the regime's social injustices. Paradoxically, the sovereign's weakness gave rise to violent criticisms of absolutism. Never before were people so stirred up. Louis XVI and Marie Antoinette were utterly dismayed. Though the King seemed to endure his fate with the gloomy indifference that alarmed his entourage, the Queen wanted to fight back, but did not know how to go about it. The open war waged against her by the Duc d'Orléans helped to completely unsettle her.

The Palais-Royal, his residence in Paris, was one of the main strongholds of the rebellion that drew more and more sympathizers. The times when the

dashing Louis Philippe Joseph, Duc de Chartres,[4] charmed the Queen's little court in the early days of the reign had long been consigned to oblivion.
His animosity could be traced back to wounded pride. Marie Antoinette had
made fun of him when he appeared triumphant at Versailles after a naval battle off the coast of Ouessant, at the beginning of the American war. The pre-
sumptuous young man claimed to have made a great contribution to the
French victory against the English, whereas he had actually jeopardized it
through an ill-considered maneuver. No doubt the King and Queen would
have forgiven his error if, out of incurable light-headedness and puerile conceit, he had not sought undeserved honors that he felt he was owed. His sub-
sequent intrigues to depose the ministers who had not supported him
doomed him as far as the royal couple was concerned. Too proud to pay
court to the sovereigns in the hope of being readmitted into their good
graces, he chose to cultivate the art of causing displeasure, and succeeded
beyond all expectation.

Since then, comments of courtiers had further inflamed relations
between the royal family and the House of Orléans. The Polignac coterie,
which was more powerful than that of the Princesse de Lamballe's, the Duc
de Chartres's sister-in-law, poured out torrents of venomous words against the
Duc de Chartres and his entourage. Courtiers on both sides exacerbated the
misunderstandings until unpardonable words had been spoken. Sulking
turned to hatred, and grievances proliferated. The Palais-Royal became a den
of malicious gossip directed against the Queen, who confined herself
increasingly to a small social circle, which now excluded the Orléans clan.
As the distance grew each day between him and the enchanted retreat to
which everyone dreamed of being admitted, the Duc de Chartres became
intensely frustrated. He was all the more cruel in his resentment against the
Queen, in that she had formerly greatly valued his companionship. With the
people in his circle, the Prince was unsparing toward Marie Antoinette; he
sought every opportunity to take revenge on a woman who had humiliated
him after having honored him with her attention. He even went so far as to
claim he had rebuffed her advances, and that this was the cause of her
extraordinary wrath. The Queen's friends enjoyed describing to her the Duc
de Chartres (now Duc d'Orléans) as the very incarnation of lustful perversity.
With each faction believing itself banished by the other, they developed a
mutual fear of each other, kindled out of all proportion by dreadful lampoons
and false reports.

Anglophile, light-headed, erratic, fickle, the Duc d'Orléans, like Marie

Antoinette, had no lust for power. He had always derived great pleasure from braving public opinion and thumbing his nose at absolutism. He fumed each time he had to request permission from the King to take a trip. And he fiercely defended what he saw as the principle of liberty. He protected artists and scholars who were followers of new ideas, and he was regarded as an enlightened man. No doubt he would have restricted himself to an attitude of provocative bravado except that, at the time, he came to represent a political stake in a society that was seething with excitement. His entourage persuaded him that he had an essential role to play. Some saw in him an alternative sovereign who accepted the principle of constitutional monarchy, while others wondered how to personally profit in making use of this cousin of the King, First Prince of Royal Blood, who owned the largest fortune in the kingdom. The magistrates in the parliament of Paris were particularly interested in him, for they could use a prestigious spokesman who would support their demands. Foreseeing that Louis XVI would need them, the most seditious paid assiduous court to the Duc d'Orléans while he let himself be intoxicated by all the agitation constantly swirling around him.

Loménie de Brienne's edicts for reform were to be presented to the parliament, which had no intention of approving them. In order to compel the magistrates to execute his wishes, Louis XVI came personally to the Palais de Justice on November 19, 1787. On the occasion of this exceptional session, the Duc d'Orléans, well coached by his advisers, had the audacity to speak out against the King. For the first time in the history of the monarchy, a prince dared to propose constitutional limits to absolutism and challenge the very essence of royalty. Flushed with rage, Louis XVI mumbled an awkward reply and walked out of the Palais de Justice in icy silence. Moments later, the Duc d'Orléans returned to the Palais-Royal in triumph.

The King and Queen felt betrayed within their very own family. The sovereign reacted immediately by exiling his cousin to his château, Villers-Cotterets. This caused turmoil in Paris. The Duc d'Orléans took on heroic stature. The parliament was jubilant; as for the other princes, they fought for their relative's cause. At Versailles intrigues were rampant. Though relieved to know that the Duc d'Orléans was far from Paris and powerless to form cabals against her, the Queen no longer knew where to turn. She questioned the sincerity of the friends on whom she had bestowed benefits. "On that score her illusions have nearly all vanished; there remain only a few momentary, superficial lapses whose effects are of little consequence; in fact necessity has closed the door to plunder and the Queen consents to no exorbitant demand," wrote Mercy. "Her heart is set on regaining the public's affection, though given the injustice and bizarreness of its judgments they would deserve to be treated with the utmost severity."[5] But the era of public relations advisers had not yet arrived. Painfully affected by calumny, the target of countless invisible enemies, the Queen avoided appearing in public. Driven by a new ardor, she turned her attention to the reforms in progress but did so, as Mercy himself put it, "with little method and no well-defined plan . . . From which there resulted a confusion which aggravated the evil instead of reducing it."[6] The problems overwhelming the King and Queen affected their health. Louis XVI came down with a serious case of erysipelas, while Marie Antoinette suffered from nonspecific ailments and put on weight.

To save money, amusements at Versailles were unexceptional, and there were fewer entertainments than usual in Paris. The only subject of conversation was politics. There was a strange climate at the masquerades of the 1788 carnival: a harlequin slapped Gabrielle d'Estrées[7] in the face, the most popular French king, Henri IV, had his hair pulled and Sully, his minister, was given a beating. These Mardi Gras incidents, which brought sympathetic smiles to the faces of many, augured much trouble to come.

Marie Antoinette trembled in fear of the day Madame de La Motte would publish a vengeful tract. It was expected at any moment, in spite of the precautions taken to avoid this kind of scandal. Entirely devoted to the Queen, Loménie de Brienne kept her abreast of political matters and described to her the parliaments' stubborn resistance, their unrelenting attacks on the King's rule and how they clamored for the convening of the Estates General. The constant conflict was turning into a test of strength. Soon, the provincial parliaments declared their solidarity with the Paris parliament. Several provinces rose up in support of the parliament members, backed by the local nobility. A movement called the "patriot party," or "national party," began to be formed. It attracted not only the supporters of the parliament but also, more importantly, all the partisans of a real constitution, which, they believed, only the Estates General was empowered to give to the kingdom. Liberal aristocrats and bourgeois quickly rallied to this party. Unable to control the situation, Loménie de Brienne seemed to sweep the King and Queen straight into the storm. On July 5, 1788, in the hope of restoring calm, he had to announce the convocation of the Estates General, though without giving a precise date.

Marie Antoinette deluded herself. She thought the government would prevail, and that they would avoid convening the Estates General. "The King is determined to uphold his laws and his authority," she wrote, full of hope, to the Emperor. On July 15, she settled at Trianon. Her usual social set kept her company, but she held no balls or fetes. They merely played games of bowls. Exhausted by his recent trials, the King went hunting in Rambouillet and slept there three nights a week, though he came to Trianon every day to dine with his family. On July 24, the Queen invited *Mesdames Tantes*. In their honor, twice as many dishes were served. The meal consisted of four soups, two main courses, sixteen first courses, four hors d'oeuvres, six roasts, two medium desserts and sixteen small desserts. It was just like the old days at Versailles—a succession of pâtés, cutlets, variety meats, fried turkey *á la ravigote*, calf sweetbreads *en papillotes*, spit-roasted suckling pig, duckling in orange sauce, chicken in white sauce, shin of veal, capon in bread crumbs, partridge, baby rabbit, Westphalian hams, scrambled and poached eggs, cream puffs, German waffles, a selection of cakes and many more offerings.

The envoys of Tippoo Sahib, King of Mysore, India, provided the great entertainment of the summer of 1788. The three representatives of this king arrived in Paris on July 16 to solicit France's protection in checking England's power. Their presence aroused the curiosity of the entire capital. After people had exhausted the future constitution and the financial crisis as subjects of conversation, they went on to discuss their customs and extravagant costumes for hours on end. All the courtiers wanted to be present at this unusual reception, which no one took very seriously. On the evening of August 12, a crowd of curious bystanders waited for the Indians at the Grand Trianon, which had been specially decked out to receive them. Accompanied by interpreters, the three ambassadors stepped out of the three coaches bearing the King's livery. They went into raptures over the beauty of the garden and palace and, as good Muslims, requested that the carpets representing human figures be removed. They were not allowed to use them for their devotions.

On the following day, for the solemn reception following mass, a throne had been set up for the King in the Hercules Room, with armchairs on either side intended for the Queen and the other members of the royal family. Amphitheaters had been erected for the public in every drawing room the ambassadors were to walk through. Preceded by the masters of ceremonies, the procession made its way through the apartments crowded with elegant women in daring low-cut dresses, which the foreigners found amazing. For this solemn occasion, the Indians had given up their native costume and kept only the headdresses. They had had a green-and-red European uniform of morocco leather made for themselves which was to serve as the prototype for a corps of sepoys. After their audience with the King, they were driven around the park in a barouche and treated to the spectacle of *les grandes eaux*—the fountains in the water garden. The ambassadors stayed in the Grand Trianon for several days, along with their turbaned slaves, who prepared for them what then seemed to the French extremely exotic dishes. New scents wafted through the gardens, of hot red pepper and curry mixed with garlic. Everyone wanted to taste these mysterious stews, but very few people, starting with the Queen, had the stomach to tolerate them.

The presence of these exotic guests distracted Marie Antoinette from her worries. She commissioned their portrait from Madame Tussaud, in order to immortalize their visit in an amusing manner. This artist of a new genre—to whom Parisians flocked to see celebrities of all ages represented in life-size wax statues—carried out the Queen's assignment to perfection. The mannequins of Tippoo Sahib's envoys, smoking their long pipes, and of their interpreter, were placed in one of the cottages in the Queen's hamlet.

While the splendors of Versailles were being offered to the Indians' astonished gazes, the financial situation had suddenly worsened dramatically. The coffers were empty. At the Stock Exchange, the royal securities were slipping from day to day. To reinstill confidence, Brienne announced the convening of the Estates General for the following May 1, but this failed to make the securities go up. On August 16, in desperation, the minister considered resorting to compulsory taxation. Panic erupted. Loménie de Brienne was held up to public obloquy. The Queen as well. She was held responsible for the minister's failures, just as if they had been her own. Louis XVI seemed incapable of making any decisions. And time was running out.

Marie Antoinette had understood that a reshuffling of the ministers was necessary. In her distress, she thought of recalling Necker, the only man deemed capable of saving the situation in the eyes of the general public. But she dreaded taking the step, for she was no more fond of the Swiss banker than the King was, and she feared his autocratic measures. Yet she felt he was their only recourse. She still had to convince Louis XVI to summon him and ensure that this former minister would accept the appointment, since he was being called back to power under disastrous conditions. The Queen needed an intermediary. Breteuil was the only person who could have spoken to the King, but he had resigned several weeks earlier because of his inability to get along with Loménie de Brienne. The Queen therefore assigned the double mission to Mercy, and he carried out her wishes. After talking to Louis XVI, who resigned himself to Necker's return, the ambassador went to see the Swiss banker. Rather reluctant at first, he asked for time to think about it before giving his reply. On August 25, he agreed to return to the cabinet, but only on condition that Loménie de Brienne resign.

Marie Antoinette was thrown into confusion. Her plan had succeeded. For the first time, she had taken a major political decision, and acted in the King's place. With Loménie de Brienne's departure, she felt she was losing the only guide she would ever follow. Suffering from a dreadful loneliness, aggravated by her ignorance of the affairs of the kingdom and assailed with gloomy forebodings, she wrote a few lines to Mercy, on the evening of August 25, the day of Saint Louis, the King's name day: "The Archbishop has left. I can't tell you, monsieur, how upset I am by the events of the day. I think this course of action was necessary, but at the same time I fear it will lead to misfortune . . . I have just written a short note to Monsieur Necker to tell him to come to see me here tomorrow at ten o'clock. There is no room for hesitation; if he can set to work tomorrow, it will be for the better. There is urgent work to be done. I tremble—forgive me this weakness—because it is I who am responsible for his return. My fate is to bring bad luck . . ."[8]

24

"DO YOU KNOW A WOMAN

MORE TO BE PITIED THAN ME?"

*I*n her inability to hide her apprehension in his presence, Marie Antoinette was very cold in welcoming the new minister. She was officially receiving a member of government for the first time, as if Louis XVI wanted to show that he included his wife in government. More sullen than ever, the King did not conceal his aversion for the Swiss banker whom he had been forced to summon. He was annoyed by this conceited, self-confident, infallible man who was idolized and whose popularity, he felt, was undeserved. "They made me recall Necker. I did not want to, but we won't be long in repenting for it. I'll do everything he tells me to do and we'll see the result,"[1] Louis XVI had cried out in impotent rage, shortly before the minister's arrival. That very evening, the Queen was particularly affable with Loménie de Brienne's close relatives. On the other hand, she treated the Baronne de Staël with haughtiness, making it obvious to her that she would have preferred to retain the Archbishop. This was an enormous blunder. In Paris, Necker's appointment had been greeted with outbursts of joy and the former minister had been burned in effigy. The King and Queen gave the cold shoulder to the man who might have been considered their savior and whose "democratic" ideas they feared. Whatever Necker did, Marie Antoinette "always felt he had been appointed by public opinion; and princes, in arbitrary governments, unfortunately become accustomed to regarding public opinion as their enemy," Madame de Staël wrote subsequently.[2]

The Queen had changed beyond recognition. Anxious, constantly on the defensive, she had lost her insouciance and gaiety. She still spent her evenings at Madame de Polignac's or Madame d'Ossun's in the presence of her friends, but she no longer spoke with the same freedom as she had in the past. She knew that her every remark would be discussed and distorted. Indeed, she had had several rather painful altercations with the Duchesse de Polignac, who had not refrained from criticizing Loménie de Brienne's policies. How could Marie Antoinette suspect that in aristocratic circles the King was now spoken of without the slightest respect, that he was mocked for his immoderate taste in hunting and for being so blind as to accept the little Duc de Normandie as legitimate?

The Queen found no comfort within the family circle. Consumed with ambition, jealous of his older brother, whom he considered unworthy of the crown, the Comte de Provence indulged in the most cruel, blunt banter when the three brothers and their wives dined together. The King did not know how to reply or how to silence him. The Comtesse de Provence, as was her habit, was extremely hypocritical in the Queen's presence, but as soon as she was out of earshot, she denigrated her openly and did not hesitate to call her, as did others, l'Autrichienne. (This is disclosed in her correspondence, which remained unpublished for many years.[3]) Moreover, this princess, to whom no one had ever paid the slightest attention, was in the midst of a passionate love affair with her female correspondent, who was actually a spy for England. Completely unaware of her lover's true character, Madame de Provence revealed to her the most intimate secrets about the royal family. As for the Comte d'Artois, who up to then had been content to lead a pleasant libertine's life, he suddenly discovered he had a political conscience, that of an extremely conservative prince, hostile to any innovative idea. His wife still stood out conspicuously as a nonentity.

At the time, the Queen was experiencing more problems than joys from her children. The Duc de Normandie had been inoculated and seemed to recover well from the procedure, but since some physicians claimed that an early inoculation was responsible for the Dauphin's heartrending state, she could not help but feel a deathly anxiety. It was probably at this time that she realized that her unfortunate older son did not have long to live. "Do you know a woman more to be pitied than me?"[4] she asked her old friend Count

Eszterhazy, whom she trusted completely and who often carried Fersen's letters to her. Fortunately, after a long absence, Axel returned to Paris in November 1788. He would remain in France until 1791, dividing his time between Versailles and his regiment.

In spite of Necker's appointment, the country was in complete turmoil. Though the minister's mere presence and his emergency measures had temporarily rekindled confidence in financial circles, the economic and social situation was still alarming. Very bad weather had been responsible for a catastrophic summer harvest and the price of bread had soared. There was a fear of shortages. Bakeries were looted; uprisings broke out in all the provinces. And the troops assigned to maintain order would sometimes shoot recklessly into the crowds. The Franco-British free trade agreement was decried in the strongest terms by French industrialists, who saw English products—cheaper than their own—flood the kingdom. Workshops shut down, and there was widespread unemployment in the manufacturing sector. This idle population, now lacking a means of subsistence, significantly increased the number of malcontents and swelled the ranks of the revolutionary masses disposed to take part in any demonstration or uprising. Everywhere throughout the land, the "patriotic party" demanded the convening of the Estates General.

Destined to play the role of Prime Minister without having the title, Necker had immediately understood that his task would go well beyond that of managing financial affairs. Though he was not an unconditional partisan of the Estates General, which he saw as possibly leading the monarchy down an unpredictable path, he insisted that the King confirm the forthcoming convocation, since the crisis had taken on proportions that no one could have predicted. With a heavy heart, Louis XVI resolved to do so. But the sovereign's conception of the Estates General did not conform at all to the aspirations of the "patriots." The King wished to proceed according to monarchical tradition, in the same spirit as in 1614, when the Estates General had last met. He regarded it as a kingdom-wide fiscal consultative assembly, whereas enlightened minds thought its function was to elect a national assembly that would draft a constitution for France.

The Estates General, an institution that dated back to the fourteenth century, had become obsolete. In order to raise exceptional taxes, ask for support or advice from his subjects, the King could assemble the deputies of the three large social categories of the realm, or orders as they were called— the clergy, the nobility and the Third Estate. Each of the three orders elected the same number of delegates, constituting three separate chambers. These chambers deliberated separately; their decisions were by majority vote. They never deliberated together; they voted as a unit and not as individuals. The absurdity of this kind of national representation at the end of the eighteenth century need not be pointed out. The Third Estate, nine-tenths of the nation, had half the number of deputies as the nobility and the clergy combined but only counted for one vote.

In a climate of general crisis, the entire country was engaged in a genuine debate concerning the nature of the regime. Everywhere the sole subject of conversation was the new constitution which would bring down despotism and wipe out privilege. Many privileged people started to panic, first and foremost the princes and the nobles at court. They insisted that the assembly be summoned as in 1614, which supposed a representation of the Third Estate that would be small in number and very elitist in social matters. But such considerations were no longer acceptable. Necker advised the King and Queen to ignore the pressures of their entourage and take measures that might secure them the sympathy of the patriots. Out of opportunism, Louis XVI and Marie Antoinette decided to favor the Third Estate over the first two orders combined. In the course of a special Council meeting, on December 27, attended, exceptionally, by the Queen and the King's brothers, Louis XVI announced his decision to double the number of representatives of the Third Estate. The Queen said nothing, but agreed with her husband. This decision was received with great disappointment by the general public, for it did not include the promise of voting as individuals.

To make matters worse, in addition to the poverty and the discontent, beginning in November, France had to endure exceptionally cold weather. The thermometer fell to minus 4 degrees Fahrenheit and dropped even lower in the course of the winter. In Paris, where the Seine was frozen over, several bridges had been swept away. The Police Lieutenant took a few measures to relieve the more destitute. Huge bonfires burned in front of the artistocrats' residences; bread was distributed. But it was the Duc d'Orléans who drew the most attention for his liberal charity. He organized the distribution of food in the street, set up heated shelters for the homeless and opened charity workshops for the unemployed. In Versailles, where the temperatures fell even lower than in Paris, there were bonfires at the crossroads and the King was often seen giving alms to the poor. In the park, the grand canal was frozen and the ice was twelve inches thick. Inside the château, people shivered under the gilded paneling. Heated with green, humid logs, the royal apartments reeked of acrid smoke.

In spite of the political disturbances and the harsh weather conditions, the first days of 1789 were marked by the ceremonies that had always rung in the new year, as far back as courtiers could remember. As in the past, shortly before midnight on December 31, the King took his seat in his Council Room. He watched the dials of the magnificent Passemant clock marking the hours, days, weeks, months and movements of the stars.[5] The birth of the new year took place under his eyes. Could Louis XVI possibly imagine that at the same time the following year he would not be watching the rotations of the enamel dials? The next morning, after the *lever*, followed by mass and the meal taken in public, the King and Queen received the best wishes of all the great bodies of the state. In the evening they dined in public again, with musical accompaniment. The immutable Versailles protocol could easily have misled the innocent visitor into thinking that nothing would ever change in the kingdom of France.

The Queen had never felt lonelier than in the first days of this new year. For several weeks she had hoped that the Estates General would take place in the provinces; but under pressure from Necker, the King had finally decided to summon them to Versailles. The task of facing a thousand—in principle hostile—representatives during all the ceremonies planned for this assembly was beyond her strength, she felt. And, above all, she worried about the power of the crown under such circumstances. An astute observer of the French court, Mercy minced no words in describing the "terror" that had taken possession of the King, the Queen and the court at the approaching Estates General, a harbinger, in his opinion, of "disastrous setbacks for the monarchy."[6]

Toward the end of March, all those who were apprehensive and feared such upheavals rallied round the Comte d'Artois. Princes and nobles advocated Necker's dismissal and his replacement by the Baron de Breteuil, who was very attached to the traditional monarchy. Since it was impossible to cancel the Estates General, the King should immediately deny them any power and thereby limit them to a mere advisory role. The Comte d'Artois discussed his recommendations with the Queen and she listened to him with interest. He then handed her a memorandum for the King outlining his plan. Louis XVI and Marie Antoinette studied it in great secrecy. Though the plan would have fulfilled their wishes, they thought it was too dangerous to implement. A change of cabinet, just a few days before the meeting of the Estates, would have been a show of strength which Louis XVI did not feel he could measure up to. Furthermore, by yielding to the Comte d'Artois and his supporters among the princes and the nobility, he ran the risk of becoming their hostage, which he wanted to avoid at all cost. Fearing the King's ambitious relatives, and trusting Necker only halfheartedly, Marie Antoinette was consumed with doubt just when the first representatives were arriving in Versailles. Yet Fersen had been with her since April 13. She had made him return from his regiment as soon as she heard that Axel's elderly father had been arrested on orders of Gustavus III. Indeed, the Swedish monarch feared being put under the supervision of the nobility and Senator Fersen was one of its most distinguished representatives.

May 4, 1789, the day of the procession marking the opening of the Estates General, was a radiantly sunny spring day. Versailles was invaded by a crowd as large as for the wedding of a prince. The windows along the road of the procession had been rented at exorbitant prices. The facades of the buildings were decorated with tapestries that were taken out only for great occasions. Musicians got ready to play at the street corners and regiments lined the main avenues. The din of a holiday grew since dawn. As of seven o'clock, the representatives of the three orders waited by the church of Notre-Dame for the King, the Queen, the princes and princesses. They stood around for three hours! Just as they were becoming impatient, the Duc and Duchesse d'Orléans drove up in a very simple carriage and were cheered at length. A hostile silence greeted the arrival of the other princes of the royal blood. At ten o'clock, the King and Queen finally drove up in their magnificent coach. Cheers went up for Louis XVI but sparse applause greeted Marie Antoinette, though she looked very beautiful in her mauve dress and elegant hairdo braided with flowers of a matching color.

The first religious ceremony was brief. They just listened to the *Veni Creator* at Notre-Dame before forming a procession and filing across town to the church of Saint Louis. The deputies of the Third Estate led the march, dressed in black and each carrying a candle. The nobility followed, proud in their plumed hats and black suits trimmed with gold cloth facing. The crowd was deeply shocked by the modest dress imposed on the people's representatives in contrast to the nobility's flaunted wealth. The representatives of the Third Estate were warmly acclaimed. After the nobility, the clergy, in their dark cassocks and purple robes, led the way for the King and the royal family. Louis XVI, appearing glum, waddled as he walked. He had the look of someone performing a tiresome formal duty. Walking behind him, in two rows, were the Queen, the princesses and the other princes.

Her lips pursed, a careworn Marie Antoinette made a vain effort to look serene. For Gouverneur Morris, the American minister who was present, she seemed to be looking with contempt on the scene as if to say: "For the present,

I submit but I shall have my Turn."[7] Throughout the day, she was constantly humiliated by the murmur of the crowds as she went by. Suddenly, at one point, some women commoners who had somehow managed to cross the security barriers started yelling: "Long live the Duc d'Orléans!" Marie Antoinette faltered and seemed about to faint. She had to be supported. Then she walked on, very pale, stung that she had not been able to control her emotion.

Finally, they reached the church of Saint Louis. But the Queen's trials were not yet over. The Bishop of Nancy, who celebrated the mass, contrasted the poverty of the people and the unrestrained luxury of the court in his sermon. He was greeted with wild applause when he denounced the Queen's puerile and extravagant tastes. Only by a small quivering of her lips was Marie Antoinette's distress revealed. Duquesnoy, a representative of the Third Estate, who watched her attentively, was surprised by this "self-confidence" and "brazen sangfroid."[8] As for Louis XVI, he had quietly dozed off during the sermon and heard nothing. At the end of the ceremony, the King and Queen returned to the château, in separate coaches. The King was again greeted with some applause, but the Queen, who delayed before instructing her coach to leave, waited in vain for any acclaim.

The King spent the whole evening rehearsing the speech he had to make the next day for the official opening of the Estates General. Overcoming her fatigue and anguish, Marie Antoinette listened to him attentively. On the morning of May 5, an extraordinary ovation greeted Louis XVI's entrance into the Salle des Menus-Plaisirs, where all the representatives of France were assembled, as well as a crowd of courtiers. The Queen, who followed her husband, took her place in an armchair near the royal throne. The King delivered his speech in a confident voice. After announcing that he had convened the assembly to restore financial order and repeating that he intended to uphold his authority and not give in to "an exaggerated desire for innovations," he yielded the floor to his Lord Chancellor, followed by Necker, whose speech was eagerly awaited.

Sitting very straight and dignified, the Queen looked impassive, but the convulsive movements of her fan betrayed her agitation. She glanced furtively at the representatives of the Third Estate, none of whom she knew. Or perhaps she was looking at the Duc d'Orléans. This prince, who had gotten himself elected as a deputy of the nobility, had had the impudence to refuse to walk with his peers in the procession; and that morning, instead of taking his place next to the members of the royal family, he had sat with the deputies. The King and the Queen were exasperated; they saw him as a dangerous agitator, fully capable of setting himself up as Louis XVI's rival. At the end of the session, when the sovereign rose, he was greeted with cheers; the deference he showed to his wife finally earned her some applause, to which she responded with a graceful curtsy.

Meanwhile, the Dauphin was slowly dying. Louis XVI and Marie Antoinette had had to face up to the sad fact. On April 15 the unfortunate child had been taken to Meudon, where the air was supposed to be healthier than in Versailles. But it was obvious that the little Prince, who was eight—and weighed only sixteen pounds fully clothed!—could never recover his health. His parents went to visit him every day. The child still played with a dog and several children who came by for his amusement. He could no longer bear the presence of Madame de Polignac. According to Madame Campan, he was convinced that his mother preferred the Duc de Normandie to him, and he kept aloof from her, to the point of even showing her some cruelty. But other memoirists assert that the Dauphin was extremely affectionate with her. A few days before his death, he requested that she be served all the dishes she most liked in his presence. Marie Antoinette was by his bedside when he breathed his last. He died on June 4, three-quarters of an hour after midnight. Louis XVI and Marie Antoinette grieved together for an entire day in complete seclusion. When they learned of their elder brother's death, Madame Royale and the Duc de Normandie burst into tears.

In accordance with the rigid etiquette, the sovereigns were kept away from the deceased child. He was embalmed, wrapped in a silver shroud and exhibited for a week in his casket. To save money, Louis XVI eschewed the grand ceremony of Saint Denis and used funds allocated for silverware to pay the costs of the funeral (the state coffers were empty). On June 7, all the people presented at court came to offer their condolences to the Queen. Her face reddened by tears, Marie Antoinette saw an endless procession of women file past her, each wearing a large black mantle flowing down in a train from the shoulders. On June 12, the Dauphin's corpse was placed in the crypt at Saint Denis.

Inconsolable over her son's death, the Queen had sleepness nights. She kept later and later hours. "One evening she sat in the middle of the room," Madame Campan writes, "recounting several unusual things that had happened during the day. There were four candles on her dressing table. The first went out on its own, I lit it again; soon the second and third also went out. At that point the Queen grasped my hand in terror, and said: 'Misfortune can make a person superstitious; if the fourth candle also goes out, I would regard it as a very bad omen.' "[9] The fourth candle went out.

25

THE FALL OF THE BASTILLE

*T*he day after the Dauphin's death, the King, the Queen and the court went to live in Marly, where Louis XVI and Marie Antoinette had no relief or rest. Political events bore down on them, forcing them to react as they were whisked into the upheaval. Ministers and delegations of the representatives came to Marly, as they had at Versailles, to appeal to them. They were allowed no period of mourning, no privacy, no time to reflect on their loss. Caught in the maelstrom that was sweeping the entire country, Marie Antoinette could do no more than have several masses celebrated so her son's soul would rest in peace.

Ever since the beginning of May, the royal couple feared the outcome of the meeting of the Estates General which Louis XVI had so reluctantly summoned. At first, their minds were put at rest by the endless procedural quarrels that followed the inaugural session. They hoped these squabbles would bring matters to a standstill. They were being far too optimistic. Determined to take on the task of regenerating France, the deputies of the Third Estate requested—in vain—that the members of the two other orders join them. Since they could say they represented 96 percent of the nation, on June 17 the Third Estate solemnly declared itself a National Assembly. Then they swore they would not disband until they had drafted a constitution for France.

Louis XVI and Marie Antoinette were utterly dismayed. It was inconceivable to them that elected officials could arrogate to themselves the legislative power that belonged solely to the sovereign, by virtue of the sacrosanct fundamental laws of the realm. Supported by Montmorin, Minister of Foreign Affairs, Necker advised the King to compromise with the Third Estate—to give in to some of its demands without recognizing the National Assembly. The Queen and the King's brothers completely disagreed. In their view, the Estates General had to be dissolved immediately and their pretensions squashed. Marie Antoinette—in her ignorance of the century's great philosophical movements and her complete lack of insight into the aspirations of the majority of the French people at a time of both economic and political crisis—naïvely believed that there was a huge plot, whose instigators were unknown, driving these men to rise up against the power of the crown. Maintained by a relatively ill-informed entourage, the premise of a national conspiracy against the monarchy was bound to appeal to the Queen. She found this simplistic explanation of the difficulties assailing the throne at once satisfying and terrifying.

As usual, the King hesitated, unable to choose between the two sides. The family dinners were stormy, and feverish secret meetings were held in every pavilion of the château. Finally, Louis XVI decided to deliver a speech at a meeting of the three orders on June 23. Shaken by his wife's and his brothers' intransigent views, but aware of the danger inherent in a show of force, he chose the middle ground. He adopted Necker's ideas in a watered-down form. In his speech, he denounced the Third Estate and declared its deliberations "null, illegal and unconstitutional." He upheld the traditional separation of the orders and did no more than recognize the principles of individual freedom, freedom of the press and equal taxation. Necker was appalled; the King had completely distorted his plan. "This was irritating the nation instead of winning it over," is how he later put it.[1]

Louis XVI had no sooner returned to his apartment than he found his minister's letter of resignation. He would have been glad to accept it, except that an emotional crowd, fearing the great man's resignation, had invaded the courtyards of the château. Marie Antoinette had to go to Necker in person and beg him to stay. "The violent agitation at Versailles allowed no hesitation on my part," Necker would write. The day ended in triumph for him. The June 23 session had made a very bad impression on public opinion, and had given rise to the fear that the Estates General—in which the French had placed all their hopes—would be dissolved. The capital was in turmoil. Both in Paris and in Versailles it was feared that the crown would make a show of strength. On June 24, a majority of the members of the clergy went over to the Third Estate; on June 25, forty-seven liberal noblemen did so as well, including the Duc d'Orléans.

According to the Marquis de Bombelles, the King and Queen were "petrified with terror." The most insane plans were concocted in their entourage. The Comte d'Artois wanted to have Necker arrested. Louis XVI and Marie Antoinette indignantly rejected the idea and wanted to leave for Compiègne. However, the trip was too dangerous without the aid of troops. Marie Antoinette was in anguish, dreading a catastrophe. "Everyone here has lost their head . . . for four days we were in imminent danger of famine, bankruptcy and civil war," Mercy wrote to Chancellor Kaunitz.[2]

Given the circumstances, were the King and Queen going to lead a royal revolution or, on the contrary, were they going to plunge headlong into the counterrevolution? On June 27, faced with the rising popular passions, they understood they would have to make concessions. Louis XVI agreed to let the three orders meet together, setting off an outburst of joy. The crowd gathered in the château courtyard and clapped their hands, calling for the sovereigns. Soon they came out on the balcony. With a graceful gesture, Marie Antoinette lifted her son in her arms and showed him to the fickle crowd, which she now found less frightening as she was greeted with cheers, something that had not happened to her for a very long time. However, this spontaneous demonstration, which continued until late in the evening, did not calm the Queen. In her heart of hearts, she had already opted for the counterrevolution, a decision stemming from her deepest and most intimate convictions. And she convinced the King to call up loyal troops to disband the deputies and maintain order while he formed a hard-line cabinet in charge of retaking control of the situation.

Having made up their minds, the King and Queen set to work. The sovereign summoned the elderly Maréchal de Broglie, who promised to assemble 30,000 men near Paris on July 13. He also received assurances that the Baron de Breteuil was ready to take power. In the meantime, the Queen was all smiles with Necker, and tried to feel out the other ministers. "Any violent measure would be dangerous," warned Saint-Priest, who suspected backroom plotting.[3] The arrival of army regiments on the outskirts of Paris was not something that went unnoticed, of course. Their presence alarmed the population and the representatives. Denouncing "the aristocratic plot," the Assembly demanded that the King order the retreat of the troops, whose presence was fomenting dangerous turmoil in the city. Louis XVI replied evasively that they were necessary to maintaining order. Anticipating violent clashes, on July 9 the Assembly proclaimed itself a Constituent Assembly. France was restless, and in Paris, where there were threatened food shortages, enraged crowds shouted angrily in the gardens of the Palais-Royal. Though not all the regiments of the army had as yet been assembled, Louis XVI was ready to strike a decisive blow.

On July 11, he sent a very dry letter to Necker requesting that he leave France as discreetly as possible. He informed the other ministers of their dismissal as well. The following day, the Assembly fought back with energetic motions while the court—including the Queen—believed in victory. The young Chateaubriand, who saw her crossing the Hall of Mirrors looking radiant, thought "she had the enchanted air of life."

In the capital, news of Necker's dismissal was a bombshell. At the Palais-Royal, a then unknown journalist by the name of Camille Desmoulins harangued the crowd and called on the people to arm themselves. In the streets, there were demonstrations in support of the dismissed minister and the Duc d'Orléans. Several hours later, with no warning, a regiment charged into a crowd at the Tuileries. Several people were wounded. Panic spread from neighborhood to neighborhood. Expecting a violent armed offensive, the Parisians raced around the city in a desperate search for weapons to defend themselves. They were restless during the following night and day, but to no avail. They managed only to loot some convents suspected of stocking grain and to open the gates of the prisons.

At dawn on July 14, as the tocsin rang out, the population was still roaming the streets. They rushed toward the Hôtel des Invalides, which had a considerable supply of weapons. But a few yards away, troops were waiting under Besenval's command. Would they charge? The fate of the uprising hinged on them. After hesitating a few minutes, the soldiers sided with the insurgents and refused to march. Besenval preferred to retreat near Saint-Cloud. The mob, now out of control, broke through the gates and seized the twelve cannons and all 40,000 guns from the cellars. The Parisians were now armed. But they were still without gunpowder and bullets. These could be found, people said, at the fortress of the Bastille, in the eastern section of Paris. So the mob rushed to this state prison, a symbol of royal despotism. The Marquis de Launay, the governor of the loathed fortress, had just reinforced its defenses, alarming the restless artisans of the Faubourg Saint-Antoine.

A series of violent acts and blunders followed. After an improvised siege for several hours, the insurgents broke into the Bastille as they were being fired on from the towers of the fortress. In spite of significant losses (about a hundred dead and seventy-three wounded), the attackers freed the seven prisoners who had been locked inside, seized the gunpowder and bullets and led the governor of the Bastille and his soldiers to the Hôtel de Ville as prisoners. Along the way, the Marquis de Launay was attacked by some madmen and brutally assassinated, and his head was cut off with a knife. Several of his subordinates suffered the same fate—as did the *prévôt des marchands* (provost of the merchants),[4] who was attacked for refusing to arm the citizens. The day ended in a hideous carnival of horror and revolutionary exhilaration: heads mounted on pikes led the procession of the "Bastille conquerors" that paraded throughout the capital.

At Versailles, the King and the Queen basked in an illusory optimism for a surprisingly long time. Louis XVI had merely given up hunting on the fourteenth of July. In the evening, the news of the fall of the Bastille hardly upset him. He regarded it as a popular insurrection no different from others that Paris had witnessed in the course of previous centuries. He thought he could count on the army to restore order the next day. He did not know that Besenval's men had deserted and had no inkling that the officers could no longer rely on their troops. "Nothing," the King wrote in his datebook. Though "nothing" meant that he had not gone hunting, it is still a disturbing remark for July 14, since Louis XVI usually recorded all the noteworthy facts in his life. On July 12, for instance, he had considered the dismissal of his ministers worthy of being recorded.

Marie Antoinette, in the company of Madame de Polignac and the Comte d'Artois, had spent the afternoon with the troops newly arrived at Versailles. According to Gouverneur Morris, they "had been all Day Tampering with the two Regiments who were made almost drunk . . . They shouted 'Vive la Reine! Vive le Comte d'Artois! Vive la Duchesse de Polignac!' and their Music came and played under Her Majesty's Window."[5] She fell asleep in a state of complete euphoria. The bubble would soon burst.

At court, the gravity of the events began to dawn on people. Some courtiers realized that the King's advisers had been under devastating illusions in believing in a show of strength and in the people's reverential fear of the monarch. Of course it would have been easy to dissolve the Assembly had Paris not rebelled. But the uprising in the capital and the desertion of the troops made Breteuil's plan impracticable. One of the more realistic aristocrats, the Duc de La Rochefoucauld-Liancourt, took it on himself to wake the King at around two in the morning to inform him of what was truly happening in Paris. "But this is a revolt," said Louis XVI, thunderstruck. "No, it is a revolution," replied Liancourt, and persuaded him to address the Assembly as soon as possible.

The representatives had remained in session since the Paris unrest had erupted. Early in the morning, one of the deputies was in the midst of a violent diatribe denouncing the conduct of the Queen and her friends with the troops when the King was announced. Everyone in the hall was stunned. Louis XVI walked in among the elected officials, unguarded, followed only by his two brothers. In an awesome silence, he improvised a short speech in an attempt to persuade the Assembly that he had not prepared a show of force and that he had just ordered the regiments to withdraw from Paris and Versailles. "Help me in this circumstance, to ensure the salvation of the state," he said; "I expect as much from the National Assembly." This was the first time the King referred to the National Assembly and not the Estates General—therefore implicitly recognizing the measures taken by the representatives. Before leaving, Louis XVI requested that the Parisians be informed of his latest decisions. The King's speech was heartening for these men, who were exhausted after a night of anxious wakefulness. Several among them rose, applauded the sovereign and followed him to the château on foot.

When they came to announce the King's decisions, the Paris population greeted the delegation of representatives enthusiastically, but they clamored for Necker to be reappointed and for the King to visit Paris as a way of acknowledging their victory. Louis XVI hesitated. Since he had not yet recalled the troops, he hoped he could reestablish his authority in Paris. But Marie Antoinette, who was overwhelmed by her fears, could no longer think about reconquering the capital. At this point she wanted the royal family to take refuge in the fortified town of Metz, near the frontier of the Austrian Netherlands. Confident of being able to convince the King that this had to be done, she had already packed her trunks and collected her jewels. Before making a decision of such importance, Louis XVI convened his council of ministers and invited his wife and brothers to be present.

For hours they procrastinated. Shaken by the betrayal of his troops, Maréchal de Broglie had to admit that the army was incapable of capturing Paris. When the Queen and the Comte d'Artois suggested they should leave for Metz, he replied that he could not guarantee the safety of the King and his family during the trip. And when they became insistent, Broglie finally said, "Yes, we can go to Metz, but what will we do when we get there?" An unimaginable dread gripped the Queen. "Well, Sirs, we must make up our minds, should I leave or should I stay?" the King finally asked. They each gave their opinion. The majority decided in favor of the royal family remaining at Versailles. Three years later, Louis XVI would admit to Fersen: "I know I missed the opportunity. I missed it on July 14. That was the time to leave and I wanted to."[6] When he came out of the council meeting, Louis XVI dismissed his cabinet and informed the Assembly that he was recalling Necker and the other dismissed ministers. He also announced that he would be going to Paris the following day. Marie Antoinette was in despair.

Versailles fell silent. The court was frightened. Amidst all the disturbing news from Paris, there was one piece of news that could not fail to terrorize the members of this insular, sheltered little world: a bounty had been put on the head of the Queen, the Comte d'Artois, the Polignacs and many others. After the slaying of the governor of the Bastille, the men in his garrison and the *prévôt des marchands*, it was hard to predict what degrees of violence the fury of the masses would unleash. Under these circumstances, the King thought it wise to request that his younger brother, the Prince de Condé, the Polignacs, Breteuil, the Abbé de Vermond and several others leave France until calm returned.

Certain that she was being spied upon by the servants at the château, whose intentions she did not know, Marie Antoinette did not even dare announce the news to Madame de Polignac. She could only send her a heartrending note, along with a gift of five hundred gold louis. At nightfall, the Comte d'Artois and his family, and most of the Queen's friends—all wearing discreet disguises—set out on the road for Belgium. They were convinced that they would soon return from this strange escapade and that their lives would then quietly resume their normal course.

At ten in the morning on the following day—July 17—Louis XVI left for Paris. Marie Antoinette had tried in vain to dissuade him from going, for she regarded his concession as humiliating and dangerous. When she had run out of arguments, she offered to accompany him on his expedition, believing there was no hope of his returning alive. He refused and asked her to remain at Versailles. After his departure, holding back tears, she cloistered herself in her apartment with her children and tried to compose a speech for the Assembly. She had decided to seek protection from the deputies in the event that Louis XVI did not return. The hours dragged on; the day was endless. The Queen asked Madame Campan to summon several people from her court, but the First Woman of the Bedchamber was obliged to tell her that most of the persons she had asked for had left their apartments. The few faithful friends she had been able to gather she sent out to get news. They returned with nothing. No one knew what was happening in Paris. Night fell. Still no news. Finally at around eleven, the King's coach drove up. Exhausted but safe, Louis XVI kissed his wife and children. He had given his support to the Paris revolution and was wearing the tricolor cockade on his hat—the national emblem in which blue and red are the colors of the city of Paris and white the color of the King. This cockade became the symbol of the union of the nation and the monarchy.

26

THE LAST SUMMER

AT VERSAILLES

A strange stillness descended on the Château de Versailles. From time to time there echoed the footsteps of the few people who still ventured down the halls, drawing rooms and antechambers that used to overflow with a dazzling crowd. People no longer spoke, they whispered. The courtiers who had had the courage to stay made themselves unobtrusive. In the course of that summer, Versailles, the former temple of the monarchy, became its sepulcher. Time hinged on the decisions of the Assembly and the rumors of the mob.

Anguished and disheartened, Louis XVI and Marie Antoinette secluded themselves in their apartments. The Queen hardly dared show herself on the terrace. The lampoons were now incredibly venomous: she was accused of wanting the people to starve and the patriots' blood to flow. The virulence of public opprobrium had made her ill. She had had to take to her bed for several days. Mercy, who continued to visit her as before, tried to explain the domestic political situation to her. He tried to make her aware of some social realities and for the present advised her to welcome Necker. Crushed by the recent events, Marie Antoinette failed to grasp that the survival of the monarchy required radical changes. She withdrew into herself and her family. "We are surrounded only by distress, misfortune and unhappy people. Everyone is fleeing and at this point I take comfort in thinking that all the people whom I most care about are far away from me. Also I see no one and I spend the whole day alone in my quarters. My children are my sole resource,"[1] she wrote to Madame de Polignac, begging her not to answer, as she was too afraid of her letters being intercepted. Of course, the Queen could not tell her friend that Fersen still came to see her in her apartment and that they met at Trianon as frequently as before. To be closer to Marie Antoinette, Axel had rented lodgings at Versailles. He was now extremely prudent in his correspondence and referred to the Queen only as "She."

After her friend's departure, the Queen had to appoint a new governess for her children. She settled on the virtuous Duchesse de Tourzel and wrote her a long epistle concerning the education of the new Dauphin, her "beloved darling": "My son is four years and four months, minus two days, old; I am not going to speak of his height or his appearance; you have only to see him. His health has always been good; but even in the cradle, we noticed that his nerves were delicate and that the slightest unusual noise affected him ... Because of his delicate nerves any noise he is unaccustomed to frightens him. For instance, he is afraid of dogs because he heard them bark next to him. I never forced him to see them, because I believe that as his reasoning faculty develops, his fears will disappear. Like all strong, healthy children, he is thoughtless, light-headed and violent in his fits of anger; but he is good-natured, gentle and even affectionate, when his thoughtlessness does not get the better of him. He has an enormous sense of pride, which, properly directed, might one day turn to his advantage. Until he feels at ease with someone, he knows how to control himself and master his impatience and anger so as to seem gentle and friendly. He is extremely reliable when he has promised something; but he is very indiscreet; he easily repeats what he has heard; and often, without intending to lie, he adds things according to his imagination. This is his greatest fault and it must be corrected. Apart from that, I repeat, he is good-natured; and by being sensitive and firm, but not too strict, one can always get him to do what one wants. But strictness would make him rebel, for he has a strong character for his age. For example, from earliest childhood, the word 'pardon' always shocked him. He will do and say anything you want when he is wrong; but he will only pronounce the word 'pardon' with tears and great difficulty.

"My children have always been accustomed to have complete trust in me and when they do something wrong, to tell me so themselves. Which means that when I scold them, I look more hurt and sad about what they did than angry. I have accustomed them to the idea that a yes or no from me is irrevocable; but I always give them a reason befitting their age, so that they do not think it is moodiness on my part. My son does not know how to read and has difficulty learning; but he is too distracted to concentrate. He has no idea of rank in his head and I would like that to continue: our children always find out soon enough who they are. He is very fond of his sister and has a good heart. Every time something makes him happy, a trip somewhere or a gift, his first impulse is to request the same thing for his sister. He was born cheerful; for his health, he needs to be outside a great deal, and I think it is best to let him play and work on the terraces rather than have him go any farther. The exercise taken by little children as they run and play outside is healthier than making them take walks, which often tires their lower backs."[2]

These were words of the Queen at a time when she was living in terror of the future, and yet could not gauge the full gravity of the turmoil shaking France. After the fall of the Bastille, the entire country succumbed to a generalized and uncontrolled panic called *"la Grande Peur,"* the Great Fear. The peasants, who represented 85 percent of the French population at the time, suspected the landowning nobility of stockpiling grain with the aim of selling it at higher prices later on, when there would be shortages. They were also convinced that the landlords would retaliate against the uprisings in Paris by letting groups of "bandits" loose in the countryside. Kindled by rumor, the terror of an "aristocratic plot" spread to every corner of the kingdom at the same time. In their unsuccessful hunt for "bandits," the peasants often attacked castles, plundered them and set them on fire. The simultaneity of the unrest, the fact that it unfolded in identical fashion in most of the French provinces, inevitably lent substance to the thesis of a plot. Poisonous lampoons ascribed criminal intentions to the Queen. People were convinced that she was conspiring against France. Everywhere, she personified the horrors of a bloody counterrevolution.

Overwhelmed by the scope of this Great Fear, the cabinet was left powerless. It was the Assembly that found a way of restoring order; on August 4, 1789, in a great surge of patriotism, the members decided to abolish all existing privileges. Inspired by the American example, the deputies set to work drafting the "Declaration of the Rights of Man and of the Citizen," which was to be the preamble to the constitution which they were drawing up. Feeling divested of his power, Louis XVI let these measures be taken, even though he disapproved of them and did not want to support them. Marie Antoinette felt crushed.

Though she now pretended not to play an active part in politics, she received Necker on July 29. Believing she was still in the era of absolute monarchy, proud as ever, she thought it appropriate to appeal to "his zeal in the service of the King as an obligation heightened by the fact that he had been recalled."³ The minister, who had just traveled through the country and seen sedition and violence everywhere, answered bluntly that "his zeal in the service of the King was a duty but he had no obligation to be grateful."⁴ Disconcerted by this answer so lacking in the submissiveness of former times, the Queen found nothing to say in reply. At that point, the Swiss banker took the liberty of taking her hand and kissing it respectfully. This was too much for Marie Antoinette. This breach in the rules of etiquette—that eternal etiquette she herself had so ardently fought against—left her stunned. She realized how weakened the throne was if a minister could allow himself such familiarity!

In spite of all the unrest, the Versailles ritual remained unchanged. The sovereigns' *lever* and *coucher* (rising and retiring) were held as usual. The King went hunting and received the ambassadors. The Queen presided over her card games with the same haughty grace she had shown for the last few years. On her name day, August 15, the same ceremonies took place. On the other hand, on the King's name day, August 25, the day of Saint Louis, anyone could see that nothing was as it used to be. Very elegant, wearing her most beautiful diamonds, the Queen was seated in a magnificent armchair and, as custom required, received the representatives of the great bodies of the state, who came to pay homage to the sovereign's wife. But since those eventful days in July, the institutions had changed. Paris had given itself a mayor—the astronomer Bailly—and a bourgeois militia called the National Guard, whose commander-in-chief was none other than the celebrated Lafayette. They had come to Versailles as well. When Bailly came before the Queen, instead of going down on one knee like the heads of the other delegations, he merely bowed. Appalled by what she considered an insult to her royal rank, Marie Antoinette responded with an extremely curt nod. The welcome she extended to Lafayette and the officers of the National Guard, whom she saw as the henchmen of the revolution, was no warmer. She stammered a few awkward words, so that these men, who had had no other wish than to be charmed by her, left very annoyed. "This unfortunate princess never fully understood the importance of the circumstances she was in; she yielded to impulse without weighing the consequences," asserted the Marquise de La Tour du Pin, who was very close to the royal couple at that time.⁵

In Versailles and Paris there was talk only of conspiracies and plots. The ministers no longer knew what to believe or how to advise a sovereign who went hunting until he was completely drained and escaped in sleep whenever their questions became too pressing. In fact, several schemes were being hatched simultaneously—one by the most conservative royalists in collaboration with the émigré princes and aristocrats. They wanted to abduct the King and his family, transfer them to a city in eastern France and force Louis XVI to dissolve the Assembly. With the help of loyal troops recruited in a variety of places (exactly how, no one knew), the old order would be restored. Though the Queen did not dislike this plan, she saw that it had two drawbacks—the danger of civil war and the more or less assured subservience of the crown to the princes and nobles. She felt it was too risky to be adopted.

Necker and Montmorin feared there would be a new insurrection in Paris at the beginning of the fall and supported a plan put forth by the moderate deputies. It involved moving the King, his family and the Assembly to Compiègne, so they would be protected from violent outbreaks in the capital. Neither Louis XVI nor Marie Antoinette accepted this plan. They were afraid that they would become hostages of the Assembly and would be abandoning the throne to the Duc d'Orléans, who, they thought, would certainly usurp it in such circumstances.

Several representatives from the *parti populaire* got wind of the secret plans and saw in them a counterrevolutionary threat. They therefore decided that the King and the Assembly should be brought to Paris. They started to stir up supporters in the capital. In the hope of maintaining order and ensuring his safety and that of his family, Louis XVI called the Flanders regiment, whose loyalty he saw as steadfast, to Versailles. Did the sovereigns have more ambitious intentions? Did they have visions of dispersing the Assembly and reconquering Paris? The King's indecisiveness discouraged his supporters while alarming his opponents. Calling up loyal troops caused no reaction among the former, but intensified the wrath of the latter.

As soon as the Flanders regiment had arrived in Versailles, Paris began to seethe once again. Nerves had been on edge since July. In the gardens of the Palais-Royal, the heart of the revolutionary movement, there was talk of marching on Versailles. In this period of "tiding over," when the new wheat harvest was not yet available and the previous one running low, people lived in fear of famine. Resentment against the hoarders, "the starvers of the people," became bitter. Adding to the fear of famine was the obsessive fear of a plot against the people.

At Versailles, the presence of a loyal regiment reinforcing the bodyguards assigned to their security, completely reassured Louis XVI and Marie Antoinette. As tradition required, the bodyguards held a banquet in honor of the newly arrived officers on October 1, in the Versailles Opera House. The two regiments fraternized in an unambiguous counterrevolutionary spirit, cheered on by the courtiers looking down from the boxes. In the midst of the libations and toasts to the health of the King and his family, some rash remarks were made against the Assembly. The impassioned ambiance excited Madame de Tessé, who ran to the Queen and begged her to join the fete. Marie Antoinette hesitated before following the young woman. Then yielding to her entreaties, she went to the opera with the King and the Dauphin. When the three appeared in the center box, the hall resounded with cries of "Long live the King!" The orchestra struck up a song by Grétry, "O Richard, ô mon roi," and everyone was delirious with enthusiasm. An officer went up to the royal box and asked the Queen if he could take the Dauphin downstairs. The child was lifted onto the table, and as he walked down its length intrepidly, smiling at everyone, he showed not the slightest fear amidst all the shouting around him. Marie Antoinette did not exhibit the same equanimity. She was very relieved when her son was returned to her; she took him in her arms and kissed him tenderly before returning to her apartment with him and the King. All the soldiers left the hall to escort the royal family. Their mood was one of inebriation mixed with uncontrolled joy. They behaved wildly, dancing under Louis XVI's windows, with one soldier climbing up on the balcony so he could cheer the monarch from close up. The King and Queen were more than pleased to hear the ovations, the sound of which they had nearly forgotten. The passionate feelings shown by the officers was unlike the happy ardor of bygone days. It was charged with provocation.

On the following day, October 2, the Flanders regiment reciprocated the bodyguards' invitation. There was the same euphoria during the toasts, and it seems they considered marching on the Assembly. The Queen felt heartened by these manifestations of loyalty to the monarchy. "I am delighted by the events of Thursday. The nation and the army must be dedicated to the King as we are ourselves," she declared with satisfaction.[6] She still believed that the army would help the King restore his former government and that the revolution was the work of a handful of seditious people paid by the Duc d'Orléans.

In Paris, people were outraged when they learned of the banquets. It was rumored that they were orgies, but this was not what mattered most. What mattered was the appearance that counterrevolution was being organized around the sovereigns. Paris flared up. On October 3, everyone demanded the departure of the Flanders regiment. By Sunday, October 4, after a turbulent night, the idea of bringing the King back to Paris had spread throughout the city: Louis XVI had to come live in the capital to quell any counterrevolutionary impulse. His presence would be a double guarantee—against a possible "aristocratic" plot and against bread shortages.

This news did not seem to perturb the royal couple; they luxuriated in these few peaceful days. Without taking any precautions against uprisings, Louis XVI continued to hunt as usual. On October 1, he successfully pursued two deer in the Meudon woods. As for Marie Antoinette, she spent time with her children, enjoyed long conversations with Fersen and began to make plans for redesigning her gardens at Trianon.

27

THE TRAGEDY

OF OCTOBER 1789

*I*n spite of the overcast sky in Versailles on the morning of October 5, 1789, Louis XVI quietly went hunting and Marie Antoinette went to Trianon, where it is possible that she saw Fersen. She returned to Versailles for lunch with her children, as planned. At the end of the meal, she was surprised to see the Comte and Comtesse de Provence, and with them Madame Elisabeth, rush into the room, in a state of great agitation. A breathless emissary from the Comte de Saint-Priest also asked to speak to the Queen. Marie Antoinette immediately realized that something grave—indeed very grave—was happening. She was not mistaken—the people of Paris were marching on Versailles! Deeply distressed, "agitated," as her daughter later said, the Queen immediately requested that several gentlemen ride off in haste to find the King. Disregarding the entreaties of her entourage, she preferred to wait for her husband to return rather than follow the ministers' suggestions and seek safety in Rambouillet.

The people had been extremely quick to rally. The tocsin had sounded throughout Paris starting in the morning. A first procession of women, from the Faubourg Saint-Antoine and the quarter of Les Halles, gathered at the Hôtel de Ville under the command of one of the "conquerors of the Bastille." These women wanted to protest to the King against unemployment and the high cost of bread that made their everyday life so difficult. At around noon, they headed for Versailles. Seething with excitement, the National Guard decided to accompany them, in spite of Lafayette's albeit timid protests. The Guard set out, followed by a mob of Parisians armed with pikes, sickles and guns. This was an entire population marching against the monarchy and voicing death threats against the Queen, the target of public condemnation. *"L'Autrichienne"* was accused of squandering the royal treasury and blamed for her supposed loose behavior; her entourage was vilified and above all she was reproached for her nefarious influence on the King.[1]

Versailles was in turmoil. Gentlemen in formal suits, women in low-cut dresses hastened to the Hall of Mirrors and the royal apartments. Many had already posted themselves in the windows of the Hercules Room to watch what would happen outside. But soon these courtiers, who had been torn from their pleasure-filled, idle lives, were overcome with panic. Though a number of aristocrats had seen combat, none were armed that day. How could they be? In the King's presence, one was required to wear only a decorative sword, in other words, an ornament.

Alarmed, the ministers congregated around Necker. The Comte de La Tour du Pin, who directed the Department of War, suggested sending the Flanders regiment to cut off the road to Paris. He was reminded that no one was entitled to take such an initiative in the absence of the sovereign. They could do no more than close the iron gates of the château, shut doors whose hinges had been unused since Louis XIV, and barricade, as best they could, passageways that had always been left open, as the King's palace welcomed all Frenchmen without distinction. "We will let ourselves be captured here and perhaps massacred without defending ourselves," thundered La Tour du Pin.[2] However, the Versailles National Guard and the Flanders regiment were assembled and lined up for battle, with their backs to the gates of the royal courtyard.

At around three o'clock Louis XVI and his retinue arrived in a cloud of dust from near Meudon, where they had finally been found. Instead of stopping to encourage the men in the Flanders regiment who were acclaiming him as he went by, the King rode past them at top speed, flew into his apartment and immediately cloistered himself in the Council Room with the Queen and his ministers. While the Parisian hordes were approaching, the sovereign hesitated about what course to adopt. The disagreements among his ministers added to his indecision. Some of his ministers, including Necker, advised him to stay at the château. Others recommended emergency measures. Saint-Priest, supported by La Tour du Pin, suggested that the Queen and the children be taken to Rambouillet under escort and that the King go with the troops to meet the Parisians. If, by misfortune, the rebels did not turn back, Louis XVI would have time to withdraw to Rambouillet and from there set off for Normandy with his family. The monarch did not want to make any decisions unless the Queen agreed, and she refused to be separated from him. She wanted to face all the dangers by his side. Fully aware of how deeply hated she was by the French, Marie Antoinette knew that her husband was her only protection, for his subjects still had a residue of sacred reverence for him.

At around four o'clock, the first demonstrators arrived without any decision having been made. These were women drenched to the bone by the pouring rain. Shouting angrily, they asked for bread and shelter, and took refuge, for the most part, at the Assembly, where they sowed discord and disorder. Their arrival created a diversion among the deputies, who had just learned, to their dismay, that the King had refused to ratify the "Declaration of the Rights of Man." Mounier, a moderate, hastened to find Louis XVI to beg him to approve the text at this crucial moment. When he reached the royal apartment, the monarch was receiving a delegation of market women. Dazzled by the royal splendor, exhausted from their long march, the fishwives were almost timid in requesting bread. One of them fainted from emotion. His fears allayed by such harmless interlocutors, the kindhearted Louis XVI calmed them by promising to supply Paris with food. Feeling reassured, the King and Queen took no security measures and kept Mounier waiting.

It was long after nightfall, around eight o'clock, when most of the people's troops swept into town. This time, the château was thrown into turmoil. In his panic, Louis XVI promised Mounier he would sign the "Declaration." Before returning to the Assembly, the deputy implored the King to leave Versailles for Normandy as soon as possible. Once in Rouen, he could summon the elected officials who would make it their duty to join him. The sovereign called another meeting of his council. Time was running out. Aware of the dangers facing the royal family, Saint-Priest and La Tour du Pin begged the King to leave immediately for Rambouillet with the Queen and the children. The ministers would talk to the insurgents and inform Louis of the outcome of their negotiations. Like Mounier, Saint-Priest suggested retreating to Normandy at a later time, should no accord be reached with the Paris rebels. Paralyzed with indecision, the sovereign kept repeating: "A fugitive king! A fugitive king!" To leave seemed to him a dreadfully cowardly act. "I do not want to jeopardize anyone," he moaned.[3] Precious time was wasted. "Sire, if you are taken to Paris tomorrow, you will lose your crown," said Saint-Priest.[4] La Tour du Pin threw himself at the sovereign's feet and urged him to leave. Greatly distressed, Louis XVI wanted to consult with the Queen in private. As long as she would not be separated from her husband, Marie Antoinette said she was prepared to brave all the dangers of this hazardous expedition. Louis XVI finally gave orders for the carriages to be prepared. Marie Antoinette walked hurriedly into her children's apartment. "We are leaving in a quarter of an hour," she said to the subgovernesses. "Pack your bags. Hurry."[5]

What possessed them to think that the crowd, which was now bivouacking in the Place d'Armes and the area surrounding the château, would not prevent the King's departure? As soon as the gates to the courtyard of the royal stables opened, a cry of rage rang out: "The King is leaving!" The mob threw itself on the carriages, cut the harnesses and led the horses away. The King and Queen were aghast. Saint-Priest and La Tour du Pin offered their own carriages. Harnessed beyond the Orangerie gates, they would permit a more discreet departure. Discouraged, Louis XVI and Marie Antoinette preferred not to leave. Very calmly, the Queen sent word to the young princes' subgovernesses: "Go and tell those ladies that everything is changed. We are staying."[6] By then it was the dead of night and the rain continued to come down unremittingly. As it was hoped that the bad weather would dampen the rebels' spirits and break up the mob, the troops lined up in the Place d'Armes were ordered to return to their barracks.

Courtiers walked the length of the Hall of Mirrors—site of all the monarchy's splendors—in fear and anguish. In the dimly lit Games Room, the ladies sat on stools and tables speaking among themselves in low voices. Madame Necker held forth; pages imparted whatever information they had and invented the rest; former officers explained strategy. While the King remained in his Council Room with his ministers, the Queen retired to her bedchamber with the Comtesse de Provence, Madame Elisabeth and several ladies of her household. Terror-struck, Marie Antoinette could now foresee that great misfortunes lay ahead and realized she was powerless to do anything about them. She had agreed with Madame de Tourzel that at the slightest sign of danger, the children would be taken to her quarters. But aware of the danger threatening her, she changed her mind. Should there be cause for alarm, she preferred that the Dauphin and Madame Royale take refuge in the King's apartment. "I prefer to expose myself to danger, if there is any, and protect the King and my children," she replied to those who urged her to spend the night with her husband.[7] At eleven o'clock, two hundred noblemen, determined to do anything they could to save the royal family, requested she give them permission to take horses from her stables. The Queen gladly acceded to their petition: "I order," she wrote, "that two hundred horses be made available to Monsieur de Luxembourg, to employ as he sees fit, should there be any danger to the King's life. But if I alone am in danger, no use should be made of the present order."[8]

Suddenly at around midnight, Lafayette was announced. Exhausted, bespattered with mud, hardly able to stand on his feet, the hero of the American war presented himself before Louis XVI: "Sire, I thought it best to die here at Your Majesty's feet than to perish pointlessly at the Place de Grève,"[9] he exclaimed.[10] The commander of the National Guard reassured the King concerning the intentions of the Parisians. Soothed by his assurances, Louis XVI entrusted him with the security of the castle and decided to retire to bed, since it seemed that calm had been restored. "Go to the Queen on my behalf," he instructed a valet. "Tell her to set her mind at rest regarding the present situation and to go to bed. I will do so as well."[11] Comforted by her husband's message, Marie Antoinette dismissed the people in her service and told the noblemen who were watching over her safety to return to their apartments. The doors were shut and the candles snuffed. At two in the morning, everyone in the Château de Versailles was asleep.

Meanwhile, Lafayette assigned the outside door of the palace to the National Guards, who were devoted to the cause of the revolution. Only the positions inside were given to reliable men — the King's bodyguards. But they were very small in number, for it had been deemed preferable to send most of these troops to Rambouillet. As for the Swiss Guards, who were stalwart in their loyalty, they had been dispatched to Rueil. Hence the defense of the château rested with the National Guards, who hated the King's bodyguards and supported the rioters. When he went around to the Assembly, at about three in the morning, Lafayette declared: "I will answer for everything; I am going to get some rest." And at this point he invited the representatives to go home, which they did at once. "I was completely trusting," he later said, "the people had promised me they would remain calm."[12]

Groups of exhausted Parisians took shelter in the taverns, stables, mansion courtyards and churches, and under canopies of the portes cocheres, but the great majority camped on the Place d'Armes in front of the château. Groups of men and women sat around bonfires eating, drinking and singing. By the reddish glow of live coals, a horse was cut up, roasted and devoured. A diffuse clamor rose from all sides augmented by the crackling sound of shots fired in the air. At around five in the morning, there was a lull; everything seemed to die down.

Suddenly, there was a call to action and drumbeats. Several women noticed that the gates to the Cour des Princes were not shut. They wandered over there to reconnoiter, while others surged into the chapel courtyard, where the gates were also open. The crowd swelled, ranting and cursing the Queen. The most aggressive demonstrators massed under the King's windows, while others ran up the Queen's stairway. A bodyguard was massacred, stabbed with pikes and dragged into the courtyard half dead. A tall man wearing a pointed hat and armed with an ax went up to the victim, stepped on his chest with one foot and sliced off his head with the ax. In the meantime, the invaders had reached the entrance to the Queen's apartment. A second bodyguard was massacred, like the first, while the doors to the room were being ripped apart with an ax.

The Queen was still in bed. She had been awakened ten minutes earlier by an indistinct noise coming from the terrace. Her chambermaids, Madame Thibault and Madame Auguié, had reassured her. They had seen several fishwives on the terrace, who had probably not found shelter for the night. No cause for alarm. Suddenly a cry rang out in the Guardroom: "Save the Queen!" At this warning cry, Marie Antoinette jumped out of bed, slipped on her stockings and quickly put on a petticoat while Madame Thibault threw a yellow cotton redingote on her shoulders. With her two servants following in her wake, the Queen ran through her inner rooms to the door of the King's second antechamber (*Oeil de Boeuf*). It was locked. A terrifying wait. "My friends, my dear friends, save me!" she sobbed.[13] Roused by her cries, a bailiff finally opened the door. She ran across the room to the King's bedchamber, only to find it empty. Then some servants led her to Louis XVI's dining hall, where, for the moment, she was safe.

Startled out of sleep by the shouts coming from the marble courtyard, Louis XVI had hastily slipped on his bathrobe and rushed to the Queen via the secret passageway connecting the two apartments. He reached her quarters just as she was dashing into the inner rooms. The guards, who had come into the room in the interim, assured him that the Queen must have gone to join him in his apartment. And what about the Dauphin? The King raced to his son's quarters. "Madame," he said to the Duchesse de Tourzel, "there is not a minute to lose; bring Monsieur le Dauphin to the King." The governess sprang up and wrapped the boy in a blanket. The King took the child in his arms and made his way back to his apartment through the maze of dark inner corridors. The candle went out. "Hold on to my bathrobe," Louis XVI said simply to the person following him. Groping their way, the little group reached the *Oeil de Boeuf*. From there, they went to the dining hall, where the Queen was waiting, pale but calm. On not seeing her daughter—whom Madame de Tourzel had not had time to warn—Marie Antoinette darted down an interior stairway to Marie Thérèse's bedroom and returned with the little Princess. Soon they were joined by *Mesdames Tantes*. They were all very worried for the Comte and Comtesse de Provence and for Madame Elisabeth. They would show up later. Since the section of the château where they lived had not been stormed, they slept peacefully through the night.

The noises coming from the *Oeil de Boeuf* were more and more alarming. In a desperate surge of energy, the bodyguards defended this last rampart separating the royal family from the assailants. The savage mob retreated. They were driven back as far as the courtyard. Then, at that moment, Lafayette appeared, proud astride his horse. Roused out of bed by the racket of the riot, he who later acquired the nickname "General Morpheus" finally raced to the scene with his men. He managed to save (with some difficulty) about thirty bodyguards who had fallen into the hands of the mob. A few minutes later, he joined Louis XVI in his Council Room.

The Queen was in the embrasure of the window, between Madame Elisabeth and Madame Royale. Standing on a chair in front of her, the little Dauphin, who had no understanding of what was going on, played with his sister's hair and complained repeatedly, "Maman, I'm hungry." With tears in her eyes, Marie Antoinette asked him to be patient and to wait until the commotion had died down. Louis XVI was consulting with his ministers in the neighboring room, where they could hear the clamor of the crowd. Lafayette convinced the sovereigns to step out on the balcony. So they went out in front of the astonished multitude—the King and the Queen, holding the Dauphin in her arms and their daughter by the hand. The general of the National Guard silenced the crowd with a gesture. He reminded them of their oath of loyalty to the King and their promise not to cause a disturbance. "We swear it!" cried the demonstrators. "Long live the King!" they added. Louis XVI was unable to utter a single word. Lafayette, who had influence over the Parisians, promised them that the King would take all possible measures to improve their living conditions and prevent bread shortages. But the orator was cut short. A huge cry rose up from the crowd: "To Paris! To Paris!" Dismayed, the sovereigns went back inside.

Lafayette tried to play for time, stepped out on the balcony again, improvised a harangue and suggested that everyone go home, but no one moved.
A voice was suddenly heard, echoed soon by many others: "The Queen on
the balcony!"

On hearing this cry, Marie Antoinette turned pale. "All the Queen's fears
were visible on her face," Madame de Staël later reported. All those who
were with her begged her not to show herself. "I will appear," she replied,
holding her head up proudly. Grasping her two tearful children by the hand,
she stepped out into the middle of the balcony and surveyed the horde of
armed fanatics. "No children," screamed a rude voice. Marie Antoinette
gently pushed the children back into the King's room and stood alone facing
the mob. She made a deep curtsy, her hands crossed on her chest. These
men and women who had been calling for her death several moments earlier
were now completely awestruck by her composure and pained dignity. They
clamored loudly: "To Paris! To Paris!" Vanquished by the Queen's charisma,
they began to shout: "Long live the Queen!"[14]

Exhausted, the Queen walked back inside the royal apartment, where
everyone stood paralyzed and dumbfounded. She took her son in her arms,
covered him with kisses and tears, then went up to Madame Necker and
whispered, sobbing: "They are going to force us to go to Paris, the King and
me, preceded by the heads of our bodyguards on pikes." Outside the mob
continued to yell: "To Paris! The King to Paris!"[15] In a dazed state that defies
imagination, Louis XVI paced between his bedchamber and the Council
Room. Saint-Priest went up to him and implored him to agree to the people's
demands. The King made no reply. "Oh! Monsieur de Saint-Priest," said the
Queen, "why did we not leave last night!" "Madame, it is not my fault!" "I
know very well," the Queen answered.[16] However, the clamor outside was
growing louder. Soon it was so menacing that it could not be ignored. The
King talked with his ministers for a few more minutes and then he and the
Queen followed Lafayette out on the balcony. "My friends," said the King in
a loud voice, "I will go to Paris with my wife and children; I entrust what is
most precious to me to the love of my good and loyal subjects." Applause
rang out, with simultaneous salvos from the musketry.

Returning to his quarters, the King hastily emptied his drawers and gathered some papers; the Queen distributed mementos and put away her diamonds in a chest that she would take with her. Meanwhile, Lafayette gave
orders and prepared the royal family's departure, for they were too distressed

to take any initiative. It was more or less calm again in the courtyard. The sun rose, its lustrous bronze rays lighting the monarchy's last hours at Versailles. At one o'clock, everything was ready for the departure. Fortunately, the King chose to leave by the small stairway; at the foot of the one the sovereigns usually took, the rebels had thrown the decapitated corpse of one of the Queen's guards. Louis XVI, Marie Antoinette, their children, Madame Elisabeth and Madame de Tourzel got into the same carriage. Before leaving, the King said to Monsieur de La Tour du Pin: "You are the master here now. Try to save for me my poor Versailles."[17]

The royal carriage set off toward the capital, surrounded by a populace drunk with fatigue, wine and bloodshed. At the end of pikes, two blood-drenched heads, twisted in atrocious grimaces, led the hearse of the monarchy. Already a consenting victim sacrificed to the national madness, the King spoke not a word during the endless journey to Paris. Men and women in mud-stained tatters sang at the top of their lungs celebrating their victory. "We're bringing back the baker, the baker's wife and the little baker's boy!"[18] they chanted, pointing to the King, the Queen and the Dauphin as they passed by astounded onlookers. Some fishwives hung on the carriage doors, hollering insults at the Queen, who remained impassive, holding her son tightly against her bosom.

As they approached the capital, the procession slowed; the entire city had come to meet the King. At the Chaillot tollgate, the sovereign was welcomed by Bailly, the Mayor of Paris, who gave him the keys to the city on a velvet pillow. "What a beautiful day, Sire, on which the Parisians will have Your Majesty and his family in their city," he said without the slightest irony. Louis XVI sighed and expressed the hope that his presence would bring peace and concord. Night had already fallen. Exhausted, the King and Queen wanted to be taken directly to the Tuileries, but such was not the plan. The people wanted to see their King. The royal family was taken to the Hôtel de Ville, amidst an overexcited, brutal and inquisitive mob. By glowing torches, the King, the Queen and the Dauphin appeared on the balcony. Captive for all intents and purposes, the sovereigns were acclaimed because they were divested of their power. It was past ten when the appeased, triumphant populace led them to the Château des Tuileries, where they were to occupy the small apartment that had served as a pied-à-terre for the Queen on her Paris jaunts. The ministers and several loyal courtiers were waiting for them. Wisely, Fersen had left several minutes earlier. "The presence of Count

Fersen, whose liaison with the Queen was well known, might have put the Queen and the King himself in danger, when the abominable escort accompanying them from Versailles would arrive," wrote Saint-Priest.[19]

Louis XVI remained silent while supper was served to the royal family. The Queen, in her black hat, had lost her haughty demeanor. She did not talk. The Dauphin, who had been asleep in the arms of his governess, had just woken up. "It's ugly here, Maman," he said to the Queen, looking surprised. Crushed by the drama they had just lived through, Louis XVI and Marie Antoinette immediately went to bed. The Comte and Comtesse de Provence left for their sumptuous Palais du Luxembourg.[20] Madame Elisabeth settled in the modest apartment on the ground floor of the Tuileries. As for Madame de Tourzel, she had to barricade the doors to the Dauphin's assigned bedroom with furniture. She sat by his bed and watched over him all night.

28

THE TUILERIES

*G*ood God, Maman, would today still be yesterday?"[1] cried the Dauphin as he ran into his mother's arms on the morning of October 7. Though the child had slept better than his parents, he had been awakened by the clamor coming from the Tuileries gardens. In spite of all the love she felt for her son, Marie Antoinette was unable to reassure him. Still shocked by the atrocities that had been committed in the preceding hours, she expected the worst, but tried to keep calm in front of this sensitive child whose life till then had been tranquil and delightfully overprotected. She put the little Prince in the care of his governess, dressed very hastily and went out on the terrace, where a horde of women were shouting angrily. They wanted to verify that the King and Queen were still present and engage them in conversation. Seething with excitement, some women demanded the dismissal of the courtiers; others asked the Queen why she had wanted to besiege Paris on July 14; still others accused her of wanting to lure the King into a criminal flight to the frontier. Marie Antoinette answered each woman calmly and intelligently. Soon these harpies changed into kindly matrons. The Queen had been so successful in convincing them of her sincerity that they asked her for the flowers and ribbons from her hat. She gave them away graciously and went back inside her apartment.

The effort she had made in confronting these women had been so great that she broke down in sobs. Her memories of the previous day were so vivid that she was unable to master herself in the presence of her friends and relatives. She trembled uncontrollably at the slightest noise. She became tearful whenever she was spoken to. The diplomats who came to pay their respects to the sovereigns, as protocol required, witnessed her distress. When the Spanish ambassador asked how the King was feeling, she answered, weeping: "Like a captive King."[2] She "could not utter a single word without being choked with sobs; it was quite impossible for us to answer her," Madame de Staël recounted.[3] Two nights before, who could have thought that the Queen of France would be welcoming guests in a room where camp beds had been set up? "You know I did not expect to come here," she said to her visitors, as if to excuse herself.

A tumultuous crowd burst into the royal apartments, bringing this strange reception to an abrupt end. Overcome with panic, the Queen took refuge in the King's study, where Lafayette had just arrived. This new demonstration was the consequence of a promise Marie Antoinette had made that morning to the women who had flocked to see her. She had promised that without their spending a penny, the objects valued under one louis (twenty-four livres) left at the state-owned pawnshops would be returned to them. Though this sum seemed trifling to the Queen, it represented a small fortune to the most penniless among them, so they ran off to the pawnshops. But of course the employees of these institutions had received no instructions and therefore refused to return the objects to their owners without payment. The women came running back to the Tuileries in droves. Yielding to Lafayette's request, Louis XVI promised to give the necessary instructions so that deposits valued under twenty-four livres, consisting only of garments, be returned to those who had pawned them. The people were pacified, but harbored resentment against the Queen, whose most praiseworthy intentions had been thereby turned against her.

On that same day, the King and Queen set about visiting the gloomy Tuileries palace in order to choose and assign apartments. Built in the second half of the sixteenth century by Queen Catherine de Médicis, this château had been completed and decorated by Louis XIV, who had made it his Paris residence before moving to Versailles in 1682. The court occupied the Tuileries again when Louis XV was a minor, from 1715 to 1722. Since then, the enormous building, which had 386 rooms, had been divided into apartments and assigned to courtiers, artists and artisans. It was an unbelievable caravansary, poorly maintained and furnished with odds and ends. The eviction of all the tenants began on the evening of October 6, to make room for the royal family and its retinue. The area around the château was congested with long rows of carriages, bringing furniture from Versailles and all the personal effects the King and Queen wanted to have in their new residence.

The first days were sheer commotion and confusion. Once the movers and workers had made the château habitable, a new life was organized. Louis XVI and Marie Antoinette now lived in close intimacy and never left their children. The King kept three rooms on the ground floor, with a view on the garden, for his own use. He installed his geography study on the entresol and his bedroom on the second floor. The Queen set up her apartment next to her husband's, on the ground floor and the entresol. Madame Royale and the Dauphin were lodged directly above her and were thus close to their parents. A drawing room, a billiard room and several antechambers completed the residence, which was decorated with tapestries meant as altar rugs rather than hangings. Madame Elisabeth and Madame de Lamballe lived in the Pavillon de Flore with a view on the Seine. The King's aunts were given permission to go to their estate in Meudon. The remaining rooms were distributed among Madame de Tourzel, the courtiers who had accompanied the royal family and the domestic servants.

The gardens were kept open for the public, for the people were driven by an insatiable curiosity to spy on the sovereigns. The latter taught their children to be amiable with the most indiscreet among them, and affable toward the National Guards, even though they distrusted them completely. The little Dauphin, who was only four years old, took great pains to faithfully carry out his parents' wishes. So every time he spoke to someone, he would rush to his mother and whisper in her ear: "Is that good?" For the young princes' amusement, two aviaries and some basins were installed at the far end of the terrace. Marie Antoinette, who devoted several hours a day to her children's upbringing, got into the habit of being present when they played. Louis XVI joined them as often as he could and occasionally made them recite their lessons. "We are living in the same apartment," the Queen wrote to Madame de Polignac. "They are nearly always with me and are my consolation. Le chou d'amour [the Queen's pet name for her son] is charming and I love him madly. He loves me very much too, in his way, without embarrassment. He is well, is growing stronger and has no more temper tantrums. He goes for a walk every day, which is extremely good for him."[4] The King and Queen now had a real family life. And yet, in spite of the recent events, the sacrosanct court ritual was maintained. Though etiquette was more slack than at Versailles, the sovereigns still had to submit to the ceremonies of the lever and coucher. Every day they were seen attending mass in the chapel of the château. On Tuesdays and Sundays, they had lunch in public; the Queen entertained on Tuesdays, Thursdays and Sundays.

However, balls, fetes, plays and concerts were now unthinkable. The King and the Queen were sulking. Given the tragic circumstances under which they had been taken to the Tuileries, they considered themselves prisoners, and behaved as such. Louis XVI obstinately refused to go out. He abstained from riding and hunting. Marie Antoinette adopted the same attitude. She restricted herself to the Tuileries, and took great pains to conceal her feelings about the crowd's lack of consideration. She dressed simply and rarely showed herself in public; her reserve was often negatively interpreted. She was considered cold and distant. She had returned her boxes at all the theaters and given up attending performances in the capital. This annoyed the Parisians. The royal couple's self-imposed reclusion only hurt their public image, and led to their being regarded as prisoners as well.

The events of October, which had revealed the power of the masses, had profoundly altered the course of the revolution and radicalized it. The National Assembly had followed the King to Paris, but it now had to take into account the threat of the revolutionary mobs. Terrified by the violence of the uprisings, several deputies had chosen to return home or even leave France. The moderate majority feared both extremes—the aggressive return of absolutism and savage outbreaks such as the ones they had just witnessed. It nevertheless continued to draft a constitution.

The Marquis de Mirabeau had dominated the Assembly ever since the opening of the Estates General. Descended from the oldest nobility of Provence, discredited by a dissolute life that had landed him in prison, he had gotten himself elected as a representative of the Third Estate. He was gifted with a keen political sense, and this man with a pockmarked face enthralled most of his colleagues by his persuasive eloquence. A confirmed royalist, Mirabeau had initially been disappointed by the King. The monarch's intransigent, excessive attachment to absolutism had suggested to Mirabeau the idea of a dynastic change. He saw the Duc d'Orléans, with his known liberal ideas and Anglomania, as the ideal candidate to succeed Louis XVI. But the Duke's inconsistency and pusillanimity had soon discouraged him. The tribune then thought of the Comte de Provence, but abandoned the idea when he failed to detect in him the qualities of a modern sovereign. Mirabeau was an advocate of a constitutional monarchy that would leave significant executive power with the king, and he finally hoped to convince Louis XVI to accept the new ideas and to share power with the nation's elective representatives. But on becoming his adviser in the hope of subsequently becoming his Prime Minister, he quite logically sought to get in contact with the sovereigns. Far from minimizing Marie Antoinette's role, he was very eager to meet her and benefit from her support. Mirabeau had struck up a friendship with the Comte de La Marck at the beginning of the revolution and asked him to act as his go-between with the royal couple. Marie Antoinette, who was usually inclined to listen to this Belgian nobleman and loyal subject of the Emperor, was indignant that he dared recommend such a man. This déclassé aristocrat, who advocated constitutional monarchy, personified, in her view, revolution and betrayal. "We will never be so unfortunate, I trust, as to be reduced to the painful necessity of seeking help from Mirabeau," she replied coldly to La Marck.[5]

However, Louis XVI and Marie Antoinette were more than ever in need of advice and enlightened opinion. Overtaken by events, the ministers restricted their activity to expediting current business. They obviously had neither the time nor the means to develop a political and social program. The King had to submit to the decisions of the Assembly. Every day his powers were reduced. Louis XVI was no longer "King of France by the Grace of God" like his predecessors, but "King of the French People by the Grace of God and the Constitutional Law of the State." He was therefore put under the joint guardianship of God and the nation, but the divine reference was now a mere concession to an ancient tradition that one dared not abolish with a stroke of the pen. The sovereign's subordination to the law was now clearly established by the representatives. "No authority in France was superior to the law; the King reigned only through it and it was only by virtue of the laws that he could demand obeisance." Powerless and unhappy, Louis XVI saw the collapse of what he regarded as the work of his ancestors. For him it was the downfall of the monarchy as conceived prior to him and as he had always envisioned it. Unable to do anything to restore his former authority, he wrote painful letters of protest to the European monarchs, trying to justify the lip service he intended to pay to the nation's representatives;[6] he was going to pose as the leader of the moderate revolution while continuing to fight, by every possible means, for the restoration of his former power. The Queen supported him actively. She asked the King of Spain and the Emperor of Austria for a concerted effort among sovereigns to restore Louis XVI's authority in his kingdom. To her great disappointment, the Spanish monarch replied very evasively. As for her brother, he preached patience and advised her to comply with the views of the majority in the Assembly.

With a heavy heart, the King and Queen were forced to make a pledge to the Assembly. On the advice of his ministers, on February 4, 1790, Louis XVI delivered a solemn speech before the representatives. While expressing his wish that the executive power be strengthened in his favor, he asserted his and the Queen's support for the constitution the representatives were drafting. He also put out an appeal to all counterrevolutionaries, imploring them to participate in the work of renovating France. This speech was greeted with thunderous applause. The deputies, who sat in the Salle du Manège, several dozen yards from the Tuileries, escorted the King to his apartment, where the Queen was waiting for him. Very moved, Marie Antoinette delivered a short prepared speech, and introduced the nation's representatives to the Dauphin, whom she held in her arms. She in turn received a sincere ovation. None of the men could suspect that when she had submitted the text of her speech to Saint-Priest that morning, she had been sobbing. The royal couple had done violence to themselves in taking a step that was diametrically opposed to their true sentiments.

Louis XVI and Marie Antoinette then attempted to end their isolation. The King reviewed the troops. He and the Queen paid a visit to the Hôpital des Enfants-Trouvés (foundling hospital) and the glass manufactory of the Faubourg Saint-Antoine. Marie Antoinette overcame her fears and apprehensions and got into the habit of taking her children for drives around the capital. As far as the Parisians were concerned, the royal couple had finally adopted a normal way of life again. February was also the month when the sovereigns decided to secretly enter into relations with Mirabeau. The King wanted to use him without the ministers' knowledge. After lengthy negotiations, it was decided that in return for substantial monetary compensation, Mirabeau would write up copious "notes" for the King and Queen explaining his opinion on the present situation. He would point out the dangers they were courting and offer means of averting them. Moreover, he promised to orient the constitution in a way favorable to the King. The sovereigns received the first of these "notes" on May 10. Mirabeau assured them of his complete devotion to their cause and asserted that he was "as distant from a counterrevolution as from the excesses to which the revolution—in the hands of clumsy and perverse individuals—had led the people."[7]

Louis XVI and Marie Antoinette studied Mirabeau's reports attentively but they trusted Breteuil and Fersen far more. Louis XVI had appointed his former minister, who had emigrated to Switzerland, as his sole genuine representative to the courts in Europe. As for Fersen, he had become the couple's most heeded adviser. He had access to Marie Antoinette at all hours of the day. To guarantee his free and easy access to her, Lafayette had given orders to leave one of the doors to the palace permanently unguarded. This unusual measure allowed the Swedish nobleman to devote most of his time to the King and Queen of France, for whom he was a confidant. He himself said that his situation was "different from everyone else's." For the first time, on December 24, 1789, he had spent the entire day with Marie Antoinette. "Imagine my joy," he wrote to his sister.[8] Fersen's love for the Queen did not prevent him from having noble-minded feelings for the King. He was moved by Louis XVI's trust, for Fersen was passionately devoted to the idea of royalty and its earthly incarnations. He felt he had a mission—that of saving the absolute monarchy at all costs. As things then stood, he thought that only by fleeing the capital could the royal couple be saved; Marie Antoinette was easily persuaded that he was right.

In spite of their distrust of Mirabeau, the royal couple had reason to be pleased with him. Indeed, he had just helped vote the approval of a decree safeguarding the King's foreign policy prerogatives. Mirabeau was then eager to meet Louis XVI so he could convince him to accept, without dissembling, the principle of constitutional monarchy, by which he would still retain significant power. But the King refused to collude with this adventurer, whom he considered one of the people responsible for the revolution. More cunning than her husband, Marie Antoinette consented to a secret meeting with this man whom she found repellent. Circumstances lent themselves to their meeting, as the Assembly had given the royal family permission to move to Saint-Cloud for the summer.

After nightfall on July 3, Mirabeau entered the Queen's apartment. She could not repress a terrified shudder when he appeared before her. They stayed together for three-quarters of an hour. Passionate about the royal cause, Mirabeau spoke a great deal, repeating in spirited fashion the arguments he had elaborated in his letters. He implored Marie Antoinette not to listen to proposals being made to her by the partisans of the counterrevolution. As he was taking leave of her, he is said to have whispered to her: "The monarchy is saved." Captivated by the courage and dignity of this woman who dared to behave like a king, he said to La Marck that "he would rather die than fail to fulfill his promises." Two weeks earlier he had written: "The King has only one man with him—his wife. Her only safety lies in restoring the royal authority. I like to think that she would not want to live without her crown; but one thing I am certain of is that she will not be able to save her life without her crown. Soon the time will come when we will have to see what a woman and a child can do in the saddle."[9] Clearly Mirabeau did not exclude the possibility of the royal family's departure from Paris. But contrary to Fersen, he thought that given the possibility, the King should put his trust in the provinces and on French troops as opposed to foreign forces.

In Saint-Cloud, where she resumed a style of life which she had been deprived of for months, the Queen's hopes were revived. She began to wear chic, light-colored dresses. She could be heard laughing. She went on long rides on horseback or in a barouche with her children. She summoned actors and musicians. She sang again and accompanied herself on the harpsichord. And every evening, Fersen, who had taken quarters not far from the château, joined her in her apartment. Tongues wagged, but she did not care. When a guard came upon this romantic consoler in the park at three in the morning, he nearly arrested him. Saint-Priest thought it behooved him to warn the Queen that Count Fersen's presence and his nocturnal visits at the château could present a danger. "Tell that to him, if you believe it," she answered the minister haughtily. "As for me, I do not care."[10] And Fersen continued to visit. All the historians intent on defending Marie Antoinette's virtue maintain that the Swedish nobleman met the Queen in the middle of the night so they could discuss political affairs with greater tranquillity.

Never had Axel's feelings for Marie Antoinette been more tender. In his letters to his sister Sophie, he constantly alluded to his loved one's misfortunes. "She is the most perfect creature I know . . . She is extremely unhappy and very courageous. She is an angel. I try to console her as best I can. I owe it to her, she is so wonderful to me. My only sorrow is not being able to fully console her for all her misfortunes and not making her as happy as she deserves to be." In the beginning of August, Fersen spent forty-eight hours in the country with Madame de Fitz-James. His mind was only on the Queen. "She was missing from my happiness, and without her, I can have no perfect happiness," he confided to Sophie.[11]

The pleasant stay in Saint-Cloud was marred by the Fête de la Fédération, which Marie Antoinette very much dreaded. Its purpose was to celebrate the first anniversary of the fall of the Bastille in a spirit of national reconciliation. Municipal delegations from everywhere in France gathered in Paris, joined by representatives from all the units of the National Guard; the reason for the fete was the desire of the participants to assert a national cohesiveness and express the will of an entire patriotic people to stave off the counterrevolution. Louis XVI and Marie Antoinette took no great pleasure in supporting a "fete" that they tended to view as an abomination.

For several weeks, the Champ-de-Mars,[12] extending from the Ecole Militaire, had been made into a large verdant amphitheater that could accommodate 400,000 people. The facade of the Ecole Militaire was hidden by a huge tent, with a stand where the King and the royal family were to be seated. Opposite, there stood an altar surrounded by four ancient vases with burning incense, and all around the edge of the amphitheater, eighty-three spears had been driven into the ground, with department banners fluttering in the wind.[13] On the quay of the Seine, a triumphal arch framed the entrance to the gigantic arena.

Beginning at dawn on July 14, all of Paris flocked to the Champ-de-Mars, the women dressed in white, with tricolor cockades brightening their hair and dresses trimmed with tricolor ribbons. At eight o'clock, in pouring rain, the King, the Queen and their children arrived in a covered carriage and took their seats. When the royal family appeared, there were enthusiastic cries and applause from all sides, while several hundred musicians mixed the melodious chant of their instruments with the crackling salvos of light arms and the thunder of artillery fire. Talleyrand, who was then Bishop of Autun, celebrated the mass, after which Louis XVI took the oath of loyalty to the law and the constitution. Though the King kept a sullen expression, loud cheers arose from the thousands present. Marie Antoinette then spontaneously lifted the Dauphin in her arms and presented him to the crowd, which began yelling: "Long live the Queen! Long live the Dauphin!" Then, since it was still raining, the Queen wrapped her son in a shawl. This simple gesture of motherly love melted the hearts of the people in the exuberant crowd.

When the ceremony ended, the royal family went quietly back to Saint-Cloud, fairly shocked by the strange nature of this fete that had no relation to those of the Ancien Régime. "It was all intoxication and noise," wrote Fersen. "The ceremony was ridiculous, indecent and consequently not imposing in spite of the site, which was glorious."[14] The King and Queen viewed what Fersen called the Fédération's "orgies and bacchanalia" with equal contempt.

29

ESCAPE PLANS

*A*fter returning to Saint-Cloud on the evening of the Fête de la Fédération, Louis XVI and Marie Antoinette no longer seemed able to enjoy true peace of mind. The permanent presence of the National Guards was a constant reminder of their state of bondage and they felt crushed by the political developments. They dreaded the moment when the King would be obliged to ratify the constitution whose very principle they objected to, and they were worried about the risks to which they were being exposed by the counterrevolution.

Hostile to the new ideas, the noblemen who had not emigrated were organizing the resistance to the revolution. In the course of the summer, they had set up a camp of 20,000 armed men in Jalès, in the Vivarais, in the South of France. They had found an eminent leader in the Comte d'Artois, who had taken refuge in Turin, Italy, with his father-in-law, the King of Piedmont. Steeped in the prerogatives of his rank, open to any quixotic dream, prepared to support the most fantastic ventures, Louis XVI's younger brother made countless incendiary proclamations against the Assembly. Meanwhile, many émigré noblemen in the German principalities rallied around the Prince de Condé, in Coblenz. They rejected the Enlightenment ideas that inspired the more moderate deputies and intended to restore the monarchy as it had been before the events of May 1789. They wanted to use force to crush the revolutionary monster. Working closely with the men in the Jalès camp, they were trying to foment an insurrection. Troops from the Piedmont were to go to the Vivarais and head north to join Condé's army. The plan was that they would stir up the provinces along the way and arrive in Paris in triumph. The fact is, these aristocrats and their leaders had nothing but contempt for Louis XVI, whose weakness and compromises they found disgraceful. Nor did the Queen find favor in their eyes. Since she paid lip service to the revolution, they called her a "democrat" and slandered her incessantly.

Terrified by the princes' statements, Louis XVI and Marie Antoinette had sent an emissary to Turin and Coblenz to restrain their relatives' blundering zeal. The Emperor had personally preached moderation to them. These secret steps had all been in vain. Meanwhile, in Paris, no one believed it possible that the King and Queen could be hostile to a counterrevolution led by the Comte d'Artois and the Prince de Condé. On the contrary. Their provocative rodomontade had aroused the wrath of the Parisians and made the sovereigns' fate considerably more precarious. Marat, a journalist who had long been noted for the virulence of his remarks, denounced Louis XVI as the leader of this counterrevolution endangering the patriots. He urged the population to go to Saint-Cloud en masse and do away with the royal family and the court. In his newspaper, *L'Ami du Peuple*, he issued very real death threats against the "perfidious conspirators." And so it was that the Parisians became increasingly accustomed to the idea that the King was a traitor to his nation who deserved to be punished by being put to death.

Marie Antoinette was still the catalyst for the public's condemnation. The tracts against her grew more and more venomous. The most wicked by far were Madame de La Motte's memoirs, which included the alleged correspondence between the Queen and the Cardinal de Rohan. Marie Antoinette was described as having had a physical relationship with de La Motte and as having subjected Rohan to her most perverse whims. She was also accused of betraying France, with Rohan as a middleman, to the benefit of her brother, the Austrian Emperor. These scurrilous writings, which delighted thousands of readers, fed the fantasies of the patriots, whose credulity was based solely on their need for a scapegoat. The Queen trembled on hearing that Monsieur de La Motte had arrived in Paris to take preliminary steps for a review of the famous trial at the Assembly. Her distress was all the more acute in that many moderate representatives saw the royal couple's divorce as the perfect solution. Because she inspired such aversion, they thought the Queen discredited Louis XVI and the regime he stood for.

In order to create the constitutional monarchy they desired, the elected representatives needed a docile, popular and respected queen. Freed of his wife, Louis XVI could become the ideal monarch.

When the royal family returned to the Tuileries at the beginning of November 1790, the King's divorce was the main subject of conversation. Lafayette bluntly told the Queen that they would try to convict her of adultery. Though she was overcome with panic, Marie Antoinette gave a cold reply to this man who had the means to trap her. She was perfectly aware that in Louis XVI's newly formed cabinet—largely made up of Lafayette's friends—several ministers openly wanted to put her on trial for adultery. Her fate would have been sealed. She would have spent the rest of her life locked up in a convent.

The Queen's loathing for the revolution grew ever more intense. Every day, she repeated to her husband that his oaths had been extorted by force and that it behooved him to use force in turn to crush the revolution. Restoring the former order was her sole goal. But she refused to lean on the nobility and the émigrés to achieve it. She did not want her husband to be indebted to the French princes and aristocrats for even the most insignificant bit of power. They would have been all too happy to impose their wishes on him. Marie Antoinette saw no other salvation but to escape from Paris. Her dear Fersen had been pressing this idea on her for several months. Nor was he alone. Having taken refuge in Switzerland right after the events of July 1789, the Baron de Breteuil urged the King to leave Paris and settle in a fortified town, and from there restore his authority with the help of loyal regiments backed up by Austrian troops. He also planned to ask the sovereign heads of France's bordering states to put armed men at the King's disposal.

Mirabeau, too, advised the royal family to leave the capital. The tribune's plans, however, differed from those of Breteuil. Mirabeau tried to warn the Queen against the errors she was in danger of committing. In his opinion, seeking assistance from foreign forces would be an irreparable mistake. He suggested that the royal couple withdraw to Fontainebleau, and with the support of loyal troops and the provinces, proceed to the dissolution of the Assembly and the election of a new chamber. Indeed, he now denounced the National Assembly as illegitimate, since it was obliged to legislate under threats from the street. New elected representatives, vested with constituent powers, could revise the legislative texts and give the executive a dominant role. Of course, elections would have to be prepared with a view to getting those men who favored a constitutional revision elected. In the interim, they had to work on public opinion, and the sovereigns had to put all their efforts into regaining their lost popularity.

Though Mirabeau and Breteuil both dreamed of restoring the power of the crown, they had different conceptions of the monarchy. Mirabeau wanted an English-style monarchy, adapted to the French context, while Breteuil wanted a return to the Ancien Régime, amended by the King's concessions of June 23, 1789.[1] This program, which had seemed inadequate at the beginning of the revolution, had very little chance of being better received in 1790. But for Breteuil as for the monarch, there was no going beyond the proposals set forth by Louis XVI. This was why the King and Queen listened to their former minister approvingly, though they were still unable to take the decisive step.

It was the religious question that gave the King the opportunity to act. The representatives feared that the clergy, among the throne's staunchest supporters, would remain loyal to the Ancien Régime. They wanted a citizen-clergy, bound to the principles of the revolution. To this end, they had introduced a decree, "The Civil Constitution of the Clergy," integrating all the ecclesiastics into state service. Elected by the citizens, the bishops and clerics would now be required to take an oath of loyalty to the nation, the law and the King. Moreover, they would have to swear to give complete support to the constitution. All those who would refuse to take these oaths would be declared "refractory." Torn by religious scruples, the King hesitated to ratify such measures. If he withheld his approval, the patriots would be capable of launching a violent "people's day" with unpredictable consequences; if he endorsed the decree, he would open the way to a schism with Rome by sanctioning a Church which the Pope condemned. With a heavy heart, Louis XVI approved the Civil Constitution of the Clergy on December 26 1790. "I would rather be King of Metz than remain King of France in such conditions," he reportedly said after signing the decree. It was then that he decided to leave the Tuileries and fight the revolution effectively.

General Bouillé seemed like the only military leader capable of supporting the royal family's plans of escape from, and reconquest of, the kingdom. In command of the army of the Rhine, Meurthe and Moselle—in other words, of all the troops in northeastern France—he had been unsparing in crushing a rebellion in Nancy the previous summer. It had created quite a stir. Loathed by the revolutionaries, who saw him as the villainous soul of reaction, Bouillé was seriously considering emigrating when he received the first appeals from the King and Queen in December 1790. The sovereigns requested that he meet with Fersen to work out the details of a plan of escape that would take them to a fortified town where they would be under his protection. Knowing that his troops, won over by the new ideas, were ready to disband, Bouillé was not optimistic. But faithful to his master's orders, he sent his eldest son to Paris to discuss the details of the royal plan with Fersen.

Secret meetings were held at Fersen's, on the rue Matignon; Fersen then brought the young officer's suggestions to the King and Queen. After much discussion, they came to an agreement. Louis XVI, Marie Antoinette, their children, Madame de Tourzel and Madame Elisabeth (the King's sister) would leave in the same carriage. They would go to Montmédy, a fortified town located in the region under Bouillé's command, where preparations could be made without arousing public suspicion. Montmédy had the advantage of being right near the frontier; it could easily be reached by outside reinforcements. If things went badly for the royal family, moving to Austrian territory would present no difficulty. Louis XVI requested that his entire trip take place solely on French territory, though, given the configuration of the frontiers, it would have been easier to cut through the Austrian Netherlands. The King did not want to alienate public opinion by taking this route, for the constitution called for his removal from office if he left French soil without the Assembly's permission. For this journey, the dangers of which escaped none of the principals involved, Bouillé had suggested—in vain—that the royal family use two lightweight, fast carriages. But the Queen refused to be separated from the King and her children. Also, instead of Madame de Tourzel, Bouillé would have liked to see a resolute officer who could make decisions in an emergency. The sovereigns felt that the governess's help was more valuable; she excelled in the children's education but had no predisposition for this sort of adventure. After careful consideration, it was decided that troops would escort the royal carriage only after it had reached Châlons-sur-Marne—in other words, more than 150 kilometers from Paris. The most difficult task was leaving the Tuileries. Fersen promised to take charge, and he kept his word.

Apparently, it had not occurred to Louis XVI that his departure might cause disturbances. He had no plan for reconquering the kingdom, and had given no thought to elaborating a program of government. He left that in the hands of Breteuil. But he had his illusions concerning the reactions of the French people and the European monarchs. He accepted the idea— indeed, even hoped for—a foreign intervention that would intimidate the French. For this, he relied on the Queen. In the name of the monarchs' time-honored solidarity against rebellious subjects, Marie Antoinette had been maintaining an intense correspondence with the courts of Europe since the beginning of the summer. But the Austrian Emperor had no desire to intervene in favor of his sister and brother-in-law. Joseph II, who had died in 1790, had been succeeded by his brother Leopold, with whom Marie Antoinette had never been close. Not only did his sister's fate matter little to him; he was pleased by the weakening of France. As for the other sovereigns, they remained deaf to Marie Antoinette's terrified appeals. The Spanish King was content to mass troops at the borders to protect himself "against the revolutionary plague." The British Prime Minister delighted in maintaining a neutrality in keeping with the English tradition of noninterference in continental affairs. The King of Piedmont lacked the means to send effective aid to Louis XVI. Only Gustavus III of Sweden proclaimed he was prepared to lead an antirevolutionary crusade, but no one rushed to join him. In fact, all the heads of state waited to see what attitude Leopold II, the new Austrian Emperor, would adopt. Mercy, who had left Paris for Brussels in October 1790, wrote to the Queen at length on March 7, 1791, explaining the situation in Europe. He reminded her that "the great powers never do anything for nothing" and told her bluntly that if they were to intervene, each of the European monarchs would demand as a payment a part of the French territory.[2] Moreover, before making any kind of commitment, the major powers wanted to be sure that a powerful royalist party existed in France, capable of staunchly supporting the monarchy. This letter—which was very compromising for the King and Queen—was intercepted and passed on to the Assembly. Though the Assembly did not proceed to an investigation, in Paris the words "conspiracy" and "coalition" were on everybody's lips. The "Austrian committee at court" was denounced more severely than ever. Pamphlets lashed out against the Queen ever more furiously. Everyone expected the departure of the royal family, and adding to the tense atmosphere in the capital was the fact that *Mesdames Tantes* had left for Rome with an imposing retinue several weeks earlier. This had been the King's decision, for he had wanted his aunts to be safe before leaving Paris himself.

In despair at not receiving a firm promise from her brother Leopold II, the Queen felt drained of nearly all her strength. "From far away," she said bitterly to the Spanish ambassador, "it is easy to advise prudence and temporizing, but not when the knife is at one's throat."[3] Racked with anguish, she lost her sangfroid and went so far as to add: "If the other courts fail to rescue the royal family from the situation it is in, it is to be feared and even hoped that they should find themselves in the same situation." In spite of continuing difficulties, she feverishly pursued her plans for escape. On March 12, Fersen informed her that the berlin the royal family was to travel in was ready.

Easter was approaching. On April 17, Palm Sunday, the King heard mass and received communion from his chaplain, who had not taken the oath to the civil constitution of the clergy. This provoked great indignation. On the following day, Louis XVI and his family were to go to Saint-Cloud with the Assembly's permission. When the King and his family took their seats inside their coaches, the National Guard prevented their departure. A large mob gathered by the railings of the palace in support of the guardsmen. Word spread that Louis XVI, violating his oaths, was going to celebrate Easter in Saint-Cloud with "refractory" priests, and he was accused of wanting to take flight. Lafayette hastened to the scene and tried to clear a passage for the carriages. In vain. Blocked by the National Guard as well, though he was their leader, and by the mob, he advised the King and Queen to return to their quarters. "You must admit that we are no longer free,"[4] the Queen cried out as she stepped out of her carriage. She took the arm of one of her ladies, who was crying. "This is no time to cry, but to show courage. I will set the example for you," she said.[5] Proud and haughty, she mounted the palace steps holding her son by the hand.

Louis XVI and Marie Antoinette's humiliations were not yet at an end. At around eight o'clock in the evening, they were told that during the night Guardsmen would make the rounds of all the rooms, including theirs, to see if there were any "refractory" priests hiding in them. This was the best way of guaranteeing that the royal family would not take flight! Outside, the mob howled death threats, as in October 1789. The Queen was so shaken that she had to take to her bed for several days. "Their Majesties are personally in great danger at this time; dreadful things are being said about them; they are no longer respected and their lives are threatened publicly and with impunity," Fersen wrote.[6]

To pacify the population, the royal family attended Easter mass celebrated by a constitutional priest at the church of Saint Germain l'Auxerrois. Louis XVI renewed his pledge to the principles of the revolution in the Assembly. But he secretly repudiated his acts in his correspondence with foreign sovereigns, who were certainly in no hurry to help him.

More determined than ever to leave the Tuileries prison, Marie Antoinette actively pursued her preparations for escape, regardless of her brother, who advised her to play a double game and wait for better days. Though they had received no assurances from the Emperor, Louis XVI and Marie Antoinette decided to leave Paris on the following June 20.

30

THE VARENNES DRAMA

n Monday, June 20, 1791, nothing about the King and Queen's behavior would have led anyone to suspect that the big day had arrived. The King spent the morning in his study while the Queen attended her children's lessons. At noon, the entire royal family gathered for mass, as always, in the chapel of the château. After lunch, Louis XVI told his sister Elisabeth of his plan, for he had preferred to keep her in ignorance of all the preparations. The Queen and her husband played their usual game of billiards. Shortly thereafter, Marie Antoinette retired to her quarters with the King. Soon, Fersen was announced. He came to give them the details of the final arrangements for their trip. "Whatever happens, I will never forget what you did for me," said the sovereign, before leaving the drawing room.[1] Once alone with her devoted admirer, Marie Antoinette wept for a long time. He consoled her, and they separated at four o'clock. The Queen then took her children for a walk in one of the most crowded gardens in Paris. Since the beginning of spring, she had been going out often so the Parisians would get used to seeing her and put their suspicions to rest.

Upon returning to the Tuileries, she still appeared completely calm and composed. Nothing had been changed in the royal family's schedule. At nine o'clock, the Dauphin and his sister went to bed, and the Comte and Comtesse de Provence arrived for dinner with the royal couple and Madame

Elisabeth. When her brother-in-law kissed her, Marie Antoinette whispered, "Take care not to make me feel moved, I do not want anyone to see that I have been crying."[2] By nine-thirty they had finished the meal; left among themselves, they discussed "the great undertaking" together.

Having been informed of the King and Queen's plans a week earlier, Monsieur and Madame de Provence had decided to leave, by different routes, that same evening. The Prince, dressed in English style, was leaving Paris for Brussels in the company of a friend, whereas his wife was taking another road with one of her lady attendants.

At ten o'clock, the Queen went upstairs to wake the children. "We are going to a fortified place where there will be many soldiers," she whispered to the Dauphin, who leaped out of bed asking for his boots and sword. He would be most disappointed several minutes later when his governess would make him put on a girl's dress. But then he resigned himself, saying to his sister, "we'll be acting in a play since we are in disguise."[3] When the Queen returned to the drawing room, the King went upstairs to kiss his children. At the same time, he handed Madame de Tourzel a note stating that she was taking the Children of France[4] away on his orders.

At ten-thirty, the great adventure began. The Queen went back upstairs, where the little princes were ready to leave. She led Madame de Tourzel and the children into the apartment that had been deserted by the Duc de Ville-quier, and where several doors had been added at various times. Their steps echoed in the dark, unfurnished rooms. They held their breath. The odd little group crossed through several rooms, until they reached a glass-enclosed room that gave out on the courtyard of the Carrousel; it was flooded with light from the torches of the valets and the carriages awaiting their owners. The Queen looked out carefully. A shadow emerged on the other side of the dusty panes, and the door was opened: it was Fersen, dressed like a coach-man. He took the Dauphin by the hand, and gestured to Madame de Tourzel to take Marie Thérèse by the arm and follow him. Reassured, Marie Antoinette retraced her steps back to the drawing room, where she joined the King, Monsieur and Madame de Provence and Madame Elisabeth. It was a quarter to eleven. Her absence could not have seemed suspicious to the servants. At eleven, the princes, very moved despite appearances, took leave of one another. They arranged to meet two days later, at the Chateau de Thon-nelles, a residence near Montmédy which Bouillé had had prepared for the royal family. Then the Comte and Comtesse de Provence went home, as they did every night, to the Palais du Luxembourg. Madame Elisabeth went to the Pavillon de Flore; and the King and Queen retired to their bedchambers for the traditional ceremony of the *coucher*.

After she had undressed and washed, the Queen got into bed and dismissed her chambermaids. As soon as they had left, she got up, went to her dressing room and put on a very simple gray silk dress and a large black hat with a long muslin veil that concealed her face. Wearing these clothes, she was supposed to go through the same rooms as she had with her children. On stepping out of her apartment, her heart stopped: a National Guardsman was on duty in front of the door to the hall leading to the Duc de Villequier's quarters. Fortunately, the man was pacing up and down. As soon as his back was turned, the Queen dashed out of her apartment and ran stealthily across the few yards that separated her from the road to freedom. When she finally reached the glass door giving onto the courtyard, she saw the silhouette of Monsieur de Malden. He was the bodyguard who was supposed to take her to Fersen's hackney, which was parked not far from the Tuileries, on rue de l'Echelle. As she went out, her heart stopped again. There, in front of her was Lafayette in his well-lit carriage; his coach brushed past her. The general did not recognize her. Trembling at the knees, for that meeting would have been a disaster, Marie Antoinette left the Tuileries leaning on Malden's arm. Unfortunately, her guide did not know Paris well. He could not find the meeting place and was obliged to ask a sentinel directions. A few minutes later, Marie Antoinette was climbing into the hackney. They all embraced and rejoiced. The King had started to worry, and had wanted to go out and find his wife. Fersen had dissuaded him. Wearing a big dark wig and a round hat, Louis XVI had left the château without incident. While his valet was putting his clothes away in the wardrobe, he had slipped out of bed, keeping the curtains drawn. He inched his way into his study, where he dressed in bourgeois clothes and walked out, as quietly as could be, with the crowd of people who had come to watch his *coucher*.

While they each described their exploit, Fersen drove his precious charge through Paris. But instead of taking the road out of Paris, he stopped in the center of the city, on rue de Clichy, where the berlin they would be using for their journey had been kept. He wanted to make sure that it had left for the outskirts of Paris to wait for its passengers. Finally, at two in the morning, the fugitives reached the Saint-Martin barrier. Fortunately, the customs clerks were feasting and reveling, so they paid no attention to these travelers who were surely new émigrés. The domestic customs barrier was crossed without incident, and they suddenly found themselves in total darkness, on the road to Bondy. But where on earth was the berlin? Fersen climbed down from his coachman's seat and went in search of the vehicle. Time went by. Impatient, Louis XVI came out of the carriage and roamed the countryside. But soon Fersen reappeared. The berlin was parked a short distance away. The royal family quickly settled inside the large green carriage with yellow wheels. The interior, upholstered in white Utrecht velvet, was particularly comfortable, with green morocco leather seats hung in matching taffeta.

Fersen had accomplished a masterly coup—the royal family's escape from the Tuileries and Paris. The expedition looked extremely promising, even though they were running two hours behind schedule. The nobleman drove the berlin at a furious pace to the Bondy relay station. There he was to take leave of the royal family, ride to Brussels by horse and join the King and Queen two days later. But while the horses were being changed, Fersen went up to Louis XVI and pleaded to be allowed to accompany him to the end of the trip. He knew that the three bodyguards would be unable to take any decisive action, should an unforeseen problem arise. With a firmness that was untypical of him, Louis XVI turned him down categorically. But he thanked him warmly. Perhaps he found it humiliating to owe his freedom to the man whom everyone took to be Marie Antoinette's lover. With a heavy heart, Fersen watched the big horse-drawn carriage lumber away in the pale light of dawn.

Inside the carriage, where they had high hopes that the adventure would come to a happy end, they agreed on the parts they would play. To avoid being recognized, the King and Queen were supposed to be in the employ of Madame de Tourzel, who was traveling under the name of Baroness de Korff, a Russian aristocrat. Marie Antoinette was supposed to be Madame Rochet, the governess of Madame de Korff's children, Amélie and Aglaé. Madame Elisabeth, now Rosalie, was the Baroness's lady's companion. As for the King, he was the lowly steward Durand. It was just like the little Trianon theater—they enjoyed playing against type. But times had changed, and today's public tended not to be very lenient.

By six o'clock, when the berlin crossed the little town of Meaux, it was broad daylight. In a lively mood, the King attacked the excellent food provisions which Fersen had had prepared. At eight o'clock, he very nearly rejoiced at the thought of Lafayette probably noticing at that very moment that the royal family had given him the slip. "Believe me, once my backside is in the saddle, I'll be very different than I've been up to now," he announced.[5]

Though Louis XVI was not the first King of France to leave the capital in order to reconquer it, none of his predecessors had done so disguised as a servant. Yet the King was convinced that he had shown his authority by leaving Paris. Since he saw himself as incarnating legitimacy, he had stubbornly refused to share his power with the people's elected representatives. In his view, he alone represented the state, and the Assembly had committed a crime in violating the fundamental laws of the kingdom. Fighting the men responsible for this heinous act—the men who were presently putting the finishing touches on the constitution—and restoring the traditional authority of the monarchy, these were now the sovereign's sacred duties. They were what justified this bourgeois escapade, in appearance devoid of glory.

For Marie Antoinette, who was tasting the exhilaration of recovered freedom, these legal considerations were secondary. Her primary consideration was to save the lives of her children, the King and herself. She preferred to brave the physical risks of this adventure, rather than continue to live with the constant threat of a riot. For her, this frantic escape to a fortified town near the border was simply a private matter—though in reality it was an affair of state, and the King was perfectly aware of it. So much so that he had committed the blunder of leaving a manifesto justifying his departure, for all to see, on his desk. In this long indictment, in which he denounced the revolution from its very beginnings, he stated that all his deeds had been wrung out of him under duress. Since he had lost all hope of seeing his subjects return to reason, he had decided to leave Paris with his family. Without making his intentions clear, he promised to forget "the wrongs" done to him when he returned, to impose the constitution of his choice.

In Paris, at about seven-thirty, as the berlin was quietly making its way through La Ferté-sous-Jouarre,[6] it was noticed that the King had vanished. There was widespread stupefaction. The King's departure had been talked about for so long that no one believed in it anymore. Every conceivable rumor made the rounds. There was a widespread belief that Louis XVI had gone to join loyal troops and that they would lay siege to Paris with Austrian troop reinforcements. At nine o'clock, the Assembly convened and assumed executive power, placing the ministers under its jurisdiction. Fearing a popular uprising, the Assembly immediately announced that it had taken all necessary measures to maintain order. As for the deputies, they were anxiously debating how to deal with the sovereign. After much discussion, an arrest warrant was sent out to the eighty-three departments[7] of the kingdom. The barely tenable thesis maintained by the arrest order was that the monarch had been abducted by counterrevolutionaries—a group whose intentions were contrasted with those of the good citizens who were working to thwart the evil designs of the enemies of the revolution. This thesis made it possible not to change the constitution if the King was found; Louis XVI would be reinstated, exonerated ahead of time by the fictitious abduction. The disclosure of the manifesto on the King's desk called everything into question. When it was read, it had the effect of a bombshell. The far-fetched fiction of an abduction collapsed. No person being abducted would have had the time to draft a statement of such length! The representatives were speechless with astonishment. Caught between the danger of counterrevolution and the democratic peril, they rallied to the abduction thesis without anyone really believing it.

Meanwhile, the King and Queen, elated by their freedom, thought they had been saved. They were far from Paris. No one was following them. So why bother to hurry? Louis XVI had not hesitated to get out and stretch his legs while the berlin inched its way up a hill. He had discussed the harvest with some peasants, while Madame de Tourzel took the children for a breath of fresh air. The Queen shared in the general euphoria. At five leagues[8] from Châlons-sur-Marne, at the relay inn of Chaintrix, a tiny village, the postmaster's son-in-law recognized the fugitives. This young man, who was the opposite of a fierce revolutionary, greeted the royal family respectfully and invited them to refresh themselves. It was oppressively hot. Why refuse such an honest offer? So the King and his family accepted. From the relay station the postilions spread the incredible news among themselves: the person they were driving to an unknown destination was the King. From that point on, the news preceded the heavy berlin, whose speed could hardly match that of galloping horse.

At Châlons-sur-Marne (170 kilometers from Paris), people looked on with curiosity at the carriage conveying the royal family. "We were clearly recognized," Madame Royale later said.[9] However, at around four-thirty, they calmly took the road to Metz. At the next relay station the King was supposed to meet the first detachment of troops that were to escort him to Montmédy. But at Pont-de-Somme-Vesle, there was no one. The passengers began to feel a vague anguish, though everything seemed calm. At Sainte-Menehould, the next stop, the inhabitants were watchful. While the horses were being changed, Louis XVI and Marie Antoinette, who had neglected to lower the blinds of the carriage, noticed a small parade of dragoons on the square. Why were they not on horseback and ready to escort the King? An officer went up to the berlin and discreetly advised the bodyguards to quickly get back on the road because, he said, "things have got off to a bad start."

As the berlin left Sainte-Menehould, the town buzzed with the report that it was the King who had just driven through. The National Guard was immediately called up. The captain of the dragoons, in spite of his protests, was considered suspect and arrested; then the postmaster, a man named Drouet, who had just changed the horses, was summoned. Contrary to a persistent version of the story, the young man had not recognized Louis XVI. When he was questioned about the passengers in the mysterious carriage, all he said was that he had noticed a fat, myopic man with an aquiline nose and a pimply face. This was enough for the municipal council to decide to catch up with the carriage. In the company of a man named Guillaume, Drouet galloped away, in the direction of Varennes, where it was known that the berlin would have to change horses.

Unaware of the turmoil they had caused, the royal family continued peacefully along the road. They were reassured by how well the trip was going, even though the troops they had expected had failed to show up; the fugitives fell asleep. They were nearing their destination, and at eleven o'clock, they arrived in Varennes, in the darkness of night. The little town was asleep. It did not have a post relay. The Sainte-Menehould postilions did not know the private coaching inn where they were supposed to change horses. Not wanting to go any further, the men stopped when they came upon the houses on the edge of the town. While one of the bodyguards wandered down a dark street looking for the overly discreet coaching inn, the King climbed out of the carriage and knocked at a door. He was unceremoniously told to continue on his way. The Queen was dismissed just as rudely. Then, as the worried sovereigns climbed back into the carriage, two galloping horsemen rode into the village. Soon several lights were lit. The King and Queen, after waiting in vain for the bodyguard to return, managed to persuade the postilions to drive to the town center. The berlin set off, but as it entered a vaulted passage, a dozen crisscrossed rifles and fixed bayonets suddenly sprang in front of the carriage, making the horses rear. Men suddenly appeared out of the darkness, menacing, and the tocsin began to sound. A municipal representative, the grocer Sauce, opened the door and asked for their passports. Madame de Tourzel handed her papers, which seemed perfectly in order. Forgetting that she was supposed to be a chambermaid, the Queen demanded that they hurry, saying she was pressed for time. Sauce returned the passports to Madame de Tourzel, and was in favor of letting the carriage proceed on its way, but at that moment, Drouet, the post-master from Sainte-Menehould, objected to their leaving. He had arrived a few minutes earlier and was the person who had sounded the tocsin. "I am sure that the carriage we have stopped is carrying the King and his family," he shouted. "If you let him escape to a foreign country, you will be guilty of trea-son."[10] This frightened Sauce. The voyagers protested; Louis XVI ordered the postilions to set off but they did not move. Some of the men cocked their rifles. All of Varennes was now awake, and an increasingly large crowd gath-ered around the carriage.

Gloomily, Louis XVI had no choice but to accept the hospitality of this Monsieur Sauce. Several minutes later, the royal family was sitting in chairs at the back of the grocery store and the royal children were tucked in the beds of the Sauce children. Greatly alarmed, Sauce went to fetch a towns-man who had lived at Versailles. Flabbergasted and moved, the newcomer bowed before Louis XVI, who stopped playing the part of the servant and embraced the good man. And Louis XVI, who had just denied being the King of France five minutes earlier, dropped his guard: "Well, yes, I am your King," he admitted, before all the members of the municipal council. They were astounded and, in spite of everything, overcome with emotion. Main-taining his calm while the Queen grew "extremely agitated," the King explained that "he had left Paris because the lives of his family were being threatened every day; that he could no longer stand living in the midst of daggers and bayonets and that he had come to seek asylum among his loyal subjects."[11] Though they were moved to compassion, the Varennois were not prepared to let the King leave. They feared the consequences of any gesture they might make. Tormented with apprehension, the Queen begged Madame Sauce to intervene with her husband so that he would consent to the royal family's resuming its trip. But the grocer's wife replied that her hus-band would be risking his life, and she valued his life more than the King's. This was where matters stood, at around one in the morning, when a shout rang out: "The hussars!"

These were Choiseul's[12] hussars, who were supposed to escort the berlin beyond Pont-de-Somme-Vesle. After waiting in vain for the carriage, Choiseul had given his men the order to pull back. Indeed, he was con-vinced that the King's escape had failed. To avoid the commotion the sight of troop movements might cause, he had taken another road to Montmédy. The lights and tocsin alerted him to the drama that was taking place in Varennes, and he galloped into the town without further delay.

In a matter of minutes, the charge of the hussars emptied the street without a single casualty. With his hand on his sword and escorted by Colonel de Damas, Choiseul stormed into the Sauce home. On seeing them, Marie Antoinette became hopeful again. She went up to them and grasped their hands effusively. "What should we do?" asked Louis XVI. "We should save you, Sire," replied Damas. "I await your orders," added Choiseul. "I have forty hussars with me. I will unseat seven; that will make one horse for you with Monsieur le Dauphin in your arms, one for the Queen, one for Madame Royale, one for Madame de Tourzel and one for Madame Elisabeth . . . The thirty-three remaining hussars will surround you . . . We will try to get through, but we must not lose a minute, for in an hour's time my hussars will be won over." But when Louis XVI asked him if he would not be exposing his family and Madame de Tourzel to danger, Choiseul swore to kill himself on the spot if any misfortune occurred. This made the King reject his offer. He did not want his family to run any risk. Besides, Louis XVI believed that Bouillé, to whom Choiseul had just sent a messenger, would arrive during the night and that the berlin would then quietly resume its journey.

The Queen kept silent during the entire exchange. Yet Goguelat, Bouillé's aide-de-camp, who was present, also begged her to leave. "I do not want to take the responsibility for anything. The King decided on this course of action; it is up to him to give orders; my duty is to follow them. Besides, Monsieur de Bouillé cannot be long in coming." She asked him openly if he thought that Fersen was safe. Thus Louis XVI and Marie Antoinette missed the opportunity to be saved.

Thereupon, the hussars scattered through the town, where the inns opened their doors. They started drinking and fraternizing with the population, who felt it was living through an utterly mad adventure. In the course of this short night, Varennes was torn between curiosity, fear, pity and patriotism. Strange rumors arose and died while the inhabitants from neighboring villages converged on the scene, armed with sickles, rifles and sticks. With food and drink, the population calmed down, but its wrathful fury was suddenly reignited when an alarming rumor began to spread: Bouillé's army was marching on Varennes! And the mob began to cry out: "To Paris! To Paris!"

At Sauce's, the King and Queen were still waiting for their savior Bouillé. At six o'clock, events took a dramatic turn; two emissaries from the Assembly rode into Varennes, armed with a decree enjoining "the good citizens to bring the King back to the National Assembly." The King and Queen were shattered. "There is no longer a king in France," murmured Louis XVI, absentmindedly placing the sheet of paper on the bed where his children were sleeping. The Queen snatched it and threw on the floor. "I will not have my children defiled by it," she exclaimed, completely exasperated.

Still convinced that Bouillé's troops would be arriving any minute, Louis XVI tried to play for time; the Queen and his children needed to rest; in fact, so did he. But the municipal representatives refused to be swayed. They insisted that the royal family set off as quickly as possible. Outside, the mob was growing dangerously rowdy. Louis XVI resigned himself. With an expression of annoyance, followed by the Queen, Madame Elisabeth, Madame de Tourzel and his children, he walked over to the berlin, which the people had harnessed and parked in front of the grocery. There were a few weak cries of "Long live the King!" and more energetic cries of "Long live the nation!" Exhausted, escorted by a huge crowd, the sovereigns began the trip back to the capital. Tossed by a human sea, the carriage drove away in a thick cloud of dust.

31

THE IMPASSE

*T*he return trip was one long nightmare. When they left Varennes, peasants brandishing rifles, scythes and sticks ran behind the berlin for the first few leagues, dreading the arrival of Bouillé's army. These men and women of modest means wanted to save their lives, their property and their villages, at the expense of a family that wanted to save its wealth and a certain conception of the French kingdom which was now outdated and no longer shared by its people. When they stopped at Sainte-Menehould, Louis XVI and Marie Antoinette still hoped that the troops would catch up with them. But it was too late. The uneasy mob began shouting: "We've been betrayed! They're waiting for Bouillé!" They were forced to leave hurriedly, while the peasants looked on in suspicion. Further along the road, in the heart of the countryside, the Comte de Dampierre, whose lands were nearby, wanted to pay his respects to the sovereigns. He was stopped. And as he tried to approach the carriage, he was massacred right before the eyes of the royal family.

In the evening, at Châlons-sur-Marne, Louis XVI turned down the suggestion made by several loyal subjects that he take flight alone. Nothing in the world could make him abandon his dear ones. The following day, in an oppressive heat, the melancholic cortege resumed its journey. The closer they got to Paris, the greater the hostility of the population. In the village of

Chouilly, where they had to make a brief stop, the rabble spit in the King's face and tore the Queen's and Madame Elisabeth's dresses. While some compassionate women mended their clothes as best they could, the two princesses sat sobbing next to the children, who clung fearfully to their skirts. Louis XVI and Marie Antoinette looked forward to being joined by the deputies sent by the Assembly to meet them. At least they would ensure their safety. To their great relief, they were met shortly after Epernay.

Representing the three principal political tendencies in the Assembly, the three elected officials greeted the King and Queen with deference. The Marquis de La Tour Maubourg, a staunch supporter of the King, climbed into the cabriolet of the ladies-in-waiting, which had been following the berlin since the beginning of the trip, while the democrat Pétion and the liberal Barnave were invited to take seats with the sovereigns. Pétion squeezed in between Madame Elisabeth and Madame de Tourzel; Barnave, between the King and the Queen. Overwrought, Marie Antoinette spoke to them hurriedly, in an oppressed voice. "The King did not want to leave France," she kept repeating.[1] Somewhat embarrassed by the mission they had been given, the two men were unable to utter a single word. They were avidly studying the royal couple, whom they had heard so much about and whom they had imagined very differently. To their amazement, they discovered a distraught couple, not particularly arrogant, expressing itself with simplicity. The family in no way matched the image being spread by all the malicious gossip. The Queen dandled the Dauphin on her knee and the child openly asked the King for his chamber pot, which the King handed him without the least sign of embarrassment. Pétion was quite taken with Madame Elisabeth. Very soon, their tongues loosened. Louis XVI talked about the constitution. The youthful Barnave, who represented the Assembly's moderate wing, answered intelligently, which made the Queen like him. Seeing that the young man was moved by her fate, she thought she might win him over.

By the time they reached Meaux, to stop for the night, the royal family were in a state of utter exhaustion. Their dirty clothes astonished everyone. The following day, Louis XVI had to borrow a shirt from a bailiff, so he could look more respectable for his arrival in Paris that evening. This was the moment they most dreaded. The Queen was informed that they would skirt the city by the northern boulevards, enter through the Etoile barrier and drive down to the Place Louis XV,[2] adjacent to the Tuileries gardens. When she expressed surprise that they would follow this route, she was told that it was better to avoid the risk of an assassination attempt and take a road where there were fewer houses. "I understand," she answered simply.

They set off at six-thirty in the morning. As they approached the capital, the crowds became truly menacing. At Bondy, a gang of madmen threw themselves on the carriage. Pétion and Barnave had to shout back that they were prepared to protect the King's life with their own. In Pantin, enraged women hurled themselves on the berlin, hollering angry words of abuse. Fortunately, Lafayette had thought to send the National Guard, who dispersed the assailants.

Yet Paris awaited the fugitive sovereigns in a state of absolute calm. "Whoever applauds the King will be flogged, whoever insults him will be hanged," could be read on the walls in the capital. The people had set themselves up as a formidable tribunal. "Keep your hat on, he will pass before his judges," a journalist had written. The National Guard stood at attention controlling a huge, silent crowd. It had been waiting for hours to catch a glimpse of the strange procession now making its entrance in a cloud of burning dust. In this oppressive silence, the King and Queen looked like they were going to their execution. From time to time Marie Antoinette buried her face in her son's hair, holding him tightly on her lap while he cried.

When the carriage stopped in front of the Tuileries, they came within a hairbreadth of tragedy. Stiff from the long journey, looking like someone lost in a nightmare, the King climbed clumsily out of the berlin and walked up the steps of the château without anyone interfering. But as soon as the Queen was seen, cries of hatred rang out, and a few crazed individuals tried to lunge at her. The National Guard stepped in just in time, and several deputies picked her up and quickly carried her into the palace. One of the elected officials had briskly taken the Dauphin in his arms, to bring him to safety as well, but for a few minutes the Queen thought that her child had been taken away from her.

Recovering from her nightmare, Marie Antoinette felt drained as she came into her husband's room, where a number of deputies were waiting. Unrecognizable, with dark rings under her eyes and covered with a layer of gray dust, she had but one desire—to take a bath. Yet she found the strength to joke with Barnave. "I confess that I never expected to spend thirteen hours in a carriage with you," she said in a tone of simulated playfulness before retiring to her apartment.[3] Then, while she rested in her bathtub, the King had to face the questions put to him by the representatives who had been appointed to interrogate him about his strange trip.

The representatives were in an awkward predicament; they were unsure what to do about Louis XVI and his family. In every city, above all Paris, the irate populace demanded the deposing of a king whose duplicity was now patently obvious. For the first time, people spoke openly of a republic. The Assembly, which had virtually finished drafting the constitution, saw its work threatened. The deputies, most of whom were constitutional monarchists, wanted to keep this weak, unlucky king on the throne, for in a sense he was the guarantor of their own power. Before reaching any verdict on the sovereign's fate, they had decided to suspend him—a unique event in the history of the French monarchy. A committee of inquiry had been appointed to investigate the circumstances behind what they persisted in calling an abduction. Louis XVI received the representatives courteously and lied to them shamelessly. Very vague as to the circumstances of his departure from Paris, he refrained from elaborating on the reasons for his leaving. He was happy, he said, to be back among the Parisians, whom he liked. He made a point of declaring his loyalty to the constitution, which he said he was prepared to ratify and defend. His statements completely contradicted the manifesto left on his desk. The investigators asked their questions in such a way that the King was exculpated before he could even feel accused. Two days later, when the same representatives questioned Marie Antoinette, she had recovered her calm and considered the answers she should give. She explained very modestly that she had not made any decisions; she had merely followed her husband and obeyed his orders.

No one was fooled by the sovereigns' statements when they were made public. The patriots were indignant. The nature of the regime was again called into question. At the Jacobins and the Cordeliers, the two big political clubs formed at the beginning of the revolution, they demanded that the King be deposed or tried. Many advocated establishing a republic. Those who had been to the United States praised the American democracy and shouted insistently that France should be a republic.

For as long as the Assembly had not reached a verdict on their fate, the King and his family continued to be considered prisoners; the Tuileries, now like a fortified camp, became their prison. The National Guardsmen camped in tents next to the château. People were searched before entering the palace. All the doors had to be double-locked and the sovereigns' every movement took place under the vigilant eyes of their jailers. Louis XVI and

Marie Antoinette were not even allowed to walk around freely in their apart-ments. Four officers escorted the Queen when she went to see the Dauphin. One of them knocked on the door and yelled: "The Queen!" The sentry on duty at the Dauphin's opened the door for the Queen and she would enter, followed by her four guards. The same procedure was adhered to when the little Prince wanted to go to his mother's. Marie Antoinette had to endure the presence of National Guardsmen right outside her bedroom door, which she was not allowed to shut, even when she went to bed. One night, one of these men had the audacity to sit on her bed so he could be comfortable while talking to her. In order to avoid such intrusions, the Queen asked her cham-bermaid to place her little bed next to hers.

In spite of the tight surveillance, Marie Antoinette regained hope. She had fully understood that the representatives wanted to keep Louis XVI in power. She managed to elude her guardians' vigilance, and, using a thou-sand ruses, to correspond with Fersen, Mercy and her brother the Emperor. Madame de Jarjayes, one of her most devoted ladies-in-waiting, smuggled out her clandestine correspondence.

The Queen's first letter was addressed to her beloved Fersen, who she knew was safe. After their hasty farewells on the road to Bondy, at dawn on June 21, Axel had made his way to Brussels, where he had joined the Comte de Provence. The news of the arrest at Varennes had driven him to despair. "Put your mind at rest; we are alive," she wrote him on June 28. "I exist . . . How anxious I have been about you and how I pity you for all your suffering at having no news of us," she wrote him the following day. "Don't write to me; it would only be exposing us; and above all don't come back here under any pretext. It is known that you got us away from here; all would be lost if you came here. We are under surveillance day and night, but I don't care . . . Don't be anxious, nothing will happen to me. The Assembly wants to treat us kindly. Farewell . . . I will not be able to write you anymore . . ."[4] The letter was probably much more tender; the ellipses indicate the illegi-ble passages that were crossed out. The following missive,[5] mentioned ear-lier,[6] escaped censorship. "I can tell you that I love you and indeed this is all I have time for," she said to him. "I am well. Do not worry about me. I would like to know you are well too." After instructing him regarding the people who were handling this secret correspondence, the Queen contin-ued: "Tell me to whom I should send my letters to you, for I cannot live without that. Farewell most loved and most loving of men. I embrace you with all my heart."[7]

Fersen exerted himself like a madman, from Brussels to Vienna, to try to get aid for the captives. The long missives he wrote to the Queen, of which only his handwritten first drafts survive, are not love messages, but political letters. "I am fine and live only to serve you,"[8] is the only liberty Fersen took in writing to the woman he loved. At least as far as we know. It is possible that in the final drafts he added more personal words that he had no reason to set down in his first drafts. It should be added that most of his letters were written in numbers or in invisible ink, which made their perusal time-consuming and complicated.

Marie Antoinette still played a double game. While secretly resuming contact with the courts of Europe, from whom she expected assistance, she had decided to use Barnave to get out of the tragic impasse facing the monarchy because of the flight to Varennes. Mirabeau having died suddenly on April 2, 1791, she wanted Barnave to intercede on behalf of the royal couple before the Assembly. Marie Antoinette saw him as a henchman of the revolution she abhorred, and thought he was a "fanatic." She did not realize that the young representative had been overtaken by a left that was increasingly attuned to the threats of the rabble, and that he was far from having any influence comparable to that of Mirabeau. At great personal risk, Barnave wrote her long reports on the political situation. Like his illustrious predecessor, he tried to persuade the royal couple that they had to accept the constitution and separate themselves from the counterrevolutionary movement to which public opinion believed the King and Queen were wedded.

On July 13, the committee appointed to investigate the King's flight submitted its findings. In their desire to preserve their legislative oeuvre, the representatives tried to give credence to the notion that Louis XVI and his family had been "abducted" by Bouillé, who had wanted to make the King "the instrument of his personal ambitions." This treasonous general[9] and his accomplices therefore had to be arrested. As for the text left by the King on the eve of his departure, it could not be taken into account, since it had not been countersigned by a minister! This report provoked heated protests among the left members of the Assembly, whose most prominent figures were Robespierre and Danton. But the left was in the minority. The moderates prevailed. Barnave attracted attention with an eloquent speech in which he declared: "Everyone must feel that the common interest lies in the revolution coming to an end." Not only were the committee's conclusions adopted, but the King was declared inviolable. Louis XVI was therefore cleared of any suspicion.

Paris was deeply shocked by these decisions. "There is a great Disposition for Riot among the People, but the Gardes nationales are drawn out and so posted as to prevent Mischief," Gouverneur Morris wrote in his journal.[10] In a stormy session, the members of the Cordeliers' club decided to take a petition to the Champ-de-Mars demanding the King's deposition. The Assembly was alarmed by this resolution, and it ordered the Mayor of Paris to break up any gathering that might disturb the public peace. Martial law was proclaimed. On July 17, while a crowd of Parisians were lining up to add their modest signatures to the petition, the National Guard invaded the Champ-de-Mars. Several individuals threw stones, a shot rang out and—no one knows how—shooting followed in spite of Lafayette's specific orders not to fire on the unarmed population. There were dozens of casualties.

Bailly, the Mayor of Paris, tried to justify the massacre by stressing that the factionists threatened the public order. Then the Assembly adopted a series of measures against incitement to murder and pillage. Several republicans were arrested. The bourgeois revolution prevailed, but triumphed without glory. The Champ-de-Mars massacre and the measures that followed it gave rise to an ineradicable feeling of hatred and a desire for revenge in the popular masses. The moderate revolutionaries from the early days, such as Lafayette, Bailly and Barnave, had now become enemies of the revolution. The King and Queen failed to grasp this.

Yet Marie Antoinette congratulated Barnave for his firmness during those days. She wanted to persuade him that she was in complete agreement with his views and those of his friends. While the Assembly was completing its draft of the constitution, Barnave asked the Queen to write to her brother the Emperor and state that she accepted the principle of a constitutional monarchy and wanted to maintain the alliance between the two powers. The Queen complied, with a heavy heart, and she sent Mercy a secret letter, asking him to warn the Emperor of the double game she was forced to engage in. "I had to give in to the requests of the party leaders here . . . It is extremely important to me that they believe I am of their opinion, at least for some time to come," she said to him.[11]

Louis XVI knew that he would have to accept this constitution, which he detested. At a loss, the Queen asked Barnave to explain the principal articles to her. She saw it as a mere "tissue of unworkable absurdities." Incapable of having a balanced opinion on a regime that she rejected a priori, exhausted by long sleepless hours spent coding and decoding messages, the Queen sank into a state of despair bordering on madness, as "the dreadful moment" approached when the legislative texts would be presented to the King. "At present we must follow a path that drives distrust away from us and at the same time can serve to foil and overturn as quickly as possible the monstrous work that has to be adopted," she said to Mercy. To her brother the Emperor she denounced "this race of tigers flooding the kingdom" and declared, pathetically: "We trust only you."[12]

More preoccupied by the risk of revolutionary contagion than the Queen of France's dramatic appeals, the European sovereigns gathered in Pillnitz, Germany. After protracted discussions, they recommended that all the European leaders turn their attention to the situation in France. This declaration, in which one could see indications of a forthcoming coalition against France, rekindled the hopes of the émigrés and increased the tensions between the revolution's partisans and opponents. It was certainly ill-timed for the royal couple, for public opinion was more and more convinced that they were colluding with the émigrés and foreign countries.

On September 13, Louis XVI informed the Assembly that he accepted the constitution. The restrictions against the King and Queen were immediately lifted, and the crowd could see the royal family attend mass. As cries of "Long live the nation! Long live the constitution!" went up, Louis XVI and Marie Antoinette could not hold back their tears. In the afternoon, a delegation from the Assembly came to the King to express its enthusiasm and announce the release of all those who had been implicated in his "abduction." Relaxed in appearance, Louis XVI turned toward his family and said: "Here are my wife and children, who share my feelings." "We share the King's feelings," the Queen replied graciously. The following day, at noon, Louis XVI went to the Assembly to take a solemn oath to the constitution. The Salle du Manège was packed; the Queen attended the session in a private box. Instead of a throne, the King was given a simple armchair decorated with fleurs-de-lis. As Louis XVI stood up, took off his hat and began to pronounce the first words of the oath, he noticed that the deputies had sat down and were wearing their hats. He suddenly turned pale, sat down and continued to read out the oath in a flat voice. In spite of the cheers that rang out, the sovereign felt more deeply humiliated than when he had been publicly insulted. On his return to the Tuileries, he broke down and wept in the arms of the Queen, who also shed tears.

However, they were obliged to continue to play the game before the representatives and the Paris population. The King and Queen had to preside over the elaborate festivities in celebration of the constitution. They attended the ballet *Psyché* at the Opera. Marie Antoinette did her best to smile. The King looked absentminded. Madame de Staël wrote that "when the Furies danced shaking their torches and the glow of the fire lit up the theater, she saw the faces of the King and Queen in the pale glow of this imitation Underworld and was suddenly overwhelmed with dire presentiments concerning their future."[13] After the opera, Louis XVI and Marie Antoinette drove up the illuminated Champs-Elysées in an open carriage. There were several cries of "Long live the King!" but whenever a cheer went up, a commoner clutching the door of the coach yelled back: "No, don't believe them: long live the nation!" No one thought of chasing away this individual about whom nothing was known. He greatly upset the sovereigns, yet they dared not complain about him.

32

THE LAST SHOW OF STRENGTH

*M*arie Antoinette, who had just turned thirty-six, agreed to sit for the painter Kucharski. This last portrait of her, which remained unfinished, shows us a very different woman from the one who had been immortalized a dozen years earlier by her favorite painter. Her face is full, her complexion radiant, but her sad gaze and scornful mouth give the painting a truthfulness that Madame Lebrun had never succeeded in capturing. Actually, the Queen had changed enormously. She had lost weight, her hair had turned gray and her cheeks were abnormally flushed. Consumed by a fear of the future, overwhelmed by a far too oppressive share of responsibilities, exhausted by sleepless nights and the continuous exertion of self-control, she was unrecognizable. "Sometimes I do not hear myself and have to stop and think if it is really me who is speaking. I don't have a moment to myself, between the people I must see, writing, and the time I spend with my children. This last occupation, which is not the most trifling, is my only joy . . .[1] and when I am very sad, I take my little boy in my arms, I kiss him with all my heart and this consoles me for a time," she wrote to Fersen.[2]

Her love for the Swedish nobleman remained her sole comfort. Fortunately, she had no idea that her beloved Axel was having an affair with Eleanore Sullivan, a very beautiful woman with a turbulent past, and the official mistress of an extremely wealthy Scotsman, Quentin Crawfurd. Staunch royalists, Mrs. Sullivan and Crawfurd had been privy to the flight to

Varennes. Ever since, from their temporary asylum in Brussels, they conspired as best they could to help the royal family. However, Fersen's liaison with Mrs. Sullivan set tongues wagging. The news even reached Sweden, where Countess Piper, Axel's sister, thought it advisable to write him: "I'm warning you, my dear Axel, for the love of Her[3] for whom, if she heard this news, it could cause a fatal blow. Everyone is watching you and talking about you. Think of unhappy Her. Spare her the most fatal pain of all."[4]

Marie Antoinette was then grappling with a political situation that seemed increasingly complex to her. By virtue of the constitution, a new Assembly had been elected, called the Assemblée Legislative. There were 264 representatives on the right, favoring a limited monarchy, 136 on the left, hostile to the aristocracy, and 345 undecided, capable of going one way or the other. The chamber greeted the King's opening speech rather warmly, and that night the sovereigns were applauded at the theater. But with the Queen's active encouragement, Louis XVI persevered in playing a double game and refused to accept his role of constitutional monarch in good faith, even though it left him room to maneuver. As if to show his hostility to the new Assembly, he kept his ministers, but without giving them any program. He let himself be carried along by events, hoping to regain his lost power, thanks to a war that would allow him to impose himself on his subjects.

Marie Antoinette regarded this Legislative Assembly as nothing more than "a heap of blackguards, madmen and beasts."[5] However, she decided to make use of the moderates, with the ulterior motive of later dispensing with them. She also pretended to listen to Barnave, who implored her to side with the people against the connivings of the aristocracy and the foreign powers. No one was duped by this duplicity. Considered to have sold out to the court, Barnave was discredited in Parisian political circles; royalists and émigrés referred to him as the Queen's evil genie. "They say the Queen is sleeping with Barnave," Fersen noted coldly in his journal. This man, though he knew Marie Antoinette well, could not understand the steps she was taking. "Do you sincerely want to side with the revolution?" he asked her.[6] "Set your mind at rest," she replied, "I am not going over to the *enragés*. If I see them or have relations with some of them, it is only in order to make use them. They inspire too much horror in me; I would never go over to them."[7] In spite of the risks, Fersen wanted to come to Paris, but the Queen dissuaded him.

At the Tuileries, the atmosphere was oppressive. Surrounded by spies, the King and Queen rarely spoke in front of the servants. And when they were alone with Madame Elisabeth, there was a veiled hostility in the air. The

King's sister kept up a regular correspondence with her émigré brothers and disapproved of the Queen's machinations. "It is hell at home; there is no way of saying anything even with the best intentions in the world. My sister[8] is so indiscreet and surrounded with intriguers, there is no way of talking to each other or we would be arguing all day," she complained to Fersen.[9] As her only entertainment, Marie Antoinette sometimes mingled with the guests at the Princesse de Lamballe's salon, where the last remaining members of the aristocratic party congregated in Paris.

The threat of counterrevolution weighing on the new regime angered the representatives. The émigrés intensified their attacks outside the country, while domestically the aristocrats tried to organize uprisings with the support of the refractory priests. The Assembly voted several decrees against these troublemakers. The émigrés, starting with the King's brothers, were ordered to return to France within two months or be accused of conspiring against the security of the state and having their assets seized. The King was to tell the princes who had welcomed the émigrés to expel them outside their borders. The refractory priests were required to take the oath to the constitution or face deportation. The ratification of the decrees forced Louis XVI to come out for or against the revolution. The King did not mind signing the decree that concerned his brothers and appealed to the foreign princes. On the other hand, he made use of his right of veto when it came to the laws concerning the émigrés and the refractory priests. This provoked a general outcry in the Assembly. The moderates were downcast and the republicans enraged, and they consequently challenged the right of veto granted to the sovereign by the constitution.

The republican offensive intensified. The counterrevolution had to be crushed, for it threatened the work accomplished in the last two years. The question arose of whether to go to war against the powers that supported the counterrevolution. Ever since the Pillnitz declaration, a widespread fear of armed conflict had emerged, with the republicans ascribing to the Emperor a zeal that was far more bellicose than it actually was. As most of the patriots saw it, war would compel everyone to take sides for or against the revolution, beginning with the King himself. Robespierre and Marat were the only ones who argued that an armed conflict would play into the hands of the King and the "Austrian committee" maintained by the Queen.

The prospect of war rekindled Louis XVI and Marie Antoinette's hopes. Pleased with the new turn of events, the King wrote to Breteuil that he wished for war. As for the Queen, she said to Mercy that "it was now up to the Emperor and the other European powers to help them."[10] Barnave, who had finally understood the royal couple's double game, had preferred to put an end to their epistolary relationship. He retired to his province, bitter and disillusioned.[11] Before leaving Paris, he sent the Queen a last message: "I see very little hope of success in the plan you are being made to follow; you are too far away from help; you will be lost before it can reach you."

For his part, Fersen had worked out new plans with King Gustavus III of Sweden, who dreamed of coming to the rescue of the King and Queen of France. He wanted them to escape from the Tuileries and be taken to Normandy, where troops would be landed. Marie Antoinette finally agreed to Fersen's trip. Her desire to see him again was dampened only by her fear of a step that was as dangerous for herself as for him.

Fersen arrived in Paris on February 13, 1792, in freezing weather, with a false passport and disguised as a courier. After having ascertained from one of the Queen's loyal friends that Marie Antoinette was expecting him in her apartment, Axel stole his way into the Tuileries and found himself by her side. His journal contains a few sparse notes attesting to this secret meeting: "Monday 13, Went to the Queen; took my usual route; afraid of the National Guard; her quarters wonderful. Stayed there. Tuesday 14, saw the King at six in the evening."[12] These two lines have caused much ink to flow. Biographers intent on upholding Marie Antoinette's virtue have maintained that she and her devoted admirer spent their time discussing politics and that Fersen slept in one of the unoccupied rooms of the château. Others, chief among them Stefan Zweig, came to the opposite conclusion: Assuming Marie Antoinette and Fersen had not been lovers prior to that evening, there is no doubt that they became lovers on that winter night. The mystery (if indeed it is one) will never really be solved. The two lovers' secret is sealed forever.

The following day, Fersen met the King only at six in the evening. Sad and discouraged, Louis XVI rejected any new escape plans. But he asked Fersen to inform all the sovereigns he met that his official statements were not to be taken at face value and that he was no longer a free person. The King retired soon, leaving his wife and her devoted admirer alone together. Axel parted from Marie Antoinette at nine-thirty, misleading her into thinking he was leaving for Spain.

The rest of the story is not quite as admirable. Instead of taking the road to Spain, the handsome Swede hailed a hackney to the rue de Clichy, where Eleanore Sullivan, now back in Paris with Crawfurd, was waiting for him. The Queen of France's romantic consoler spent over a week hidden in the attic, coming down to join his mistress whenever Crawfurd went out. He left Paris on February 21, without ever seeing Marie Antoinette again.

The Legislative Assembly's bellicose intentions calmed the Queen. The French intensified their incitements of the great powers, and the Minister of War, who had just formed two armies, let it be thought that France could stand up to all of Europe. Just then, they learned of Emperor Leopold II's sudden death, on March 10. This news greatly upset Marie Antoinette. She was far from suspecting that Leopold's twenty-four-year-old successor, Francis II, was "a military man at heart" and quite eager to cross swords with revolutionary France, which he loathed. As soon as she learned of her nephew's intentions, she sent him a secret emissary to tell him of the royal couple's "dreadful situation" and requesting prompt aid. Furthermore, the messenger was supposed to inform the Emperor of the following: one, that war would soon be declared against him; two, that Louis XVI and Marie Antoinette could count on the support of the majority of the French people from the beginning of the conflict; three, that the allies would be greeted as liberators as long as they respected the constitution, to which the King promised to bring the changes he deemed necessary. Lastly, the Emperor was asked to keep the émigrés as the army's rear guard; the King promised he would subsequently make them the elite corps of the future French army.

In view of the imminent conflict, Louis XVI thought it wise to form a new cabinet that would include members of the moderate left, called the Girondins.[13] Dumouriez, the new Minister of War, wanted to avert the enemy offensive without delay. Responding to her husband's entreaties, the Queen met with Dumouriez. She received him in her bedchamber and strode up and down the room, her face drawn. Haughty, curt, she went straight to the point without mincing words. "Monsieur," she said to him, "you are all-powerful at present, but this is through the favor of the people who break their idols. Your existence depends on your conduct. You must consider that neither the King nor I can accept all the innovations, or the constitution. I tell you so frankly; make the best of it." Unperturbed, Dumouriez replied: "Madame, I am sorry about the painful secret Your Majesty just confided in me. I will not betray it; but I am caught between the King and the nation and I belong to my country. Allow me to impress on you that the King's salvation, yours and that of your august children is tied to the constitution. I would be serving you badly, and him too, if I spoke to you differently." Irritated by these remarks, the Queen declared that the constitution would not last. "Believe me, Madame, I have no interest in misleading you, I abhor anarchy and crime as much as you do. Believe me, I have experience. I am in a better position than Your Majesty to judge events. This is not, as you seem to think, a passing popular movement. It is the almost unanimous insurrection of a great nation against inveterate abuses."[14] Dumouriez's remarks failed to frighten the Queen and she hastened to acquaint Mercy and Fersen of the general disposition of the troops at the frontiers and the military staff's plans of attack.

On April 20, 1792, Louis XVI, with great satisfaction, made the Assembly adopt the declaration of war against the Emperor, which the majority of the chamber had long wanted. On April 28, the French offensive in Belgium instantly turned to disaster. After this promising start, the Austrian Emperor and the King of Prussia, who had joined forces with him, appointed the Duke of Brunswick as commander-in-chief of the allied armies and decided to march on Paris. Kept informed of the Austro-Prussian plans by Fersen, the Queen advised him of the French troop movements. Though nothing specific was known of the King and Queen's machinations, it was rumored that the sovereigns were betraying the nation. Fear of the Ancien Régime's triumphant return inflamed patriotic passions. The masses were haunted by the idea of an aristocratic plot, and began to arm themselves.

Not for a moment doubting that everything she was doing was legitimate, Marie Antoinette despaired of ever seeing the arrival of those foreign armies that were supposed to liberate her. Her letters to Fersen rang out with desperate appeals regarding her ever "more dreadful" situation. She was being insulted right outside her windows. Her more moderate critics talked of locking her up in the Val de Grâce; the others clamored for her death. In constant fear of assassination, she had a little dog sleep under her bed to warn her in case an intruder entered her bedroom. Every day new scurrilous pamphlets nourished the fantasies of a people in search of culprits. Considered for years to be the "mother of all vices," the Queen had now become the "female monster" thirsting for blood, which the French imagination adored. In Paris, people rushed to applaud a play whose subject was the assassination of kings.

In order to meet the counterrevolutionary danger, the Legislative Assembly adopted three decrees: refractory priests, denounced by their fellow citizens, were to be punished by deportation; the King's guard, suspected of colluding with the counterrevolution, was to be dismissed; a camp of 20,000 National Guardsmen was to be set up in Paris to defend the capital against any attempt on the part of generals suspected of being tied to the court. This roused Louis XVI from the gloomy despair he had been plunged in for several weeks. He agreed to ratify the decree concerning his guard, but aggressively vetoed the two others. With the Queen's encouragement, he remained inflexible in spite of his ministers' pleas. On June 12, feeling strengthened by the support of the army's high-ranking officers, he dismissed his Girondin ministers and formed a moderate cabinet; this was considered a provocation.

On June 20, an enormous crowd armed with pikes, axes and sticks with metal tips left the outlying districts and marched toward the Assembly to deposit petitions demanding that the King withdraw his veto. The deputies were terrified by this horde of armed and menacing men, and heard only a few petitioners. Turned away from the Salle du Manège, which they could not enter, the demonstrators gathered in the Tuileries gardens and the area near the palace. Soon the gates were forced open without the National Guard making any real attempt to keep the mob out. Indeed, many of the guardsmen were fraternizing with the rioters, whose numbers were steadily growing.

Inside, the Queen, Madame Elisabeth and the children had taken refuge, trembling, in Louis XVI's room. Though Marie Antoinette sobbed incessantly, the King remained calm. At three o'clock, there was a frightening din as the doors to the château were smashed by the blows of the assailants, with no resistance on the part of the attendants in charge of defending the château. In a matter of minutes, the palace was invaded by the mob. The clamor of the riot, the noise of the doors being axed apart, completely horrified the royal family. The few faithful friends who were still with the sovereigns dragged the protesting Queen and the children into the Dauphin's apartment, while Louis XVI, with his sister clinging to his coattails, faced the invaders. A few grenadiers pushed the King and Madame Elisabeth against the embrasure of a windows in order to better assure their protection. The Queen stayed in the Dauphin's room for two hours. Several times, she asked if she could join her husband. But when she was reminded that she would be exposing the King and her son to danger, she resigned herself to staying put. But soon sinister sounds could be heard again. More doors were torn down. The rioters were coming closer. They invaded the Queen's apartment and ransacked it. To escape from the madmen, Marie Antoinette and her children now had to withdraw to the King's bedroom and wait for what seemed another endless period of time. The invaders were clamoring for the Queen in increasingly threatening tones. Under the protection of several loyal grenadiers, holding her son in her arms and fighting back her tears, Marie Antoinette walked through her husband's bedroom and into the Council Room. She and the young princes were pushed into a corner of the room and a heavy table dragged in front of them as a barricade against the raging mob. Santerre, who commanded a battalion of the National Guard, watched over her. For several hours, she had to withstand miniature gallows and guillotines jiggled in front of her, threats and unending verbal abuse. The Dauphin sobbed. He had put on the patriots' red bonnet, just like his father, whom he could not see for he was in the neighboring room.

Throughout the entire day, Louis XVI tried to converse with the people who demanded that he withdraw his veto. He consistently and calmly answered that he would not go back on his decision. At ten in the evening, the courtyards and gardens were finally evacuated. The King, the Queen, Madame Elisabeth and the children hugged each other and sobbed. The Queen, exhausted, threw herself in an armchair. Then they thought of having a light meal.

"I still exist, but it is by a miracle. The 20th was a dreadful day. It is no longer against me that they are most bitter, but against my husband's very life; they do not hide it anymore," Marie Antoinette wrote to Fersen. "He showed a firmness and strength that impressed them for the moment, but the dangers could once again arise at any time. I hope you are receiving news of us. Farewell. Take care of yourself for our sake and do not worry about us."[15] Though she was under increasingly close surveillance, the Queen still received Fersen's letters. He reassured her as best he could, giving her the latest news concerning commander-in-chief Brunswick. The latter was getting ready to march on Paris. Moreover, Fersen said triumphantly, he planned to precede his entrance "with a very strongly worded manifesto, in the name of the allied powers, which would hold all of France, and Paris in particular, responsible for the royal persons."[16] Convinced that threats would suffice to paralyze revolutionary action, he saw this manifesto, which he himself was actively working on, as the royal family's last hope.

While Fersen was busy in Brussels, a semblance of court life resumed at the Tuileries. Terrorized, Marie Antoinette lived in the mad hope of being delivered by the foreign armies. She felt comforted by the idea of the manifesto. "Our position is dreadful," she wrote to Fersen on July 3, "but do not be too worried; I feel courageous and something in me tells me that we will soon be happy and saved. This idea alone sustains me . . . When will we see each other again quietly?"[17]

33

THE FALL OF THE MONARCHY

A show of strength was imminent and the Queen was frightened. The situation of the army was deteriorating. Given the magnitude of the peril, the Assembly declared "the country in danger"; this meant a mass mobilization against the foreign despots and against the King, accused of being in league with them. The National Guards from all the departments, called the *fédérés*, poured into the capital by the thousands. Republican, staunchly patriotic, they were prepared to drive the enemy out of France and do away with the monarchy. The atmosphere at the Tuileries was becoming more and more oppressive. Convinced that the King was in danger of being assassinated, Marie Antoinette had a metal breastplate made for him as a protection against stab wounds. Louis XVI refused to wear it, except on the occasion of the 14th of July celebration. On that day, the crowd on the esplanade of the Champ-de-Mars seemed to be preparing for a riot, rather than a patriotic ceremony. Only a single row of guardsmen separated the royal family from the menacing spectators. There was a moment of supreme mockery when Louis XVI took an oath utterly devoid of meaning, while the public jeered. The Queen, looking very elegant in a white dress embroidered with sprigs of lilac, tried in vain to smile through her tears. Several hours earlier, she had let slip her last opportunity to escape. Dismayed by the violence of June 20, Lafayette had left his command and hastened to Paris to put his sword in the service of the King.

He offered to take him and the royal family to Compiègne. But Marie Antoinette had dissuaded her husband from accepting this plan. She feared that in agreeing to be kept in power thanks to this revolutionary general, the King would be obligated to him. She preferred to owe her freedom to the Austro-Prussian armies. For the moment, she waited impatiently for the manifesto Fersen had promised. She was far from suspecting that this incendiary proclamation would hasten the fall of the monarchy.

The manifesto, to which the Duke of Brunswick had put his signature, was known throughout Paris by August 3. Incredibly violent, it threatened to subject the capital to total subversion and bring death to its inhabitants if they did not submit immediately to their King. It seemed obvious that the sovereign had colluded with the enemies of the nation. Driven by an irrepressible desire for revenge, the Parisians in the local assemblies demanded the King's deposition and trial.

Outstripped by the demands of the people and the turmoil in the streets, the Assembly stalled for time. In order to save the moribund monarchy, it suggested that the King abdicate in favor of his son, who would be assigned a tutor and a patriotic cabinet. Louis XVI refused. During that time the sections[1] were arming themselves. The events of June 20 had shown that it was easy to storm the Tuileries. Now it was essential to go much further. Powerless, the Assembly let events follow their course.

In the Tuileries, the royal family were in a state of constant fear. The King thought that he would soon be brought to trial. He had destroyed quantities of documents and set up a hiding place in the panels of a corridor for other papers. The Queen had left her ground-floor apartment and slept in a room between the rooms of her husband and her son. Awake at dawn, she was haunted by dark thoughts, though she still hoped they would be rescued by the foreign troops. One morning, she confided to Madame Campan that she knew the armies' marching plan.

Never were the Tuileries courtiers more numerous than at the mass of Sunday, August 5. The last defenders of the monarchy wanted to show their loyalty to the King and Queen. Their deep concern for Louis XVI and Marie Antoinette could be seen by the distressed looks on their faces. They must have thought that they might be seeing them for the last time. Hubert Robert has left us a remarkable painting, in warm but faded colors, of this last religious service of the monarchy, showing the royal family from the back, kneeling and lost in prayer.

No insurrection was more actively prepared for than that of August 10,

1792. On August 8, Mandat, the commander of the National Guard, summoned the Swiss Guards stationed in Rueil and Courbevoie. These were elite troops the King could count on; they were devoted to his cause and determined to wage battle. To these nine hundred Swiss could be added nine hundred gendarmes and two thousand National Guardsmen. The latter were far less reliable, as had been apparent the previous Sunday. Several among them had yelled "No more King" at the entrance to the chapel. On the afternoon of the 9th, Louis XVI learned that the storming of the palace was imminent. Convinced that the last battle to save the royalty was about to be waged, approximately three hundred noblemen came to the Tuileries that evening. Armed with swords, rifles or simply ordinary shovels and fire tongs, they came prepared to sacrifice their lives for their deeply held convictions.

Having taken refuge in the King's apartment, the royal family and its last defenders kept silent. At eleven, Roederer, the Prefect of the Commune, came to tell them that all Paris was in revolt. Soon Pétion, the recently elected mayor, arrived to guarantee the "preservation" of the royal family, as he put it. Then, muffled drumrolls were heard in the distance; a tocsin rang out in one church tower, followed by two, and then three others. They stood by the windows and listened, calling out the names of the patron saints of all the churches, like a litany, as they recognized each mournful peal one by one. The monarchy's death knell was tolling in the depth of the night. Louis XVI ordered the doors to the terrace closed. They waited. Some in the group wanted to keep Pétion as a hostage, but they let him go to the Assembly. Soon they were informed that the faubourgs were in ferment. Roederer sat down on a stool between the Queen and Madame Elisabeth. The others sat wherever they could, on chairs or on the floor. Yet several courtiers pointed out that it was contrary to etiquette to sit down in the presence of the King.

Suddenly the tocsin stopped ringing. An oppressive silence descended on the château. Louis XVI took advantage of this apparent lull to flop down on his bed fully dressed. The Queen and her sister-in-law lay down on the two couches in an antechamber, while the ladies-in-waiting kept watch. At four o'clock, the first hint of daylight appeared in the sky. Madame Elisabeth rose and walked slowly up to a window. There were red streaks in the eastern sky. "Sister, come and see the dawn," she said to the Queen. Like an automaton, Marie Antoinette took a few steps and joined Elisabeth by the window. The King came into the room, his hair unpowdered and completely flattened. They continued to wait.

Paris was waking up. The inhabitants of the faubourgs and the *fédérés* were advancing. Soon they could be seen, preceded by several cannons; they lined up and took up positions for battle near the château. The Queen grew frightened and asked Roederer what to do. Without losing his composure, he replied that they should seek refuge in the Assembly without further delay. It was the only place where the royal family would be safe. "Monsieur, we have forces here; it is time we found out who will prevail—the King, the constitution or the rebels?" she replied, proudly and haughtily.[2] Roederer tried to press his point, but in vain.

In the meantime, the insurgents were crowding in front of the palace gates in growing numbers. The King decided to go and encourage his men. He walked clumsily down into the courtyard to review the troops. The Swiss cheered him, but the National Guardsmen greeted him with boos. "Like flies pursuing an animal that they are eager to torment," several gunners shouted him down, yelling: "Down with the King! Down with the veto!" The Queen, who watched the scene from a window, began to cry. Louis XVI returned to his apartment and sat down without saying a word. How could they wage battle against the popular forces when their own troops were so divided?

Roederer was even more firmly convinced that the King should ask the Assembly for protection. "Resistance is impossible. All of Paris is coming," he said again to the Queen, who wanted a final showdown. Roederer insisted: "Sire," he said, "there is no time to lose; there is only one thing to do now. We request permission to take you away." Shattered, the King said simply: "Let us go." The Queen did not reply, but she was so overcome with emotion that Madame de Tourzel saw "her face and bosom become flushed."[3] It was eight-thirty.

Preceded by Roederer and the officer of the Swiss troops who led the march, they formed a sad procession. The King came first. The Queen followed him, holding the Dauphin by the hand. Then came Madame Elisabeth with the young Marie Thérèse at her arm, sobbing; the Princesse de Lamballe and the Duchesse de Tourzel, the ministers and several noblemen. Louis XVI walked straight ahead, his face livid; the Queen, distraught, furtively wiped away the tears she could not hold back; the Dauphin, who did not understand what was happening, kicked piles of dead leaves with his feet. "They are falling early this year," the King mumbled, while the crowd jeered him. When he entered the Salle du Manège—fortunately not far from the château—he went up to the president, stood on his left and said: "I have come here to avoid a great crime and I will always think of my family and myself as safe among the nation's representatives. I will spend the day here."[4]

Dismayed by this unexpected arrival, the deputies confined Louis XVI and his family in a stifling little room behind the president's seat. While the riot was raging outside, they dared not come to a decision regarding the fate of the man who had been King of France. The sound of gunfire, followed by cannons, could be heard outside. The battle was raging at the Tuileries. The *fédérés* and the people from the faubourgs were fighting the Swiss and the monarchy's other champions.

On leaving the château, Louis XVI had put the elderly Maréchal de Mailly in command of the forces, promising he would return as soon as calm was restored. He had not given orders to surrender. The Assembly had tried to send a delegation warning the insurgents that there was no reason to invade the château since the King had taken refuge among the representatives. But the delegation had been obliged to retrace their steps. The insurgents had already charged through the courtyard and broken inside the palace, convinced that the defense would capitulate. The Swiss, who had taken the offensive, greeted them with heavy gunfire. The assailants retaliated with cannon fire. While they were defending the château, the Swiss received Louis XVI's written order to cease fighting. Seething with rage, they handed their arms to the rioters and were massacred by them. The insurgents and the *fédérés* complained loudly of treason; the defenders of the château, they claimed, had lured them inside in order to ambush them. This was an inexcusable crime; its authors deserved neither forgiveness nor pity, for it was the ultimate proof of a counterrevolutionary, royal plot.

The King and Queen could do nothing but sit idly by and watch the legal collapse of the monarchy. While the Queen cried incessantly and the Dauphin moaned to be taken out for a walk, the King remained impassive and ate his meals with a hearty appetite. In the evening, they were taken to the narrow cells of the Couvent des Feuillants, whose walls were papered in green, and they tried to get some rest. Several devoted attendants, including Madame Campan, were allowed to join them. "We are lost, we will die in this horrible revolution,"[5] the Queen cried out, in an attack of nerves, upon seeing her lady-in-waiting. She got up suddenly and strode up and down the room, cursing her fate. The royal family spent three days in the stifling cubicle at the Assembly and three nights in the convent.

Placed in an awkward predicament by the King's fate, the representatives merely voted Louis XVI's temporary suspension. They felt that the gravity of the situation demanded another institutional setting, and they decided to disband. They called on a new constituent assembly to define the nature of the regime that the French wanted to adopt. In the interim, before the future elected representatives reached their verdict concerning the fate of the King, they decided he would be transferred to the Temple. The mayor came to fetch the royal family at five o'clock on August 13. They were squeezed into a court carriage with Madame de Lamballe and Madame de Tourzel. In a sinister mockery of a parade, the carriage made its way slowly across the capital, escorted by National Guardsmen on foot, waving the white flag. All along the road, the deposed monarch was met with threats and abuse. They were deliberately taken to the Place Vendôme so Louis XVI could see the overturned statue of Louis XIV. "This is the way tyrants are dealt with!" the people yelled, intoxicated by their victory.

Finally, at around seven o'clock, the carriage rolled into the Temple courtyard. The heavy doors closed behind them and the clamor of the crowd was no longer heard. The Temple consisted of an elegant seventeenth-century mansion called the palace. It had been magnificently restored and furnished in the eighteenth century by the Prince de Conti, the setting of his sumptuous receptions. A few yards away there was an enormous dungeon, surmounted with four turrets and an adjoining, less imposing building, the small Temple tower. The royal family was taken inside the palace, which the King and Queen knew very well. They had been invited there several times by the Comte d'Artois, its last owner. It will be recalled that Louis XVI and Marie Antoinette had dined there on the occasion of the celebrations for the first Dauphin's birth. Relieved at finding themselves in this pleasant retreat, they took a walk in the garden. They were already allotting the rooms when they were told that dinner was being served. The presence of the slovenly-looking municipal guards, smoking their pipes ostentatiously, reminded them that the grand old days were over. Soon they lost their very last illusions. At around eleven o'clock, they were taken to the sinister dungeon and temporarily lodged in the apartment of the guard of the archives, in the little tower, while the big tower was being prepared for them, a dwelling that would actually be their prison.

Several days after their arrival at the Temple, they were no longer allowed the servants they had initially been granted, except for one valet who remained in Louis XVI's service. On August 19, at around midnight, Madame de Tourzel and Madame de Lamballe were taken away and incar-

cerated at the prison of La Force. The Queen and her two friends wept bitterly on parting. The vise was tightening around the prisoners.

A strange family life was soon organized under the iron rule of the municipal guards who kept watch over the illustrious prisoners. The days went by,
monotonously. The King rose and dressed at six o'clock. After his prayer, he
read until nine. The Queen rose later and helped the Dauphin dress, then she
and the children joined the King and Madame Elisabeth for breakfast. The
King taught his son to read and write, and instructed him in Latin, history and
geography, while the Queen and her sister-in-law drew and gave music lessons
to Madame Royale. When they had permission from Santerre, the new commander of the National Guard, they would take walks in the garden. The
Dauphin was delighted; he could play ball or quoits until mealtime. Then
they went up to the King's quarters and had a quick lunch in the Queen's
room. Louis XVI played a game of backgammon or piquet with his sister and
then dozed off in an armchair. Meanwhile, Marie Antoinette and Elisabeth
did some needlework or knitting and the children studied their lessons. At
seven o'clock one of the two princesses read out loud. They dined at eight
o'clock, after putting the Dauphin to bed. The King went up to his room and
read until midnight. Marie Antoinette stayed with Elisabeth until they were
given the order to separate, and the Queen was locked into her room.

The conditions of their detention soon became more unpleasant. Louis
XVI's sword was confiscated. To avoid a daily search, the King asked his valet
to turn his pockets inside out at night after he had undressed. For fear that the
prisoners might correspond with the outside, their bread was sliced before
being served to them and their food thoroughly examined. In spite of all
these precautions, which they pretended not to find insulting, Louis XVI and
Marie Antoinette were kept informed of events on the outside. Louis XVI's
valet reported everything he heard, and some news vendors, bribed by the
royalists, read out the news in a loud voice by the walls of the Temple. The
King and Queen still entertained the hope that they might be freed by the
foreign armies. They were delighted by the series of French defeats they were
told about, and heard with satisfaction about the birth of royalist movements
in several provinces.

On September 2, feeling more serene thanks to the latest news, they were
quietly walking in the garden with their children when they were suddenly
hurried inside. Drumbeats could be heard as well as a confused noise that
was growing louder and louder. Paris was in turmoil. The French defeats

gave substance to the thesis of an aristocratic plot. The counterrevolutionary danger had never seemed more terrifying than now, when the nation's future was in jeopardy because of hostile forces it could not contain. A vengeful panic soon took possession of the population. In a tidal wave of sudden rage, crazed by the certainty of treason, the mob stormed the prisons where the aristocratic royalist sympathizers, the last surviving Swiss and refractory priests were being held since August 10. There followed a hideous massacre. From September 2 to 6, the wails of slaughtered victims rang out in the streets of Paris and the gutters ran with streams of blood. The government formed after August 10 was more concerned with retreating south of the Loire than with stopping the killing.

Given this paroxysm of violence, there was good reason to fear the royal family would be assassinated. On September 3, the King was denied permission to walk in the garden. He had no inkling of what was going on in the city. When the royal family sat down to eat, a frightening din could be heard outside. A municipal guard and four commoners burst into the room. They asked the King and Queen to stand at the window. Other guards tried to prevent them from doing so. The prisoners were alarmed. "They want to hide from you the head of Lamballe, which has been brought here to show you how the people take revenge on their tyrants," said one of the men, sniggering. "I advise you to appear if you do not want the people to come up here." Marie Antoinette fainted; the children started to cry. "We expect anything, Monsieur, but you might have spared the Queen knowledge of this dreadful misfortune," the King said calmly.[6]

The people's delegates left. The Queen regained consciousness. Through the blinds, the head of the Princesse de Lamballe could be seen at the end of a pike, her face twisted into a grimace and her long blond hair flowing in the wind, caked with blood. Her naked, mutilated body had been dragged through the streets by her assassins; it lay on the ground among a group of madmen; they had torn out her heart and brandished it at the end of a sword like a trophy.

34

THE DEATH OF THE KING

*T*he King, the Queen and Madame Elisabeth stoically endured the insolent behavior of the municipal guards; every day they saw the walls covered with a fresh crop of threatening graffiti and obscene drawings. On September 21, they suddenly heard a stampede that made them all start. Had their saviors come to their rescue at last? A loud voice was heard outside, proclaiming the official abolition of the monarchy and the birth of the republic. The King did not interrupt his reading. The Queen took to her bed in despair.

That same day, the Prussian army had been defeated at Valmy. The French victory, though it was not decisive, dispelled the specter of defeat for the French army. Considered hostages since the first days of their incarceration, the King, the Queen and their children were now political prisoners, and negotiating their liberation was out of the question. The conditions of their detention worsened. On September 29, paper, pens and pencils were taken from them. Several hours later, Louis XVI was moved into the big tower of the Temple. He was taken alone, in spite of the Queen's tears and her insistence that she wanted to go with him. The following morning, she begged her jailers to let the family be reunited, at least at mealtimes. Permission was granted two days later. During the day, Cléry, the valet who was still in the King's service, conveyed news back and forth between the two apartments. By the end of October, the Queen, Madame

Elisabeth and the children were also transferred to the big tower of the Temple.

Every precaution had been taken to make escape impossible; a new wall had been built to enclose the dungeon; it had two doors with iron bars and huge bolts. The apartments were on two floors, each divided into four modestly furnished rooms. The painted wallpaper in the entry represented the inside of a prison. There was no light from the windows that were fitted with enormous bars and splays. In spite of the stove, it was cold. The King soon fell ill and was bedridden; then the Dauphin became ill. The Queen nursed both her husband and her son. The surveillance over the prisoners was tightened. In the beginning of December, knives, scissors, penknives and all other sharp objects were taken from them.

These aggravated daily humiliations presaged a change in the prisoners' situation. Indeed, after much discussion, the newly elected assembly, called the Convention, had decided to set itself up as a tribunal and to try Louis XVI. A committee of inquiry was preparing the King's trial. When his "iron strongbox" was discovered—the secret hiding place he had used in his Tuileries apartment—his fate was sealed. The documents hidden away in this casket were proof of his double game since the beginning of the revolution, of his ties with the émigrés and of his negotiations with the foreign powers.

Cléry tried to be as gentle as possible in revealing to his masters that the King was going to be summoned before the Convention. On December 11, early in the morning, the roll of the drums could be heard. The King and Queen immediately understood what this meant. Impassive during lunch, they hardly dared speak to each other. Oblivious as children usually are at that age, the Dauphin asked his father to play with him. The King agreed. He was interrupted in the midst of a game of siam (a form of ninepins) and forced to follow the Mayor of Paris, who told him bluntly that he had come to take him before the representatives, now his appointed judges. Marie Antoinette awaited her husband's return in torment. But that evening he failed to join them as he had previously. He was not allowed any contact with his family for the duration of the trial. Permission had been granted for his son to move in with him, but only on condition that the child stop seeing his mother, his aunt and his sister.

Louis XVI was not so cruel as to ever separate the Dauphin from the Queen. So he resigned himself to remaining in solitude while Marie Antoinette gave in to despair. She hardly ate and wasted away, scarcely speaking and crying for hours. On Christmas Day, she was not allowed to see her husband and he took advantage of that sad day to draw up his will. The King had no illusions as to his the fate. Preoccupied with the salvation of his soul, he was absorbed in prayer. Aside from his lawyers, he had obtained permission to see the priest of his choice—a refractory priest, of course. Taking Holy Communion from this man was a great comfort to him. On January 1, 1793, the royal family exchanged their wishes for a "happy" new year through Cléry.

The Queen's anguish was excruciating. She knew that her husband's sentencing was imminent. She was prepared for the worst on the evening of January 20, when she was finally allowed to see him along with Madame Elisabeth and the children. She entered first, holding the Dauphin by the hand. The two princesses followed. The King himself told them that he had been sentenced to be guillotined in public, on the scaffold at the Place Louis XV, now renamed the Place de la Révolution.[1] "They all threw themselves into the King's arms; for several minutes there was a gloomy silence, broken only by sobs," Cléry recounts. They soon sat down, very close together, and spoke in a low voice for nearly two hours. The municipal guards, who watched them through the glass door, could not hear their heartrending conversation.

At around ten-fifteen, the King stood up. Louis XVI and Marie Antoinette held the Dauphin by the hand and the princesses clung to the condemned man's arms. They all wept. "I assure you," the King said to them, "that I will see you tomorrow morning at eight o'clock." "Do you promise?" they all asked together. "Yes, I promise." "Why not at seven?" the Queen asked. "Well, fine! At seven then," the King replied. "Farewell . . ."[2] He kissed them at length and went into his room. The princesses sobbed as they went down to their quarters. Marie Antoinette lay on her bed completely dressed and shaking like a leaf. As of six in the morning, she waited to be taken to the King. But no one came to fetch her. Abbé Edgeworth, who ministered to the King in his last moments, had advised him against seeing his family again. He feared that a new meeting would make parting too inhuman. Obeying his confessor, the King summoned Cléry: "Tell the Queen, my dear children and my sister that I had promised to see them this morning, but that I wanted to spare them the pain of such a cruel separation; it grieves me very much to go without receiving their last embraces . . . I give you the task of making my farewells." He handed him his seal for his son and his wedding ring for his wife. "Please tell her that I leave her with sorrow," he told him.[3] He also gave him a parcel of hair for Marie Antoinette. Cléry had to elude the guardians' surveillance in order to transmit the King's messages and give these precious objects to the Queen.

Louis XVI left for the scaffold shortly after nine o'clock. The drumrolls informed Marie Antoinette that she would never see her husband again. At the Temple, breakfast had been served as on any other morning. The children refused to eat in spite of their mother's pleas. Heartsick, they awaited the fatal moment. At ten twenty-two, they knew from the renewed drumrolls and the cannon shots that the King had just been beheaded. The royal family surrendered to their despair. Several minutes later, the Queen kneeled before her son and hailed the accession of Louis XVII.

After the King's death, Marie Antoinette fell into a state of complete prostration. She refused to eat or go outside, and was subject to frequent convulsive attacks which left her exhausted. She was unrecognizable. At thirty-seven, the Queen had become an old woman in frail health. One of the municipal guards, moved by the calamities that had befallen her, had to force her to take an occasional walk. Since she refused to go down into the garden because she did not want to pass by Louis XVI's door, on the days when he was on duty he took her to the circular gallery girding the tower, where she sat with her children and sister-in-law.

During the King's trial, the role of the Queen had never been alluded to. This woman who, for years, had been the catalyst for French animosity seemed forgotten. As for her relatives and former friends, they gave very little thought to her fate. Her nephew the Emperor had no intention of asking the French authorities for her liberation; he would have considered such a gesture a strategic error. The émigrés were indifferent to her misfortunes. Only Fersen attempted the impossible to save her. Shortly after the King's execution, it was rumored that the entire royal family had been slaughtered. Prostrated by this news, he had written a poignant letter to his sister: "The one who made my happiness, for whom I lived—yes, my tender Sophie, for I have never ceased loving her—the one I loved so much, for whom I would have sacrificed a thousand lives, is no more. Never will her adored image be erased from my memory."[4] When he learned that the Queen was still alive, Fersen was still very worried about her fate. "Sometimes I have hopes, sometimes I despair, and my compulsory inaction, the limited means there are of serving her, add even more to my sorrow. In my social circle, we speak only of her, of ways of saving her, and do nothing but grieve and cry over her fate," he wrote to his sister.[5] He considered every conceivable stratagem to save

Louis XVI's widow. With the very modest support of Mercy, he tried to bribe Danton to arrange her escape from the Temple. It seems the Convention representative did indeed receive money, but no promise was kept in exchange.

In Paris, a few loyal supporters of humble descent also tried to save the Queen, her sister-in-law and the children. Moved by the former sovereign's distress, two municipal guards, Toulan and Lepître, developed a kind of veneration for her. They made contact with Jarjayes, who had formerly handled her secret correspondence, and devised an escape plan. The Queen and Madame Elisabeth were to be smuggled out of the Temple in guards' clothes, Madame Royale was to be dressed like the lamplighter's son and the little King carried out in a laundry basket. The plans dragged out during the months of February and March, with the Queen's prospective saviors worried about where to house the royal family after their escape from the Temple.

By the end of March, the Queen was suspected of having accomplices inside the Temple. The personnel was changed. The plan as initially conceived became unworkable. Instead, Lepître offered to help the Queen escape alone. She refused, but took advantage of the opportunity to entrust Jarjayes with a new secret mission. She arranged for him to give the King's seal and his wedding ring to the Comte de Provence. She also sent him on a mission to Fersen. "When you are in a safe place," she said to Jarjayes, "I would very much appreciate it if you gave news of me to my great friend who came to see me last year. I don't dare write but here is an impression of my motto. When you send it, tell the person that it has never been more true." Fersen did not receive the letter until January 21, 1794! He explains the motto in the entry for that date in his journal: "This motto was from a seal showing a pigeon in flight with the motto *Tutto a te mi guida*. Her idea, in those days, had been to take my emblem and we had taken the flying fish for a bird. The impression was on a piece of paper. Unfortunately, it had been completely erased in the heat. In spite of that I keep it carefully in my casket with the note and the drawing of the seal."[6] Everything leads me to you . . . Never had the motto been more true.

Marie Antoinette was living under illusions. She thought her family was going to undertake negotiations to liberate her. Indeed, Louis XVI's execution was an affront to all those sovereigns who saw republicanism as a despicable form of government and France as a dangerous nation. But they were not in the least troubled at the thought that the Queen might be executed. A second victim, as regal as the first, further justified their action. The representatives were fully aware that the Queen was an insignificant hostage. On March 27, Marie Antoinette's fate was invoked for the first time before the Convention. "The time has come," said Robespierre, "for patriots to rekindle their vigorous and immortal hatred for those who are called kings. Will the punishment of one tyrant, obtained after so many odious debates, be the sole homage we pay to liberty and equality? Will we tolerate that a person who is just as guilty, equally accused by the nation, and who has been spared up till now, quietly reap the fruit of her crimes? A great republic, so insolently offended, so audaciously betrayed, expects you to deliver the impetus that will revive a holy antipathy for royalty in the hearts of all and give new strength to the public spirit."[7] He demanded that the former Queen of France be brought before the revolutionary tribunal "for having participated in violations against the liberty and security of the state."

Marie Antoinette, whom the patriots had always abhorred, would now become their victim. But whatever their aversion, they still had to find a pretext for bringing her to trial before the revolutionary tribunal, a court which had been created on March 10 to try aristocrats and persons suspected of royalist sympathies. Since foreign armies were endangering the national territory, and several provinces were rebelling against the excesses of the new regime, representative Cambon denounced General Dillon's plot; he claimed that the general planned to abduct Louis XVI's son and proclaim him King Louis XVII. This was sufficient reason for the members of the Convention to decide to separate the child from his mother and his aunt.

On July 3, at around ten o'clock, several municipal officers burst into the Queen's room and disrupted the three princesses' peaceful occupations. One of the officers pompously read a decree. The Queen did not immediately understand it; then the horrible truth became all too obvious—her son was to be taken away from her. Suddenly summoning all her remaining strength, this ailing woman rose up like a fury and furnished every possible argument for keeping her child. Adamant, the men approached the Prince's bed. He awoke and gave out piercing cries. His mother embraced him tightly. But when the municipal officers threatened to call in the guards to take the boy away by force, the Queen yielded. She helped him get up, dressed him and wept as she kissed him and gave him over to the brutes. She was completely disconsolate the next day on learning that her son's "tutor" was an alcoholic cobbler by the name of Simon. For two days she heard her son cry in Louis XVI's former bedroom, which was now his. On the third day, the child went down into the garden. Like a ghost in her mourning clothes, the Queen roamed silently around her apartment. She now had but one interest in life—to climb up to the top of the tower and watch through a slit in the wall for a glimpse of her child passing by at a distance.

Meanwhile, the allies continued to advance and the domestic insurrection, especially in the Vendée, was becoming a serious and alarming threat for France's new rulers. Anticipating a European coalition, the members of the Convention took radical measures aimed at striking terror in the hearts of all the enemies of the revolution. In a climate of uncontrolled panic, the deputies put out ringing appeals to fight all the enemies of the revolution. First among them was Marie Antoinette, who was now referred to exclusively as the widow Capet.[8] People clamored for her to be brought before the revolutionary tribunal to account for her crimes.

On August 2, the princesses were suddenly awakened at two in the morning: the Queen was going to be taken to the prison of the Conciergerie. Like an automaton, without protesting, Marie Antoinette got up, dressed and packed a little bundle with the few things she was allowed to take. She kissed her daughter and sister-in-law tenderly. Then without looking back, in her long black garment, which made her pallor all the more striking, the Queen left the Temple.

35

THE CONCIERGERIE

ifteen minutes later, the cabriolet carrying the Queen stopped in front of the grim towers of the Conciergerie. Without any consideration, the former sovereign was pushed in front of a wicket gate and submitted to the formalities of imprisonment like a common criminal. Registered under the name of "widow Capet," she became the 280th prisoner of that institution. Before being taken to her cell, her bundle was opened and the clerk carefully noted down its contents. The jailers then led her into her new quarters, a dungeon of fifteen square meters whose walls were covered with an old cloth stained by humidity. A narrow window, level with the ground, let in a pale light. Marie Antoinette's only furniture was a camp bed, a table, two chairs with straw seats, a convenience chair and a bidet. A screen hid her from the gaze of two soldiers who were supposed to watch her, day and night.

She was forbidden to leave her cell, though the other prisoners were allowed to walk in the courtyard and corridors. Up at six in the morning, she washed and dressed, with the help of Rosalie, a kind girl who did everything she could to improve the conditions of her captivity. But, of course, her means were very limited. The Queen, who had no right to a pen, paper or pencils, would have been doomed to complete inactivity had she not been given several novels, which she devoured avidly. The rest of the time she watched the two gendarmes play backgammon, as she twirled her rings on her fingers.

The Conciergerie was called death's antechamber—and for good reason. When Fersen learned that she had been transferred there, he tried desperately to find a way of saving her. He wanted to send a large cavalry force to Paris to free her. But the steps he took before the highest Austro-Prussian military authorities were all in vain. "I am no longer alive, for it is not living to live as I do now, suffering so much pain," he wrote to his sister Sophie. "If I could only do something for her deliverance, I think I would suffer less, but not being able to do anything except by appealing to others is awful. I can't do anything, and all I can think of is that unfortunate and worthy princess's misfortune. My greatest happiness would be to die for her. I begrudge myself the very air I breathe when I think she is locked up in a horrible prison."[1] Meanwhile, Madame de Staël published anonymously a sentimental booklet entitled *Réflexions sur le procès de la reine, par une femme* [Reflections Concerning the Queen's Trial, by a Woman]. Appealing to women, Necker's daughter refuted the calumnies that Marie Antoinette had been the victim of since her halcyon days, and pleaded her cause as an unfortunate mother.

The Queen's weariness was extreme. She was exhausted by serious hemorrhaging and she seemed numb to everything. Strangers streamed into her cell every day. She hardly noticed the men and women who stared at her as though she were a strange beast. By letting anyone who wanted to see "*l'Autrichienne*" in prison spend a few minutes in her presence, the concierge had found a way of supplementing his income. However, one day Marie Antoinette was unsettled. Among her visitors, she recognized the Chevalier de Rougeville, one of the officers who had protected her on that horrible day, June 20, 1792. Taking advantage of a moment's inattention on the part of her guards, he made a sign to her, and threw two carnations at her feet, which she quickly picked up. They contained a message, informing her that the Chevalier planned to abduct her. With beating heart, the Queen tried to answer him by tracing letters on the paper with pinpricks. The gendarme on duty noticed what she was doing, took the incriminating evidence away and gave it to his immediate superiors. Rougeville had managed to run away.

The Queen was racked by such anxiety that she had to be given herbal tea to calm her. Much more than captivity, she feared the consequences of the Chevalier's mad attempt at a time when the members of the Convention were compiling evidence against her. Her fears were completely justified. As soon as the incident was known, throughout Paris people said that there was a new plot to abduct the "widow Capet" and restore the monarchy. Fouquier-Tinville, the public prosecutor, who complained of not having received the evidence he needed to make his indictment, did not fail to exploit the affair. After a formal search of the Queen's cell, her remaining jewels and her watch were confiscated. Two deputies were then appointed to interrogate her.

They appeared before her on September 3, 1793. At first they questioned her as though a minor matter were involved, but they soon went on to more general questions.[2] They asked her if she knew that the French troops had won some victories, and if she had maintained "relations on the outside by secret means." Stressing her situation as a prisoner, Marie Antoinette told them that she had never had any news other than the things cried out by the peddlers on the other side of the Temple wall. "Are you interested in the success of our enemies' troops?" she was asked abruptly. "I am interested in the success of the troops of my son's nation; when one is a mother, that is the primary relationship," she replied, rather cleverly. And Marie Antoinette asserted that her only concern was for France's happiness. "May France be great and happy, that is all we desire," she declared calmly to these men who tried to extract incriminating statements from her. After she had asserted that she had always done her duty, they broached a specific topic—the flight to Varennes. Marie Antoinette repeated what she had said to the deputies conducting the investigation after June 21, 1791; as a submissive and obedient wife, she had followed her husband, who had not wanted to leave France but to "return freely among the people." She had only done her duty. To clear herself, she had decided to depict herself as a subservient woman who had respected the absolute supremacy of her husband's decisions.

They investigated her briskly concerning the "carnation plot." Plied with questions, the Queen finally admitted that she had indeed received a note from the mysterious visitor. She said it contained only some rather vague sentences, and she had simply replied that she was under surveillance. The halfhearted unraveling of this so-called conspiracy was a mere pretext. Following the same pattern of questioning they had used during the first cross-examination, the investigators did not limit themselves to merely routine questions. They asked Marie Antoinette if she had had relations with the deputies of the Legislative Assembly, and whether she had been apprised of political affairs before August 10. Once again she hid behind the role of the submissive wife obedient to the monarch's will. "I only knew what I was told by the person to whom I was exclusively attached," she said, before asserting that the King's sole desire was the people's happiness.

When the inquiry was over, it was considered more prudent to transfer the Queen into another cell. The Conciergerie dispensary was rearranged for

that purpose and all its exits carefully barricaded. Racked by chronic hemor-
rhages, Marie Antoinette was becoming weaker and weaker. Some members
of the Convention were in no rush to conduct the trial, probably hoping that
she would die a natural death. However, France was still threatened with
invasion and just as in 1789, at the same time of year, there was a fear of food
shortages. There were stormy popular demonstrations in the capital, and the
provinces were in turmoil. Given this climate, the "carnation plot" had
revived feelings of hatred that were scarcely dormant. She was the perfect
culprit, the person whom it would be most appropriate to immolate during
this period of unrest. Petitions piled up at the Convention demanding the
execution of the "Austrian she-wolf." On October 5, after the representative
Billaud-Varenne made a particularly violent diatribe against the widow
Capet, who was, he said, "the shame of humanity and of her sex," Marie
Antoinette was indicted by decree.[3]

Normally months of work were needed for the preliminary investigation
in this kind of trial. It required reviewing all the documents used in Louis
XVI's trial, poring over the papers of the Queen that had been seized after the
storming of the Tuileries, conducting a complex inquiry into all her activities
and gathering credible, trustworthy witnesses. Though Louis XVI's trial had
been conducted very hastily before the representatives of the Convention
officiating as self-appointed judges, it had been a real trial. But the Revolutionary Tribunal—an emergency court if ever there was one—did not burden itself with normal legal procedures, especially not in dealing with a
defendant whose fate had already been decided. It had literally been created
to terrorize by pronouncing death sentences and was a court that could render only a parody of justice. In the Queen's trial, the "preliminary investigation" merely turned up a group of hastily assembled underling stooges
masquerading as witnesses. Out of the forty-one people who were called to
the stand, barely five or six had statements of any importance to make. On
October 13, two days before the opening of the hearings, Fouquier-Tinville
arranged to have the documents "concerning the Capet trial and those that
were to be used for his widow's trial" delivered to him. Since the complete
dossier could not be found, but only the papers seized in the Queen's quarters in the Tuileries during the flight to Varennes, he had to make do with
those! It would seem he did not even consult them.[4]

Moreover, in order to fully convince public opinion of just how evil
"l'Autrichienne's" crimes were, Fouquier-Tinville wanted to use the filthy
accusations made by the little Louis XVII against his mother. It is a despica-

ble story. The cobbler Simon, who was in charge of the child-king's "educa-tion," had caught him masturbating and had questioned him concerning his bad habits. Without any hesitation, the child answered that his mother had taught him these practices. Simon notified the authorities of his discovery. On October 6, an official committee, made up of the mayor, the district pros-ecutor, two members of the general council and a police administrator, went to the Temple to cross-examine Louis XVII, his sister and his aunt.

Sitting in a big armchair, swinging his little legs that did not even touch the floor, the child asserted that his mother and aunt had had secret meetings with certain municipal guards, whose names he provided. He said that these men brought the ladies information from the outside, and paid peddlers to shout the latest news loudly in the street. He added that at the Tuileries "Pétion, Bailly and Lafayette had behaved very mysteriously with the women" and that he thought his mother had received letters from them when she was at the Temple. Finally, he obligingly told them that he had been instructed in "his very pernicious habits by his mother and aunt and that several times they had amused themselves watching him repeat the prac-tices in their presence and that very often this took place when they made him go to bed between them. From the way in which the child explained things," it said in the report, "he made it clear that once his mother made him come close to her; that this resulted in copulation and a swelling in one of his testicles, for which he wears a bandage, and that his mother advised him never to speak of it; that this act took place several times since."[5]

On the following day, October 7, Marie Thérèse was questioned by these same investigators, who were now joined by the painter David, who was a member of the Comité de Sûreté Générale. The little girl denied that her mother had had secret dealings with the municipal guards on duty. She merely recalled hearing the peddlers shout when she was in bed. Several times, her brother gave specific details proving that she was not telling the truth. Marie Thérèse found no other response than to say that her brother was cleverer than she and gifted with a greater sense of observation. Finally, when she was asked if her mother and aunt had been in bed with the boy between them, she answered no. According to the minutes, Louis XVII had nothing more to add.

The children were sent away and Madame Elisabeth was summoned. Naturally, she denied having had any meetings with the municipal guards to get information or transmit messages. The little Prince was called in and he maintained the opposite. Then they read the child's statement "concerning the indecencies mentioned" by him. The Princess was appalled. "This was too great an infamy and too far-fetched to merit a reply; that this was a habit the child had had for a long time; and that he must certainly recall that she and his mother had scolded him for it several times." As the child persisted in his statements, the Princess refused to add anything. The Prince was pressed with new questions. Who had initiated him into such practices? "Both together," he answered. Was this during the day or at night? He couldn't remember, but he thought it was in the morning.[6]

In the Conciergerie, Marie Antoinette, it seems, had no idea that "evidence" was being gathered for her trial. On October 12, at six o'clock, Hermann, the president of the Revolutionary Tribunal, summoned "the widow Capet" to appear in the large courtroom, in the presence of Fouquier-Tinville and the clerk Fabricius. This was a secret cross-examination in preparation for the hearing which was to take place two days later. Hermann went straight to the point. In fact, the questions did not require answers; they were accusations.

"Before the revolution you maintained political relations with the King of Bohemia and Hungary and these relations were contrary to the interests of France, which was bestowing on you enormous advantages," declared Hermann. Marie Antoinette answered that she had had only "friendly relations" with her brother. She had never discussed politics with him. Indeed, since the beginning of the revolution, she "had forbidden herself all correspondence abroad and had never meddled in internal affairs." She asserted that she had never employed secret agents in order to correspond with her family or other foreign powers. She denied having been the moving spirit of the counterrevolution at the Tuileries. And, of course, she denied having transmitted money to the Emperor. In this, her answer was accurate.

After clearly alluding to high treason, Hermann accused the Queen of having had a pernicious and decisive influence on Louis XVI. "It was you who taught Louis Capet the art of dissembling by which he so long deceived the good French people, who were far from suspecting that villainy and perfidy could reach such extremes." "Yes, the people have been deceived," she answered; "they have been cruelly deceived, but not by my husband or me." This was a perfectly sincere answer on the part of Marie Antoinette, who remained convinced that the only legitimate power was that of the King; that he incarnated the state and that whoever dared rebel against him was a criminal deserving of capital punishment. The logic of the monarchy and that of the revolution were diametrically opposed — and irreconcilable.

Hermann also accused her of having been "the prime instigator of Louis Capet's treason. It is because of your advice and perhaps your persecution that he wanted to flee France and put himself at the head of the defiant men who wanted to tear their country apart." Marie Antoinette retreated to the position she had taken during the previous interrogations. She had obeyed her husband, who had had no intention of crossing the borders. She was even so bold as to state that "had he intended to, she would have employed all means to dissuade him." Since Hermann accused her of having encouraged the King to declare war, she reminded him that Louis XVI had been pressured to do so by the majority of the representatives. The subject of the declaration of war led her to deny once again that she had had any relations with foreign countries. The president then brought up the events of October 1789, Marie Antoinette's responsibilities in triggering and preparing the bloodshed of August 10 and, lastly, the carnation affair.

At the conclusion of the cross-examination, the president asked the accused if she wanted the help of a lawyer for her trial, which was to start in two days. Exhausted, the Queen answered that she knew no one she could call on. The tribunal appointed two lawyers, Chauveau-Lagarde and Tronçon-Ducoudray. Thrown into a panic by the mission incumbent upon them—even though they were fully aware of the Revolutionary Tribunal's intentions and the hopelessness of pleading before it—the two men begged the Queen to request a delay so they could become acquainted with the dossier. The Queen's letter asking for a delay remained unanswered. The trial was to open on the morning of October 15.

36

TRIAL AND DEATH

OF THE QUEEN

*A*t eight in the morning on Wednesday, October 15, 1793, in the former Grand Chambre of the Palais de Justice, where the parliament used to sit, the woman who had been the Queen of France stepped forward, pale and majestic. She was appearing before the Revolutionary Tribunal. Dressed in black and wearing a widow's bonnet in white lawn and trimmed with black mourning crepe, she sat down in the armchair that had been prepared for her in front of the public prosecutor's table and the other assisting judges. The jury members had just taken their seats behind the judges. They were all followers of Robespierre and Fouquier-Tinville and included a surgeon, a bookseller, a wig maker, a clog maker, a café owner, a hatter, a musician, two carpenters, an auctioneer, a journalist and a former prosecutor, as well as the Marquis d'Antonelle, a former representative in the Legislative Assembly and an early supporter of the revolution. A plain balustrade separated the court from the public eager to look at *"l'Autrichienne"* whose conviction they expected. People who had seen Marie Antoinette on previous occasions had trouble recognizing her, for she was now an emaciated woman whose face was ravaged by suffering.

After ordering her to state her name, surname, age and profession, the clerk read out the indictment—a masterpiece of revolutionary rhetoric. Comparing Marie Antoinette to the wicked queens of antiquity and the Middle Ages, the public prosecutor made her responsible for all of France's ills since her arrival in the country. From this very long statement, essentially three charges were made against her: "depleting the national treasury," "maintaining secret relations and correspondences" with the enemy and "plotting conspiracies against the internal and foreign security of the state." Marie Antoinette was quite clearly being tried for high treason. But the child-king's statements were also being used to charge the former Queen with the crime of incest with her son. Impassive, with a faraway look in her eye, the Queen drummed her fingers on the arm of her chair while her "crimes" were read out. Her facial muscles betrayed no emotion whatsoever.

The procession of forty-one witnesses then began. They were all abject stooges whose depositions would never have been seriously upheld by any court worthy of the name. A surgeon named Rossillon, for instance, claimed that, after the events of August 10, he had found bottles of wine for encouraging the troops under the Queen's bed at the Tuileries. Without the slightest proof, he accused her of being the instigator of the Champ-de-Mars massacre and of sending money out of the country for her brother. A servant by the name of Reine Millot maintained that in 1788 she had heard the Duc de Coigny say that the Queen was smuggling out two hundred million to her brother the Emperor. Another witness said that she wore pistols in order to assassinate the Duc d'Orléans.

The Queen defended herself vigorously. Not once did the president catch her lying or contradicting herself. The hearings continued, lengthy and hollow. The room remained silent. The proceedings were almost tedious. Then came Hebért's turn. Editor-in-chief of *Le Père Duchesne*, a scurrilous newspaper that issued calls to murder every day, he was the person who had urged the cobbler Simon to tell Fouquier-Tinville about the Queen's scandalous conduct with her son. Looking self-satisfied, he repeated in a loud, clear voice the monstrous accusation and deemed it useful to add an explanation. "There is reason to believe," he said, "that this criminal sexual intercourse was not dictated by pleasure, but by the political hope of enervating the physical condition of the child, whom they still liked to think of as destined to occupy a throne and over whose mind, therefore, they wanted to be sure of having power."

The Queen remained impassive. Then one of the members of the jury demanded an explanation from the accused on this specific point. Now very agitated, Marie Antoinette rose and replied in a loud voice: "If I did not reply, it is because nature refuses to answer such a charge against a mother. I appeal to all the mothers who may be here present."[1] The common women in the courtroom—though they loathed the former Queen, who had been depicted to them for years in the blackest terms—were suddenly moved to compassion for her as a shamelessly maligned mother. This vile accusation against Marie Antoinette made them all feel under attack. The courtroom became disorderly and Hermann had to suspend the hearing for ten minutes. "Was there too much dignity in my reply?" the Queen whispered to her lawyer. He set her mind at rest: "Madame, be yourself and you will always be perfect." Her question, Chauveau-Lagarde later said, proved that she still had hopes of not being sentenced to death.[2] When he later heard of this incident, Robespierre cursed Hebért and reproached him for allowing the Queen to have her "last public triumph."

At four-thirty in the afternoon, having been in continuous session since morning, the hearings were interrupted for one hour. The Queen had just enough time to drink some broth and exchange a few words with her lawyers, who were very intimidated by her, despite the resigned gentleness she showed them. The hearings resumed. The witnesses who testified were just as mediocre as the previous ones. After they had been examined, the president asked the Queen if she had any statement to make in her own defense. "Yesterday," she replied, "I did not know the witnesses. I did not know what they would say. Well, no one has uttered anything positive against me. I conclude by remarking that I was only Louis XVI's wife, and I had to submit to his will."

The debates were over. After a brief adjournment, Fouquier-Tinville made a closing speech in which he stated that he considered "Antoinette the declared enemy of the French nation." Her lawyers were finally allowed to speak. Since they had only had time to jot down some notes, they were obliged to improvise.

Chauveau-Lagarde argued against the charge of her "alleged conspiracy with the foreign powers," Tronçon-Ducoudray against her "alleged conspiracy with internal enemies." In examining the main grievances made against the Queen, they stressed the absence of proof to substantiate the seriousness of the accusations. "I myself saw those two devil's advocates not only walk on hot coals to try to prove the slut's innocence, but also dare to weep over the death of the traitor Capet and say to the judges that it was enough to have punished the fat pig, that they should have mercy on his hussy," *Le Père Duchesne* wrote the following day. Moved by Chauveau-Lagarde's ardor, Marie Antoinette thanked her defense attorney warmly.[3]

However, the defense would not have the last word. The defendant was instructed to leave the room, and before the jury retired to deliberate, Hermann, the president of the tribunal, made a long speech that was in effect a second indictment.[4] Likening the Queen's trial to the King's, he accused Marie Antoinette of having been "the accomplice or rather the instigator of most of the crimes of which this last tyrant of France had been guilty." He submitted four questions to the jury:

"1. Is it established that there were plots and secret dealings with foreign powers and other external enemies of the republic, which plots and secret dealings were aimed at providing these enemies with monetary help, giving them entry into the French territory and facilitating the progress of their armed forces there?"

"2. Is Marie Antoinette convicted of having cooperated in these machinations and having maintained these secret dealings?"

"3. Is it established that there existed a plot and conspiracy to ignite a civil war within the republic?"

"4. Is Marie Antoinette of Austria . . . convicted of having participated in this plot and conspiracy?"

The jury retired to deliberate. The Queen was exhausted, but hoped she would be sentenced to deportation. Marie Antoinette certainly believed she was innocent of the crimes of which she was accused, for she had done everything within her power to save the monarchy as she conceived it. But today, thanks to an abundance of archival material, we know that she had indeed been guilty of high treason when she released France's military plans of attack. However, though the republicans' accusation was justified, it was unproved. No proof of treason had been produced. Legally, the trial was iniquitous. But these considerations hardly troubled the members of the jury. They made believe that they were deliberating for an hour to give the appearance that the verdict was not predetermined.

Outside the walls of the Palais de Justice, in spite of the biting cold, a large, anxious crowd milled around waiting for the verdict. When the end of the deliberations was announced, a deep hush fell over the packed courtroom. "Antoinette, here is the jury's declaration," Hermann said to her. In a resonant voice, Fouquier-Tinville proclaimed that the defendant was sentenced to death for the crime of high treason. The jury had answered in the affirmative the four questions that had been put to them.

The Queen heard the ruling against her without a word or gesture. "She showed no sign of fear, indignation or weakness," said one of her lawyers. She crossed the courtroom in a state of shock. When she reached the balustrade, where the people were, she lifted her head majestically. Suddenly, in the corridor, she faltered. "I can't see my way,"[5] she had to admit to the gendarme on duty. He gave her his arm, for which he was arrested the next day.

As soon as she arrived in her cell, the Queen asked for a pen, paper and ink and sat down to write a long farewell letter to Madame Elisabeth: "It is to you, my sister, that I write for the last time. I have just been sentenced, not to a shameful death, for it is shameful only for criminals, but to join your brother. Innocent like him, I hope to show the firmness he showed in these last moments. I am calm as one is when one's conscience is clear; I deeply regret having to abandon my poor children; you know that I lived only for them and for you, my good and loving sister. You who have out of friendship sacrificed everything to be with us. In what a position I leave you! . . . May my son never forget his father's last words, which I expressly repeat to him, that he never seek to avenge our death. I have to speak of something which pains my heart. I know how much distress this child must have caused you. Forgive him, my dear sister, remember his age and how easy it is to make a child say anything one wants, and even things he does not understand . . .

"It remains for me to confide my last thoughts to you . . . I die in the Catholic, Apostolic and Roman religion, the religion of my fathers, the one in which I was brought up and which I always professed. I expect no spiritual consolation, not even knowing if there still are priests of that religion, and furthermore the place where I am would expose them to too much danger, if they were to visit me . . . I forgive all my enemies the harm they have done me. I here bid farewell to my aunts and to all my brothers and sisters. I had friends. The thought of being separated from them forever and their sorrow is among my greatest regrets in dying; may they know, at least, that I thought of them up to the very last. Farewell, my good and loving sister, may this letter reach you! Think of me always. I embrace you with all my heart as well as those poor, dear children. My God! How heartbreaking it is to part with them forever. Farewell! Farewell! . . ." This letter would never reach its addressee. It was given to Fouquier-Tinville by the prison concierge. Under the Restoration, in 1815, a former Convention deputy, who had preserved many important papers, arranged to give it to Louis XVIII when he ascended to the throne. Today it is in the National Archives.

Day was breaking when the young servant Rosalie found the Queen in tears, lying on her bed in her mourning dress. Since she refused to take any food, the young girl begged her to accept a bit of soup, but she could swallow only a few spoonfuls. At around eight o'clock, she helped her change. The

Queen was not allowed to go to the scaffold in her mourning dress. "Her Majesty stood in the small space which I usually left between her camp bed and the wall. She gestured to me to stand in front of the bed so the gendarme would not see her body; she crouched in the space and took off her dress to change her undergarments for the last time. But the officer of the Gendarmerie came closer, stood by the bolster and watched the Princess change. Her Majesty quickly put her fichu back on her shoulders and with great gentleness said to the young man: 'In the name of decency, monsieur, allow me to change my undergarments without witnesses.' 'I cannot give my consent,' the gendarme answered . . ."[6] Helped by Rosalie, the Queen put on a white piqué negligee and a small lawn bonnet.

At around ten o'clock, Larivière, the turnkey, came into the Queen's cell. "You know they are going to put me to death?" she whispered to him. He did not have time to answer. The judges and the clerk had arrived to read out the bill of indictment to the condemned woman for the second time. Then Henri Sanson, the executioner, entered. He went up to the Queen and said to her: "Hold out your hands." She recoiled in horror and, very upset, said: "Will my hands be bound? Louis XVI's were not bound." But the judges said to Sanson: "Do your duty."[7] The executioner brutally tied the Queen's hands behind her back, removed her bonnet and cut her hair to the nape of her neck. She was ready—ready to go to the scaffold.

It was eleven in the morning when the prison gates opened and let the victim out. The call to arms had started at dawn; the armed forces had been mobilized, cannons lined the squares and the intersections; patrols scoured the streets. Thirty thousand men were to accompany the former Queen of France to her execution. Held at the end of a long rope by the executioner, Marie Antoinette climbed into the dingy cart that was to bring her to the scaffold, on the Place de la Révolution. A constitutional priest sat next to her and lavished her with exhortations, to which she did not respond. For her, a constitutional priest was no more than a traitor. According to a believable legend, the Queen had received the ministrations of a refractory priest during her detention at the Conciergerie.

The cart moved slowly in the midst of a very dense crowd of people who had been waiting since dawn to watch it go by. At the corner of the rue Saint-Honoré, with a cruel stroke of the pencil, the painter David sketched the last image of the Queen of France for all eternity. Sitting very straight, pale but with cheeks flushed with fever and bloodshot eyes, her coarsely cut white hair sticking out of her bonnet, Marie Antoinette was oblivious to everything and everyone. It seemed that she did not even hear the cries of "Long live the Republic! Down with tyranny!" When they arrived at the former Place Louis XV, the Queen looked toward the Tuileries gardens, saw the scaffold and grew pale. Still ignoring the priest and his final words to her, she climbed out of the cart with a light step and mounted, "with bravado," the steep steps leading to the guillotine. With an abrupt movement of the head, she let the bonnet fall and surrendered herself to the executioners. Preparations for the execution lasted an endless four minutes. The board tipped and the blade came down. Sanson picked up the bleeding head and the crowd yelled: "Long live the Republic!" It was twelve-fifteen.

On the very day of the execution the Queen's mutilated body was taken to the small cemetery of the Madeleine, where the King's body had been left nine months earlier. On November 1, a gravedigger buried the remains of the victim and sent the following note to the municipal authorities: "The widow Capet. 6 livres for the coffin. 15 livres, 35 sols for the grave and the gravediggers." These words described the funeral of the last Queen of France.[8]

Epilogue

WHAT BECAME OF THEM?

ews of the Queen's execution soon spread throughout Europe. The courts went into mourning, but this tragic death aroused little emotion. Fersen alone grieved over Marie Antoinette's death. "Though I was prepared for it and expected it since the transfer to the Conciergerie, I was devastated by the reality," he wrote in his journal, on October 20, 1793. "I did not have the strength to feel anything. I went out to talk about this misfortune with my friends and Madame de Fitz-James and the Baron de Breteuil, whom I did not find. I wept with them, especially with Madame de Fitz-James . . . I thought about her constantly, about all the horrible circumstances of her sufferings, of the doubt she might have had about me, my attachment, my interest. That thought tortured me. Then I felt all that I was losing in so many different ways: feeling, interest, existence, everything was joined in her and all was lost . . . I even had moments of distaste for Eleanore. It was not the same feeling, that consideration, that care, that tenderness . . ."

October 21: "I could only think of my loss. The fact that she was alone in her last moments, without consolation, with no one to talk to, no one to whom she could give her dying wishes, it is horrifying. What monsters from hell! No, without revenge, never will my heart be content."

On that same day, he sent his sister a grief-stricken letter: "She for whom I lived, since I have never ceased to love her, she I loved so much, for whom

I would have given a thousand lives, is no more. Oh, my God! Why overwhelm me thus, what have I done to deserve your wrath? She is no more. I am in an agony of pain and I do not know how I go on living; I do not know how I can bear my suffering. It is extreme and nothing will ever erase it. She will always be present in my memory and I will never cease to mourn her."

And Fersen, usually so laconic, covered the pages of his journal with his heartbreaking regrets:

October 24. "Her image, her sufferings, her death and my feeling are always present in my head, I can think of nothing else."

October 26. "Every day I think about it, and every day my sorrow increases. Every day I am even more aware of all that I have lost."

November 5. "Oh, how I blame myself for my wrongs toward her, and how I know now that I loved her. Eleanore will never replace her in my heart. What gentleness, what tenderness, what kindness, what care, what a loving, sensitive, tactful heart!."

Axel's grief was not appeased with the passage of time. A year after the Queen's death, his pain became even more intense: "This day was a memorable and terrible day for me. It is the day I lost the person who loved me most in the world and who truly loved me."[1]

He remained faithful to the memory of Marie Antoinette all his life, in spite of his many female conquests. For a while, he thought of marrying Eleanore Sullivan, but she chose to marry Crawfurd, instead. Laden with honors, Grand Marshal of the Kingdom of Sweden, he was massacred by the mob in Stockholm while he was following the funeral procession of the heir apparent to the throne. He was suspected of having poisoned the Prince. The date of this calamity was June 20, 1810—the anniversary of the flight to Varennes! Several months after his death he was rehabilitated by the Supreme Court and given a solemn funeral.

The only persons to remain ignorant of the Queen's fate were the prisoners in the Temple tower. Madame Elisabeth and Madame Royale lived together until May 9, 1794. On that day, they came to fetch Louis XVI's sister and brought her before the Revolutionary Tribunal. She was guillotined the following day. Before going to the scaffold, she learned of her sister-in-law's tragic end from her companions in misfortune.

The young Marie Thérèse remained at the Temple, after seeing all those dearest to her leave. The conditions of her detention became inhuman. For over a year, she did not see a single person. Food was given to her through a wicket gate. In December 1795, France and Austria negotiated an exchange of prisoners; she was freed and taken to Vienna. She lived in exile with her uncle, the Comte de Provence, who had proclaimed himself King and taken the name Louis XVIII. Then she married her cousin, the Duc d'Angoulême, the eldest son of the Comte d'Artois. She returned to France with them in 1814, following the fall of Napoleon I and the Restoration of the monarchy. After the revolution of 1830, she went into exile again, where she died in 1851.

The fate of little Louis XVII, who had been placed under the guardianship of the cobbler Simon, is one the great enigmas of French history. Officially, according to a record of his death, he died on June 8, 1795, of a "scrofulous disease." However, doubt was soon cast on the identity of the young boy who died at the Temple, and there was much talk of an escape and another child being substituted. But all these rumors remain unfounded. Many false Dauphins came forward in the beginning of the nineteenth century, particularly during the Restoration. The Duchesse d'Angoulême, who never saw her brother again after he had been torn away from the Queen, in July 1793, never wanted to meet any of these pretenders. An abundant literature grew out of what is commonly called the "enigma of the Temple," but it is more concerned with romantic intrigue than with historical truth.

With the Restoration of the monarchy, in 1814, there developed in France the cult of the "martyr Queen," carefully nurtured by the royalists. The very people who had helped tarnish Marie Antoinette's reputation while she was alive became the unconditional defenders of her virtue. First among these was her brother-in-law, the Comte de Provence, who became King Louis XVIII. It was under his reign that an expiatory chapel was erected on the cemetery site where the sovereigns' corpses had been thrown after their execution. In those days, "good French society" lived in a climate of mourning in expiation for the regicide, and the lives of the two lofty victims were idealized. On the other hand, the republicans tended to justify the double execution by nurturing the "black legend" of the Queen.

Today the last Queen of France is no longer considered one of history's great criminals. Instead, she tends to arouse interest and compassion. After her death on the scaffold, Marie Antoinette entered the world of legend and became a mythic figure. We seek to penetrate the secrets of her romantic and tragic life. Though repeatedly and tirelessly put on trial, this sentimental and frivolous princess, who was completely unprepared for her heroic fate, knew better than any other sovereign how to bring to perfection the aristocratic art of living of prerevolutionary France.

ABBREVIATIONS

NOTES

BIBLIOGRAPHY

INDEX

ABBREVIATIONS

A.A.E.: Archives du Ministère des Affaires Étrangères de France.

A.F.: *Correspondance secrète du comte de Mercy-Argenteau avec l'empereur Joseph II et le prince de Kaunitz*, published by the Chevalier d'Arneth and Jules Flammermont.

A.G.: *Correspondance secrète entre Marie-Thérèse et le comte de Mercy-Argenteau, avec les lettres de Marie-Thérèse et de Marie-Antoinette*, with an introduction and notes by the Chevalier d'Arneth and A. Geffroy.

A.N.: Archives Nationales de France.

B.N.: Bibliothèque Nationale de France.

NOTES

I. DAUGHTER OF MARIA THERESA

1. This kingdom, with Prague as its capital, included the present-day Czech Republic and Slovakia.
2. This kingdom, with Budapest as its capital, extended far beyond today's Hungary and included part of today's Romania.
3. Cited by V.-L. Tapié, in *L'Europe de Marie-Thérèse*, pp. 58–59.
4. Cited by Marguerite Jallut and Philippe Huisman, from *La Correspondance de Léopold Mozart*, in *Marie-Antoinette*, p. 28.
5. Alfred Arneth, *Geschichte Maria-Theresia's*, vol. VII, p. 551.
6. The goddaughter of Louis XV and his wife, Queen Maria Leszczynska, Maria Carolina of Naples would be an opponent of the revolution and of Napoleon. However, as the grandmother of Archduchess Marie Louise, who was Napoleon's second wife, she held her great-grandson, the King of Rome, on her knees during a trip to Vienna in 1814. In 1808, in Palermo, her daughter Maria Amalia married the Duc d'Orléans, who ruled France from 1830 to 1848 under the name Louis Philippe I.
7. Arneth, *Geschichte Maria-Theresia's*, vol. VII, p. 353.

2. GREAT EXPECTATIONS

1. Vienna, Haus Hof und Staatsarchiv, *Familienkorrespondenz*, 37.
2. A.A.E., *Correspondance politique Autriche*, 307.

3. Arneth, *Maria-Theresa und Marie-Antoinette, ihr Briefwechsel während des Jahre 1770–1780*, pp. 361–62.
4. *Cavagnole*, a kind of lotto, was all the rage in the courts of Europe at the time.
5. Arneth, *Maria-Theresa und Marie-Antoinette, ihr Briefwechsel während des Jahre 1770–1780*, pp. 361–62.
6. A.F., vol. II, p. 358.
7. Arneth, *Maria-Theresa und Marie-Antoinette, ihr Briefwechsel während des Jahre 1770–1780*, pp. 361–62.

3. A ROYAL MARRIAGE

1. The building of this castle, according to the plans of the architect Gabriel, had not been entirely completed in 1770.
2. This pavilion had been given to the young Louis XV by the Regent. The King had made it into a pleasure retreat. It was torn down in the middle of the nineteenth century.
3. Princes of royal descent who are neither sons nor grandsons of the King are called princes of royal blood. Their wives are entitled to the title princess of royal blood.
4. This tree-lined avenue running alongside the Seine starts at the present location of the Place de l'Alma and ends at the Louvre. It was in the underpass giving out on the Place de l'Alma (built after the Second World War) that the accident occurred that was to cost the life of Diana, Princess of Wales, in August 1997.

4. THE VERSAILLES COURT

1. Arneth, *Maria-Theresa und Marie-Antoinette, ihr Briefwechsel während des Jahre 1770–1780*, pp. 354 ff.
2. A.G., vol. I, p. 7.
3. Jules Flammermont, *Correspondance des agents diplomatiques* . . . , Report of Aranda, ambassador of Spain, pp. 474–79.
4. A.G., vol. I, p. 12.
5. This residence eight kilometers to the north of Marly was destroyed during the revolution. Only the gardens still exist.
6. The castle of Choisy had been acquired and embellished by Louis XV, who liked to use it for pleasure parties. It consisted of several buildings that were also destroyed during the revolution.
7. A.G., vol. I, p. 26.
8. Ibid.
9. Ibid., p. 12.
10. Ibid., p. 17.
11. Ibid., p. 27.
12. Ibid., p. 14.

13. Ibid., p. 17.
14. Vienna, Haus Hof und Staatsarchiv, *Frankreich Berichte*, 147.
15. This referred to a network resembling "checks and balances" where the parliaments played a key part. The parliaments acted simultaneously as a court of justice and a chamber for recording royal edicts. Aside from the Paris parliament—whose breadth of jurisdiction and competence made it the most important—there were a dozen other parliaments in the French kingdom. Since the fourteenth century, they addressed "remonstrances" to the King on administrative questions and general policy. The Paris parliament was suspended by Louis XIV, exiled several times under Louis XV, dismembered in 1771 by Chancellor Maupeou and reinstated by Louis XVI at his accession in 1774. The young King thought he could make it his ally.

5. MADAME LA DAUPHINE

1. Vienna, Haus Hof und Staatsarchiv, *Frankreich Berichte*, 147.
2. A.G., vol. I, pp. 203–4.
3. Ibid., p. 221.
4. Ibid., p. 243.
5. Ibid., p. 264.
6. Ibid., p. 261.
7. A.F., vol. II, pp. 402, 405.
8. Vienna, Haus Hof und Staatsarchiv, *Frankreich Berichte*, 147.
9. Ibid.
10. Ibid.
11. Ibid.
12. Ibid.
13. Ibid., 154.
14. A.A.F., *Correspondance politique Sardaigne*, 255.
15. This palace was built west of the Louvre at the end of the sixteenth century and was altered during the following century. Louis XVI and his family would be made to reside in it from October 6, 1789, to August 1792 (see below, Chapter 28). Napoleon I, Louis XVIII, Charles X and Napoleon III would make it their principal residence. Set on fire during the Commune, in 1871, the building was torn down shortly thereafter.
16. *Correspondance entre Marie-Thérèse et Marie-Antoinette*, ed. by Georges Girard, p. 97.

6. END OF A REIGN, END OF AN ERA

1. A.G., vol. II, p. 140.
2. A.G., vol. I, p. 455.

3. Ibid., p. 446.
4. Ibid., p. 442.
5. Ibid.
6. A. Geffroy, *Gustave III et la cour de France*, vol. I, p. 359.
7. This was a common illness in the eighteenth century, characterized by a high fever and a rash that developed into pustules.
8. For accounts of the death of Louis XV, cf. Pierre Darmon, *La Variole, les nobles et les princes*, pp. 85–146.
9. A.G., vol. II, p. 137.
10. This is the communion ceremony given to the dying in the Catholic religion.
11. The Cent-Suisses or Hundred Swiss (actually 127) were elite men selected from the Swiss regiments of the army.

7. A HAPPY ACCESSION

1. Jacob-Nicolas Moreau, *Mes souvenirs*, vol. I, p. 362.
2. A.G., vol. II, p. 140.
3. Ibid., p. 149.
4. Ibid., p. 147.
5. Ibid.
6. A.F., vol. II, pp. 453–55.
7. A.G., vol. II, p. 176.
8. Ibid., p. 150.
9. Ibid., p. 187.
10. All that remains of this castle in Touraine, near Amboise, built by the Princesse des Ursins at the end of the eighteenth century, is a pagoda in a park. The building was torn down in 1823.
11. *Droit de joyeux avènement*, tax on a new sovereign's accession to the throne.
12. *Droit de ceinture*, tax on wines entering Paris and intended for the upkeep of the Queen's household.
13. A.G., vol. II, p. 204.

8. "LITTLE TWENTY-YEAR-OLD QUEEN"

1. Madame Campan, *Mémoires*, vol. I, p. 69.
2. Baudeau, *Chronique secrète de Paris sous le règne de Louis XVI*.
3. A reference to the popular Henri IV. At Louis XVI's accession, *Resurrexit* (He is resurrected) was inscribed on the pedestal of the statue of Henri IV on the Pont-Neuf in Paris, near the fountain of La Samaritaine, a water pump decorated with an image of the woman of Samaria offering Jesus a drink of water.
4. Duc Emannuel de Croÿ, *Journal inédit*, vol. III, p. 132.
5. Ibid.

6. Abbé Soulavie, *Mémoires historiques et politiques du règne de Louis XVI*, vol. I, ch. 5.
7. The present-day Parc Monceau is what remains today of that former estate.
8. Abbé de Véri, *Journal*, vol. I, p. 240.

9. THE CORONATION

1. A.G., vol. II, p. 306.
2. Ibid., p. 307.
3. Ibid., p. 313.
4. The Comtesse d'Artois, who was several months pregnant, did not take part in the coronation ceremonies.
5. Croÿ, vol. III, p. 174.
6. A.G., vol. II, p. 346.
7. Ibid., p. 343.
8. Ibid., p. 362.

10. THE QUEEN'S CIRCLE

1. A.G., vol. II, p. 360.
2. Ibid., pp. 364–66.
3. Ibid.
4. Ibid., p. 380.
5. Ibid., p. 363.
6. Besenval, *Mémoires*, ed. by G. de Diesbach, p. 181.
7. Lauzun, *Mémoires*, p. 206.
8. Ibid., p. 217.
9. Ibid., p. 219.
10. Ibid., pp. 221–22.
11. Ibid., p. 226.
12. Ibid., p. 229.
13. A property located about forty kilometers southeast of Paris.
14. Prince de Ligne, *Fragments de l'Histoire de ma vie*, ed. by Leuridant, vol. I, p. 118.
15. A.G., vol. II, p. 404.

11. VENUS AND VULCAN

1. A.G., vol. II, p. 361.
2. Madame Campan, who left interesting memoirs describing the court of Louis XVI, was Marie Antoinette's First Woman of the Bedchamber. Campan, pp. 72–73.
3. Comte de Tilly, *Mémoires*, vol. I, pp. 13–14.
4. Letter of Horace Walpole to Lady Ossory dated August 18, 1775, Horace Walpole's *Cor-*

respondence, ed. by W. S. Lewis, Yale University Press, New Haven, 1965, vol. XXXII, p. 254.

5. Véri, vol. I.
6. A.G., vol. II, p. 357.
7. According to the fundamental laws of the monarchy, the devolution of the crown was by order of male primogeniture. Hence if Louis XVI were to die, the Comte de Provence would be first in succession. If the Comte died, the crown would go to the Comte d'Artois. And at his death, it would go to the little Duc d'Angoulême.
8. A.G., vol. II, p. 366.
9. Ibid., p. 373.

1 2. THE QUEEN'S INTRIGUES

1. A.G., vol. II., p. 501.
2. Ibid., p. 490.
3. Ibid., p. 446.
4. Lauzun, p. 259.
5. Ibid.
6. Ibid., p. 261.
7. A.G., vol. II, p. 525.
8. Besenval, p. 181.

1 3. THE BROTHER'S VISIT

1. A.G., vol. II, p. 460.
2. Ibid., p. 531.
3. Ibid., p. 485.
4. Ibid., p. 492.
5. Ibid., p. 534.
6. Croÿ, vol. IV, p. 8.
7. The Hôtel des Invalides, founded by Louis XIV to house disabled ex-servicemen, was built according to the plans of Jules Hardouin-Mansart. In 1840, it received Napoleon's ashes; today it is the seat of the Musée de l'Armée.
8. The royal tapestry workshop created by Louis XIV.
9. Created in 1604, this was a workshop devoted to Oriental-style carpets and was housed in the Chaillot district, in a former soap (*savon*) factory, hence its name, Manufacture de la Savonnerie.
10. Vienna, Haus Hof und Staatsarchiv, *Familienakten Sammelbände*, 7.
11. Ibid.
12. Ibid.
13. Ibid.

14. Vienna, Haus Hof und Staatsarchiv, *Familienakten Sammelbände*, 55: *Réflexions données à la reine de France.*
15. Ibid.
16. *Correspondance entre Marie-Thérèse et Marie-Antoinette*, ed. by Girard, p. 206.
17. Vienna, Haus Hof und Staatsarchiv, *Frankreich Berichte*, 163.

14. MOTHERHOOD

1. *Correspondance entre Marie-Thérèse et Marie-Antoinette*, ed. by Girard, p. 215.
2. Vienna, Haus Hof und Staatsarchiv, *Familienkorrespondenz*, 26.
3. A.G., vol. III, p. 200.
4. Ibid., p. 162.
5. Ibid., p. 169.
6. Ibid., p. 191.
7. Ibid., pp. 200–1.
8. Ibid., p. 213.
9. A.F., vol. II, pp. 528–29.
10. A.G., vol. III, p. 221.
11. Ibid., p. 234.
12. Ibid., p. 311.
13. Ibid., vol. III, p. 235.
14. Campan, vol. I, ch. 9, p. 150.
15. A.G., vol. III, p. 285.

15. FERSEN

1. Alma Söderhjelm, *Fersen et Marie-Antoinette*, pp. 54–55. The author of this book was the first person to have access to the archives of the Fersen family in Löfstadt and Stasfund, Sweden. She quotes extensively from his *Intimate Journal*, his *Correspondence Book* and his correspondence with his sisters.
2. Baron Klinckowström, *Le comte de Fersen et la Cour de France, extraits des papiers du Grand Maréchal de Suède, comte Jean-Axel de Fersen*, vol. I, p. XXXII.
3. Söderhjelm, p. 61.
4. Comte de Saint-Priest, *Mémoires*, vol. II, p. 67.
5. Croÿ, vol. IV, p. 79.
6. Klinckowström, vol. I, p. XXXV.
7. A.G., vol. III, p. 306.
8. Comte Valentin Esterhazy, *Mémoires*, p. 181.
9. A.G., vol. III, p. 323.
10. Ibid, p. 339.
11. Ibid., p. 338.

12. Ibid.
13. Ibid., p. 407.

16. QUEEN OF TRIANON

1. Tilly, *Mémoires*, vol. I, pp. 13–14.
2. Silk fabric whose weave is thicker and stronger than taffeta.
3. Comte d'Angiviller was the King's Buildings Director from 1774 to 1789. The Buildings Administration was in charge of the upkeep and construction of the royal residences while also being the instrument of patronage.
4. Those Louis XVI and Marie Antoinette liked best were by the architect Paris and have been preserved at the Besançon library.
5. Comte Félix d'Hézecques, *Souvenirs d'un page de la Cour de Louis XVI*, p. 261.

17. BIRTH OF A DAUPHIN

1. A.G., vol. III, p. 482.
2. *Correspondance de Marie-Thérèse et Marie-Antoinette*, ed. by Girard, p. 324.
3. Arneth, *Marie-Antoinette, Joseph II und Leopold II, ihr Briefwechsel*, p. 22.
4. In those days, the Bois de Boulogne, where the Château de La Muette was located, was outside the city limits.

18. FERSEN'S RETURN

1. Born Catherine von Württemberg, she had been rebaptized in Russia and given the name Maria Feodorovna.
2. Campan, vol. I, p. 174.
3. Baronne d'Oberkirch, *Mémoires sur la Cour de Louis XVI et la société française avant 1789*, p. 198.
4. Comte F. U. Wrangel, *Lettres d'Axel de Fersen à son père pendant la guerre d'indépendance d'Amérique*, p. 170.
5. Ibid., p. 145.
6. Ibid., p. 176.
7. Ibid.
8. Ibid., p. 182.
9. Söderhjelm, p. 77.
10. Ibid.
11. Ibid., pp. 81–82.
12. The italics are added.
13. Probably the Château de Dangu in Normandy, which belonged to the Baron de Breteuil, Fersen's faithful protector.

14. Madame de Matignon was Baron de Breteuil's daughter. Since she was a widow, there was talk of a marriage between her and Fersen.
15. In his journal, written in French, Fersen always referred to the Queen as *Elle* with a capital E.
16. Brussels was the capital of the Austrian Netherlands.

19. LAST ILLUSIONS

1. A.F., vol. II, p. 264.
2. Oberkirch, p. 354.
3. She was the daughter of a chambermaid and a bailiff, and her real name was Marie Philippine Lambriquet. The Queen preferred to give her the first name of Ernestine, which was the name of the heroine of a novel by Madame Riccoboni, which was very fashionable at the time. The child went home to her parents every evening, but at her mother's death in 1788 Marie Antoinette took her completely in her care. During the Terror, she was saved by her grandparents and she died in 1814.
4. Marquis de Bombelles, *Journal*, vol. I, pp. 208–9.
5. Ibid, p. 293.
6. Arneth, *Marie-Antoinette, Joseph II und Leopold II, ihr Briefwechsel*, pp. 39–40.

20. SCANDAL IN THE AIR

1. A.G., vol. I, p. 568.
2. Klinckowström, *Le comte de Fersen et la Cour de France.*
3. A.N., AP 440.
4. Ibid.
5. Ibid.
6. Saint-Priest, *Mémoires*, vol. II, p. 80.
7. Söderhjelm, p. 104.
8. All that remains today of this château west of Paris, which had belonged to the Ducs d'Orleans, is the park. The buildings were severely damaged in 1871 during the fighting preceding the fall of the Commune and they were razed shortly thereafter.
9. Campan, vol. I, p. 198.
10. Ibid., p. 201.
11. The Minister of the King's Household was in charge of all internal affairs.
12. A.N., X2B 1417, Bassenge's deposition.

21. THE DIAMOND NECKLACE AFFAIR

1. This dialogue comes from Madame Campan's memoirs, which in this instance perfectly match the memoirs of Georgel, the Cardinal's personal secretary.

2. This second dialogue is taken from Georgel's memoirs.
3. Thanks to the Maréchal de Castries's unpublished journal, it is possible to follow the beginning of the investigation in detail.
4. B.N., Département des Manuscrits, Fonds Joly de Fleury, 2089.
5. This was how the Comtesse de Provence was referred to.
6. Journal of the Maréchal de Castries, A.N., AP 306.
7. Ibid.
8. Ibid.
9. Arneth, *Marie-Antoinette, Joseph II und Leopold II, ihr Briefwechsel*, p. 93.
10. Ibid., p. 96.

2 2 . " M A D A M E D E F I C I T "

1. A.F., vol. II, p. 80.
2. Besenval, vol. II, pp. 255–56.
3. Arneth, *Marie-Antoinette, Joseph II und Leopold II, ihr Briefwechsel*, p. 113.
4. Bombelles, vol. II, pp. 204–5.
5. Arneth, *Marie-Antoinette, Joseph II und Leopold II, ihr Briefwechsel*, p. 113.
6. Saint-Priest, vol. II, p. 80.
7. Söderhjelm, pp. 108–9.
8. A.N., O1 1802–3.
9. Besenval, ed. by Mercure de France, p. 303.
10. Hézecques, p. 154.

2 3 . " M Y F A T E I S T O B R I N G B A D L U C K "

1. Söderhjelm, p. 113.
2. Madame de Staël, *Considérations sur les principaux événements de la Révolution française*, vol. I, p. 165.
3. On this national assembly, see below, Chapter 24.
4. Son of Louis Philippe, Duc d'Orléans (1725–85), the Duc de Chartres had taken the title Duc d'Orléans at his father's death in 1785.
5. A.F., vol. II, p. 141.
6. Ibid.
7. Mistress of King Henri IV.
8. A.F., vol. II, p. 211.

24. "DO YOU KNOW A WOMAN MORE TO BE PITIED THAN ME?"

1. Sallier, *Annales françaises* . . . , vol. I, p. 126.
2. Madame de Staël, vol. I, p. 165.
3. Cf. Evelyne Lever, *Louis XVIII*, Fayard, Paris, 1988.
4. Bombelles, vol. II, p. 214.
5. This clock can be seen in the Château de Versailles today and is still in perfect working order.
6. A.F., vol. II, p. 232.
7. *A Diary of the French Revolution by Gouverneur Morris, Minister to France During the Terror*, ed. by Beatrix Cary Davenport, Houghton Mifflin, Boston, 1939, vol. I, p. 66.
8. Adrien Duquesnoy, *Journal*, vol. I, pp. 5–6.
9. Campan, vol. I, pp. 230–31.

25. THE FALL OF THE BASTILLE

1. Jacques Necker, *Histoire de la Révolution française*, in *Oeuvres de Necker*, vol. I, pp. 271–72.
2. A.F., vol. II, p. 255.
3. Saint-Priest, vol. II, p. 83.
4. A position that was equivalent to Mayor of Paris.
5. *A Diary of the French Revolution by Gouverneur Morris*, vol. I, p. 150.
6. Söderhjelm, p. 242. See also the letter written by Fernan Nuñez, the Spanish ambassador to France, to Florida Blanca, in Albert Mousset, *Un Témoin ignoré de la Révolution*, p. 83.

26. THE LAST SUMMER AT VERSAILLES

1. Comtesse Diane de Polignac, *Mémoires sur la vie et le caractère de Mme la duchesse de Polignac*.
2. Duchesse de Tourzel, *Mémoires*, vol. I, p. 242.
3. Saint-Priest, vol. II, p. 84.
4. Ibid.
5. Marquise de La Tour du Pin, *Journal*, pp. 111–12.
6. Dom H. Leclercq, *Les Journées d'octobre*, p. 30, n. 4.

27. THE TRAGEDY OF OCTOBER 1789

1. Legend has it that when the Paris mob stormed Versailles, Marie Antoinette said, "If they don't have any bread, let them eat brioche." This heartless comment is one of

those famous historical statements that was never made. However, it isn't completely invented. There is an anecdote in Book VI of Jean-Jacques Rousseau's *Confessions* that was probably used by the Queen's enemies. In 1741, Rousseau was staying with Madame de Mably, where, on the sly, he used to drink excellent Arbois wine that stimulated his appetite. But he did not dare walk into a bakery in his gentleman's clothes; it would have been demeaning. "Then," Rousseau writes, "I remembered a great Princess's suggestion when she was told that the peasants didn't have any bread: Let them eat brioche, she said. So I bought myself a brioche." Rousseau doesn't name the princess, but it certainly wasn't the Queen of France.

2. La Tour du Pin, p. 115.
3. Ibid., p. 117.
4. Saint-Priest, *Abrégé des circonstances du départ de Louis XIV pour Paris, le 6 Octobre 1789*, p. 306.
5. J. Weber, *Mémoires*, p. 267.
6. Ibid.
7. Tourzel, ed. by Mercure de France, Paris, 1986, p. 25.
8. Marquis de Ferrières, *Mémoires*, vol. I, p. 315.
9. Place de l'Hôtel de Ville in Paris.
10. La Tour du Pin, p. 118.
11. François Hüe, *Souvenirs*, p. 20.
12. J. de Salmour, *Rapport sur les journées des 5 et 6 octobre 1789*, in Jules Flammermont, *Les Correspondances des agents diplomatiques étrangers en France avant la Révolution*.
13. *Procédure du Châtelet*, 387ème et 388ème *dépositions*.
14. Staël, vol. I, p. 272.
15. Ibid.
16. Saint-Priest, *Mémoires*, vol. II, p. 89.
17. La Tour du Pin, p. 123.
18. For the Parisians, the King's return to Paris meant an end to the threat of bread shortages, which explains the nicknames of baker for the King, baker's wife for the Queen and baker's boy for the Dauphin.
19. Saint-Priest, *Mémoires*, vol. II, p. 90.
20. Today the seat of the Senate.

28. THE TUILERIES

1. Campan, vol. II, p. 33.
2. Saint-Priest, *Mémoires*, vol. II, p. 90.
3. Staël, vol. I, p. 346.
4. Marie Antoinette to Madame de Polignac, November 19, 1789, in *Lettres de Marie-Antoinette*, published by M. de La Rocheterie, Paris, 1895–96.
5. La Marck, *Correspondance entre le comte de Mirabeau et le comte de La Marck*, vol. I, p. 107.

6. On October 12, he wrote to the King of Spain: "I owe it to myself, I owe it to my children, my family and my entire House, not to allow the debasement of the royal prerogatives which have been established in my dynasty over many centuries . . . I choose Your Majesty as the repository of the solemn protest I hereby raise against all the acts contrary to the royal authority which have been imposed on me by force since July 15 of this year . . ."
7. Guy Chaussinand-Nogaret, *Mirabeau . . . Notes à la Cour . . .* , pp. 77–80.
8. Söderhjelm, p. 138.
9. Chaussinand-Nogaret, p. 46.
10. Saint-Priest, *Mémoires*, vol. II, p. 92.
11. Söderhjelm, pp. 151–54.
12. This is where the Eiffel Tower is today.
13. In 1790, the Assembly had decided to divide France into eighty-three new administrative districts called "departments."
14. Klinckowström, vol. I, p. 77.

29. ESCAPE PLANS

1. See above, Chapter 25.
2. Arneth, *Marie-Antoinette, Joseph II und Leopold II, ihr Briefwechsel*, pp. 147–50.
3. Mousset, p. 244.
4. Klinckowström, vol. I, p. 105.
5. A.G., vol. II, p. 526.
6. Klinckowström, vol. I, p. 108.

30. THE VARENNES DRAMA

1. Söderhjelm, p. 181.
2. Louis XVIII, *Relation d'un voyage à Bruxelles et à Coblence*, 1791. After the revolution and the Empire, and after wandering throughout Europe for over twenty years, the Comte de Provence would mount the throne of France in 1814 as Louis XVIII. *Relation d'un voyage* is the account he left of his escape from Paris on June 20, 1791.
3. Marie Thérèse de France, *Journal*, p. 21.
4. *Enfants de France* was the term used for the children of the sovereign.
5. Tourzel, p. 195.
6. A large market town about seventy kilometers from Paris.
7. These were the new administrative districts of France.
8. A league equals about four kilometers.
9. Marie Thérèse de France, *Journal*.
10. Récit de Drouet à l'Assemblée, *Archives parlementaires*, vol. XXVII, p. 508.
11. Marie Thérèse de France, p. 27.

12. The young Duc de Choiseul-Stainville was the nephew of Louis XV's former minister. The quotations at the end of this chapter are taken from *La Relation du départ de Louis XVI, le 20 juin 1791*, written after these events.

31. THE IMPASSE

1. Pétion, *Le Retour de Varennes*, in Mortimer-Ternaux, *Histoire de la Terreur*, vol. I, p. 357.
2. Today the Place de la Concorde.
3. Mousset, p. 278.
4. Söderhjelm, p. 204.
5. A.N., AP 440.
6. See above, Chapter 20.
7. A.N., AP 440.
8. Klinckowström, vol. I, pp. 147–48.
9. Bouillé had emigrated several days after the King's arrest at Varennes.
10. *A Diary of the French Revolution by Gouverneur Morris*, vol. II, p. 218.
11. Arneth, *Marie Antoinette, Joseph II und Leopold II, ihr Briefwechsel*, pp. 196–97.
12. Ibid., pp. 200–6.
13. Staël, vol. I.

32. THE LAST SHOW OF STRENGTH

1. The ellipses stand for the famous deletions that make it impossible to decipher anything.
2. Söderhjelm, p. 229.
3. This was how Fersen and those close to him referred to the Queen. They referred to Eleanore as El.
4. Söderhjelm, p. 229.
5. Klinckowström, vol. I, p. 208.
6. Ibid., p. 199.
7. Ibid.
8. The word "sister" was often used for a sister-in-law.
9. Klinckowström, vol. I, p. 207.
10. Arneth, *Marie-Antoinette, Joseph II und Leopold II, ihr Briefwechsel*, p. 234.
11. He returned only to appear before the Revolutionary Tribunal, which would condemn him to death on November 29, 1793.
12. Fersen's journal from February 11 to 23, 1792, is reproduced in its entirety in Söderhjelm, pp. 241–47.
13. Indeed, most of the moderates originated from the department of the Gironde.
14. Dumouriez, *Mémoires*, vol. II, pp. 163–65.
15. Klinckowström, vol. II, p. 319.

16. Ibid., p. 323.
17. Ibid., p. 317.

33. THE FALL OF THE MONARCHY

1. Paris had been divided into forty-eight sections by a decree of May 21, 1790. The citizens of each section convened in assemblies approximately every ten days. But beginning in July 1792, these assemblies were in session almost permanently, convening on their own authority. They played a major role throughout all the revolutionary days, and the events of August 10, 1792, were planned during their sessions.
2. Comte P. L. Roederer, *Chronique de cinquante jours*, in his *Oeuvres*.
3. Tourzel, p. 364.
4. Ibid., p. 365.
5. Campan, vol. II, p. 151.
6. J.-B. Cléry, *Journal de ce qui s'est passé à la Tour du Temple pendant la captivité de Louis XVI*.

34. THE DEATH OF THE KING

1. Today the Place de la Concorde.
2. Cléry, p. 187.
3. Ibid.
4. Söderhjelm, pp. 277–78.
5. Ibid., p. 281.
6. Ibid., p. 323.
7. *Le Moniteur*, Robespierre's speech of March 27, 1793, pp. 816–17.
8. Since August 10, 1792, the revolutionaries who no longer wished to call Louis XVI "Majesty" or "Sire" had given him the name of Capet, in memory of Hugues Capet (tenth century), founder of the dynasty of which the Bourbons were a branch.

35. THE CONCIERGERIE

1. Söderhjelm, pp. 298–300.
2. The following cross-examination is taken from *Actes du Tribunal Révolutionnaire*, published by G. Walter, Paris, new ed., 1987, pp. 64 ff.
3. *Le Moniteur*, issue of October 5, 1793, reporting on the session of October 3.
4. A.N., W 290, dossier 179.
5. A.N., W 297, dossier 261.
6. Ibid.

36. TRIAL AND DEATH OF THE QUEEN

1. G. Walter, *Marie-Antoinette*, pp. 81–88.
2. Notes of Chauveau-Lagarde, in G. Lenôtre, *La Captivité et la mort de Marie-Antoinette*, p. 344.
3. Arrested in the courtroom, he was freed after the Queen's execution, but was first subjected to a cross-examination.
4. See *Le Moniteur*, issue of October 28, 1793.
5. Notes of Chauveau-Lagarde, cited by Lenôtre, p. 348.
6. Account of Rosalie Lamorlière, *La Captivité* . . .
7. Ibid.
8. The King and Queen's mortal remains were taken with great pomp to the Saint Denis basilica on January 21, 1815. This is where they rest today.

EPILOGUE: WHAT BECAME OF THEM?

1. Excerpts from Fersen's journal in Söderhjelm, pp. 310, 311, 315.

BIBLIOGRAPHY

MANUSCRIPTS

ARCHIVES NATIONALES
BB 30, 82.
C 45, 182, 186, 192, 220–23.
K 160–64, 505–6, 528.
O1 598, 1708, 1873–87, 3250–64, 3276, 3745, 3790–99.
F7 6413, 3870.
X2 B 1417.
W 290.
AD1 74–76, 108.
AP 440.
AP 306, Fonds Castries.

ARCHIVES DES AFFAIRES ÉTRANGÈRES
Correspondance politique Autriche, vols. 285–363.
Correspondance politique Prusse, vols. 188–212.
Mémoires et documents, France, vols. 426, 429, 1897.

BIBLIOTHÈQUE NATIONALE
Joly de Fleury Collection, mss. 2088–89.

BRETEUIL ARCHIVES

HAUS HOF UND STAATSARCHIV, VIENNA

Familienakten Vermalhungen, 54–55. These dossiers mainly concern the education of the archdukes and archduchesses, including the "instructions given to the Queen of France" by Joseph II.

Familienakten Vermalhungen, 50, concern the preparations for the marriage of Marie Antoinette and the Dauphin.

Familienakten Sammelbände, 7, include Joseph II's letters concerning the Bavarian succession. Several of the Emperor's letters concerning his sister at the time of Louis XV's death are interesting. Joseph's letters to Leopold contained in this box shed light on the intimate relations of Louis XVI and Marie Antoinette.

Familienkorrespondenz, 26, includes Marie Antoinette's letters to Joseph II and Leopold II, Leopold II's answers, as well as several letters of Louis XVI.

Familienkorrespondenz, 27A, includes several letters of Louis XVI and of Marie Antoinette dated 1788.

Frankreich Berichte: The series contains the correspondence of Mercy-Argenteau with Maria Theresa, Joseph II, Leopold II, Kaunitz, Colloredo, Neny, Cobenzl. This correspondence, written in French (except for Mercy's official reports, long excerpts of which have been translated by Flammermont), gave rise to several publications essentially due to the Chevalier d'Arneth, A. Geffroy and J. Flammermont (see below, "Published Sources"). These scholarly works—whose authors, however, failed to give specific references—are still the fundamental source material for any serious study of Marie Antoinette. Most of the Queen's biographers used the confidential letters of the Empress and the ambassador to depict the Queen's everyday life and the young couple's intimacy, but neglected their political significance. A new interpretation of these texts seemed called for.

1769, box 141.

1770, boxes 142, 144.

1771, box 147.

1772, box 148.

1770–80, boxes 149, 150. These two boxes include all of Maria Theresa's letters to Mercy.

1773–74, box 154.

1775–76, box 155.

1777, box 157.

1778, box 158.

1779, box 160.

1780, box 162. This bundle also contains Mercy's letters to Joseph II for the years 1773, 1774, 1776, 1777, 1778, 1779, 1780.

1773–80, box 163. Includes Mercy's confidential letters to Maria Theresa.

1781, box 165.

1782, box 166.

1783, box 168.

1784, box 169.

1784–85, box 173.

1787–88, box 176.

1788–89, box 177.

1790–92, box 178.
1791–93, box 180.

PUBLISHED SOURCES

CORRESPONDENCE, NEWSPAPERS, MEMOIRS

Allonville, Armand-François, Comte d', *Mémoires secrets de 1770 à 1830*, Paris, 1838–41, 6 vols.

Amiguet, Philippe, *Lettres de Louis XV à son petit-fils, l'infant de Parme* . . . , Paris, 1938.

Anonymous, *Journal pour servir à l'histoire du XVIII siècle*, Paris, 1788–89, 4 vols.

——. *Bulletin à la main pour les années 1787–1789*, 3 vols. (B.N. Réserve, Lc2 2225).

Argenson, René-Louis de Voyer, Marquis d', *Journal et Mémoires*, published by E. J. B. Rathery, Paris, 1859–67, 9 vols.

Augeard, J.-M., *Memoires secrets de J.-M. Augeard, secrétaire des Commandements de la reine Marie-Antoinette*, published by E. Bavoux, Paris, 1866.

Bachaumont, Louis Petit de, *Journal ou Mémoires secrets pour servir l'Histoire de la République des Lettres depuis 1762*, London, 1777–89, 36 vols.

Bailly, Jean-Sylvain, *Mémoires*, Paris, 1804, 4 vols.

Barentin, Charles-Louis-François de Paule de, *Mémoire autographe de M. de Barentin, Chancelier et Garde des Sceaux, sur les derniers Conseils du Roi Louis XVI*, published by M. Champion, Paris, 1844.

Barnave, Pierre-Joseph-Marie, *Introduction à la Révolution française*, Paris, 1960. (See also Marie Antoinette.)

Baudeau, Abbé, *Chronique secrète de Paris sous le règne de Louis XVI*, published by Taschereau, in *Revue Rétrospective*, Paris, 1833–38, première série, vol. III.

Beauchamp, Comte de, *Les Comptes de Louis XVI*, 1909.

Beaucourt, Marquis de, *Captivité et derniers moments de Louis XVI, récits originaux et documents officiels*, collected and published by the Société d'Histoire Contemporaine, Paris, 1892. (See vol. I, *Récits originaux*.)

Bertrand de Moleville, A. F., *Histoire de la Révolution de France pendant les dernières années du règne de Louis XVI*, Paris, 1801, 3 vols.

Besenval, Pierre Victor, Baron de, *Mémoires du baron de Besenval*, published by Berville et Barrière, Paris, 1821, 2 vols.

Beugnot, Comte, *Mémoires du comte Beugnot*, published by Comte A. Beugnot, his grandson, 1866, 2 vols.

Boigne, Adèle d'Osmond, Comtesse de, *Mémoires . . . Récits d'une tante*, ed. J.-Cl. Berchet, vol. I: *Du règne de Louis XVI à 1820*, Paris, new ed., 1979.

Boislisle, A. de, *Choix de lettres adressées à Mgr de Nicolay, évêque de Verdun par le dauphin, la dauphine et divers princes, princesses ou personnages de la Cour (1750–1767)*, Nogent-le-Rotrou, 1875.

Bombelles, Marc de, *Journal du marquis de Bombelles*, vol. I, Geneva, 1977; vol. II, Geneva, 1982.

Bouillé, Marquis de, *Mémoires du marquis de Bouillé*, ed. F. Barrière, Paris, 1859.

Brienne, Comte de Loménie de, *Journal de l'Assemblée des Notables de 1787, par le comte de Brienne et Etienne-Charles de Loménie de Brienne, archevêque de Toulouse*, published by Pierre Chevallier, Paris, 1960.

Brissot, J.-P., *Correspondance et Papiers*, published by C. Perroud, Paris, 1912.

———, *Mémoires*, published by C. Perroud, Paris, 1910, 2 vols.

Burcke, Edmund, *Reflexions pour être envoyées à la Reine de France par l'intermédiaire du comte de Mercy-Argenteau . . .*, in *Revue Rétrospective*, vol. I, deuxième série.

Campan, Jeanne-Louis Genet, Madame, *Mémoires sur la vie privée de Marie-Antoinette*, Paris, 1822, 2 vols.

Cars, Jean-François de Pérusse, Duc des, *Mémoires*, Paris, 1890, 2 vols.

Chateaubriand, Vicomte René de, *Mémoires d'outre-tombe*, Paris, 1949.

Choiseul, Claude-Antoine-Gabriel, Duc de, *Relation du départ de Louis XVI, le 20 juin 1791*, Paris, 1822.

Cléry, J.-B., *Journal de ce qui s'est passé à la Tour du Temple pendant la captivité de Louis XVI, roi de France*, London, 1798.

Croÿ, Emmanuel, Duc de, *Journal inédit . . .*, Paris, 1906, 4 vols.

Desmoulins, Camille, *Correspondance inédite*, published by Matton, 1836.

Dufort de Cheverny, Comte Jean-Nicolas, *Mémoires*, ed. R. de Crévecoeur, Paris, 1909, 2 vols.

Dumouriez, Charles-François, *Mémoires du général Dumouriez, ecrits par lui-même*, Paris, 1821.

Duquesnoy, Adrien, *Journal d'Adrien Duquesnoy, député du Tiers Etat de Bar-le-Duc, sur l'Assemblée Constituante*, Paris, 1894, 2 vols.

Escherny, Comte François-Louis d', *Correspondance d'un habitant de Paris avec ses amis de Suisse . . .*, Paris, 1791.

Esterhazy, Comte Valentin, *Mémoires . . .*, Paris, 1905.

Ferrières, Marquis de, *Mémoires*, Paris, 1822.

———, *Correspondance inédite*, published by H. Carré, 1932.

Fersen, Comte Axel de, *Le comte de Fersen et la Cour de France, extraits des papiers du Grand Maréchal de Suède, comte Jean Axel de Fersen, publiés par son petit-neveu, le baron R. M. de Klinckowström*, Paris, 1877, 2 vols. Baron Klinckowström "censored" many passages in Fersen's papers. The archivist Alma Söderhjelm later published many previously unpublished texts in what is today the basic reference work, *Journal intime et Correspondance du comte Axel de Fersen*, Paris, 1930.

Flammermont, Jules, *Les Remontrances du Parlement de Paris au XVIII siècle*, Paris, 1898.

———, *Louis XVI et le baron de Breteuil*, Paris, 1885.

———, *Les Correspondances des agents diplomatiques étrangers en France avant la Révolution*, Paris, 1896.

Frénilly, Auguste-François Fauveau de, *Souvenirs du baron de Frénilly, pair de France . . .*, Paris, 1908.

Geffroy (A.), *Gustave III et la Cour de France*, Paris, 1867, 2 vols.

Genlis, Félicité du Crest de Saint-Aubin, Comtesse de, *Mémoires sur le XVIIIème siècle*, Paris, 1825, 10 vols.

Georgel, Abbé, *Mémoires pour servir à l'histoire des événements de la fin du XVIIIème siècle*, Paris, 1820, 6 vols.

Goguelat, François, Baron de, *Mémoires*, Paris, 1823.

Goret, Charles, *Mon Témoignage sur la détention de Louis XVI et de sa famille dans la
Tour du Temple . . .*, Paris, 1825.

Goubert, Pierre, and Michel Denis, *Les Français ont la parole: Cahiers des Etats
Généraux . . .* [1789], Paris, 1964.

Grégoire, Abbé Henri-Baptiste, *Mémoires de Grégoire, ancien évêque de Blois . . .*, Paris,
1837, 2 vols.

Grimm, Diderot, Raynal, Meister, *Correspondance littéraire, philosophique et critique*, ed.
Tourneux, Paris, 1877–82, 16 vols.

Hardy, *Mes loisirs ou Journal d'événements tels qu'ils parvinrent à ma connaissance, de
1764–1789*, BN. Ms.fs. 6680–87.

Hézecques, Félix, Comte d', *Souvenirs d'un page de la Cour de Louis XVI*, Brionne,
Gérard Montfort, reprint, 1983.

Holland, Lord Henry Richard, *Souvenirs diplomatiques*, published by his son and translated by H. de Chomski, Paris, 1851.

Hüe, Baron François, *Dernières années du règne et de la Vie de Louis XVI*, Paris, 1860.

———, *Souvenirs du baron Hüe, officier de la chambre du roi Louis XVI et du foi Louis
XVIII*, Paris, 1903.

Joseph II, *Correspondance secrète du comte de Mercy-Argenteau avec Joseph II et le prince
de Kaunitz*, published by Arneth and Flammermont, Paris, 1889–91, 2 vols.

———, *Joseph II und Graf Ludwig Cobenzl, ihr Briefwechsel*, edited by Adolf Beer and
Joseph Ritter von Fiedler, Vienna, 1901, 2 vols.

———, *Joseph II und Leopold von Toscana, ihr Briefwechsel von 1781 bis 1790*, edited by
Alfred Ritter von Arneth, Vienna, 1872, 2 vols. (I: 1781–85; II:1786–90).

———, *Joseph II, Leopold II und Kaunitz, ihr Briefwechsel*, edited by Adolf Beer, 1873.

———, *Marie-Antoinette, Joseph II und Leopold II, ihr Briefwechsel*, edited by Alfred Ritter
von Arneth, Leipzig, 1866.

———, *Marie Theresia und Joseph II, ihre Correspondenz, sammt Briefen Josephs an seinen
Bruder Leopold*, edited by Alfred Ritter von Arneth, Vienna, 1867–68, 3 vols. (I:
1761–72; II: 1773–July 1778; III: August 1778–1780).

———, *Correspondances intimes de l'empereur Joseph II avec son ami le comte de Cobenzl et
son premier ministre le prince de Kaunitz . . .*, with an introduction and historical notes
by Sébastien Brunner, Mainz, F. Kirchheim, 1871.

Lafayette, Gilbert Motier, Marquis de, *Mémoires, Correspondances et Manuscrits du
Général Lafayette*, published by his family, Paris, 1837, 6 vols.

Lage de Volude, Béatrix Etiennette d'Amblimont, Marquise de, *Souvenirs d'émigration . . . 1792–1794*, Paris, 1869.

La Marck, Prince Auguste d'Arenberg, Comte de, *Correspondance entre le comte de
Mirabeau et le comte de La Marck, pendant les années 1789, 1790, 1791*, published by
A. de Bacourt, 1851, 3 vols.

Lameth, Alexandre de, *Histoire de l'Assemblée Constituante (1789–1790)*, Paris, 1828, 2 vols.

Lameth, Théodore de, *Mémoires*, published by E. Welvert, Paris, 1913.

La Tour du Pin-Gouvernet, Lucie Dillon, Marquise de, *Journal d'une femme de cinquante ans*, Paris, new ed., 1989.

Lauzun, Armand-Louis de Gontaut, Duc de Biron et Duc de, *Mémoires*, edited and with a preface by G. d'Heylli, Paris, 1880.

La Vauguyon, Paul-François de, *Portrait de feu Monseigneur le Dauphin*, 1766.

Lefebvre, Georges, *Recueil de documents relatifs aux séances des Etats Généraux, mai–juin 1789*, vol. I: *Les Préliminaires, la séance du 5 mai*, Paris, C.N.R.S., 1953; vol. II: *La Séance du 23 juin*, Paris, 1962.

Lescure, M. de, *Correspondance secrète inédite sur Louis XVI, Marie-Antoinette, la Cour et la ville de 1777 à 1792*, published by Lescure, Paris, 1866, 2 vols.

Lévis, Gaston, Duc de, *Souvenirs et portraits (1780–1789)*, Paris, 1813.

Liedekerke-Beaufort, Comte de, "Souvenirs d'un page du comte de Provence," *Revue de Paris*, 1952, pp. 52–84.

Ligne, Charles-Joseph-Lamoral, Prince de, *Fragments de l'Histoire de ma vie*, Paris, 1928.

———, *Oeuvres*, published by Lacroix, Brussels, 1860, 4 vols.

Louis XVI, *Description de la Forêt de Compiègne telle qu'elle était en 1765 . . .* , Versailles, 1766.

———, *Maximes morales et politiques tirées de Télémaque*, Versailles, 1766.

———, *Réflexions sur mes Entretiens avec M. le duc de La Vauguyon*, by Louis Auguste Dauphin, with an introduction by M. de Falloux . . . , Paris, 1851.

———, *Journal*, ed. L. Nicolardot, Paris, 1873.

Luynes, Duc de, *Mémoires du duc de Luynes sur la Cour de Louis XV (1735–1758) . . .* , Paris, 1860.

Mallet du Pan, Jacques, *Journal historique et politique*, Geneva, 1784–87, 12 vols.

———, *Mémoires et correspondances pour servir à l'histoire de la Révolution française*, collected and edited by A. Sayous, Paris, 1851, 2 vols.

Malouet, Pierre-Victor, Baron, *Mémoires de Malouet*, 2nd ed., Paris, 1874, 2 vols.

Maria Theresa (see also Joseph II and Marie Antoinette), *Briefe der Kaiserin Maria Theresia an ihre Kinder und Freunde*, edited by Alfred Ritter von Arneth, Vienna, W. Braumüller, 1881, 4 vols.

———, *Maria-Theresa und Marie-Antoinette*, Vienna, 1866. This edition includes Vermond's letters.

Marie Antoinette (see also Joseph II), *Correspondance secrète entre Marie-Thérèse et le comte de Mercy-Argenteau, avec les lettres de Marie-Thérèse et de Marie-Antoinette*, published with an introduction and notes by Alfred von Arneth and M. A. Geffroy, Paris, Firmin Didot Frères, Fils et Cie, 1874, 3 vols.

———, *Correspondance entre Marie-Antoinette et Marie-Thérèse*, published by Georges Girard, Paris, 1933.

———, *Marie-Antoinette, Joseph II und Leopold II, ihr Briefwechsel*, edited by Alfred Ritter von Arneth, Leipzig, Paris and Vienna, 1866.

———, *Marie-Antoinette et Barnave, Correspondance secrète (juillet 1791–janvier 1792)*, published by Alma Söderhjelm, Paris, 1934.

Marie-Thérèse de France (Madame Royale), *Journal de la duchesse d'Angoulême, corrigé et annoté par Louis XVIII*, Paris, 1893.

Marmontel, Jean-François, *Mémoires*, published by M. Tourneux, Paris, 1891, 3 vols.

Martange, *Correspondance inédite*, published by Charles Bréard, Paris, 1898.

Mercier, Louis-Sébastien, *Tableau de Paris*, Amsterdam, 1781–89, 12 vols. *Le Nouveau Paris*, VII, 6 vols.

Métra, *Correspondance secrète* . . . , Paris, 1787–90, 18 vols.

Miot de Melito, Comte, *Mémoires*, Paris, 1858, vol. I.

Mirabeau (see below, "Other Works": Chaussinand-Nogaret).

Montbarey, Prince de, *Mémoires autographes de M. le Prince de Montbarey*, Paris, 1826, 3 vols.

Montjoye, *Histoire de la conjuration de Louis-Philippe-Joseph d'Orléans, surnommé Egalité*, Paris, 1796, 3 vols.

Montlosier, Comte de, *Mémoires de M. le comte de Montlosier sur la Révolution française* . . . , Paris, 1830.

Montyon, Baron Antoine de, *Particularités et observations sur les ministres des Finances de France les plus célèbres, depuis 1660 jusqu'à 1791*, Paris, 1812.

Moreau, Jacob-Nicolas, *Mes souvenirs*, published by C. Hermelin, Paris, 1898–1901, 2 vols.

Morellet, Abbé, *Mémoires inédits de l'Abbé Morellet sur le XVIII siècle et sur la Révolution*, Paris, 1822, 2 vols.

——, *Lettres à Lord Shelburne*, Paris, 1898.

Morris, Gouverneur, *A Diary of the French Revolution by Gouverneur Morris, Minister to France During the Terror*, ed. by Beatrix Cary Davenport, Houghton Mifflin, Boston, and Riverside Press, Cambridge, Mass., 1939.

Mouffle D'Angerville, *La Vie privée de Louis XV*, London, 1781, 4 vols.

Mousset, Albert, *Un témoin ignoré de la Révolution: Le comte Fernan Nuñez, ambassadeur d'Espagne à Paris*, Paris, 1924.

Necker, Jacques, *Oeuvres de Necker*, published by Baron de Staël, 1820–21, 15 vols.

Nicolardot, Louis, *Journal de Louis XVI*, Paris, 1873.

Nougaret, P. J. B., *Anecdotes du règne de Louis XVI*, Paris, 1791, 6 vols.

Oberkirch, Baronne d', *Mémoires sur la Cour de Louis XVI et la société française avant 1789*, published by Suzanne Burkard, Paris, 1970.

Papillon de La Ferté, Denis Pierre Jean, *Journal 1766–1780*, Paris, 1887.

Pasquier, Etienne-Denis, *Histoire de mon temps. Mémoires* . . . , vol. I, 6th ed., Paris, 1894.

Pilcher, Baron de, see Maria Theresa, *Maria-Theresa und Marie-Antoinette*, 1866 ed.

Polignac, Comtesse Diane de, *Mémoires sur la vie et le caractère de Madame la duchesse de Polignac*, Paris, An V (1796).

Rabaut-Saint-Etienne, *Oeuvres*. . . . , published by Collin de Plancy, Paris, 1825, 2 vols.

Rochambeau, Jean-Baptiste Donatien de Vimeur, Comte de, *Mémoires militaires, historiques de Rochambeau*, Paris, 1824, 2 vols.

Roederer, Comte P. L., *Oeuvres*, published by his son, Baron A. M. Roederer, Paris, 1853–59, 8 vols.

Roland, Madame, née Marie-Jeanne Phlipon, *Mémoires de Mme Roland*, ed. Paul de Roux, Paris, 1966.

Sabran, Comtesse de, *Correspondance inédite (1778–1788)*, Paris, 1875.

Saint-Priest, Guillaume Emmanuel Guignard, Comte de, *Mémoires*, Paris, 1929, 2 vols.

———, *Abrégé des circonstances du départ de Loius XVI pour Paris, le 5 octobre 1798, à la suite des Mémoires de Madame de Campan*, Paris, 1928.

Sallier, *Annales françaises depuis le commencement du règne de Louis XVI jusqu'aux Etats généraux (1774–1789)*, Paris, 1813.

Ségur, Comte Louis Ph. de, *Mémoires ou Souvenirs et Anecdotes*, Paris, 1843, 5th ed., 2 vols.

Sénac de Meilhan, Gabriel, *Le Gouvernement, les moeurs et les conditions en France avant la Révolution*, ed. Lescure, Paris, 1862

Söderhjelm, Alma, *Fersen et Marie-Antoinette*, Paris, 1930.

Soulavie, Abbé, *Mémoires historiques et politiques du règne de Louis XVI*, Paris, 1801, 6 vols.

Staël, Madame de, *Considérations sur les principaux événements de la Révolution française*, posthumous work published by the Duc de Broglie and the Baron de Staël, Paris, 1843.

Staël-Holstein, Baron de, *Correspondance diplomatique du baron de Staël-Holstein . . .*, published by L. Léouzon le Duc, Paris, 1881.

Stedingk, Field Marshal Curt von, *Mémoires posthumes . . . , rédigés sur les lettres, dépêches et autres pièces authentiques . . .*, published by the Comte de Björntstjerna, Paris, 1844–47.

Talleyrand, Charles-Maurice de, *Mémoires*, Paris, 1957, 2 vols.

Terray, Abbé, *Mémoires*, Paris, 1776.

Thiébault, Paul Charles François, Général Baron, *Mémoires*, Paris, 1893–95.

Tilly, Comte Alexandre de, *Mémoires*, Paris, 1929, 2 vols.

Tourzel, Louis-Joséphine de Croÿ d'Havré, Duchesse de, *Mémoires . . .*, published by the Duc des Cars, Paris, 1883.

Tourzel, Pauline de, *Souvenirs de quarante ans (1789–1830)*. Her account of the days following the events of August 10, 1792, were published in the *Mémoires* of the Duchesse de Tourzel.

Turgot, *Oeuvres*, Paris, 1913–23, 5 vols.

Véri, Joseph-Alphonse, Abbé de, *Journal*, published by Baron Jehan de Witte, Paris, 1928, 2 vols. Several fragments after 1781 were published by the Duc de Castries in *La Revue de Paris*, November 1953.

Vivenot, *Vertrauliche Briefe von Thugut*, Vienna, 1872.

Walpole, Horace, *Correspondence*, ed. by W. S. Lewis, Yale University Press, 1965.

Weber, Joseph, *Mémoires concernant Marie-Antoinette*, London, 1804–9.

Wrangel, Comte F. U., *Lettres d'Axel Fersen à son père*, Paris, 1929.

Young, Arthur, *Voyages en France en 1787, 1788 et 1789 . . .*, Paris, 1931, 3 vols.

OTHER WORKS

Actes du colloque sur le bicentenaire de Vergennes, 1–2 octobre 1987, Revue d'Histoire diplomatique, Paris, 1987, 3–4.

Alméras, Henri d', *Marie-Antoinette et les pamphlets royalistes et révolutionnaires*, Paris, 1907.

Antoine, Michel, *Louis XV*, Paris, 1989.

———, *Le Dur Métier de roi: Etudes sur la civilisation politique de la France d'Ancien Régime*, Paris, 1986.

Arnaud, Claude, *Chamfort*, Paris, 1988.

Arnaud-Bouteloup, Jeanne, *Le Rôle politique de Marie-Antoinette*, Paris, 1924.

——, *Marie-Antoinette et l'art de son temps*, Paris, 1924.

Arneth, Alfred Ritter von, *Geschichte Maria-Theresia's*, Vienna, 1863–79, 10 vols.

Aulard, Alphonse, *Histoire politique de la Révolution française*, Paris, 1901.

——, *La Société des Jacobins: Recueil de documents pour l'histoire du club des jacobins de Paris*, Paris, 1889–97, 6 vols.

Babelon, Jean-Pierre, *La Vie quotidienne à Paris dans la seconde moitié du XVIII siècle*, Paris, 1973.

Badinter, Elisabeth, *Les Romontrances de Malesherbes (1771–1775)*, Paris, 1978.

Badinter, Robert and Elisabeth, *Condorcet, un intellectuel en politique*, Paris, 1988.

Baecque, Antoine de, *La Caricature révolutionnaire*, Paris, 1988.

Baker, Keith Michael, *The Political Culture of the Old Regime*, Oxford, 1987.

——, *Condorcet*, University of Chicago Press, 1975.

——, *Inventing the French Revolution*, Cambridge and New York, 1990.

Barret-Kriegel, Blandine, *Les Historiens et la monarchie*, Paris, 1968, 4 vols.

Barton, H. Arnold, "The Origins of the Brunswick Manifesto," *French Historical Studies*, No. 5, 1967.

——, *Count Hans Axel von Fersen*, Boston, 1975.

Bérenger, Jean, *Histoire de l'Empire des Habsbourg*, Paris, 1990.

Bertaud, Jean-Paul, *Les Origines de la Révolution français*, Paris, 1971.

——, *Les Amis du roi: Journaux et journalistes royalistes en France de 1768 à 1792*, Paris, 1984.

Bluche, François, *Le Despotisme éclairé*, Paris, 1968.

——, *La Vie quotidienne de la noblesse française au XVIII siècle*, Paris, 1973.

——, *La Vie quotidienne au temps de Louis XVI*, Paris, 1980.

Bluche, Frédéric, *Danton*, Paris, 1984.

——, *Les Massacres de septembre*, Paris, 1987.

Bodinier, Gilbert, *Les Officiers de l'armée royale, combattants de la guerre d'indépendance des Etats-Unis, de Yorktown à l'An II*, Paris, 1983.

Bottineau, Yves, *L'Art d'Ange Jacques Gabriel à Fontainebleau*, Paris, 1962.

Bourgeois, Emile, *La Diplomatie secrète au XVIII siècle*, Paris, n.d., 3 vols.

Boutry, Maurice, *Autour de Marie-Antoinette*, Paris, 1907.

Breillat, Pierre, *Ville nouvelle, capitale modèle, Versailles*, Versailles, 1986.

Broglie, Duc de, *L'Alliance autrichienne*, Paris, 1895, 2 vols.

——, *Marie-Thérèse, impératrice*, Paris, 1888.

Butler, Rohan, *Choiseul, Father and Son*, Oxford, 1980.

Campardon, Emile, *Marie-Antoinette et le procès du collier*, Paris, 1863.

——, *Marie-Antoinette à la Conciergerie: Pièces originales conservées aux Archives, suivies du procès imprimé de la reine*, Paris, 1864.

Capefigue, G. B., *Louis XVI, son administration, et ses relations diplomatiques avec l'Europe*, Paris, 1844, 4 vols.

Caron, Pierre, *Les Massacres de septembre*, Paris, 1935.

——, "La Tentative de contre-révolution de juin–juillet 1789," *Revue d'Histoire Moderne et Contemporaine*, vol. VIII (1906–7).

Carré, Henri, Philippe Sagnac and Ernest Lavisse, *Louis XVI (1774–1789)*, Paris, 1911.

Chagniot, Jean, *Paris et l'armée au XVIII siècle*, Paris, 1985.

Chaumié, Jacqueline, *Le Réseau d'Antraigues et la Contre-Révolution*, Paris, 1965.

Chaussinand-Nogaret, Guy, *La Noblesse au XVIII siècle: De la féodalité aux Lumières*, Paris, 1976.

——, *Mirabeau*, Paris, 1982.

——, *Mirabeau entre le roi et la Révolution: Notes à la Cour suivies de discours*, Paris, 1986.

Chevallier, Jean-Jacques, *Barnave ou les deux faces de la Révolution*, Paris, 1936.

Chevallier, Pierre, *Histoire de la Franc-Maçonnerie française*, Paris, new ed., 1984, 3 vols.

Cobban, Alfred, *The Social Interpretation of the French Revolution*, New York, 1968.

Crankshaw, E., *Maria-Theresa*, London, 1969.

Darmon, Pierre, *La Variole, les nobles et les princes*, Paris, 1989.

Darnton, Robert, *The Literary Underground of the Old Regime*, Harvard University Press, 1982.

——, *La Fin des Lumières*, Paris, 1984.

Dechêne, Abel, *Un enfant royal, le duc de Bourgogne*, Paris, 1933.

——, *Le Dauphin, fils de Louis XV*, Paris.

Desjardins, Gustave, *Le Petit Trianon*, Paris, 1885.

Diesbach, Ghislain de, *Madame de Staël*, Paris, 1983.

——, *Histoire de l'émigration*, Paris, 1975.

Doyle, William, *Origins of the French Revolution*, Oxford University Press, 1980.

——, "The Parliaments of France and the Breakdown of the Old Regime," *French Historical Studies*, No. 6, 1970, pp. 415–58.

Egret, Jean, *La Révolution des notables: Mounier et les monarchiens*, Paris, 1950.

——, *Louis XV et l'opposition parlementaire (1715–1774)*, Paris, 1970.

——, *Necker, ministre de Louis XVI*, Paris, 1975.

Ernouf, Alfred-Auguste, *Maret, duc de Bassano*, Paris, 1878.

Eude, M., "Breteuil, Bombelles, Castries en 1791," *Annales Historiques de la Révolution Française*, vol. XXXIV (1962).

Fagniez, Gustave, "La Politique de Vergennes et la diplomatie de Breteuil (1774–1787)," *Revue Historique*, Paris, 1922.

Faure, Edgar, *La Disgrâce de Turgot*, Paris, 1961.

Faÿ, Bernard, *L'Esprit révolutionnaire en France et aux Etats-Unis à la fin du XVIII siècle*, Paris, 1925.

——, *Louis XVI ou la fin d'un monde*, Paris, new ed., 1981.

Fayard, Jean-François, *La Justice révolutionnaire*, Paris, 1988.

Fejtö, François, *Joseph II*, Paris, 1953.

Filleul, Paul, *Le Duc de Montmorency-Luxembourg*, Paris, 1939.

Flammermont, Jules, *Négociations secrètes de Louis XVI et du baron de Breteuil avec la cour de Berlin, décembre 1791–juillet 1792*, Paris, 1885.

Fleischmann, Hector, *Les Maitresses de Marie-Antoinette*, Paris, 1910.

——, *Les Pamphlets libertins contre Marie-Antoinette*, Slatkine Reprints, Geneva, 1976.

Fleury, Vicomte, *Les Derniers Jours de Versailles*, publication data unspecified.

Franqueville, Comte de, *Le Château de La Muette*, Paris, 1915.

Funck-Brentano, Franz, *La Mort de la reine*, Paris, 1901.

——, *Marie-Antoinette et l'énigme du collier*, Paris, 1926.

Furet, François, *Penser la révolution française*, Paris, 1978.

——and Denis Richet, *La Révolution française*, Paris, 1973.

——and Mona Ozouf, *Dictionnaire critique de la révolution française*, Paris, 1988.

Gaxotte, Pierre, *Le Siècle de Louis XV*, Paris, 1933.

——, *La Révolution française*, new ed., 1962.

Girault de Coursac, Pierrette, *L'Education d'un roi, Louis XVI*, Paris, 1972.

Godechot, Jacques, *La Contre-Révolution*, Paris, 1961.

——, *La Prise de la Bastille*, Paris, 1965.

——, *Les Révolutions, 1770–1779*, Paris, 1963.

Griffiths, Robert H., *Le Centre perdu: Malouet et les monarchiens dans la Révolution française*, Grenoble, 1988.

Grosclaude, Pierre, *Malesherbes, témoin et interprète de son temps*, Paris, 1961, 2 vols.

Gruber, Alain-Charles, *Les Grandes Fêtes et leurs décors à l'époque de Louis XVI*, Geneva and Paris, 1972.

Harris, R. D., *Necker and the Revolution of 1789*, London, 1986.

Hazard, Paul, *La Pensée européenne au XVIII siècle: De Montesquieu à Lessing*, Paris, 1963.

Hours, Bernard, *Madame Louise, princesse au Carmel*, Paris, 1987.

Huart, Suzanne d', *Brissot, la Gironde au pouvoir*, Paris, 1986.

Hunt, Lynn, *The Family Romance of the French Revolution*, Berkeley, California, 1992.

——, "The Many Bodies of Marie-Antoinette: Political Pornography and the Problem of the Feminine in the French Revolution," in *Eroticism and the Body Politic*, Baltimore and New York, 1991.

Jallut, Marguerite, *Marie-Antoinette et ses peintres*, Paris, 1955.

Jullien, Adolphe, *La Cour et l'Opéra sous Louis XVI*, Paris, 1878.

Kermina, Françoise, *Hans-Axel de Fersen*, Paris, 1985.

Khevenhüller-Metsch, Joseph, *Aus des Zeit Maria-Theresia's: 1742–1776*, Vienna, 1907–17, 5 vols.

Labourdette, Jean-François, *Vergennes, ministre de Louis XVI*, Paris, 1990.

Lacour-Gayet, Robert, *Calonne, financier, réformateur contre-révolutionnaire (1734–1802)*, Paris, 1963.

Landes, Joan B., *Women and the Public Sphere in the Age of French Revolution*, Cornell University Press, 1988.

Lecestre, Léon, *Les Tentatives d'évasion de Marie-Antoinette au Temple et à la Conciergerie*, Paris, 1886.

Leclercq, Dom H., *Les Journées d'octobre et la fin de l'année 1789*, Paris, 1924.

——, *La Fédération (janvier–juillet 1790)*, Paris, 1929, 2 vols.

——, *L'Eglise constitutionnelle (juillet 1790–avril 1791)*, Paris, 1934.

——, *La Fuite du roi (avril–juillet 1791)*, Paris, 1936.

——, *L'Oeuvre de la Constituante (juillet–décembre 1791)*, Paris, 1938.

——, *Feuillants et Girondins (août 1791–avril 1792)*, Paris, 1940.

Lefebvre, Georges, *La Révolution française*, Paris, new ed., 1963.

Lenôtre, G., *La Captivité et la mort de Marie-Antoinette*, Paris, new ed., 1951.

——, Le Vrai Chevalier de Maison-Rouge, Paris, new ed., 1959.

Lever, Evelyne, Louis XVI, Paris, 1985.

——, Louis XVIII, Paris, 1988.

——, Marie-Antoinette, 1991.

——, Philippe-Egalité, 1996.

Lombares, Michel de, Enquête sur l'échec de Varennes, Paris, 1988.

Mansel, Philippe, Louis XVIII, Paris, 1983.

——, La Cour sous la Révolution, Paris, 1989.

Mathiez, Albert, La Révolution française, new ed., 1960.

——, "Etude critique sur les journées des 5 et 6 octobre 1789," Revue Historique, vol. 67, 1898, pp. 241–81; vol. 68, pp. 258–94; vol. 69, 1899, pp. 41–66.

Maugras, Gaston, La Disgrâce du duc et de la duchesse de Choiseul: La vie à Chanteloup, Le retour à Paris, La mort, Paris, 1903.

——, La Fin d'une société: Le duc de Lauzun et la Cour de Marie-Antoinette, Paris, 1893.

Mauzi, Robert, L'Idée du bonheur dans la littérature et la pensée française aux XVIII siècle, Paris, 1960.

Maza, Sarah, Private Lives and Public Affairs: The Causes Célèbres of Prerevolutionary France, Berkeley, California, 1993.

Methivier, Hubert, L'Ancien Régime en France, XVIème, XVIIème, XVIIIème siècles, Paris, 1981.

Mortimer-Ternaux, Histoire de la Terreur, Paris, 1862–69, 8 vols.

Mossiker, Frances, The Queen's Necklace, New York, 1961.

Mousnier, Roland, Les Institutions de la France sous la monarchie absolue: 1698–1789, Paris, 1974–80, 2 vols.

Nolhac, Pierre de, Histoire du château de Versailles, Paris, 1911–18, 3 vols.

——, Versailles et la cour de France, Paris, 1925–30, 10 vols.

——, Le Trianon de Marie-Antoinette, Paris, 1914.

Nordmann, Claude, Gustave III, un démocrate couronné, Paris, 1986.

Orateurs de la Révolution française: Les Constituants, annotated by François Furet and Ran Halévi, Paris, 1989.

Petitfrère, Claude, Le Scandale du "Mariage de Figaro," Brussels, 1989.

Pimodan, Comte de, Le Comte de Mercy-Argenteau, ambassadeur impérial à Paris sous Louis XVI, Paris, 1911.

Poignant, Simone, Les Filles de Louis XV, l'aile des princes, Paris, 1970.

Poisson, Georges, Choderlos de Laclos, ou l'obstination, Paris, 1985.

Price, Munro, The Comte of Vergennes and the Baron of Breteuil: French Politics and Reform in the Reign of Louis XVI, Cambridge University, Ph.D., typed ms.

——, "The 'Ministry of a Hundred Hours': A Reappraisal," French History, No. 4 (September 1990), pp. 317–39.

Proyart, Abbé, Louis XVI et ses vertus aux prises avec la perversité de son siècle . . . , Paris, 1805, 5 vols.

Quétel, Claude, Histoire vraie d'une prison légendaire, Paris, 1988.

Rampelberg, R. M., Le Ministre de la maison du roi, baron de Breteuil, 1783–1788, Paris, 1975.

Reinhard, Marcel, *La Chute de la royauté*, Paris, 1969.

Renouvin, Pierre, *Les Assemblées provinciales de 1787 . . .* , Paris, 1921.

Revel, Jacques, "Marie-Antoinette in Her Fictions: The Staging of Hatred," in *Fictions of the French Revolution*, ed. by Bernadette Fort, Evanston, Illinois, 1991.

Rousselet, Marcel, *Les Souverains devant la justice*, Paris, 1946.

Rudé, Georges, *The Crowd in the French Revolution*, Oxford, 1959.

Sagnac, Philippe, *La Chute de la royauté*, Paris, 1907.

Ségur, Marquis de, *Au couchant de la monarchie*, vol. I: *Louis XVI et Turgot*: vol. II: *Louis XVI et Necker*, Paris, 1909.

Seligman, Edmond, *La Justice en France pendant la Révolution*, Paris, 1901–13.

Sevin, A., *Le Défenseur du roi, Raymond de Sèze*, Paris, 1936.

Soboul, Albert, *La Révolution française*, Paris, 1964, 2 vols.

———, *Le Procès de Louis XVI*, presented by Albert Soboul, Paris, 1966.

Solé, Jacques, *La Révolution en questions*, Paris, 1988.

Solnon, Jean-François, *La Cour de France*, Paris, 1987.

Sorel, Albert, *L'Europe et la Révolution française*, Paris, 1885–1911, 8 vols.

———, *La Question d'Orient au XVIII siècle*, Paris, 1878.

Sorg, Roger, "Fersen officier français et Marie-Antoinette," *Mercure de France*, July 15, 1933.

———, "Le véritable testament de Marie-Antoinette," in *Historia*, August–September 1955.

Stryienski, Casimir, *La Mère des trois derniers Bourbons: Marie-Josèphe de Saxe et la cour de Louis XV, d'après les documents inédits tirés des archives royales de Saxe*, Paris, 1902.

———, *Mesdames de France, filles de Louis XV*, Paris, 1910.

Sutherland, Donald M. G., *France 1789–1815, Revolution and Counter-Revolution*, London, 1985.

Sydenham, M.-J., *The Girondins*, London, 1961.

Tackett, Timothy, *La Révolution, l'Eglise, la France*, Paris, 1986.

Taillemite, Etienne, *La Fayette*, Paris, 1989.

Tapié, Victor-Lucien, *L'Europe de Marie-Thérèse: Du baroque aux Lumières*, Paris, 1973.

Thomas, Chantal, *La Reine scélérate: Marie-Antoinette dans les pamphlets*, Paris, 1989.

Tocqueville, A. de, *Coup d'oeil sur le règne de Louis XVI*, Paris, 1952.

Tulard, Jean, Jean-François Fayard and Alfred Fierro, *Histoire et dictionnaire de la Révolution française, 1789–1799*, Paris, 1987.

Vaissière, Pierre de, *La Mort du roi*, Paris, 1910.

Vatel, Charles, *Histoire de Madame du Barry*, Versailles, 1883, 3 vols.

Verlet, Pierre, *Le Château de Versailles*, Paris, 1985.

———, *Le Mobilier royal français*, Paris, 1946–55, 2 vols.

Vidalenc, Jean, *Les Emigrés français, 1789–1795*, Caen, 1963.

Vinot, Bernard, *Saint-Just*, Paris, 1985.

Vovelle, Michel, *L'Etat de la France pendant la Révolution, 1789–1799*, Paris, 1988.

———, *La Chute de la Monarchie, 1787–1792*, Paris, 1972.

Vuaflart and Bourin, *Les Portraits de Marie-Antoinette*, Paris, 1909.

Waddington, Richard, *Louis XV et le renversement des alliances*, Paris, 1896.

Wallon, H., *Histoire du tribunal révolutionnaire*, Paris, 1880–82, 6 vols.

Walzer, Michael, *Regicide and Revolution: Speeches at the Trial of Louis XVI*, Cambridge University Press, 1974.

——, "Le Procès du roi et la culture politique," in *The French Revolution and the Creation of Modern Political Culture*, vol. II, 1988, Pergamon Press.

Welvert, Eugène, "L'Eminence grise de Marie-Antoinette," in *Revue d'Histoire de Versailles*, 1921–22.

Winock, Michel, *1789: L'Année sans pareille*, Paris, 1988.

——, *L'Echec au roi (1791–1792)*, Paris, 1991.

Wrangel, F. V., *Origines et débuts du Royal-Suédois*, 1914, other publication data unspecified.

PRINCIPAL BIOGRAPHIES OF MARIE ANTOINETTE

Among the best-known biographies of Marie Antoinette are the following:

Castelot, André, *Marie-Antoinette*, new ed., 1956.

Chalon, Jean, *Chère Marie-Antoinette*, Paris, 1988.

Dunlop, Ian, *Marie-Antoinette*, London, 1993.

Goncourt, Edmond and Jules de, *Histoire de Marie-Antoinette*, Paris, 1859.

Huisman, Philippe, and Marguerite Jallut, *Marie-Antoinette, l'impossible bonheur*, Paris and Lausanne, 1970.

Kunstler, Charles, *La Vie privée de Marie-Antoinette*, Paris, 1938.

Lever, Evelyne, *Marie-Antoinette*, Fayard, Paris, 1991.

Nolhac, Pierre de, *Marie-Antoinette dauphine*, Paris, 1929.

——, *La Reine Marie-Antoinette*, Paris, 1929.

Vallotton, Henri, *Marie-Antoinette et Fersen*, Paris and Geneva, 1952.

Walter, Gérard, *Marie-Antoinette*, Paris, 1946.

Webster, Nesta, *Marie-Antoinette intime*, Paris and Geneva, 1957.

Zweig, Stefan, *Marie Antoinette*, Insel Verlag, Leipzig, 1932; The Viking Press, New York, 1933.

INDEX

Abraham, Nicolas, 90

Adélaïde, Madame, 21, 25, 33, 52–53, 57, 145; *see also* Mesdames

Adhémar, Comte d', 96, 136

Aiguillon, Duchesse d', 193

Aiguillon, Emannuel Armand, Duc d', 34, 38, 51, 52, 57–61, 97

Albert, Prince of Sachsen-Teschen, 9, 184

Alcestis (Gluck), 135, 141

Alvensleben, Herr, 192

American War of Independence, 124, 127, 138, 140–41, 144, 149–50, 167, 194, 227

Ami du Peuple, L' (newspaper), 243

Andlau, Comtesse d', 96, 104

Angiviller, Charles Claude, Comte d', 131

Anglais à Bordeaux, L' (Favart), 136

Angoulême, Duc d', 93, 142, 169, 308

Anne of Austria, 56

Antonelle, Marquis d', 299

Artois, Charles Philippe, Comte d', 21, 79, 85, 118, 175, 189, 201, 204, 210, 308; and birth of Dauphin, 142; birth of son of, 93; at coronation of Louis XVI, 73; counterrevolutionary schemes of, 242, 243; and death of Louis XV, 54, 55; and fall of Bastille, 212–14; friendship of Marie Antoinette and, 42–43, 65–67, 80, 175, 177, 183; inoculation against smallpox of, 63; Louis XVI's distrust of, 57; marriage of, 41; in private theatricals, 42, 43, 136; rapprochement with Prussia advocated by, 162; romantic liaisons of, 96, 101; at siege of Gibraltar, 149; Temple palace of, 145–46

Artois, Marie Thérèse, Comtesse d', 41–43, 54, 64, 92, 93

Aubry, Etienne, 132

Auguié, Madame, 228

Aumale, Madame d', 157

Aumont, Louis Marie Céleste, Duc d', 133

Bachaumont, Louis Petit de, 50
Bailly, Sylvain, 219, 231, 266, 296
Barber of Seville, The (Beaumarchais), 169, 170, 176
Barnave, Antoine, 261, 262, 265, 266, 270–72
Barrington, Richard, 125
Barrymore, Lady, 100–1
barrystes, 38, 47, 51, 61
Bassenge, Paul, 169–72, 175–76
Bastille, 99, 168, 175; fall of, 211–15, 218, 240
Bavarian Succession, War of, 114–17
Beaudau, Abbé, 64
Beaumarchais, Pierre Augustin Caron de, 167–69
Beauvau, Maréchale de, 193
Berthe (playwright), 136
Bertin, Rose, 69–70, 88, 148, 183
Besenval de Bronstadt, Pierre Victor, Baron de, 79, 92, 95, 98, 103, 123, 126, 187, 189, 212
Beugnot, Comte, 179–80
Bibliothèque Royale, 47
Billaud-Varenne, Jacques Nicolas, 295
Böhmer, Charles, 169–72, 174–76
Bombelles, Marc Marie, Marquis de, 157, 158, 166, 187, 210
Bouillé, François Claude, Marquis de, 245–46, 251, 258–60, 265
Bouillon, Princesse de, 82, 193
Boulainvilliers, Marquise de, 175
Bourbon, Duchesse de, 135
Bourbon, Louis Henri Joseph de Condé, Duc de, 189
Bourgogne, Duc de, 90
Brandeiss, Countess of, 8
Breteuil, Louis Auguste Le Tonnelier, Baron de, 198, 210, 244–46, 271, 306; as ambassador to Vienna, 62; and diamond necklace affair, 170–77, 179, 180; and fall of Bastille, 212, 214; as Louis XVI's representative to courts

of Europe, 238; Necker replaced by, 204
Brissac, Duc de, 44, 45
Broglie, Madame de, 38, 193
Broglie, Victor François, Maréchal de, 210, 213
Brunswick, Karl Wilhelm Ferdinand, Duke of, 274, 276, 278

Cagliostro, Joseph Balsamo, Comte de, 172
Calonne, Charles Alexandre de, 184–87, 189, 192
Cambon, Joseph, 290
Campan, Jeanne Louise Genêt, 88, 120, 132, 169, 170, 174, 189, 207, 214, 278, 281
Campan, Monsieur, 131, 136
Caraman, Comte de, 66
Carmelite order, 21
Castries, Maréchal de, 175–77
Catherine II, Empress of Russia, 80, 82, 118, 148, 155
Charles Joseph, Archduke of Austria, 4, 7, 9
Charles VI, Emperor of Austria, 4, 7
Chartres, Duc de, *see* Orléans, Louis Philippe Joseph, Duc d'
Chartres, Duchesse de, 24, 69, 78
Chauveau-Lagarde (lawyer), 298, 301
Choiseul, Etienne François, Duc de, 38, 57, 60, 75–76, 80, 92, 97, 170; du Barry's opposition to, 34–35; and flight to Varennes, 257–58; and "flour wars," 71; Lauzun and, 83; and Louis XV's death, 51; Maria Theresa's attitude toward, 58; Marie Antoinette's marriage negotiated by, 20; Princesse Guéméné and supporters of, 79
choiseulistes, 51, 79, 99, 116
Civil Constitution of the Clergy, 245
Clermont-Tonnerre, Marquise de, 62
Cléry (valet), 285–88

Clotilde, Madame, 22, 54, 84
Coigny, Marie François Henri, Duc de,
    79, 95–96, 100–1, 104, 108, 118, 123,
    126, 143, 187, 300
Coigny, Marquise de, 193
Collège Louis-le-Grand, 44
Comédie-Française, 46, 67, 168, 169
Comité de Sûreté Générale, 296
Compiègne, Château de, 20, 21, 32,
    64–65, 73
Conciergerie, prison of, 291–94, 297
Condé, Louis Joseph, Prince de, 157, 214,
    242–43
Condorcet, Marie Jean Antoine Nicolas
    Caritat, Marquis de, 193
Contat, Mademoiselle, 94
Conti, Louis François Joseph, Prince de,
    145
Convention, 286, 289–91, 293, 295, 303
Cooper, Alfred Duff, first Viscount
    Norwich of Aldwick, 160
Cordeliers, 263, 266
Cornwallis, Charles, first Marquis, 144
Cossé, Duchesse de, 83
Crawfurd, Quentin, 269, 272–73, 307
Crébillon, Prosper Jolyot de, 165
Croÿ, Emmanuel, Duc de, 64, 95, 107, 124
Czartoryska, Princess, 80

Daguerre (purveyor of decorative objects),
    133
Damas, Colonel de, 258
Dampierre, Anne Elzéard du Val, Comte
    de, 260
Danton, Georges Jacques, 265
David, Jacques Louis, 132, 296, 304
Deane, Silas, 124
Declaration of the Rights of Man and of
    the Citizen, 218, 225
Desfarges (silk manufacturer), 130
Devin du village, Le (Rousseau), 136
Dillon, Dominique, 78, 79, 81, 84

Dillon, General Théobald, 290
Dormeur éveillé (Marmontel), 160
Drouet, Jean Baptiste, 256
du Barry, Jeanne Bécu, Comtesse, 12, 22,
    41, 47, 57, 59, 99, 149; and death of
    Louis XV, 50, 52, 169; exile of, 60, 61;
    Gluck and, 49; Marie Antoinette's
    animosity toward, 34, 36–39; political
    influence of, 34–35; Rohan and, 62
Ducreux, Joseph, 14
Dumouriez, Charles, 273–74
Du Pont de Nemours, Pierre Samuel, 184
Duquesnoy, Adrien, 206

Edgeworth de Firmont, Abbé Henri
    Essex, 287
Elisabeth, Madame, 22, 145, 235, 246,
    261, 283; death of, 307; escape plan for,
    289; and fall of monarchy, 279, 280;
    during flight to Varennes, 250–53, 258,
    259; governess of, 78; imprisonment of,
    285, 286, 288; and Louis XIV's
    accession, 54; and Louis XVI's death,
    287; Marie Antoinette's farewell letter
    to, 303; overnight stays at Trianon of,
    134; in private theatricals, 136; during
    riot of June 1792, 275–76; testimony at
    Marie Antoinette's trial of, 296, 297;
    during tragedy of October 1789, 223,
    226, 229, 231; at Tuileries, 232, 270–71
Enlightenment, 242
Enville, Duchesse d', 193
Escars, Comtesse d', 193
Estates General, 193, 196, 198, 202,
    204–6, 208–9, 213, 236
Eszterhazy, Count Valentin, 75, 96, 126,
    201–2

Fabricius (court clerk), 297
Fausse Infidélités, Les (Berthe), 136
Favart, Charles Simon, 136

Ferdinand, Archduke of Austria, 4, 6, 7, 17, 84
Ferdinand, Duke of Parma, 11
Fersen, Count Axel, 49, 122–24, 128, 149–54, 157, 183, 184, 191, 214, 293; in American War of Independence, 124, 125, 127, 128, 149–50; attractiveness to women of, 123; and Brunswick's manifesto, 276, 278; correspondence of Marie Antoinette and, 152–54, 159–60, 164–65, 188, 202, 264–65, 269, 271, 274, 276; de Staël and, 151; escape plans of, 244, 246, 248, 272; after execution of Louis XVI, 288–89; on Fête de la Fédération, 241; on flight to Varennes, 250–53, 258; gossip about, 163–64; Gustavus III and, 159, 160, 205; during last summer at Versailles, 217, 222; liaison of Sullivan and, 269–70, 272–73; and Marie Antoinette's death, 306–7; nature of Marie Antoinette's relationship with, 164–67; and tragedy of October 1789, 231–32; at Tuileries, 238–40; Versailles quarters of, 188–89
Fête de la Fédération, 240–42
Fitz-James, Duchess of, 125, 240, 306
Flanders regiment, 220, 222, 224
"flour wars," 71, 81, 93, 97
Fontainebleau, Château de, 65, 81, 101–3, 132, 178
Foster, Elizabeth, 160
Fouquier-Tinville, Antoine Quentin, 293–95, 297, 299, 300, 302, 303
Fragonard, Jean Honoré, 66
Francis I, Emperor of Austria, 3–9
Francis II, Emperor of Austria, 273, 274, 288
Franco-British trade agreement, 202
Franklin, Benjamin, 124–25, 127, 144
Frederick II, King of Prussia, 114, 116, 117, 161
Frederick William II, King of Prussia, 192, 274

French Guard, 112
French National Archives, 165, 303
Fronsac, Duc de, 136

Gabriel, Jacques Ange, 23, 59, 66, 133, 135
Gageure imprévue, La (Sedaien), 136
Gamain ("Locksmith to the King's Chambers"), 90
Gautier-Dagoty (miniaturist), 130
Georgel, Abbé, 174
Girondins, 273, 275
Gluck, Christoph Willibald, 7, 49–50, 68, 135, 141
Gobelins, Manufacture des, 107
Goethe, Johann Wolfgang von, 18
Goguelat (Bouillé's aide-de-camp), 258
Gontaut, Marquise de, 193
Gouthière (bronzesmith), 133
Gramont, Duchesse de, 83
Grancher (purveyor of decorative objects), 133
Grasse, Admiral de, 147
Great Fear, 218
Grétry, André Ernest Modeste, 135, 221
Greuze, Jean Baptiste, 132
Grimm, Friedrich Melchior, Baron, 177
Guémémé, Marie Louise, Princesse de, 78–79, 81–85, 96, 108, 121, 149
Guémémé, Prince de, 79, 149
Guiche, Duc de, 138
Guines, Comte de, 96, 99–100, 126
Gustavus III, King of Sweden, 49, 118, 122, 125, 150–52, 159, 160, 163, 205, 247, 272

Habsburg, House of, 11–12, 48
Haydn, Joseph, 7
Hébert, Jacques René, 300, 301
Hénin, Princesse d', 193
Henri II, King, 72, 171, 175, 181

Henri III, King, 27
Henri IV, King, 56, 67
Hermann, Armand Martial Joseph,
    297–98, 301, 302
Hesse-Darmstadt, Princess von, 8, 135
Hézecques, Félix d', 132, 189
Hofburg Palace, 6, 7, 9, 10, 106

Iphigénie in Aulide (Gluck), 49–50, 68
Isabella of Parma, 7

Jacob, Georges, 133
Jacobins, 263
Jarjays, Madame de, 264, 289
Jefferson, Thomas, 193
Joseph II, Emperor of Austria, 3–5, 17,
    67, 77, 112, 144, 147, 160, 183, 186,
    197, 237; accession of, 11; and
    American War of Independence, 141;
    counterrevolutionary noblemen
    supported by, 243, 251; death of, 247;
    and father's death, 9; in France,
    105–11; imperial ambitions of, 114–15,
    148, 155–56, 161–62; marriage of, 8;
    and mother's death, 139–40; musical
    interests of, 7, 49; portrait at Versailles
    of, 88; Rohan and, 61
Josephina of Bavaria, 8, 9

Kaunitz, Count Wenzel Anton von, 39,
    58, 106, 210
Klinckowström, Baron, 165
Kornmann (banker), 193
Kucharski (painter), 269
Kunsthistorisches Museum, Vienna, 7

La Bruyère, Jean de, 30
La Châtre, Comtesse de, 193
Laclos, Pierre Choderlos de, 165

Lafayette, Marie Joseph Yves Gilbert du
    Motier, Marquis de, 219, 234, 244, 248,
    262, 266, 277–78, 296; in American
    War for Independence, 144–46; and
    Estates General, 193; Fersen and, 239;
    and flight to Varennes, 252, 253; and
    tragedy of October 1789, 224, 227, 230
La Ferté, Duc de, 66–67, 72, 83
La Force, prison of, 283
La Harpe, Jean François de, 143
La Marck, August Marie Raymond,
    Prince d'Arenberg, Comte de, 237, 239
Lamballe, Marie Thérèse de Savoie-
    Carignan, Princesse de, 63, 84, 85, 194,
    271, 280; death of, 284; favors bestowed
    on, 104; Fersen and, 128; friendship of
    Marie Antoinette and, 78; gambling at
    home of, 102; imprisonment at La
    Force of, 282–83; Joseph II's opinion of,
    108; Lauzun and, 81, 101; in London,
    189–90; at royal births, 119, 120, 142;
    at Tuileries, 235
Lameth, Comtesse de, 193
La Motte, Comte de, 175–76, 179, 243
La Motte-Valois, Comtesse de, 171,
    174–76, 179–81, 189, 196, 243
La Muette, Château de, 21, 60, 67;
    ceremony of "mourning bows" at, 62
Larivière, Charles de, 304
La Rochefoucauld-Liancourt, François
    Alexandre Frédéric, Duc de, 193,
    212–13
La Tour du Pin, Henriette Lucy,
    Marquise de, 219
La Tour du Pin, Jean Frédéric, Comte de,
    224, 225–26, 231
La Tour Maubourg, Victor de Fay,
    Marquis de, 261
Launay, Bernard René Jordan, Marquis
    de, 211–12
Lauzun, Armand Louis, Duc de, 80–85,
    93, 95, 100–2, 123, 144, 150
La Vauguyon, Duc de, 15, 38

Le Brun, Charles, 131
Lee, Arthur, 124
Legislative Assembly, 270, 271, 273, 274, 277–81, 294, 299
Le Moyne, François, 131
Le Nôtre, André, 134
Léonard (hairdresser), 88
Leopold II, Emperor of Austria, 4, 5, 8, 11, 109, 247, 249, 264, 266, 267, 271, 273, 275
L'Epée, Abbé de, 107
Lépicié (artist), 132
Lepître (municipal guard), 289
Lerchenfeld, Countess of, 10
Lespinasse, Julie de, 50
Leszczynska, Queen Marie, 87, 131
Ligne, Charles-Joseph, Prince de, 85, 96, 99
Loménie de Brienne, Etienne Charles de, 144, 186–87, 191–93, 195, 196, 198–201
Lorraine, House of, 25
Louis XIII, King, 56, 72
Louis XIV, King, 25, 27–28, 32, 55, 56, 72, 130, 131, 234
Louis XV, King, 28–30, 32, 47, 58, 66, 78, 79, 83, 87, 162; accession of, 72; Beaumarchais and, 167; and consummation of grandson's marriage, 40–41; death of, 50–55, 57, 122; du Barry and, 22, 33–39, 50, 59, 62, 169; "entrance" into Paris arranged by, 43–45; gardens of, 66; Marie Antoinette presented to, 20–21, 91; marriage negotiations of Maria Theresa and, 10, 12–17, 20; Mercy's attitude toward, 48; at Petit Trianon, 133–34; and private theatricals, 42; Richelieu and, 94; at Tuileries, 234; Versailles apartments of, 89; at wedding of Marie Antoinette and Louis Auguste, 22–25
Louis XVI, King of France; accession of, 54–60, 62, 69; and American War of

Independence, 124–25, 127, 140–41, 144–45, 167–68; birth of children of, 119–21, 141–43, 145–46, 163, 184; celebration of marriage of, 22–27; charges against Marie Antoinette for influencing, 297–98; and Choiseul's audience with Marie Antoinette, 75–76; and Choiseul's dismissal, 35; and constitution, 218, 266–68; coronation of, 66–67, 71–75, 79; and court protocol, 89–91; death of, 287–89, 304, 305; and death of Louis XV, 50–54; demands for deposition of, 263, 266; and diamond necklace affair, 169–77, 180–82; divorce advocated by moderates for, 243–44; Duc d'Orléans as leader of opposition to, 193–95; "entrance" into Paris of, 43–45; escape plans for, 245–49, 272, 277–78; and Estates General, 196, 202–6, 208; fall of, 277–82; and fall of Bastille, 212–16, 218; favors bestowed on Marie Antoinette's friends by, 78, 104–5, 138–39; Fersen and, 122–24, 166; and Fête de la Fédération, 240–42; during financial crisis of 1787–88, 184–87, 195–96, 198–200; flight to Varennes of, 250–62, 265; during "flour wars," 71, 97; gambling allowed by, 102; gossip about, 86, 118; Gustavus III's visit to, 160; hunting as favorite pastime of, 31, 81, 87, 89, 100, 190; incarceration at Temple of, 282–86; and Indian envoys, 197–98; inoculation against smallpox of, 63; and Joseph II's imperial ambitions, 155–56, 161–62; Joseph II's visits to, 105–11, 141; during last summer at Versailles, 216–22; Lauzun and, 80–82; and Marie Antoinette's arrival in France, 20–22; during Marie Antoinette's pregnancies, 114–16, 118–19, 183; marriage negotiations for, 10–16; Maurepas as mentor to, 58, 98; Maximilian's visit to, 67–68; mechanical hobbies of, 87, 89–90; Mirabeau and, 238–40, 244–45; and National Assembly, 208–11, 236–38; and older son's death, 207; at Parisian entertainments, 46–47; and peace negotiations with Britain, 147–48; physical appearance of, 91; private theatricals performed for, 42, 43, 135, 137; prospect of war greeted by, 271–74; proxy wedding of, 16–17; and publications denouncing Marie Antoinette, 63–65, 143, 164, 190; riot of June 1792 against, 275–76; sexual inadequacy of, 24, 30–32, 36–37, 40–41, 92–94, 108–13, 124, 139; during tragedy of October 1789, 223–32; trial of, 286–87; Tsarevitch's visit to, 148–49; at Tuileries, 231–36, 262–64, 270–72; Turgot's influence on, 97–100; Versailles apartment of, 131; and War of Bavarian Succession, 114–18

Louis XVIII, King of France, *see* Provence, Comte de

Louis Auguste, Dauphin, *see* Louis XVI, King of France

Louise, Madame, 21

Louis Joseph Xavier, Dauphin, 145, 162, 178; birth of, 142–43, 169, 282; death of, 207, 208; illnesses of, 156, 183, 187–88, 201; in painting by Vigeé-Lebrun, 184

Louvre, 107, 132

Lully, Jean Baptiste, 24

Luxembourg, Chevalier de, 79, 105, 227

Mackau, Baroness de, 156, 157

Mailly, Maréchal, 281

Maintenon, Madame de, 56

Malden, Monsieur de, 252

Malseherbes, Chrétien Guillaume de Lamoignon de, 65

Mandat, Jean Antoine, Marquis de, 279

Marat, Jean Paul, 243, 271

Maria Amalia, Duchess of Parma, 4, 10, 11, 160

Maria Anna, Archduchess of Austria, 4, 7

Maria Antonia, Archduchess of Austria, *see* Marie Antoinette, Queen of France

Maria Carolina, Queen of Naples, 4, 8, 9, 160

Maria Christina, Archduchess of Austria, 4, 6, 7, 9, 184

Maria Elisabeth, Archduchess of Austria, 4, 9, 12

Maria Feodorovna, Grand Duchess of Russia, 148–49

Maria Johanna, Archduchess of Austria, 4, 9

Maria Josephina, Archduchess of Austria, 4, 9–10

Maria Theresa, Empress of Austria, 3–10, 27, 35, 36, 46, 58–60, 70, 75–77, 92, 121; accession to throne of, 4–5; and American War of Independence, 127; birth of heir encouraged by, 93, 124; birth of youngest daughter of, 3–4; and consummation of Marie Antoinette's marriage, 32, 41; death of, 139–40; and death of Louis XV, 57; and du Barry problem, 37–39; family life of, 5–7; and husband's death, 8–9, 11; Joseph II sent to France by, 105–6; marriages of children of, 8–14, 16, 17; Maximilian sent to France by, 67; Mercy's reports to, 31, 48, 80, 96, 99–100, 104, 137, 184; Mesdames and, 33; music enjoyed by, 7–8, 49; portrait at Versailles of, 88; Rohan and, 61–62, 170, 171; Vermond and, 13–14; Viennese court of, 7; and War of Bavarian Succession, 114, 115, 117, 118

Maria Theresa of Spain, 55

Marie Antoinette, Queen of France: and accession of Louis XVI, 54–60; and American War of Independence, 127;

Marie Antoinette (*cont.*)
arrival in France of, 18–22; Artois and, 41–42, 67, 80; Beaumarchais and, 167–69; beauty and charm of, 91–92, 129–30; Besenval and, 79–80, 85, 103; birth of, 3–4; birth of children of, 119–21, 124, 141–43, 145–46, 163, 184; celebration of marriage of, 22–27; childhood of, 6–9; children's relationship with, 156–57, 187–88, 217–18; Choiseul's meeting with, 75–76; in Conciergerie prison, 292–94, 297; and constitution, 266–68; and coronation of Louis XVI, 66–67, 71–75; correspondence of Fersen and, 152–54, 159–60, 164–65, 188, 202, 264–65, 269, 271, 274, 276; and court protocol, 30, 65–68, 88–89; death of, 303–9; and death of Louis XV, 50–54; and diamond necklace affair, 169–82; divorce advocated by moderates for, 243–44; du Barry snubbed by, 34–39; Duc d'Orléans as leader of opposition to, 193–95; enemies at court of, 61–63; "entrance" into Paris of, 43–45; escape plans for, 245–49, 272, 277–78; and Estates General, 196, 203–7, 208; fall of, 277–82; and fall of Bastille, 212–16, 218; fashions worn by, 69–70, 88, 134–35, 153; Fersen becomes favorite of, 122–25, 128; and Fersen's return to France, 151–54; and Fête de la Fédération, 240–42; during financial crisis of 1787–88, 184–87, 189, 190, 195–96, 198–200; first meeting of Fersen and, 49; flight to Varennes of, 250–62, 265; gambling by, 102; as Gluck's patron, 49–50, 135; gossip about, 85–86, 104; and Guéméné circle, 78–79; Gustavus III's visit to, 160; incarceration at Temple of, 282–91; and Indian envoys, 197–98; jewelry purchased by, 105, 169; and

Joseph II's imperial ambitions, 155–56, 160–62; Joseph II's visits to, 105–11, 141; journey from Austria to France of, 17–18; during last summer at Versailles, 216–22; Lauzan and, 80–85, 93, 100–2, 123; Louis XV and, 33, 36, 39–40, 45, 47, 48; marriage negotiations for, 10, 12–16; Maximilian's visit to, 67–68; measles suffered by, 125–26; Mercy's political influence on, 47–48, 58–59, 140, 143–44, 162, 186, 191–92; and Mesdames, 33–34, 38, 47; Mirabeau and, 238–40, 244–45; and mother's death, 139–40; and National Assembly, 208–11, 236–38; nature of Fersen's relationship with, 164–67; and older son's death, 201, 207, 208; at Parisian entertainments, 46–47, 95; and peace negotiations with Britain, 147–48; and Polignac coterie, 84–85, 95–98, 101–2, 104–5, 108, 123, 138–39, 189–90; portraits of, 129, 153, 183–84, 191, 269; pregnancies of, 114–16, 118–19, 123, 140, 141, 163, 183; private theatricals of, 42–43, 135–37; prospect of war greeted by, 271–74; proxy wedding of, 16–17; publications denouncing, 63–65, 143, 164, 190; redecoration of apartments by, 130–33; and redesign of Petit Trianon, 59–60, 70–71, 133–34, 157–59, 167; riot of June 1792 against, 275–76; sexual relations of Louis XVI and, 24, 30–32, 36–37, 40–41, 64, 92–94, 108–14, 127–28, 139; during tragedy of October 1789, 223–32; trial of, 290, 293–302; during trial and execution of Louis XVI, 286–89; Tsarevitch's visit to, 148–49; at Tuileries, 231–36, 262–64, 270–72; Turgot's dismissal instigated by, 98–100; and War of Bavarian Succession, 114–18

Marie Antoinette Holding a Rose (Vigée-
    Lebrun), 128
Marie Thérèse, Madame Royale, 127,
    156–57, 188, 280; birth of, 120–21,
    124, 133, 142; and brother's death, 207;
    escape planned for, 289; and father's
    death, 287; on flight to Varennes, 251,
    255, 258; imprisonment of, 283–86,
    288, 307–8; marriage of, 308; in
    painting by Vigeé-Lebrun, 184; during
    riot of June 1792, 275–76; testimony at
    mother's trial of, 296; during tragedy of
    October 1789, 226, 229, 231; at
    Tuileries, 235
Marivaux, Martin de, 16
Marmontel, Jean François, 160
Marriage of Figaro, The (Beaumarchais),
    168
Marsan, Princesse de, 78–79, 83, 171
Masonic lodges, 193
Matignon, Madame de, 153
Maudoux, Abbé, 52
Maurepas, Jean Frédéric Phélypeaux,
    Comte de, 58, 65, 91, 97–100, 115–17,
    128, 143, 144, 185–86
Maximilian Francis, Archduke of Austria,
    4, 6, 7, 67, 106
Mecklenburg, Princess of, 8
Médicis, Catherine de, 72, 234
Médicis, Marie de, 56
Mercklein (furniture maker), 133
Mercy-Argenteau, Count, 62, 65, 77–78,
    92, 102, 113, 126, 195–96, 274, 289;
    Artois criticized by, 80; birth of heir
    encouraged by, 93; on birth of Madame
    Royale, 120; and coronation of Louis
    XVI, 72, 74; and death of Louis XV, 52;
    and diamond necklace affair, 180, 182;
    and du Barry incident, 38; and Estates
    General, 204, 210; and Fersen liaison,
    127, 166; friendship between Marie
    Antoinette and Madame de Polignac
    opposed by, 85, 96, 104, 139; and

Joseph II's visit to France, 106, 108–10;
    Leopold II and, 247, 266, 267, 271; as
    Maria Theresa's information source, 31,
    32, 37, 39, 99–100, 184; during
    marriage negotiations, 14–15; Necker
    and, 198–99, 216; political influence
    of, 47–48, 58–60, 140, 143–44, 162,
    186, 191–92; and private theatricals,
    137; and Tsarevitch's visit to Versailles,
    149; during War of Bavarian
    Succession, 116, 117
Mère confidente, La (Marivaux), 16
Mesdames, 25, 34, 36–38, 46, 47, 51, 57,
    60, 64–66, 197, 229, 247
Metropolitan Museum of Art, New York,
    133
Meytens, Martin van, 4, 6
Mignard, Pierre, 130
Millot, Reine, 300
Mique, Richard, 66, 70, 158
Mirabeau, Honoré Gabriel Riqueti,
    Marquis de, 165, 236–40, 244, 245, 265
Miromesnil, Armand Thomas Hue de,
    173, 176, 177
Monmouth, battle of, 144
Montesson, Madame de, 135
Montmorin Saint Hérem, Armand Marc,
    Comte de, 209, 220
Morris, Gouverneur, 205–6, 212, 266
Mozart, Leopold, 8
Mozart, Wolfgang Amadeus, 7–8, 135

Napoleon I, Emperor, 308
National Assembly, 208–11, 220, 225,
    246, 248, 261, 263, 265, 266;
    Declaration of the Rights of Man and
    of the Citizen drafted by, 218;
    declared by Third Estate, 208; divorce
    of royal couple advocated by, 243; and
    flight to Varennes, 254, 258; Louis
    XVI's acceptance of constitution drafted
    by, 267; Mirabeau's denunciation of,

National Assembly (*cont.*)
244; move to Paris of, 236; powers of
monarchy curtailed by, 237–38; support
for Necker in, 213, 214, 216
National Guard, 248, 262, 266, 272, 274,
277, 279, 280, 283; and flight to
Varennes, 252, 256; formation of, 219;
during riot of June 1792, 275–76;
during tragedy of October 1789,
223–24, 227, 229; at Tuileries, 235,
242, 263, 264
Necker, Germaine, *see* Staël, Baronne
Germaine de
Necker, Jacques, 151, 152, 192, 193, 218,
220, 224; during American War of
Independence, 140; dismissal of, 211;
and Estates General, 202–6, 209–10;
National Assembly support for, 213,
214, 216; recall of, 198–200
Necker, Madame, 226, 230
Noailles, Comtesse de, 18, 22, 30, 36, 63,
65, 83
Normandie, Duc de (Dauphin *after older
brother's death*), 188, 217–18, 221, 231,
250, 251, 261, 262; accusations made
against mother by, 295–97, 300; birth of,
163; and brother's death, 207; and
collapse of monarchy, 280, 281; death
of, 308; escape plan for, 289; and father's
death, 287, 288; on flight to Varennes,
258, 259; imprisonment of, 283–86; in
painting by Vigeé-Lebrun, 184; during
riot of June 1792, 275–76; rumors about
paternity of, 201; taken into custody of
municipal officials, 290–92; and tragedy
of October 1789, 226, 228–29, 231; at
Tuileries, 232, 233, 238
Nouvelles de la cour, 86
Noverre, Jean Georges, 16

Oberkirch, Baroness d', 149
Oeben (cabinetmaker), 133

Oliva, Mademoiselle d', 179, 180
On ne s'avise jamais de tout (Sedaine),
136, 137
Orléans, Louise Marie Adélaïde,
Duchesse d', 205
Orléans, Louis Philippe, Duc d', 21, 63,
67, 68, 132, 135
Orléans, Louis Philippe Joseph, Duc d'
(*formerly* Duc de Chartres), 21, 43, 220,
236; Anglo-Chinese garden of, 66; charity
given to poor and homeless by, 203; and
death of Louis XV, 52; at Estates
General, 205, 206, 210; Lauzun and, 80,
101; during Maximilian's visit, 67, 68;
rebellion supported by, 193–95, 221
Ossun, Comtesse d', 187, 201

Paris Opera, 46, 49–50, 67, 68, 95, 111,
116, 128, 135, 141, 146, 268
Paul, Grand Duke of Russia, 148–49
Penthièvre, Duc de, 78
Père Duchesne, Le (newspaper), 300, 301
Pernon (silk manufacturer), 130
Perseus (Lully), 24
Pétion, Jérôme, 261, 262, 279, 296
Petit (anatomist), 188
Petit Trianon, 59–60, 92, 126, 133–35;
gardens of, 70–71, 112, 133–34; hamlet
at, 157–59, 167; theater at, 135–37
Piccinni, Nicolò, 135, 160
Piedmont, Prince of, 84
Pillnitz declaration, 271
Piper, Countess Sophie (Fersen's sister),
152, 166–67, 239, 240, 288, 293
Poinsinet (playwright), 136
Poix, Princesse de, 193
Polastron, Comtesse de, 96
Polignac, Cardinal de, 104–5, 138
Polignac, Comtesse Diane de, 96, 136
Polignac, Duc de, 95, 101, 138, 139, 187
Polignac, Duchesse Jules de, 84, 114,
120, 125, 162, 201, 217, 235; Besenval

and, 95; and fall of Bastille, 212, 214; favors bestowed on, 101, 104, 138–39; Fersen and, 123, 128; as Governess of the Children of France, 139, 157, 207; Joseph II's dislike of, 108; in London, 189; overnight stays at Trianon of, 134; performance of *Marriage of Figaro* supported by, 168; Vaudreuil's liaison with, 84–85, 95–96, 138; Vermond's opposition to Marie Antoinette's friendship with, 96–97

Polignac, Marquis de, 104

Pompadour, Jeanne Antoinette Poisson, Marquise de, 42, 58, 59, 80

Ponts-et-Chaussées, offices of, 107

Poux-Landry, Ambroise, 90

Pragmatic Sanction, 4, 5

Provence, Louis Stanislas Xavier, Comte de, 21, 42, 46, 118, 120, 232, 236, 250–51, 289; accession of, as Louis XVIII, 303, 308; and accession of Louis XVI, 54; and birth of Dauphin, 142; at coronation of Louis XVI, 73; escape to Brussels of, 251, 264; inoculation against smallpox of, 63; marriage of, 36, 37; in private theatricals, 43; relationship of Louis XVI and, 57, 201; and tragedy of October 1789, 223, 229; on visit to wife's family, 84

Provence, Marie Joséphine, Comtesse de, 37, 41, 42, 93, 120, 126, 232, 250–51; and accession of Louis XVI, 54; at coronation of Louis XVI, 73; hostility toward Marie Antoinette of, 64, 201; and tragedy of October 1789, 223, 226, 229; visit to family of, 84

Psyché (Lully), 268

Quinault, Philippe, 24

Racine, Jean, 49

Raynal, Abbé Guillaume, 144

Restoration, 303, 308

Réteaux de Villette, 179, 180

Revolutionary Tribunal, 295–302, 307

Rheims, Archbishop of, 23

Rheims Cathedral, 72–73

Richelieu, Jean Armand du Plessis, Duc de, 51, 94

Riesener, Jean Henri, 133

Robert, Hubert, 132, 278

Robespierre, Maximilien de, 44, 265, 271, 290, 299, 301

Robin (clockmaker), 133

Rochambeau, Jean Baptiste Donatien de Vimeur, Comte de, 150

Roederer, Pierre Louis, Comte de, 279, 280

Rohan-Guémémé, Cardinal Louis Edouard de, 53, 61–62, 142, 170–82, 186, 243

Roi et le femier, Le (Sedaine), 136

Roman Catholic Church, 8, 71, 145, 303

Rose et Colas (Sedaine), 136

Rosenberg, Count, 67, 76, 78, 87

Rossillon (surgeon), 300

Rougeville, Chevalier de, 293

Rousseau, Jean Jacques, 50, 136

Sacchini, Antonio Maria Gaspro Gioacchino, 135

Saint Denis, convent of, 21

Saint-James, Boudard de, 172, 176

Saint-Priest, François Emmanuel, Comte de, 123–24, 166, 186, 188, 210, 223–26, 230, 232, 238, 240

Salieri, Antonio, 135

Santerre, Antoine Joseph, 276

Sauce, Jean Baptiste, 256–58

Savonnerie tapestry workshop, 47, 107

Schönbrunn Castle, 6–7, 9, 22, 65

Sedaine, Michel Jean, 136

Sèvres porcelain, 133

Simon, Antoine, 290, 296, 300, 308

Söderhjelm, Alma, 153
Sophie, Madame, 21, 25, 131–32; see also
    Mesdames
Sophie Hélène Béatrice, 184
Sorcier, Le (Poinsinet), 136
Staël, Baron de, 151, 152
Staël, Baronne Germaine de, 151, 152,
    192, 200–1, 230, 234, 268, 293
Starhemberg, Prince of, 17, 31
Stedingk, Count von, 128
Stendhal (Henri Beyle), 91
Stuart, Charles Edward, 160
Sullivan, Eleanore, 269–70, 272–73,
    307
Suvée (artist), 132
Swieten, Dr. van, 6
Swiss Guards, 28–29, 53, 79, 227, 279

Talleyrand-Périgord, Charles Maurice,
    Duc de, Prince de Bénévent, 241
Temple palace, 145–46; imprisonment of
    royal family at, 282–84
Tessé, Comte de, 82
Tessé, Madame de, 221
Théâtre des Italiens, 46, 67, 191
Thibault, Madame, 228
Third Estate, 202–3, 205, 206, 208–10,
    236
Tilly, Comte de, 91, 130, 166
Tippoo Sahib, King of Mysore, 197–98
Torok, Maria, 90
Toulan (municipal guard), 289
Tourzel, Louise Elisabeth, Duchesse de,
    226, 228, 229, 246, 261, 280; appointed
    governess, 217; on flight to Varennes,
    251, 253, 255, 258, 259; imprisonment
    at La Force of, 282–83; at Tuileries,
    232, 235
Tronçon-Ducoudray (lawyer), 298, 301
Tuileries, Château des, 44–45, 231–36,
    250, 262–64, 270–72, 277, 278; riot of
    June 1792 at, 275–76

Turgot, Anne-Robert Jacques, Baron de
    l'Aulne, 65, 71, 72, 78, 97–100
Tussaud, Madame, 198

U.S. Congress, 144
U.S. Constitution, 193

Vaudreuil, Joseph Hyacinthe François,
    Comte de, 84–85, 95–96, 123, 138,
    149, 187, 189
Vaux, Comte de, 125
Vergennes, Charles Gravier, Comte de,
    60, 82, 149, 192; and American War of
    Independence, 141, 144, 168; death of,
    185; and diamond necklace affair, 173,
    175–77; Fersen and, 128; and Joseph
    II's imperial ambitions, 114–17, 148,
    155–56, 161; in peace negotiations with
    Britain, 147–48
Véri, Abbé Joseph Alphonse de, 68, 91
Vermond, Abbé Jacques de, 17, 40, 91, 104,
    119, 126, 214; and coronation of Louis
    XVI, 72; and death of Louis XV, 52; and
    diamond necklace affair, 170, 172; and
    Joseph II's visit, 106; Loménie de
    Brienne and, 144, 186; in London, 190;
    Louis's failure to consummate marriage
    confided to, 24, 31, 37; Madame Royale
    and, 157; and Maria Theresa's death,
    139–40; as Maria Theresa's spy at
    Versailles, 13–14, 105; Marie Antoinette's
    friendship with Madame Polignac
    opposed by, 96–97; in Vienna as tutor to
    Marie Antoinette, 13, 16
Vermond, Dr., 119, 120
Versailles, 27–35, 56, 164; balls and
    parties at, 36, 66, 67, 146; births at,
    119–20, 141–43; churches at, 100;
    courtiers in residence at, 29–30; death
    of Louis XV at, 50–54; Fersen at, 122,
    123, 188–89, 202; gardens at, 66; gossip

about royal couple at, 41; Gustavus III
at, 160; Hall of Mirrors at, 29; Indian
envoys at, 197–98; Joseph II at, 106–11,
141; King's Antechamber (*Oeil-de-
boeuf*) at, 28; last summer at, 216–22;
Lauzun at, 81; march of people of Paris
on, 223–31; Marie Antoinette's arrival
at, 22, 43; mass in honor of Queen at,
173–74; Necker at, 140; Polignacs at,
85; protocol at, 27–28, 68, 88–89, 107;
Queen's apartment at, 87–88, 130–32;
Schönbrunn Castle modeled on, 7;
Tsarevitch at, 148–49; wedding
celebrations at, 22–25
Victoire, Madame, 21, 25; *see also*
Mesdames

Vien, Joseph, 132
Vigée-Lebrun, Elisabeth, 129, 131, 132,
153, 183–84, 190, 269
Villequier, Duc de, 251, 252

Wagenseil, Georg Christoph, 7
Wallace Collection, London, 133
Walpole, Horace, 91
Westphalia, Treaty of, 161

Yorktown, battle of, 144–45, 150

Zweig, Stefan, 272

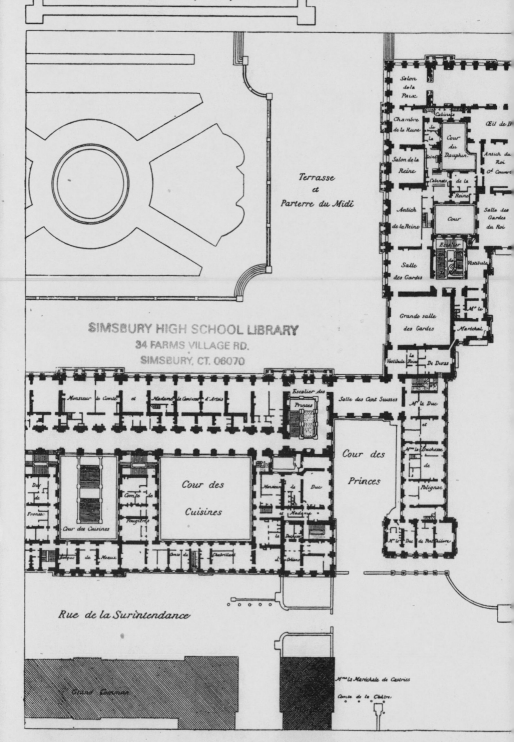

1ᴱᴿ ÉTAGE

Plan de la partie principale

CHATEAU

Terrasse
et
Parterre du Midi

Salon
de la
Paix

Cabinet

Chambre
de la Reine

Œil de B⁻

Cour
du
Dauphin

Salon de la
Reine

Antich du
Roi
G⁴ Couvert

Cabinet
de la
Reine

Antich
de la Reine

Cour

Salle des
Gardes
du Roi

Salle
des Gardes

Vestibule

M⁻ le
Maréchal

Vestibule

la
Reine

De Duras

M⁻ le Duc
et

Escalier des
Princes

Salle des Cent Suisses

Nᵐᵉ la Duchesse
de
Polignac

Monsieur le Comte et Madame la Comtesse d'Artois

Cour des
Princes

Duc
de
Fronsac

Comte

Monsieur le Duc

Cour des
Cuisines

et Madame

Cour des Cuisines

Fougères

la Duchesse

M⁻ le Duc de Penthièvre

Évêque de Meaux

Comte de Chabrillant

l'Orléans

Rue de la Surintendance

Grand Commun

Nᵐᵉ la Maréchale de Castries

Comte de la Châtre